EXPLORING The NEW TESTAMENT WORLD

Foreword by Bruce M. Metzger

ALBERT A. BELL, JR

Publishers Since 1798

THOMAS NELSON PUBLISHERS

Nashville

Exploring the New Testament World
Copyright © 1998, Thomas Nelson, Inc.

Published in Nashville, Tennessee, by Thomas Nelson, Inc.

Unless otherwise indicated, Scripture quotations are from the *New Revised Standard Version Bible*, copyright © 1989 by the Division of Christian Education of the National Council of Churches of Christ in the USA. Used by permission.

Verses marked "RSV" are taken from the *Holy Bible: Revised Standard Version*, second edition, copyright © 1946, 1951, 1972 by the Division of Christian Education of the NCCCUSA.

Verses marked "KJV" are from the *King James Version, The Holy Bible*.

The scene on page 203 is from William Fuller and Jane Ray, *Old and New Testament Coloring Book* (New York: Modern Promotions, 1981), page 271, used in critique. The quotation on pages 93–95 is from Betty Radice, trans., *The Letters of the Younger Pliny*, Penguin Classics Series (New York: Viking Penguin), 1963, used by permission of Viking Penguin.

The Publisher has made a good faith effort to observe the legal requirements with respect to the rights of the suppliers of photographic material. Nevertheless, persons who have claims are invited to apply to the Publisher.

Book text designed by BookSetters, White House, Tennessee

Library of Congress Cataloging-in-Publication Data

Bell, Albert A., 1945-
    Exploring the New Testament world / Albert A. Bell, Jr.; foreword by Bruce M. Metzger.
        p. cm.
    Includes bibliographical references and indexes.
    ISBN 0-7852-1424-0
    1. Bible. N.T.—History of contemporary events. I. Title.
    BS2410.B355   1998
    225.9'5—dc21   98-8168
                                                         CIP

Printed in the United States of America

3 4 5 6 7—03 02 01 00 99

*In memory of my mother
and in honor of my father*

Contents

FOREWORD

PREVIOUS GENERATIONS OF students were instructed and entranced by T. R. Glover's classic book, *The World of the New Testament*, published by the Cambridge University Press in 1931. That book, no longer in print, will now be replaced for other generations of readers by the present volume written by Dr. Albert A. Bell, Jr., whose broad knowledge in classics and history is focused on the New Testament world in still more extensive vistas—for the Dead Sea Scrolls and other documents have come to light in the years following the publication of Glover's book.

Writing in a style that will appeal to the general reader, Bell has a knack of putting things in simple, yet memorable phrasing. Beginning his survey with the Judaic background, Bell describes the several Jewish sects that lived in Palestine during the New Testament period. Within this environment, he locates the place of Jesus and the early church. Then the scope widens and the reader is introduced to the Roman authorities who ruled during the first century. After providing thumbnail sketches of leading personalities, the author focuses on the Roman theory of law and the powers of governors to carry out criminal procedures. A discussion of how one could obtain citizenship is balanced by a consideration of the plight of slaves, who numbered perhaps half the population of Rome.

Turning from politics, Bell next guides the reader through the intricacies of Greco-Roman religions, including the mystery cults that spread from the East. This is followed by a succinct discussion of the several philosophical schools of classical times, succeeded later by Hellenistic philosophies. Here the commonly held understanding of Epicureanism as a self-indulgent philosophy is corrected and its true character, along with that of Stoicism, is set forth. A discussion of Neopythagoreanism and Neoplatonism rounds out the chapter.

From religion and philosophy, the author turns to consider the structures of Greco-Roman society. Here one finds a detailed account of the social classes (patrons, clients, slaves, freedmen, and women), as well as a description of the daily schedule of the ordinary person—including information about meals, housing, and clothing. The chapter on morality and personal relations (including family life, divorce, sexual deviance, and suicide) provides a nuanced discussion of features that led to the ultimate weakening of the social fabric of the Empire.

The multitudinous facts of Greco-Roman history are treated with a completeness and proportion that make the book a veritable marvel of craftsmanship. In spite of all the compression that had to be exercised in delineating the history of New Testament times within the scope of some three hundred pages, Bell has escaped the danger of merely setting down a succession of facts. Each one of the topics considered in the book will assist the reader of the New Testament to understand more fully something of the society in which the early church found itself, something of the dominating personalities who played a part in this development, and something of the daily conditions of ordinary people in street and home.

—*Bruce M. Metzger*
Professor of New Testament, Emeritus
Princeton Theological Seminary

Author's
Preface

This book has been in development, I now realize, since I was in high school. My interest in the world of ancient Rome was stimulated by my Latin teacher and my minister. At some point I made the connection that the people who wrote the literature I was reading in Miss Kay's class lived in the same world as the people who wrote the books I studied on Sunday. Knowing something about one of them, I somehow perceived, should help me understand the other. Without making a conscious decision to do so, I began a pilgrimage that has had as its goal the gathering of as much information as I could find about life in the first century A.D. Over the years I've detoured to explore other topics, but I always come back to one of those roads that leads to Rome.

As a teacher I have the opportunity to share what I've learned with a new crop of students every year. I also speak from time to time in Sunday school classes. Encouragement from those audiences has prompted me to think that enough people might share my interest in these matters to justify putting together a book. This is not the only book that could be written on this subject, as will be evident from the bibliography in chapter 1. If I were to start over from scratch, I might even write a different book, but I have enjoyed collecting and presenting this material.

Much of the content of this book originally was published by Herald Press under the title *A Guide to the New Testament World*. That material now has been updated and revised. A substantial number of illustrations have been added to give a new dimension to the book and make it even more reader-friendly.

The book is intended primarily for a lay readership, i. e., people studying the New Testament on their own or in Bible study groups. If it also proves useful for students in colleges or seminaries, that will be a bonus. I don't assume anything on the part of the reader except an interest in the New Testament and an openness to exploration.

None of the topics in this book is treated as fully as it could be. As John discovered when trying to write about Jesus' life, you just can't put everything in (John 21:25). Some features of this book are designed to give the reader some direction to the next point on the pilgrimage. The textboxes which appear throughout the book are designed to supplement the text alongside which they appear and to let the ancient authors speak for themselves at a bit more length than they can in the short quotations which appear in the text. I hope readers will be intrigued enough to consult the full text from which these snippets are extracted. The first Appendix tells a bit more about those authors and how to gain access to their works in translation.

If you come to the end of a section and think, *I want to know more about this,* the bibliographies can make that next step easier. Bibliographic items are numbered by the chapters in which they first appear. When an item is referred to in the text, the number is printed in **bold** to distinguish it from numbers referring to the works of ancient authors or verses in the Bible. A reference in parentheses in the form (**5.102**) would mean that the reference is to chapter 5, item 102. If I've used a direct quotation from that source, the page number will be given after a colon, e. g., **5.102**:37.

I would like to take the opportunity to thank some people who have helped me in significant ways during this process of exploration:

- Prof. Archie Nations, who introduced me to the study of the Greek language and for whom I wrote a term paper that eventually became my first published article. Not surprisingly, it was about using Roman historians to establish a date for the book of Revelation (**3.84**).

- Rev. Robert McClernon, who was my pastor and friend during some difficult graduate school years.

- Profs. George Kennedy and George Houston, my advisors in graduate school at the University of North Carolina at Chapel Hill and for whose friendship I am still grateful.

- My father and mother, for the models of faithful living they have always provided for me.

- My wife and children for their patient support and love over the years.

List of Abbreviations

AClass	*Acta Classica*	*FNT*	*Filologia neotestamentaria*
AJA	*American Journal of Archeology*	*G&R*	*Greece and Rome*
AJAH	*American Journal of Ancient History*	*GRBS*	*Greek, Roman and Byzantine Studies*
AJPh	*American Journal of Philology*	*HeyJ*	*Heythrop Journal*
AmBenRev	*American Benedictine Review*	*HibJ*	*The Hibbert Journal*
AmerBaptQ	*American Baptist Quarterly*	*HistPolTho*	*History of Political Thought*
AmHistR	*American Historical Review*	*HSCP*	*Harvard Studies in Classical Philology*
AmPhQ	*American Philosophical Quarterly*	*HT*	*History Today*
AncHist	*Ancient History (formerly AncSoc)*	*HThR*	*Harvard Theological Review*
AncSoc	*Ancient Society (now AncHist)*	*HUCA*	*Hebrew Union College Annual*
AncW	*The Ancient World*	*ICS*	*Illinois Classical Studies*
AndUnivSemStud	*Andrews University Seminary Studies*	*IntPhQ*	*International Philosophical Quarterly*
AngThR	*Anglican Theological Review*	*IrBibStud*	*Irish Biblical Studies*
ANRW	*Aufstieg und Niedergang der römischen Welt*	*IrJur*	*The Irish Jurist*
BAR	*Biblical Archaeology Review*	*IrTheolQ*	*Irish Theological Quarterly*
BiblArch	*Biblical Archaeologist*	*IsrExplJ*	*Israel Exploration Journal*
BibRes	*Biblical Research*	*JbAc*	*Jahrbuch für Antike und Christentum*
BibRev	*Bible Review*	*JBiblEqual*	*Journal of Biblical Equality*
BibT	*Bible Today*	*JBL*	*Journal of Biblical Literature*
BibTrans	*Biblical Translator*	*JEH*	*Journal of Ecclesiastical History*
BJRL	*Bulletin of the John Rylands Library*	*JerPer*	*Jerusalem Perspective*
BTB	*Biblical Theology Bulletin*	*JEvangThSoc*	*Journal of the Evangelical Theology Society*
BurHist	*Buried History*	*JHI*	*Journal of the History of Ideas*
C&M	*Classica et mediaevalia*	*JHPh*	*Journal of the History of Philosophy*
CB	*Classical Bulletin*	*JHS*	*Journal of Hellenic Studies*
CBQ	*Catholic Biblical Quarterly*	*JJewSt*	*Journal of Jewish Studies*
CF	*Classical Folia*	*JMS*	*Journal of Mithraic Studies*
ChHist	*Church History*	*JPh*	*Journal of Philosophy*
ChrT	*Christianity Today*	*JQR*	*Jewish Quarterly Review*
CJ	*Classical Journal*	*JRel*	*Journal of Religion*
ClassAnt	*Classical Antiquity (formerly CSCA)*	*JRelHist*	*Journal of Religious History*
CompLit	*Comparative Literature*	*JRS*	*Journal of Roman Studies*
CPh	*Classical Philology*	*JSemStud*	*Journal of Semitic Studies*
CQ	*Classical Quarterly*	*JSJ*	*Journal for the Study of Judaism*
CSCA	*California Studies in Classical Antiquity (now ClassAnt)*	*JStudNT*	*Journal for the Study of the New Testament*
CSSH	*Comparative Studies in Society and History*	*JStudPseud*	*Journal for the Study of the Pseudepigrapha*
CTM	*Currents in Theology and Mission*	*JTheolSAfr*	*Journal of Theology for South Africa*
CW	*Classical World*	*JThS*	*Journal of Theological Studies*
DownRev	*Downside Review*	*LexThQ*	*Lexington Theological Quarterly*
EMC	*Échos du monde classique*	*LuthTheolJ*	*Lutheran Theological Journal*
EphThL	*Ephemerides theologicae Lovanienses*	*MedHist*	*Medical History*
EvangQ	*Evangelical Quarterly*		
ExposT	*Expository Times*		
Faith&Ph	*Faith and Philosophy*		

N&C	Nigeria and the Classics	RHD	Revue d'histoire du droit
Neotest	Neotestamentica	ScandJTh	Scandinavian Journal of
NewBlackfr	New Blackfriar		Theology
NovT	Novum Testamentum	ScotJTh	Scottish Journal of Theology
NTS	New Testament Studies	SDHI	Studia et documenta historiae et
P&P	Past and Present		iuris
PACPhA	Proceedings of the American	SEAJTh	Southeast Asia Journal of
	Catholic Philosophical		Theology
	Association	SecCent	Second Century
PalExQ	Palestine Exploration Quarterly	SJPh	Southern Journal of Philosophy
PAPhS	Proceedings of the American	SR	Studies in Religion
	Philosophical Society	StudLiturg	Studia liturgica
PAS	Proceedings of the Aristotle Society	StudPatr	Studia patristica
PBSR	Papers of the British School at Rome	StudTh	Studia theologica
PCA	Proceedings of the Classical	SWJourTheol	Southwestern Journal of Theology
	Association	Syll Class	Syllecta Classica
PCPhS	Proceedings of the Cambridge	TAPhA	Transactions of the American
	Philological Society		Philological Association
QuartRev	Quarterly Review	TheolEd	Theological Educator
RefRev	Reformed Review	TheolEvang	Theologia evangelica
RefThRev	Reformed Theological Review	TorJTheol	Toronto Journal of Theology
REJ	Revue des Études Juives	TynBull	Tyndale Bulletin
RelEd	Religious Education	VetTest	Vetus Testamentum
RelStud	Religious Studies	VigChr	Vigiliae Christianae
RelStudRev	Religious Studies Review	VoxRef	Vox Reformata
RelTrad	Religious Traditions	ZNTW	Zeitschrift für neutestamentliche
RestorQ	Restoration Quarterly		Wissenschaft
Rev&Expos	Review and Expositor	ZPE	Zeitschrift für Papyrologie und
Revbib	Revue biblique		Epigraphik
RevQum	Revue de Qumran		

About the Author

Albert A. Bell, Jr., is professor of classics and history and chairperson of the history department at Hope College in Holland, Michigan, where he has taught since 1978. Born in Laurens, South Carolina, he grew up in nearby Greenville and in Chattanooga, Tennessee. He graduated from Carson-Newman College in Jefferson City, Tenn., and holds an M.A. from Duke University, an M.Div. from Southeastern Seminary, and a Ph.D. from the University of North Carolina at Chapel Hill.

Bell is an ordained Baptist minister and served as a campus minister at Syracuse University. In addition to articles and reviews in a number of scholarly journals, he has published articles and stories in newspapers and magazines such as the Detroit *Free Press* and *Jack and Jill*. He is also the author of a Christian historical novel, *Daughter of Lazarus* (Abbey Press).

Albert and his wife, Bettye Jo, are the parents of two sons and two daughters.

CHAPTER 1

WHY THIS BOOK?

ANYONE WHO READS a book wants to get as much out of it as possible. This is true for a reader of the New Testament as for no other document. To grow in faith through the reading of the New Testament requires that we comprehend it to the fullest degree possible. How can we believe something we don't understand? Can we be satisfied with a faith based on books whose meaning we only partially perceive? Christianity has often been called a religion of the book. But if we don't understand the book, we find ourselves in the predicament of the Ethiopian eunuch (Acts 8:26–40). He was trying to puzzle out the meaning of a passage in Isaiah when the apostle Philip approached his chariot and asked, "Do you understand what you are reading?" The Ethiopian replied, "How can I, unless someone guides me?" Then he invited Philip to join him while he traveled.

I hope this book will become a valuable companion on your intellectual and spiritual journey, assisting you as you grow in your faith or as you try to understand the New Testament on a new level. The book is intended as a first step for people who want to know more about the New Testament but don't know where to turn for information. I believe that, before making faith assertions, we must study the New Testament as objectively as possible to be certain that we understand what *it* really means to say and not let cultural baggage—its or ours—get in the way. People who do that can experience the vitality of what they read and can carry the very life of the text over into their own lives.

For the sake of clarity, I need to specify what this book is not about as well as what it aims to do. It does not deal with the theological interpretation of the New Testament text, nor with questions of the authorship or canonicity of certain books. It does not attempt to advocate or repudiate any particular interpretation of the New Testament. Its focus is the political and social background against which those books were written, the *context* which is fundamental to the fullest possible understanding of all aspects of the text.

Text and Context

A crucial part of understanding any written text is knowing something about the historical background of the author and the original audience. To put it in more formal terms, every text has a context. Every written document—whether a piece of graffiti on a wall or a prize-winning play—has certain cultural assumptions built into it. Those assumptions affect an author's choice of theme, vocabulary, images, and every other aspect of one's writing. It is important to emphasize this because authors assume their readers will be familiar with the culture which underlies their writings. Hence, they seldom go into detail explaining their social customs or political institutions. This has always been true. As C. S. Wansink notes, "Ancient authors often did not relate situations with which their readerships were familiar; some things were just 'not of sufficient importance' to merit their notice" (**1.63**:11).

The problem arises when someone from another culture or a later time reads that work. The Ethiopian eunuch was separated from the prophet Isaiah by hundreds of years and hundreds of miles. If a North American from our era were to read a story written in seventeenth-century Japan or eighteenth-century Germany, that reader would find some of it unintelligible because the authors assume that the reader knows certain things or shares certain assumptions arising naturally from the culture. We would wonder, for example, why a Japanese warrior would kill himself rather than face disgrace and why his suicide would be committed according to an elaborate ritual. References to the German nobility would likely baffle us. Why are some of them called Electors? Relations between church and state would appear to be different from our own familiar setting. How could a German ruler order his subjects to be members of the Lutheran or Catholic church?

To some degree, every word we say is culturally conditioned. Even our jokes have a context, and if the reader (or listener) doesn't know that context, the joke has no meaning. This is particularly true with humor that involves puns or other forms of word play. For instance, in an "Arlo and Janis" comic strip, Arlo tells his son Gene a positively ancient joke that concludes with a punch line about Dale Evans seeing a cougar near the ranch and saying, "Pardon me, Roy, is that the cat who chewed your new shoes?" Gene looks at Arlo as though he's speaking a foreign language. Arlo tries to help him by adding, "There's this old song . . . ."

Gene could not appreciate the pun—and some readers of this book may not—because he did not know the cultural context of the joke. To share his father's laughter, to derive the same meaning as the person communicating the idea to him, he would have to be familiar with Glenn Miller's old song, "Pardon Me, Boy, Is That the Chattanooga Choo-Choo?" (We won't even get into the possible racist overtones of the term 'boy'.) Gene would also have to know who Dale Evans and Roy Rogers were. Without that cultural context, he could make no sense of the text of his father's joke.[1]

Even when we speak the same language in which a text is written, we can have difficulty understanding it if we are far enough removed in time from the origin of the text. Consider this line from Shakespeare's Othello: "He robs himself that spends a bootless grief." Some phrases from the King James Version of the Bible, written by people who heard and understood Shakespeare, have meaning for us only because we have heard them explained so many times. The meaning of many English words has changed in the four centuries which separate us from Elizabethan England. A good example would be "suffer the little children to come unto me" (Matt. 19:14 KJV). The meaning of "allow" or "let" is only an obscure usage of the word "suffer" today.

If it can be that hard to understand an older text written in our own language, how much greater the problem that confronts us when reading books from cultures which use a language different from ours. The Ethiopian eunuch was almost certainly using a Greek translation of Isaiah, putting him at an immediate disadvantage (**1.15**). Like him, we have to rely on a translation (or spend several years learning the original language of the text). If we stop to think about it, we might wonder how accurate is the translation we're using. Translation is an art, not just a matter of looking up a word in a dictionary and finding its equivalent in another language (**1.14**). Words and idioms have subtle shades of meaning which a non-native speaker has trouble picking up. Consider the difference between blowing up a photograph, blowing up a balloon, and blowing up a bridge. How would we translate the intent of those phrases into another language? (**1.2; 1.5**).

To look at the problem from the other side, imagine you were reading a French novel in which the phrase *l'esprit de l'escalier* appeared. Translated literally as "the wit of the stairway," it would mean nothing to modern English-speaking readers. A dictionary and commentary would help us to understand that it describes the sensation of thinking of a perfect comeback to someone when it's too late, usually as you're going up the stairs to your room. Then an inspiration hits and you think, "*That's* what I should have said."

All literature contains such culturally conditioned material. A few marginal notes can't provide readers from outside the culture or from a later time period with all the insight they need to get the full meaning from a document. It is not necessary to understand the culture fully to benefit from reading the document, but having even a degree of insight into the culture can enrich one's reading significantly and help one guard against erroneous interpretations.

This claim is not a new one. As long ago as A.D. 200 (on B.C./A.D., see chapter 9), Clement of Alexandria had to deal with criticism from those who wanted to read only the Bible: "Some, who pride themselves on their innate wisdom, will not study philosophy or logic and refuse to learn natural science. They insist on faith alone, as if they could immediately harvest fruit without taking care of the vine. . . . I call those truly learned who apply all facets of knowledge to the study of the truth" (*Stromata* 1.9; see appendix 1 under "Clement"). In the mid-eighteenth century, Anglican Bishop Joseph Butler advised his readers that the New Testament writings "have all a particular reference to the condition and usages of the Christian world at the time they were written. . . . They cannot be thoroughly understood, unless that condition and those usages are known and attended to" (*Sermon on Human Nature* 1.1). The scholars who today are putting some emphasis on this aspect of the study of various New Testament books are thus advocating nothing new.

When applied to the New Testament, this approach is not intended to undermine anyone's faith. Some devout Christians seem to fear that reading *about* the New Testament, instead of just reading the New Testament, will have that effect. Billy Graham, in his newspaper column, used to advise people just to read the New Testament itself and not bother with books about the New Testament. He is not alone in this opinion. I have in my files a newspaper ad for a new splinter denomination, proclaiming their belief that the Scriptures are "not culturally conditioned." Such a view seems to imply that the world in which the New Testament writers lived was so like ours, or had so little influence on the New Testament writers, that the modern reader's understanding of the texts will be unhindered by cultural differences.

Can we truly believe that things have changed so little in two thousand years? Dig out a *Time* magazine from the late 1960s. If you're under forty, ask your parents to explain that world, that cultural context. If you're over forty, try to put hippies, Woodstock, paisley ties, "Laugh-In," or Vietnam in terms that your children can understand. Another way to experience just how much our culture has changed in a generation is to watch reruns of "Donna Reed" or "Dick Van Dyke." Anything written in the 1960s shared *that* cultural background, and unless we know something about that culture, we cannot fully comprehend material written at that time.

Understanding material written in America in the 1960s or Japan in the sixteenth century is an interesting intellectual exercise but not of life-altering importance. Understanding the New Testament is quite a different matter, isn't it? Christians believe that the New Testament contains a message which changes people's lives. How important it is, then, to understand as much about the New Testament as we possibly can so that we can be sure of the validity of our interpretation and communicate the message as fully as possible. We can do this only if we know something about the context of a particular text. This is happening as scholars come to see the importance of studying the background of particular texts (**1.6**; **1.8**; **1.11**; **1.13**). As B. J. Malina says (**1.39**:2), "Any adequate understanding of the Bible requires some understanding of the social system embodied in the words that make up our sacred Scripture" (cf. **1.10**). Bruce Metzger concurs by saying that "every serious attempt to understand the Scriptures must be historically oriented" (**1.9**:7).

From the Ivory Tower to the Pew

From teaching adult Sunday school classes in various churches, I have come to realize that people are eager to know such things but intimidated by how much there is to learn. I repeatedly hear, "How can I find out about these things without going to seminary? . . . Don't you have to be a Ph.D. to understand all this stuff?"

Likewise, more scholars today seem to be aware that the New Testament cannot be studied as though it were produced in a vacuum. In recent years several books on this subject have appeared, with sociological analyses proving particularly popular (**1.24**; **1.32**; **1.54**; earlier ones are reviewed in **1.28**; **1.31**). But most of them are aimed at audiences on the college and seminary level, not for a general readership. Malina's informative book, for example, is intended for "freshman and sophomore college students as they come to grips with the data presented in introductory New Testament courses" (**1.39**:v). Stambaugh and Balch assure us that "students in colleges and seminaries and at more advanced levels" will find their book helpful (**1.53**:1).

What about the people in the pews? Where can a lay person serious about the study of the New Testament turn for help? Is it necessary to go to seminary or graduate school? This book is intended for such people, to point them to material which presents scholarly information in a way that non-professional readers can understand, either working on their own or in a group setting.

The professionals who make the study of the New Testament their life's work do what experts in any area do: they develop a special vocabulary for talking about their field, and they share a fund of knowledge not readily available to those outside that field. A few seem actually to mistrust the lay public. One scholar has advocated the publication of two separate translations of the New Testament, one for specialists and the other for an untutored public who need a cleaned-up version since they can't comprehend the subtleties of the original (**1.21**).

Most scholars, however, don't deliberately try to conceal their knowledge from lay people. Yet it has become almost second nature for many of them to envelope the New Testament in a layer of arcane scholarship, most of which seems to be written in German. They talk about *traditionsgeschichte* and pericopes and redaction criticism[2] in tones which suggest that they regard the New Testament as their private preserve, open only to the initiated. Michael Grant, for example, cautions that "the study of the highly idiosyncratic Gospels requires that all the normal techniques of the historian should be supplemented by a mass of other disciplines, though this is a counsel of perfection which few students, if any, can even begin to meet" (**1.29**:197).

As if that were not enough intimidation, other scholars suggest that anyone hoping to understand the New Testament must first master the voluminous collection of rabbinic traditions, or the literature written between the Old Testament and the New Testament. Still others advise the prospective student of the New Testament to learn something about archaeology and coins. On top of all that, Wayne Meeks complains about the "isolation of New Testament study from other kinds of historical scholarship—not only from secular study of the Roman Empire, but even from church history" (**1.41**:1). Perhaps even the specialists are guilty of taking too narrow a view of their subject and do not know enough about a variety of related fields. E. A. Judge seems to think so. He accuses scholars interested in this period of being "handicapped by disciplinary boundaries" (**1.35**:23). Gasque says that "concentration on one testament or the other is bound to lead to a lack of balance" (**1.28**:74).

The result of all this specialization has been the creation of a chasm between scholars and the general public. S. J. Patterson described the situation succinctly (**1.49**:16):

> As scholars, we are not generally encouraged to share our work with a wider public. . . . Rather, we tend to communicate with each other through our own rather arcane media. . . . What has resulted is, on the one hand, a professional guild that rather naively assumes that it may confine itself to historical or literary matters without the slightest expectation that anyone would find our work of any great theological or cultural significance and, on the other hand, a general public with little awareness of what scholars are doing.

Parish ministers might seem to be the ideal bridge between scholars and the laity. They've been to seminary, and they have daily contact with lay people. But few ministers become biblical scholars in seminary. Their course work emphasizes training for their service in a church. Once they're on the job, the majority of their time is divided among sermon preparation, pastoral care, and church administration. Nor is a twenty-minute sermon the ideal format for presenting this kind of background information. Anyone studying the historical-cultural background of the New Testament needs time to reflect on what is read and absorb it. The minister's primary interest in a text is usually its applicability to the lives of parishioners. When ministers do talk about the background of a biblical text, they may have only limited information from a commentary and little time to browse in a library, even if one is nearby.

I once heard a minister describe Paul's imprisonment in Rome during the course of a sermon. The congregation was given a graphic picture of the apostle clanking around in chains in a dank, foul-smelling dungeon that would have made the Tower of London look like a luxury hotel. The account was so vivid we could practically hear rats scurrying around in the straw on the floor. It was also totally inaccurate: that's not the way the Romans treated people in prison. This is an isolated incident, but it illustrates the problem. The minister's misunderstanding of the culture of New Testament times was affecting his interpretation of the text (Phil. 1). He was reading into it things not there in an effort to make his point about how God helps us bear up under adversity. At the same time, he was missing some of the real meaning of the passage.

My hope is that any lay person seriously wanting to learn something about the New Testament will find this book useful. I have tried to write in a style that will enable high-school graduates with interests in studying the New Testament to understand the material. I also hope that ministers and other professionals who want to integrate their knowledge of some part of the ancient world into a larger whole will find the book helpful. It won't answer every question you may have. No single source can. It is intended to provide brief introductions to the major questions which arise when you begin to examine the cultural context of the New Testament.

To help you find more information, it also includes, at the end of each chapter, references to books and articles in English which you can read to explore a particular topic further. The items in the bibliography are of varying difficulty, but anyone with a desire to learn can profit to some degree from reading any of them. I don't pretend that this is an exhaustive bibliography, but it should help you take a second step in your quest for understanding the New Testament. When items in the bibliography are referred to in parentheses in the text (in **bold** numbers), this is not meant to imply that the author of the article agrees with the point I'm making, merely that the source says something on the same point. The ancient writers cited most frequently are discussed in Appendix 1.

Theology and History

Exploring the cultural background of the New Testament is not the same as studying its theological meaning, but the theological meaning is often influenced by the cultural context of a passage. The cultural context is intimately bound up in the original language of the text. The text which most people read today is a translation, not the original.

Scripture references in this book are from the New Revised Standard Version unless otherwise noted. The very fact that we aren't reading the text in the original language removes us one step from a full understanding even as we open the book. As W. Meeks says, "Even so simple a task as translating a sentence from an ancient language into our own requires some sense of the social matrices of both the original utterance and ourselves. . . . If we translate without that awareness, we are only moving bones from one coffin to another" (**1.41**:5). Let's study some specific examples of how a clearer understanding of the social-cultural background of the New Testament enables us to interpret the text more accurately.

Stone Walls and Prisons

Let's look again at the question of Paul writing from prison. That very phrase, "writing from prison," conjures up in our minds a man in a small cell with no freedom of movement. It may even evoke an image of someone like Dietrich Bonhoeffer writing letters from a Nazi prison. We read that into the passage because it is the cultural baggage (or the "social matrix," to use Meeks's more refined term) which we associate with the concept.

But the Roman social matrix of imprisonment was quite different. As the *Oxford Classical Dictionary* (2nd ed., p. 879) notes, "Roman criminal law did not recognize the imprisonment of free persons as a form of punishment." The *Digest*, part of the first collection of Roman laws published in A.D. 533 and reflecting much earlier practices, admits that provincial governors sometimes imprisoned people, "but they should not do so, for such penalties are forbidden; prisons are for holding men for trial, not for punishing them" (48.19). How long an individual might be detained for questioning or until a trial was held could vary. There was no right of *habeas corpus* or guarantee to a speedy trial. Family or friends, however, were not likely to be denied access to prisoners (**1.61**). Some magistrates did gain reputations for treating prisoners cruelly, but this was a matter of individual personalities, not of Roman policy (**1.63**).

Once sentence had been passed, a person might be incarcerated until punishment was inflicted. That usually followed close on the heels of the trial. After conducting a trial of Christians in the province of Bithynia in A.D. 112, Pliny the Younger—normally a humane person, to judge from his treatment of social inferiors in other situations (**1.55**)— ordered those who refused to recant to be taken away and executed (*Ep.* 10.96).[3] The severity of punishment varied according to the guilty person's social status (**4.51**; **7.51**). Fines could be imposed, particularly on wealthier people. Forced labor was a common penalty for the lower classes, but they were not necessarily locked up each night. Pliny discovered several cases of men who had walked away from the mines and quarries to which they had been condemned and who "in their old age, from all reports, are living modestly and quietly" (*Ep.* 10.31).

Paul's imprisonment could more accurately be described as house arrest, confinement to an ordinary house. An attentive reading of the New Testament makes this clear. Philippians 1 merely refers to Paul's imprisonment in Rome. Acts 28:16 gives us more information: "When we came into Rome, Paul was allowed to live by himself, with the soldier who was guarding him." He stayed for two years "at his own expense" (Acts 28:30; cf. **1.58**). The NRSV gives "in his own hired dwelling" as an alternative rendering of that phrase. During that time people "came to him at his lodging in great numbers" (Acts 28:23), and he was "proclaiming the kingdom of God and teaching about the Lord Jesus Christ with all boldness and without hindrance" (Acts 28:30). Being "in prison" in ancient Rome begins to sound more like a minor inconvenience than a fate to be dreaded (though we shouldn't make light of it).

Roman sources reveal more generally how prisoners were treated during Paul's lifetime. The biographer Suetonius says that, after the emperor Tiberius exiled his niece Agrippina the Elder and her two sons, "whenever he moved them from one place to another, they rode in closed litters, in chains and under guard" (*Tib.* 64). They were in chains, though, only while being moved. Tiberius was regarded as particularly cruel to his ex-wife Julia because he imprisoned her in a house and would not permit her to have visitors (*Tib.* 50). If Paul was ever chained, as he claims in Acts 28:20, it would have been during one of his moves or to keep him from escaping when crowds of people came to see him. There is no mention of chains, however, when he was being transported from Palestine to Rome. The accompanying centurion even "treated Paul kindly" (Acts 27:3).

Except for sheds known as *ergastula*, where slaves were sometimes penned up (**1.56**), there were no facilities for long-term imprisonment in an ancient town. When Paul was arrested in Jerusalem, he was locked up in the soldiers' barracks (Acts 23:16). Even when he was beaten and imprisoned in Philippi, the beating, not the imprisonment, was his punishment. If Paul was kept under house arrest in Rome for a long time, it was because his case was slow to receive a hearing. The Roman judicial system could grind almost as slowly as our own if the government wasn't particularly interested in a case.

The closest the Romans came to punishing someone by lengthy imprisonment was exile to some island or remote part of the Empire. Exile could be of two types. In one, the person was ordered to keep a certain distance from Rome but could move about as he/she chose. Cicero was sentenced to that type of exile; he was required to stay at least four hundred miles from Rome. The emotional impact of such a sentence was probably greater than any physical discomfort suffered (**1.59**; **1.62**).

In the other type of exile, the person was confined ("relegated") to a particular spot. Persons in exile would live in a house in some small town where they could be watched, but they were not usually kept under lock and key. Augustus relegated the poet Ovid to a small town on the Black Sea, a place that is now an Eastern European version of the Riviera. Ovid complained bitterly and made it sound like a living hell (see box), but he learned the native dialect and continued to write poetry. Augustus also exiled Archelaus, the deposed king of Judea, to Gaul. (Spending a few years in a villa in France sounds like the prison sentences some white-collar criminals receive in our day.)

Exile was a punishment usually reserved for persons of some status, a fact which should shed light on our reading of the book of Revelation. Its author, John, was in exile on the island of Patmos (Rev. 1:9). He was not, it seems, some petty criminal in the eyes of the Roman government. The pages of the historian Tacitus are filled with people, almost always aristocrats, exiled to small towns or islands or to one of their country estates when the emperor even suspected them of misconduct. They were usually recalled when the next emperor came to power. Caligula once asked a returned exile how the man had spent his time. Trying to flatter the new emperor, the man replied, "I prayed constantly to the gods for Tiberius' death, and for your accession; and my prayer was answered." Fearful that the people he had exiled were praying for his own death, Caligula "sent agents around to the islands and had them kill all the exiles" (Suetonius, *Calig.* 28).

Lower-class criminals could be sent to work in mines in various places around the Mediterranean. But if that was John's fate on Patmos, he would not have had writing materials or the privacy necessary to compose his book. He would have been forced to work each day until he dropped. Thus it seems unlikely that he was a prisoner of that class; he was "in exile."

An Exile's Anguish

Spare me, father of our country! Don't forget my name and snatch from me the hope that I might someday placate you. I'm not asking to be allowed to come home, although I believe that the great gods have granted greater prayers. If you would give me a milder place of exile, one closer to Rome, a large part of my punishment would be lifted. My suffering couldn't be any worse, cast out into the midst of enemies. No exile is farther away from his homeland. I alone have been sent to the seven-mouthed Danube, whose waters scarcely keep out the crowd of barbarians. Although others have been exiled for more serious reasons, no one has been sent to a more remote spot than I. No place is farther away than this, except for the cold and the enemy and the sea whose waters solidify with the cold. . . . I ask only a safer and somewhat more peaceful place of exile, so that my punishment may be equal to my crime.

Ovid, *Tristia* 2.179–191, 577–578

This is just one case where reading ancient source material shows us that a concept—imprisonment, in this instance—which means one thing to us meant something quite different in antiquity. Yet misconceptions about this and other background matters persist among lay and clerical readers of the New Testament. Where do they come from?

Many of them have been created by writers and artists who knew nothing of how people actually lived, ate, or died in the first century A.D. They read their own cultural experiences back into the New Testament. Many of the concepts which underlie today's commentaries and Sunday school lessons were formulated in this way by the time of the Reformation. They have been handed down without critical examination since.

The Last Supper

Sometimes all it takes is one picture to fix an image in our minds. Consider our conception of the Last Supper. Few of us, I dare say, can visualize that event without thinking of Leonardo da Vinci's painting, completed in 1498. Some churches even stage living tableaux with people posing as da Vinci painted the apostles and Jesus. Because of the pervasive influence of this portrayal, it has become part of our unspoken assumption about the Last Supper that everyone present was sitting around a table.[4] Most English translations of the Bible use the word "sitting" in this passage, thus reinforcing the image from another side (as in Mark 14:18, KJV).

What do we make, then, of the passage which says that "one of his disciples—the one whom Jesus loved—was reclining next to him" (John 13:23), "close to the breast of Jesus" (RSV)? Some misinformed interpreters have taken this as an indication that there was an intimate relationship between the two. This is one of the passages, along with the friendships of David and Jonathan, Naomi and Ruth, and Paul and Timothy, usually adduced as supporting evidence in discussions of a favorable biblical attitude toward homosexuality (**1.64–66**; **1.70**). Others find a clear condemnation of such practices (**1.69**), while some emphasize the ambiguity of the passages (**1.67–68**; see also chapter 8).

Many Christians are uncomfortable with the notion of a homosexual Savior. How do they answer the charge? One well-intentioned writer tried to argue that Jesus' culture was more open to touching and that Jesus himself "didn't hesitate to let the apostle John rest his head on his bosom nor shake him away because of what people might think" (**1.69**:1400). That argument is obviously circular. If the society was more open to touching, no one would think anything about their posture, and Jesus would not have to be concerned with shaking John away.

The resolution of the question, though slightly different, is culturally based. Jesus and his disciples ate the Passover not sitting in chairs around a table but reclining on couches.[5] The Greek verbs used in all the Gospels mean "to recline," not "to sit."[6] The phrase "to lean (recline) on someone's breast" is an idiom in Greek meaning no more than "to sit next to someone" in English. So we find that even a quick insight into the cultural setting of the narrative resolves what appeared to be a difficulty for interpretation. Arguments based on a misreading of the text can be recognized as deceptive.

Images of the Crucifixion

Another small point of confusion arises with regard to the crucifixion. Medieval artists have left us with an inaccurate impression about an important facet of how Jesus was crucified. When we read in the Gospels that nails were driven into Jesus' hands, we visualize marks in the palms of his hands. We have probably sung that old hymn, "Place your hands in the nail-scarred hands," and have conjured up in our minds an image of a man's palms. St. Francis of Assisi even claimed to bear the *stigmata*, the marks of Christ's crucifixion, with scars in his palms.

Instances are known today of devout people who have bled from their palms after periods of intense meditation or prayer. Occasionally individuals have themselves crucified as an act of devotion, and the nails are always driven into the palms of the hands. An illustration from a newspaper ad shows how pervasive this image has become.

Resurrection Celebration

GOOD FRIDAY SERVICE
April 1
1:00 - 2:00 p.m.

Popular perception of Jesus' crucifixion wounds

From archaeological finds, however, we now know that the Romans drove nails in behind the wrist bone because the fragile bones of the hand would not support the weight of a human body hanging on a cross. The Greek word for hand covers the wrist. The Latin word *manus* does not. Few artistic representations of the crucifixion were created before A.D. 600. The Roman government outlawed that form of execution ca. A.D. 400. When medieval artists read their Latin New Testament—or, more likely, heard it read to them—and began painting pictures of the crucifixion, no one living had seen anyone crucified, so they painted what they thought they could deduce from the text. From archaeological finds we now know how the hands would have been fastened and that the body would have been positioned on the cross with the legs drawn up and turned to one side so that a single nail could have been driven through both heels (**1.80**).

Drawing based on remains of a crucified man from the first century A.D., found in a cave in Jerusalem. Both feet were pierced with one spike just below the heel
(Drawing by Gaalyeh Cornfeld)

In light of the fact that medieval artists did not know where the Romans drove in the nails during a crucifixion, the relic known as the Shroud of Turin, which is alleged to be Jesus' burial shroud (cf. Mark 15:46; John 20:6) presents an interpretive problem. This piece of linen with a faint image of a man on it has been the center of intense study and controversy since the late nineteenth century (**1.78**; **1.80**). No one has yet been able to explain to everyone's satisfaction how the image was put on the cloth. The shroud itself was subjected to carbon-14 testing, which established a date for the cloth of ca. 1300 A.D. (**1.75**; **1.82**). Some scholars have expressed doubts about the claims for reliability of the date and reservations about the way the tests were done (**1.76**; **1.79**).

Several features of the shroud continue to excite questions. The image, when photographed, appears to be a photographic negative, i.e., its features appear more lifelike when viewed on the negative film. Could a medieval artist have created such an illusion five hundred years before the invention of photography? Perhaps more significantly, the image shows a blood stain not in the back of the man's right hand (his hands are crossed over his lower abdomen) but higher up, in his right wrist. No medieval artist ever painted the nail wounds in that position. Furthermore, the man's thumbs are not visible, a fact which becomes significant when one learns that driving a spike in behind the wrist strikes a tendon which causes the thumb to draw down into the palm. If this shroud is a fourteenth-century forgery, how did this particular artist know things known by no one else on the face of the earth at that time? (**1.74**)

The Zero Factor

Sometimes people base important parts of their theology on a misunderstanding of the cultural background of the New Testament.

Herbert W. Armstrong, founder of the Worldwide Church of God and Ambassador College and publisher of the *Plain Truth* magazine, argued that Jesus could not have been crucified on Friday and resurrected on Sunday because three days won't fit between Friday and Sunday. Any grade-school child can see that his arithmetic makes sense. Given the way we count, from Friday afternoon to Sunday morning is a day and a half, at most. But not if you count like the Jews and Romans did. They lacked a zero in their mathematical systems; the zero was not used as a numeral until the early seventh century A.D., by an Indian mathematician named Brahmagupta (cf. **1.85**:69–72). Without a zero, the Jews and Romans counted the day on which something occurred as the first day. In Luke 13:32, Jesus counts in exactly this fashion: "Listen, I am casting out demons and performing cures today and tomorrow, and on the third day I finish my work."

Furthermore, a portion of a day was counted as a whole day. So, if Jesus spent any part of a day in the tomb, it would count as a full day. He was placed in the tomb before sunset on Friday, and the day began at sunset. Thus, by the counting system in use in New Testament times, Friday was the first day, Saturday the second, and Sunday—which began at sundown on Saturday—was the third, no matter how small a part of each day Jesus was in the tomb.

Conclusion

These are examples of only a few passages in the New Testament which have been misunderstood or misinterpreted because people had inadequate knowledge of the Greco-Roman world in which the New Testament was written. They illustrate the point that an understanding of the cultural background of the New Testament can have an impact on one's theological understanding of it. At the risk of being repetitious, understanding the context affects our interpretation of the text. As Allan Janssen put it, "Not only are we indebted to a contextual reading; we cannot escape it. Nor, perhaps, were we ever meant to!" (**1.86**:24).

What follows is an effort to introduce lay people to the wealth of information which can enrich their study of the New Testament. Since the most immediate context of the life of Jesus is Judaism, we will begin by looking at various facets of that religion and culture, then examine the political structure of the Roman Empire before studying certain aspects of Roman culture in more detail.

Notes

1. This strip itself is built on some cultural in-jokes. The title characters are named after Arlo Guthrie and Janis Joplin, popular figures of the late 1960s. Gene is the namesake of Senator Eugene McCarthy, popular but unsuccessful Democratic presidential aspirant in 1968. Knowing even that much about the background of the strip enables the reader to enjoy it on a different level.

2. The German phrase *traditionsgeschichte* means "history of tradition." It refers to the study of the historical context in which the Bible was written. A pericope is an individual story about the life of Jesus (cf. p. 43 below). Redaction criticism is the study of the process by which books of the Bible were thought to be edited over the years.

3. For fuller discussion of this letter, see chapter 3.

4. It is unlikely, though, that they would all have been sitting on one side of the table, as da Vinci shows them. Not even the people of his own day ate that way. He could not, however, have shown any apostle with his back to the viewer. Similarly, on TV shows and in theatrical productions today people usually don't sit all the way around a table when they eat. Performers want their faces instead of their backs toward the camera or the audience.

5. Dinner customs in the Greco-Roman world will be discussed in detail in chapter 7.

6. The verb "to sit" does occur in the New Testament, often in connection with the posture which Jesus assumed when teaching, as in Matthew 5:1; 13:1–2; 23:2; Mark 13:3.

Bibliography

Text and Context

1.1.   Collins, A. Y. "Insiders and Outsiders in the Book of Revelation and Its Social Context." In *"To See Ourselves As Others See Us": Christians, Jews, "Others" in Late Antiquity.* Ed. by J. Neusner et al. Chico, CA: Scholars Press, 1985: 187–218.

1.2.   Crim, K. R. "Translating the Bible: An Unending Task." *RelEd* 85(1990): 201–210.

1.3.   De Vries, P. G. R. "The Medium Is the Message: Luke and the Language of the New Testament Against a Graeco-Roman Background." *Neotest* 24(1990): 247–256.

1.4.   Dockery, D. S. "Author? Reader? Text? Toward a Hermeneutical Synthesis." *TheolEd* 38(1988): 7–16.

1.5.   Ellington, J. "Up on the Housetop." *BibTrans* 41(1990): 238–243.

1.6.   Esler, P. F. *Community and Gospel in Luke-Acts: The Social and Political Motivations of Lucan Theology.* New York: Cambridge University Press, 1987.

1.7.   Hodgson, R., Jr. "Valerius Maximus and the Social World of the New Testament." *CBQ* 51(1989): 683–693.

1.8.   Horsley, R. A. *The Liberation of Christmas: The Infancy Narratives in Social Context.* New York: Crossroad, 1989.

1.9.   Metzger, B. M. *The New Testament: Its Background, Growth, and Content.* Nashville: Abingdon Press, 1965.

1.10.   Osei-Bonsu, J. "The Contextualization of Christianity: Some New Testament Antecedents." *IrBibStud* 12(1990): 129–148.

1.11.   Oster, R. E. "When Men Wore Veils to Worship: The Historical Context of 1 Corinthians 11:4." *NTS* 34(1988): 481–505.

1.12.   Radcliffe, T. "Time and Telling: How to Read Biblical Stories." *NewBlackfr* 72(1992): 131–139.

1.13.   Robbins, V. K. "Text and Context in Recent Studies of the Gospel of Mark." *RelStudRev* 17(1991): 16–23.

1.14.   Salevsky, H. "Theory of Bible Translation and General Theory of Translation." *BibTrans* 42(1991): 101–114.

1.15.   Spencer, F. S. "The Ethiopian Eunuch and His Bible: A Social-Science Analysis." *BTB* 22(1992): 155–165.

1.16.   van der Horst, P. W., and G. Mussies. *Studies on the Hellenistic Background of the New Testament.* Utrecht: Rijksuniv. fac. der Godgeleerdheid, 1990.

From the Ivory Tower to the Pew

1.17.   Alexander, P. S. "Rabbinic Judaism and the New Testament." *ZNTW* 74(1983): 237–246.

1.18.   Barnett, P. *Behind the Scenes of the New Testament.* Downer's Grove, IL: InterVarsity Press, 1990.

1.19.   Beckwith, R. "Intertestamental Judaism, Its Literature and Its Significance." *Themelios* 15, no. 3, (1990): 77–81.

1.20.   Blaiklock, E. M. "Archaeology and the New Testament." *BurHist* 9, no. 2, (1973): 36– 71.

1.21.   Borowsky, I. J. "The Need for Two Translations of the Bible, One for Scholars and a Second 'Hate-Free' Edition for the Public." *Explorations* 11, no. 2, (1997), 3.

1.22.   Court, J., and K. Court. *The New Testament World.* Cambridge University Press, 1991.

1.23.   Eybers, I. H. "The Value of Archeological Excavations for Biblical Studies." *TheolEvang* 14(1981): 3–9.

1.24.   Fenn, R. K. "Sociology and Social History: A Preface to a Sociology of the New Testament." *JStudPseud* 1(1987): 95–114.

1.25.   Fields, W. *Thirteen Lessons on New Testament Backgrounds.* Joplin, MO: College Press, 1977.

1.26.   Gager, J. G. *Kingdom and Community: The Social World of Early Christianity.* Englewood Cliffs, NJ: Prentice-Hall, 1975.

1.27. Garner, G. G. "Archaeology as a Tool." *VoxRef* 50(1988): 39–47.

1.28. Gasque, W. W. "Background to the New Testament." *ChrT* 17(1972): 74–79.

1.29. Grant, M. *Jesus: An Historian's Review of the Gospels.* New York: Scribner's, 1977.

1.30. Grant, R. M. *Early Christianity and Society: Seven Studies.* New York: Harper & Row, 1977.

1.31. Harris, O. G. "The Social World of Early Christianity." *LexThQ* 19(1984): 102–114.

1.32. Holmberg, B. *Sociology and the New Testament: An Appraisal.* Minneapolis: Fortress Press, 1990.

1.33. Horbury, W. "Keeping Up with Recent Studies, V: Rabbinics." *ExposT* 91(1980): 233–240.

1.34. Horsley, G. H. R. "The Inscriptions of Ephesos and the New Testament." *NovT* 34(1992): 105–168.

1.35. Judge, E. A. "St. Paul and Classical Society." *JbAC* 15(1972): 19–36.

1.36. Kee, H. C. *The New Testament in Context: Sources and Documents.* Englewood Cliffs, NJ: Prentice-Hall, 1984.

1.37. Koester, H. *Introduction to the New Testament:* vol. 1, *History, Culture and Religion of the Hellenistic Age;* vol. 2, *History and Literature of Early Christianity.* Berlin: de Gruyter, 1982.

1.38. Malherbe, A. *Social Aspects of Early Christianity.* Baton Rouge: Louisiana State University Press, 1977.

1.39. Malina, B. J. *The New Testament World: Insights from Cultural Anthropology.* Atlanta: John Knox Press, 1981.

1.40. Marms, F., and E. Alliata, eds. *Early Christianity in Context: Monuments and Documents.* Jerusalem: Franciscan Printing Press, 1993.

1.41. Meeks, W. A. *The First Urban Christians: The Social World of the Apostle Paul.* New Haven, CT: Yale University Press, 1983.

1.42. Millard, A. *Discoveries from the Time of Jesus.* Batavia, IL: Lion Publishing Corp., 1990.

1.43. Nash, R. H. *Christianity and the Hellenistic World.* Grand Rapids: Zondervan, 1984.

1.44. Niswonger, R. L. *New Testament History.* Grand Rapids: Zondervan, 1988.

1.45. Nock, A. D. *Early Gentile Christianity and Its Hellenistic Background.* New York: Harper & Row, 1964.

1.46. Osiek, C. *What Are They Saying About the Social Setting of the New Testament?* 2nd ed. Mahwah, NJ: Paulist Press, 1992.

1.47. Oster, R. "Numismatic Windows into the Social World of Early Christianity: A Methodological Inquiry." *JBL* 101(1982): 195–223.

1.48. Packer, J. I., et al. *The World of the New Testament.* Nashville: Thomas Nelson, 1982.

1.49. Patterson, S. J. "Bridging the Gulf Between Bible Scholarship and Religious Faith." *BibRev* 6, no. 6, (1990): 16, 44.

1.50. Pervo, R. I. "Wisdom and Power: Petronius' *Satyricon* and the Social World of Early Christianity." *AngThR* 67(1985): 307–325.

1.51. Roetzel, C. J. *The World that Shaped the New Testament.* Atlanta: John Knox Press, 1985.

1.52. Spencer, R. B. "Is Biblical Scholarship Really Objective?" *Homiletic and Pastoral Review* 89, no.7, (1989): 52–58.

1.53. Stambaugh, J. E, and D. L. Balch. *The New Testament in Its Social Enviroment.* Philadelphia: Westminster Press, 1986.

1.54. Tidball, D. *The Social Context of the New Testament: A Sociological Analysis.* Grand Rapids: Zondervan, 1984.

Stone Walls and Prisons

1.55. Bell, A. A., Jr. "Pliny the Younger: The Kinder, Gentler Roman." *CB* 66(1990): 37–41.

1.56. Fitzgibbon, J. C. *"Ergastula."* *EMC* 20(1976): 55–59.

1.57. Forbes, C. A. "The Education and Training of Slaves in Antiquity." *TAPhA* 86(1955): 333–359.

1.58. Mealand, D. L. "The Close of Acts and Its Hellenistic Greek Vocabulary." *NTS* 36(1990): 583–597.

1.59.   Narducci, E. "Perceptions of Exile in Cicero: The Philosophical Interpretation of a Real Experience." *AJPh* 118(1997): 55–74.

1.60.   Rapske, B. M. *The Book of Acts and Paul in Roman Custody.* Grand Rapids: Eerdmans, 1994.

1.61.   ———. "The Importance of Helpers to the Imprisoned Paul in the Book of Acts." *TynBull* 42(1991): 3–30.

1.62.   Robinson, A. "Cicero's References to His Banishment." *CW* 87(1994): 475–480.

1.63.   Wansink, C. S. *Chained in Christ: The Experience and Rhetoric of Paul's Imprisonments.* Sheffield, UK: Academic Press, 1996.

The Last Supper

1.64.   Bartlett, D. L. "Biblical Perspective on Homosexuality." *Foundations* 20(1977): 133–147.

1.65.   Ide, A. F. *Battling with Beasts. Sex in the Life of St. Paul: The Issue of Homosexuality, Heterosexuality and Bisexuality.* Las Colinas, TX: Tanglewuld, 1991.

1.66.   ———. *Zoar and Her Sisters: Homosexuality, the Bible and Jesus Christ.* Oak Cliff, TX.: Minuteman, l991.

1.67.   Johnson, R. O. "What the Bible Says About Homosexuality." *Dialog* 28(1989): 149–150.

1.68.   Lance, H. D. "The Bible and Homosexuality." *AmerBaptQ* 8(1989): 140–151.

1.69.   Scanzoni, L. "On Friendship and Homosexuality." *ChrT* 18(1974): 1397–1402.

1.70.   Smith, A. "The New Testament and Homosexuality." *QuartRev* 11(1991): 18–32.

1.71.   Wright, D. F. "Homosexuality: The Relevance of the Bible." *EvangQ* 61(1989): 291–300.

Images of the Cruxifixion

1.72.   Heller, J. H. *Report on the Shroud of Turin.* Boston: Houghton Mifflin, 1983.

1.73.   Hoare, R. *The Turin Shroud Is Genuine: The Irrefutable Evidence.* New York: Barnes & Noble, 1994.

1.74.   Kohlbeck, J. A., and E. L. Nitowski. "New Evidence May Explain Image on Shroud of Turin." *BAR* 12, no. 4, (1986): 18–29.

1.75.   Nickell, J. *Inquest on the Shroud of Turin.* Rev. ed. Buffalo, NY: Prometheus Press, 1987.

1.76.   Paci, S. M. "The Shroud of Turin: The Case Is Not Closed!" *30 Days* 3, no. 6, (1990): 36–40.

1.77.   Picknett, L., and C. Prince. *Turin Shroud: In Whose Image? The Truth Behind the Centuries-Long Conspiracy of Silence.* New York: HarperCollins, 1994.

1.78.   Smith, D. M. "Mark 15:46: The Shroud of Turin as a Problem of History and Faith." *BAR* 9, no. 4, (1983): 251–254.

1.79.   Stevenson, K. E., and G. R. Habermas. *The Shroud and the Controversy.* Nashville: Thomas Nelson, 1990.

1.80.   Tzaferis, V. "Crucifixion – The Archeological Evidence." *BAR* 11, no. 1, (1985): 44–53.

1.81.   Weaver, K. F. "The Mystery of the Shroud." *National Geographic* 157 June 1980): 730–756.

1.82.   Wild, R. A. "The Shroud of Turin: Probably the Work of a 14th-Century Artist or Forger." *BAR* 10, no.2, (1984): 30–46.

1.83.   Wilson, I. *The Shroud of Turin: The Burial Cloth of Jesus Christ?* Rev. ed. Garden City, NY: Doubleday, 1979.

The Zero Factor

1.84.   Richardson, W. F. *Numbering and Measuring in the Classical World: An Introductory Handbook.* Oakland, N. Z.: St. Lanyards Publ., 1985.

1.85.   Scott, J. F. *A History of Mathematics: From Antiquity to the Beginning of the Nineteenth Century.* New York: Barnes & Noble, 1969.

Conclusion

1.86.   Janssen, A. "More than Words on a Page." *Perspectives* June/July 1997, 24.

CHAPTER 2

THE JUDAIC BACKGROUND OF THE NEW TESTAMENT

SOME CHRISTIANS DON'T like to be reminded that Jesus was a Jew. When I mentioned that fact in my grandmother's hearing, she immediately said, "Only on his mother's side." But Matthew and Luke both included genealogies at the beginnings of their gospels to lay claim to Jesus' Judaism in no uncertain terms. There is much debate over what relationship Jesus saw between himself and Judaism, but it does appear that he saw himself primarily as trying to reform Judaism, not trying to start another religion (**2.81**:363). There was, in his view, nothing inherently wrong with Judaism; the problem lay in the way people had distorted God's purpose over the centuries. He seems to have identified himself with prophets such as Amos and Micah, who protested against the emphasis on ritual and legalism at the expense of what Jesus called "the weightier matters of the law" (Matt. 23:23).

What makes it even more difficult to determine Jesus' attitude toward Judaism is that the Gospels were written at a time when the Christians were trying to establish an identity for themselves separate from the Jews, who had staged a long, bloody revolt against Rome in A.D. 66–73. The Jews, in turn, wanted no part of the *minim* (heretics) who recognized an executed criminal as the Messiah. Among the Eighteen Benedictions regularly recited in the synagogues was one which asked God to "let the Nazarenes and the heretics perish as in a moment, let them be blotted out of the book of the living." The Gospel of John, many scholars feel, reflects a decidedly negative view of the Jews, typical of Christians by the end of the first century. The earlier Gospels, especially Matthew, depict Jesus as sympathetic to Judaism, if not to its leaders. In Matthew 23:1–3 Jesus acknowledges the authority of the scribes and Pharisees, but cautions people to "do whatever they teach you and follow it; but do not do as they do, for they do not practice what they teach." We will return to this topic at the end of this chapter.

When we read the New Testament, we encounter the terms "scribes" and "Pharisees" frequently in the Gospels and early chapters of Acts, and they evoke a largely negative response. But who were the scribes and Pharisees? Who were some of the other Jewish groups, such as the Sadducees and Herodians, who are mentioned now and again in the Gospels? To understand more adequately what Jesus saw as his mission and why the early Christians eventually separated themselves from the Jews, we need to survey, however superficially, the state of Judaism in the early first century A.D.

Judaism: Hellenistic and Judean

Paul may have believed that in Christ there was no distinction between Jew and Greek (Gal. 3:28), but few Jews or Greeks (or Romans) of his day would have agreed. The Jews were accused by the Greeks and Romans of being aloof, separatist, priding themselves on maintaining their identity (cf. chapter 3). At a time when ethnic distinctions were being blurred under the *pax Romana*, Tacitus (*Hist.* 5.5) considered Jewish customs "perverse and disgusting" and claimed that the Jews "hate all others as though they were enemies" (cf. **2.2**; **2.11**).

But the Jews were divided among themselves by the first century (**2.10**). It was once fashionable to talk of the distinction between the Jews of Palestine and those of the Diaspora, the Jews scattered across the Mediterranean world (cf. James 1:1 and 1 Peter 1:1). The picture was simple: Palestinian Jews were conservative, clinging to the Hebrew Torah, untouched by Hellenistic influences. Diaspora Jews were virtually indistinguishable from their pagan neighbors in appearance, ignorant of Hebrew, and willing to write new devotional literature in Greek (which eventually became the Old Testament Apocrypha, with books like Tobit and 1–2 Maccabees).

Today, however, it no longer appears possible to insist on such clear-cut demarcations. Some scholars see Palestine itself as Hellenized, learning Greek customs and language (**2.7**); others are less certain (**2.4**). There is a new emphasis on the diversity of opinions among Diaspora Jews (**2.6**). Others see messianic fervor as a connector between Palestinian Jews and lower-class Jews in the Diaspora (**2.13**). R. Murray suggests that new distinctions need to be drawn up, based on criteria other than geography. He uses the terms 'Jew' and 'Judaism' for those who focused on the temple. Other groups, such as the Essenes, who were critical of the priests managing the temple rituals, Murray calls 'Hebrews' (**2.273**). In the discussion that follows, we will use the categories 'Diaspora Jews' and 'Palestinian Jews', even though they are not clearly defined in every case.

Conservative Jews such as the Essene community in Palestine practiced baptism for purification. (Photo by Gustav Jeeninga)

What made Palestinian Jews different from Diaspora Jews, even if only to a degree, was the use of the Hebrew/Aramaic language and the presence of the center of worship in *eretz Israel*, the land of Israel (**2.8**; **2.12**). This doesn't mean that Palestinian Jews didn't use Greek, only that the Hebrew/Aramaic language and ways of thinking dominated in Palestine, while Diaspora Jews had to be more aware of the dominant Greek culture around them. Only when those distinctions were lost, after the destruction of Jerusalem in A.D. 70, did ancient Judaism become unified (**2.3**). Then it was Palestinian Judaism which dominated, rejecting the "contagion" of the Greco-Roman world which had nearly destroyed it.[1]

The Diaspora

Diaspora Jews were descendants of those driven into exile when Jerusalem fell in 586 B.C. Some had gone to Babylon, others to Egypt, such as the prophet Jeremiah, who was dragged unwillingly into Egypt (Jer. 42:18–43:7). After 538 B.C. some Jews returned to Judea and began the rebuilding process, as recorded in the books of Ezra and Nehemiah. Others remained in their newly established homes. The Egyptian Jews built another temple on an island in the upper Nile at

Elephantine. Palestinian Jews regarded it as an abomination and it was destroyed in 410 B.C. When the city of Alexandria was established ca. 325 B.C., many Jews migrated there. By the time of the birth of Christ,

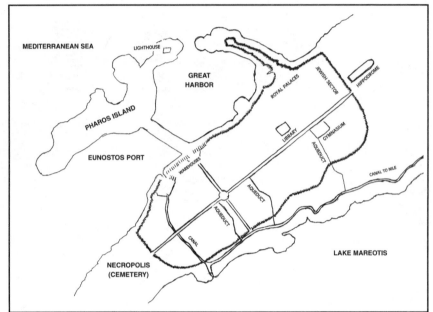

Map of Alexandria

it is estimated, at least a quarter of that city's population was Jewish, perhaps as much as 30 percent (**2.24**). The city was the home of one of the greatest Hellenistic Jewish thinkers, Philo, a member of a prominent family who served as an ambassador to the emperor Caligula (**2.15**; **2.45**).

With so many Jews spread around the Mediterranean, it is little wonder that the Greeks and Romans became aware of them and curious about their religion. If the author of Acts is right—and pagan literature does not refute him—the Greeks spent much of their time talking about new ideas (Acts 17:21). Many Gentiles appear to have attended synagogue services. Some synagogues were predominantly Hellenistic and provided the first inroads for Christian missionaries (**2.17**; **2.47**; **2.51**). The Jews who welcomed Paul to Corinth in Acts 18:7–8 bear suspiciously Greco-Roman names like Titius Justus and Crispus.

Justus is described by Luke as "a worshiper of God," a phrase used to denote Gentiles who attended the synagogues without fully converting to Judaism. These "Jewish sympathizers" (**2.27**) or "God-fearers" have been the subject of some controversy (**2.26**; **2.29**; **2.30**; **2.35**; **2.49**), but their presence can hardly be doubted. Some of them eventually converted to Judaism (**2.19**). Women converts went through an initiation bath, called *miqva'ot*, a ritual which may have had some impact on the Christian rite of baptism (**2.22**; **2.36**; **2.42–43**;

2.46). Circumcision was the stumbling block for many males (**2.20**; **2.31**). Many remained on the fringe of Judaism, reluctant to undergo that surgery (without anesthesia, remember). When what appeared to be an alternative form of Judaism—i. e., Christianity—presented itself, many of these "god-fearers" were apparently drawn to it.

Since Diaspora Jews were not as cut off from their neighbors as Palestinian Jews were, we might wonder how much, if any, intermarriage there might have been. The strictest interpretation of who is a Jew has long been that only the children of a Jewish mother qualify (**2.21**). Once a Gentile man converted to Judaism, he could marry a Jewish woman, and their children would be Jews. This may have happened more than we suspect. One papyrus from Alexandria, a loan agreement, closes with a physical description of the two men who are making a contract. Both are Jews. Apollonios is "tall, fair, with rather bright eyes and protruding ears." The other, Sostratos, is "of middle

Synagogue from Capernaum

height, fair." They probably would have mingled easily in the streets of the city. Ancient writers rarely comment on anything distinctive about the appearance of the Jews. They looked different only when they frequented the gymnasium or a public bath, where nudity was commonplace. In those contexts circumcision quickly identified the Jewish males.

Because of their lack of contact with Jerusalem, Jews in the Diaspora developed some features in their faith which their orthodox coreligionists in Judea saw as bordering on heresy (**2.29**). In cities around the Mediterranean, inscriptions record the participation of Jews in pagan cults, sometimes as officials (**2.17**). Contact between Jews and Greeks in the major cities, especially Alexandria, was so extensive and intensive that "the prevailing approach in Alexandrian Jewish apologetics" came to be "to show that Greek philosophers had borrowed from the Bible" (**2.29**:220). The more imaginative Jewish writers saw a connection between Moses and the legendary Greek sage and poet Musaeus (**2.14**; **2.32**). Many pagan intellectuals were attracted to Jewish monotheism and ethical practices. Even Tacitus, in the passage already cited, concludes his denunciation of the Jews with grudging admiration for their form of worship. Christians later used some of the same arguments.

Jews spread to other parts of the Mediterranean world as well and seem to have mingled with the pagan population wherever they went, to a greater extent than previously recognized. Inscriptions reveal their presence in Athens soon after 400 B.C. The poet Horace (ca. 30 B.C.) complained about the large numbers of Jews in Rome, and

Scale model of Herod's Temple
(Photo from Matson Collection, The Episcopal Home)

Ovid, writing a few years later, mentions the synagogue as a likely place for a man to meet young women (*Art of Love* 1.75). Diaspora Jews seem to have been eager to win converts, but a passage in Horace often cited as evidence of their aggressive proselytizing may point instead to their efforts to protect their political rights (**2.40–41**). The Romans allowed money sent to Jerusalem for the support of the temple to be counted as a tax payment. Once the temple was destroyed, however, the government continued to collect this *fiscus Judaicus*; whether or not an individual paid it was one test of his identity as a Jew (**2.33**).

Jewish customs were widely known, if often despised. The emperor Augustus joked in a letter that he was fasting like a Jew on the Sabbath (Suetonius, *Aug.* 76). He obviously didn't understand what Jews did on the Sabbath, but he could allude to their observation of the day and expect his reader to know roughly what he meant. Petronius mocked their table manners (**2.18**). Tacitus could parody the Exodus account and dismiss Jewish rituals and customs as deliberately contrary to the practices of sensible people (*Hist.* 5.3–5). The vocabulary used by a number of Roman poets indicates a greater familiarity with Judaism than one might at first suspect (**2.16**).

The Septuagint

Although these widely scattered Jews considered themselves devout children of Abraham, they could not avoid influences from the culture around them. The area in which they were most seriously affected was probably language. By the time they had lived outside Judea for a few generations, they had come to speak the languages of the people around them, in particular Greek. Alexander the Great's conquests had spread Greek culture and language all over the eastern Mediterranean. Hebrew was not immediately forgotten, as the Scriptures continued to be read in the original language, but the language of daily life was Greek. Soon many Jews found themselves unable to understand the Scriptures when they were read in the synagogue services.

During the third century B.C., the Jewish Scriptures were translated into Greek, a process begun in Alexandria. Whether it was instigated by Ptolemy II, the Greek king of Egypt who wanted to acquire as complete a royal library as possible (**8.93**), cannot be determined with certainty. When they learned what was happening, Jews in Judea held a national day of mourning, one apocryphal story says, because they considered Hebrew the only acceptable language for the reading and study of the Scriptures (**2.53**).

But this Greek version, eventually known as the Septuagint (abbreviated LXX) because it was allegedly done by seventy(-two) scholars, became the standard text for Diaspora Jews, just as the King James Version became a sacred text in its own right for many people who could not read the Hebrew or Greek originals. Some brilliant Jewish scholars, such as Philo, wrote extensive treatises on the Scriptures without being able to read Hebrew. Philo's claim that the Greek version was a verbatim translation of the Hebrew, equally inspired (see box), simply shows his lack

How the Septuagint Was Translated

They [the translators] were mindful of what a monumental task it was to make a faithful translation of laws which came from the mouth of God. They must not add or delete or change anything but were required to retain the original shape . . . . They fell under a kind of divine possession or inspiration so that they did not each produce their own translation but each wrote the same thing, word for word, like scribes taking dictation from an unseen reader. It's common knowledge that in any language, but especially in Greek, there are many terms with similar meanings, so that one idea can be expressed in many ways, differing by only a word or by a whole phrase. But in this case the Greek version was an exact match for the Chaldean [Hebrew], perfectly expressing the original meaning . . . . Chaldeans who have learned the Greek language, or Greeks the Chaldean, when they read both versions, the Chaldean and the translation, hold them in awe and reverence as sisters, or indeed as one and the same in subject matter and in words, and they regard the authors not as mere translators but as priests and prophets of the mysteries.

Philo, *Life of Moses* 2.34, 37–40

of familiarity with the Hebrew text. The *Letter of Aristeas* adds to the mystique of the LXX by claiming that it was translated in seventy-two days (**2.54**).

The LXX differs from the original in its readings in a number of passages. In fact three versions of the LXX eventually came into existence, as it was copied, edited, and corrected by various people. By the third century A.D. the Christian scholar Origen tried to reconcile them and establish a standard text. His compilation, known as the Hexapla, survives only in fragments. The LXX is useful to biblical scholars today because it is based on a Hebrew text older than any copy of the Old Testament which we have. Comparison of the Greek with the Hebrew can help in understanding and translating the latter (**2.55**).

As a Diaspora Jew, Paul was certainly more comfortable with Greek than with Hebrew. The author of Acts claims that Paul studied in Jerusalem under Gamaliel (Acts 22:3). Paul himself never mentions this in his letters, even when talking about his zeal for the Law (as in Gal. 1:14). If we grant that he did study in Jerusalem, he must have known Hebrew, but when he refers to Old Testament passages in his letters, he quotes the LXX, the version his readers knew.

Some Diaspora Jews may have known both versions of the Scriptures, but the Greek was the only one non-Jews could read. One pagan writer on style, Longinus, cites Genesis 1:3 and 1:9–10 (*De Sublimitate* 9.9). His wording is not exactly the same as the LXX and may indicate that there was some general knowledge of the text among the Greeks and Romans (**2.56**). The satirist Juvenal makes light of the "obscure volume of Moses" (*Sat.* 14.100–104).

Judaism and Hellenism in Judea

It's tempting to draw a sharp line between the Diaspora Jews and the more conservative, traditional Jews of Judea, but as already noted, that would not be entirely accurate. To begin with, Judean Jews used Hebrew only in the synagogues (**2.94**). In everyday life Aramaic, a related Semitic tongue, had long since become the spoken language of the land. When the New Testament says "Hebrew," it really means Aramaic (John 19:20; Acts 21:40). It was even necessary to publish Targums, Aramaic translations of the Hebrew Scriptures (**2.85**; **2.101**), a process well attested by the first century A.D.

Greek was so widely spoken by the first century A.D. that it might be more accurate to describe Palestine as multilingual (**2.90**). Hellenistic influences had permeated many areas of life in Judea. The Jews fought the Maccabean revolt in 167–164 B.C. to assert their freedom from the Greek king Antiochus IV Epiphanes, who insisted that all his subjects worship the Greek gods (**2.63**; 1 Macc. 1). But after winning that war, at least one family of Jewish high priests began taking names like Jason and Menelaus, which come from Greek mythology (**2.79**). Archaeologists have unearthed the tombs of the high priest

Caiaphas and his family and have found coins inserted in the mouths of the deceased, a Greek practice to pay for the ferry across the river Styx in the underworld (**2.70**). Even in the last throes of their fight for independence, under siege at Masada, someone scratched something in Greek on a broken piece of pottery (**2.65**).

Greek institutions like the wrestling schools and baths sprang up in Jerusalem itself. The wrestling school was built on the very temple hill (1 Macc. 1:14–15). And the Jews seem to have attended these places regularly (**2.73**). Some were so eager to blend in with their Greek overlords and neighbors that they resorted to surgery to remove the evidence of circumcision, which they could no longer hide when they stripped to exercise or bathe, as the Greeks always did (**2.72**; **2.96**:25; 1 Macc. 1:11–15; 2 Macc. 4:9–17). The details of the operation are spelled out by the Roman doctor Celsus (ca. A.D. 30) in his *De medicina* 7.25.1 (**2.93**). Herod the Great adopted a policy of deliberate Hellenization. He staged games on the Greek model, rebuilt and renamed cities (e. g., Caesarea), gave his children a Greek education, and encouraged his non-Jewish subjects to participate in the imperial cult (see chapter 5). Many upper-class Jews adopted the Greco-Roman custom of reclining on couches to eat their meals (**2.99**; see chapter 8).

Although this process of Hellenization began in earnest after the Seleucid conquest of the area in 200 B.C., in the view of V. A. Tcherikover:

> Hellenism was not introduced into Israel by the forces outside; part of the Jewish public itself developed an attachment to alien customs and became eager for Hellenistic modes of life to obtain a foothold in Jerusalem. . . . The bearers of the idea of Hellenization among the Jews were not distributed among various classes of Jewish society, but were entirely confined to one class, namely, the ruling aristocracy of Jerusalem (**2.102**:118).

The debate over the degree to which Greek manners and ways of thought might have influenced Palestine is an example of how supposedly objective scholars can become personally involved in their subjects. Tcherikover's view is seconded by M. Hengel (**2.76**), who argues that Hellenization began even before Alexander the Great's time, with the arrival of Greek mercenaries in Palestine as part of the Persian army. But L. H. Feldman, an Orthodox Jewish scholar, can refute Hengel at virtually every point (**2.66**) and maintains that any Greek influences in Palestine were late and superficial (**2.67**). As S. Sandmel points out (**2.95**), even the most serious scholars sometimes come down on the side of theories that they simply feel comfortable with. Only rarely do they admit their subjectivity as openly as S. Pomeroy did when, concluding an argument, she said, "While there is no firm evidence to confirm the hypothesis, I find it easier to believe that . . ." (**7.113**:37).

The New Testament gives somewhat ambiguous evidence of this Hellenistic influence on Judean Judaism. Jesus came from a portion of Palestine called "Galilee of the Gentiles," supposedly because of the predominance of non-Jewish elements there (Matt. 4:15). Feldman argues that the Greek cities in the district were almost exclusively on the border and that the interior was un-Hellenized. On this interpretation, only the lower part of Galilee, where Jesus came from, appears to have been touched by Greek influences (**2.67**:95). Klausner, though, reached a different conclusion, which he put forth unequivocally (**2.81**:363):

> Jesus of Nazareth, however, was a product of Palestine alone, a product of Judaism unaffected by any foreign admixture. There were many Gentiles in Galilee, but Jesus was in no way influenced by them. In his days Galilee was the stronghold of the most enthusiastic Jewish patriotism. Jesus spoke Aramaic and there is no hint that he knew Greek.

Klausner, it must be noted, had not seen the results of archaeological excavations at Sepphoris, a city built by Herod Antipas and called by Josephus the "ornament of all Galilee." This city of some 30,000 people had all the accoutrements of a Greek city: agora (marketplace), baths, gymnasium, and theater. One hour's walk to the south lies Nazareth. The excavations, begun in 1983, indicate that Greek influences pervaded Galilee to a degree that scholars had not previously suspected (**2.58**; **2.64**; **2.84**; **2.89**). It is highly unlikely that Jesus could have been totally untouched by contact with this center of Greek culture, though there is admittedly no direct mention of this city in the New Testament (**2.91**).

The evidence is obviously capable of widely different interpretations. There is even a middle ground. S. Freyne (**2.68–69**) has shown that the Jews of Judea regarded Galilee as less purely Jewish than their own area. The two districts were separated geographically by Samaria, and direct communication was difficult. The people of Galilee, however, seem to have been devoted to the Jerusalem temple cultus, even if pharisaic teaching, with its constant references to the opinions of earlier teachers, did not dominate the way it did in Judea (**2.82**). It was the decidedly un-pharisaic quality of Jesus' teaching—with its emphasis on his personal authority—that made him so popular with the people of Galilee (Mark 1:22), and that still makes some Jews uncomfortable with him (**2.103**).

In spite of what Klausner says, it is highly likely that Jesus spoke Greek; any tradesman in that area would have needed at least a working knowledge of the language to survive (**2.98**). The large number of Greek and bilingual (Greek and Aramaic) inscriptions found in Palestine "prove beyond any reasonable doubt that the majority of Jewish families could read and write Greek and did so even for strictly family business" (**2.87**:82). Josephus says, in a curious passage (*Ant.* 20.263), that knowledge of Greek was more common among lower-class people. He himself had to have assistants help him in his writing because he normally spoke Aramaic. Most of Jesus' teaching in Judea was more likely to have been done in Aramaic. Some scholars see in his vocabulary and sentence structure an Aramaic origin for his parables and short, pithy sayings (**2.98**). Others suspect he was influenced by performances in the Greek theater (**2.59**).

Suggestions of Greek influences can be found in the Gospels. The names of two of Jesus' disciples—Philip and Andrew—are Greek. When Pilate questioned Jesus at his trial, there does not seem to have been any lack of communication, unless they were using an interpreter of whom we're not informed. In situations where they had to deal with "barbaric" people such as the Celts and Carthaginians, the Romans did make use of interpreters and refer to them in their literature (**2.57**). But they did not regard Greek as a "foreign" language; it was "the other language." Roman boys learned it in elementary school right along with Latin.

Pilate, like any educated Roman of the day, would have spoken Greek fluently. Latin was the official language of the Empire but little used in the eastern Mediterranean. When relations between Jews and Romans grew heated, they did fall back to their native languages. Titus's speech to the Jews shortly before he conquered Jerusalem was delivered in Latin and translated into Aramaic (Josephus, *War* 6.327). But, under normal circumstances, both sides could have used Greek. If we admit the possibility that Jesus knew some Greek, he and Pilate could have carried on a conversation (**2.92**). For official purposes when Jesus was crucified, Pilate put a sign over him in three languages: Latin, Greek, and Aramaic (John 19:20).

The early Christians did not escape these linguistic problems. In Acts 6 the Jerusalem church was troubled by a dispute between the Hebrews (old-line Judean Jews) and the Hellenists (those who had come back from the Diaspora or were Greek converts to Judaism) (**2.77**; **2.100**). To keep peace, seven men, all with good Greek names, were appointed deacons.

Even more interesting is Acts 6:9, which mentions that Jews from various synagogues (a Greek word, incidentally; **2.83**) began to dispute with Stephen over the Christian message. Their synagogues bear revealing names: "of the Freedmen . . . , Cyrenians, Alexandrians, and others of those from Cilicia and Asia." The presence of enough Alexandrian Jews in Jerusalem to warrant a synagogue of their own suggests that there was probably more contact between Palestine and Egypt than is usually assumed. Cyrene was a Greek city in North Africa; Cilicia and Asia were Greek-speaking provinces in what is now Turkey. So, even in the very heart of Judaism, people from a Hellenistic background were numerous. Some of those people provided a bridge between the synagogues and the first churches in Palestine (**2.78**; **2.86**). Those early churches quickly took on a Greek identity (**2.71**).

Aramaic, however, was still the native language of the people, and most business in the street was conducted in that tongue. Much like a modern American city, with signs in English and Spanish, Jerusalem was a city which had to say everything important in at least two languages. Archaeologists have uncovered a bilingual inscription in the temple warning Greeks not to enter the inner courtyard (**2.61**; **2.97**). When Paul was thought to have violated this rule, he was mobbed and only barely rescued by Roman soldiers. The tribune in charge seemed surprised that his prisoner spoke Greek. Paul then asked to address the crowd and did so in Hebrew/Aramaic (Acts 21:27–22:21).

In spite of the Gentile cultural influences pressing upon them, Judean Jews struggled to retain their identity. If they appear in the New Testament to be overly conservative and self-righteous, we must note two things. First, the picture we have of them was drawn by those of an opposing party. Second, they were trying to preserve their religious heritage. They had fought a war with Antiochus Epiphanes (1–2 Maccabees). They had forced Herod to remove some images from a theater in Jerusalem (Josephus *Ant.* 15.8.2). They had made Pilate take out of Jerusalem legionary standards, banners depicting Caesar, contrary to the second commandment (Ex. 20:4–6; Josephus, *Ant.* 18.3.1). Having faced all those challenges successfully, they were not about to let a lone individual like Jesus "subvert" the faith they had struggled so hard and long to preserve.

Oral Tradition in Judaism

Students of the New Testament often encounter references to Mishnah, Talmud, *halakah*, and other unfamiliar terms describing documents relating to Jewish interpretation of the Old Testament. An old tradition among Jewish scholars of antiquity held that Moses began a process of explaining the meaning of the Law. Noted scribes such as Ezra were believed to have passed along this body of oral teaching. Since the Jews of the pre-Christian era had not settled on a canon of sacred books and since they did not adhere to a literal reading of their scriptures, they could dispute the meaning of any passage. The interpretation given by a majority of rabbis was supposed to be binding, but the minority opinions were also preserved. These authoritative pronouncements are called *halakah*. This rabbinic style can be observed in Paul's letters (**2.113**). The *halakah* came to be organized by subject matter in a collection of treatises known as the *Mishnah*, from a Hebrew word meaning to "repeat" or "study." (One studied by repeating the material until it was memorized.) The Mishnah was committed to writing by the end of the second century A.D., under the direction of the highly revered Rabbi Judah, called the Patriarch or the Prince. But the process of explaining the Law didn't stop there. Later groups of rabbis, known as the *Amoraim* ("speakers") created a commentary on the Mishnah, known as the *Gemara* or completion. The Mishnah and Gemara were combined, in the fifth and sixth centuries, into the Talmud, another word meaning "study" or "instruction." The Talmud exists in two versions, the Babylonian and Jerusalem (or Palestinian). The Babylonian Talmud is about four times as long as the Jerusalem Talmud and is generally recognized as *the* Talmud (**2.105**; **2.112**).

Another category of interpretive material not included in the Talmud is the *Midrashim*, commentaries on various biblical passages, primarily from Exodus, Leviticus, Numbers, Deuteronomy, and Psalms. These sometimes take the form of legal proscriptions, sometimes of sermon-like explanations. The dates of this material range from the early Christian era to the twelfth century A.D. (**2.110**). A major problem in using any of Talmudic or Midrashic evidence in the study of first-century Judaism is that one cannot be certain of the date of origin of any particular passage. An opinion attributed to one rabbi may have been merely his statement of a view that had been in circulation long before, or it may be a later view attributed to an earlier, more authoritative rabbi in order to give it more weight. This material also reflects a concern with Palestinian Judaism alone, not with the Diaspora.

Perhaps more important for students of the New Testament are the *targumim*, or Aramaic paraphrases of the Hebrew scripture. The need for these paraphrases arose as early as ca. 500 B.C. because Aramaic had replaced Hebrew as the everyday language of Palestine and people could no longer understand their scriptures when read in their original version. In Nehemiah 8:8 we find a likely allusion to an oral targum: "They [the priests] read from the book, from the law of God, with interpretation. They gave the sense, so that the people understood the reading." Some of these targums were eventually written down and provide an important witness to the form of the biblical text of about the first century. They circulated widely; the quotation of Psalms 68:18 in Ephesians 4:8 is actually from a targum, not from the Hebrew or the Septuagint (**2.104**; **2.108**).

Jewish Factions

Even in their struggle to preserve and transmit their faith, the Jews were split into several factions or parties, what one scholar calls "a society divided by religion" (**2.117**). Christians tend to think just of "the Jews" without realizing that there were divergent and even conflicting viewpoints within Judaism, just as there are today. Defining "orthodoxy" in first-century Judaism has proved difficult (**2.114**; **2.116**; **2.119**). As E. Ferguson says, "At any given time it would be possible to find Jews believing almost anything and everything, and this is especially true at the beginning of the Christian era. To list the elements of Jewish 'orthodoxy' is an all but impossible task" (**2.5**:502). Instead of a monolithic Judaism, it might be more accurate to talk about "multiple Judaisms" (**2.115**). Putting it more positively, one scholar has described Judaism in the New Testament period as "so alive, so progressive, so agitated by controversies, that under its spacious roof the most contrasting views could be held—until a greater uniformity was reached after A.D. 200" (**2.120**:53). Most of the parties of first-century Judaism are mentioned in the New Testament. It will help us to understand their opposition to Jesus if we see them first as upholders of their religious tradition, however they may have differed among themselves over its interpretation.

Those differences were extremely important while the Jews enjoyed their existence as a nation. The writers of the first three Gospels are usually specific when they mention a certain party of Jews as opposing Jesus. Only when Paul's missionary work spreads into the Greek world do we find Christian writers making a broad contrast between "Jew and Greek." To outsiders, the factional disputes seemed, in Gallio's words, "a matter of questions about words and names and your own law" (Acts 18:15 RSV).

As we look at specific groups that constituted Judaism in Jesus' day, we should bear in mind that they represent several approaches to religion which might be found in any tradition. The Sadducees emphasized formalism, devotion to the temple and its rituals, a strain which survived in Palestine even during the exile. The Pharisees were typical of a group which tries to adjust to changed circumstances. When the Jews did not have the temple during the Babylonian exile, they developed synagogues and teachers to instruct the people. After the destruction of the temple in A.D. 70, they focused on the study and transmission of the Torah and its interpretation. The term *Pharisee* may not have been used after 70, but the approach of the rabbis was the same (**2.118**).

The Essenes were the ascetics, emphasizing self-denial and self-discipline and demanding more of themselves than most members of their larger religious group. The Sicarii and Zealots were the radicals, those unwilling to accept any compromise with their belief that only God is Lord over Israel. These approaches to Judaism appear to have existed throughout its history, though the groups which embodied them may have been called by different names at different times (**2.121**). We can thus trace Sadducean and Pharisaic attitudes back to Old Testament times, even if the groups called by those names in the New Testament do not have that long a history.

Sadducees

Starting at the top of the social scale, we encounter first the group known as the Sadducees from their alleged descent from David's high priest Zadok (2 Sam. 8:17; 1 Kings 2:35), or perhaps from the word *saddiq*, meaning "righteous" (**2.124**). They took an ultra-conservative stance, recognizing only the authority of the Torah (the five books of Moses) and refusing to sanction any doctrine not explicitly taught therein. Sadducees could not deny the existence of angels which appear in the Torah, but they were cool to elaborate beliefs about angels and demons that flourished in the period after the Babylonian exile. They did not see resurrection in the Torah (though others might: Heb. 11:19). Thus they rejected belief in resurrection either in the form of angels or of spirits (**2.126**; Acts 23:8).[2]

Knowing that helps us understand why the Sadducees ask Jesus the question about the woman married to seven brothers in succession (Mark 12:18–27). Whose wife will she be in the "resurrection"? We can almost hear them snickering as they pose the problem. Within their own circle, they probably regarded it as reducing to absurdity the whole case for a bodily resurrection. Jesus answers them with a text from "the book of Moses," the only Scripture they acknowledge, and teaches that the dead raised are like angels, who don't marry. Later the Sadducees attacked the apostles for preaching "that in Jesus there is the resurrection of the dead" (Acts 4:1–3; 5:17). They didn't believe in his resurrection because they rejected the general notion of resurrection. Paul was able to create dissension between the Sadducees and Pharisees on the Sanhedrin by voicing his belief in the hope of the resurrection (Acts 23:6–8).

The Sadducees had little contact with the ordinary people of Judea and no concern with popularity. Josephus says that "even towards each other [they] show a rather harsh spirit, and they treat others like themselves as rudely as they do foreigners" (*War* 2.166). In another passage he says they "have the support of the rich only but no following among the masses; the Pharisees, on the other hand, enjoy popular support" (*Ant.* 13.298). The Sadducees, then, were an aristocratic, high-priestly group, concerned almost exclusively with running the temple (**2.123**). After it was destroyed in 70, the Sadducees disappeared from history, unable to adapt to the changed circumstances in which Judaism found itself (**2.125**).

Pharisees/Scribes

Trying to arrive at a precise definition of who the Pharisees were is an exercise only for those with a high tolerance for frustration (**2.137**). To begin with, we have very few documents which we know beyond doubt were produced by the Pharisees, so we have little evidence for determining what they thought they were about. We have to base our study of them largely on the opinions of their opponents, the Sadducees and the Christians (**2.131**). All we can say for certain is that they weren't priests, and the term rabbi was not yet commonly used. They were teachers and interpreters of the Torah, "a scholar class dedicated to the supremacy of the twofold Law, the Written and the Unwritten" (**2.155**:247; **2.160**).

The very meaning of their name is debatable. Manson (**2.124**) thought it was a corruption of Persian, an allusion to the theological doctrines—resurrection, expanded belief in angels and demons—which they were accused of picking up from the East. Others argue that the Semitic root of the word means "heretic" or "separated one" (**2.155**). The term was allegedly used at first in a derogatory way because the Pharisees accepted as Scripture some books outside the Torah. Another suggestion is that the name comes from the Hebrew word meaning to "specify" or "be exact," alluding to their concern with the fine points of the Law (**2.128**). In the Talmud the name is used only in opposition to the term Sadducee. Otherwise the Pharisees are called "sages" or "scribes."

The Gospels often speak of "scribes and Pharisees," as though the two were separate groups. This may not have been the case. The confusion possibly arose out of difficulties in translation caused by changes in the meanings of words.

A class of scribes (*soferim*; singular *sofer*) had existed in Judaism probably since the time of Ezra, who led the people of Israel back to a strict observance of the Law after their return from the Babylonian exile (538 B.C.). Scribes were copyists of the Law and regarded themselves as its preservers and protectors, rather than inspired interpreters. One Talmudic tractate urges the *sofer* to "be deliberate in giving judgment, and train many disciples, and make a fence around the Law" (Mishnah Aboth 1.1). When the LXX was translated, the Greek word *grammateus* (scribe in the literal sense) was used for the Hebrew *sofer*, and the meaning was clear.

By the late second century B.C., the Hebrew *sofer* had taken on a new meaning, seen in the apocryphal book of Ben Sirach or Ecclesiasticus, which says that the scribe "seeks out the wisdom of all the ancients. . . . He will show the wisdom of what he has learned, and will glory in the law of the Lord's covenant" (Sirach 38:24–39:11). By that time the term *sofer* had come to signify an interpreter of the law, "an intellectual, not a scribe; a scholar, not a copyist" (**2.157**:139). The Greeks, however, still translated the word as *grammateus*, and that word had not changed its meaning. The term Pharisee, whatever it may have meant, seems to have been applied to these scribes at first in a derogatory sense, just as Christian seems to have arisen as a term of abuse for Jesus' early followers in Antioch (Acts 11:26).

Other terms are used in the Gospels to make clear who the Pharisees were, to describe their function to those unfamiliar with Palestinian Judaism. They are "those skilled in the law" and "teachers of the law." When the word *grammateus* is used, it is often followed in Greek by *kai Pharisaioi*. The word *kai* usually means "and," but it can also mean "even" or "namely." Apparently the first generation of Christians were aware of the need to clarify that these scribes were different from what was normally meant by the Greek word *grammateus*.

They were "the scribes, namely the Pharisees." This distinction, however, was lost on later commentators and translators until a wholly artificial and meaningless separation was created. In fact, a separate group was created which never existed as a discrete entity in Palestinian Judaism.

According to Josephus, who may have been one (**2.148**), the Pharisees were "considered the most authoritative in their explanations

The Wailing Wall, part of the temple wall in Jerusalem, remains a popular place of prayer for modern Jews. (Photo by Ben Chapman)

of the Law and esteemed as the leading sect" (*War* 2.162). Jesus said that they "sit on Moses' seat," and he urged people to follow their teaching, if not their practice (Matt. 23:2–3). Several recent studies (e. g., **2.133**) have focused on Jesus' relationship to the Pharisees, with results that might surprise many modern Christians, who know the group only as an object of contempt (**2.134**; **2.139**). That attitude is certainly not new. Even before the birth of Christ, Nicolaus of Damascus condemned them as hypocritical, greedy, and devious. But he was Herod the Great's court historian, and the Pharisees opposed Herod bitterly, so his account is no model of objective reporting.

The Pharisees could be called the "liberals" of their day. In contrast to the Sadducees, they were "congenial to one another and desirous of concord with the people" (Josephus, *War* 2.166; cf. **2.153**). They accepted the books of the prophets as authoritative Scripture along with the Torah, though most were not yet prepared to canonize the Writings, the group of miscellaneous books including Esther, Psalms, Proverbs, Daniel, and several others. The Pharisees placed great stress on a continuing oral interpretation of the Scripture as conditions changed or new insights were achieved. Jesus referred to this body of oral law, which eventually became the Mishnah and was incorporated into the Talmud, when he criticized the Pharisees for teaching "human precepts" in place of the commandments of God (Mark 7:6–8).

Along with new interpretations of the Law, the Pharisees welcomed new rituals not ordained by the Torah and thus not observed by the Sadducees. They celebrated Hanukkah, established in 164 B.C. by the Maccabees to commemorate the cleansing of the temple from its defilement by King Antiochus IV Epiphanes (**2.154**); and Purim, the joyous re-enactment of the Jews' rescue by Esther. The practice of baptizing proselytes is pharisaic, as is much Jewish doctrine about angels, demons, the Messiah (**2.231**), and bodily resurrection. One scholar has described modern Judaism as "the monument of the Pharisees" (**2.149**:1).

The particular groups known to us as Sadducees and Pharisees both developed out of the Maccabean period (160s B.C.). The Pharisees seem to have come from a group called the "Hasidim," or the "Pure Ones." (This term is also used of several later Jewish mystic groups, especially one founded in the eighteenth century.) These devout Jews refused to break the Law by fighting on the Sabbath (1 Macc. 1:29–42). As a result, not many of them survived the war. Those remaining seem to have liberalized their views a bit, though not their devotion to preserving the Law (**2.141**; **2.150**). The Pharisees, as they came to be called, professed "to be more religious than other sects, propounding the laws more accurately," as Josephus says (*Vita* 191). There may be an implicit criticism in his statement that accords with the New Testament view of the group.

In Jesus' day the Pharisees themselves were divided into two strongly opposing groups which had arisen in the generation immediately before Jesus' lifetime. One, headed by Hillel, took a fairly lenient view of the Law and a conciliatory stance in most controversies, whether with Gentiles or other Jews. Scholars have long recognized (**2.81**:361ff.) that Jesus' teaching closely resembles that of Hillel, who formulated the so-called negative golden rule: "Do not do unto others what you would not have them do unto you."[3] Gamaliel, who advised the Sanhedrin to "consider carefully what you propose to do to these men" (Acts 5:33ff.), was a follower of Hillel, whose opinions were in the minority at that time. Paul was a student of Gamaliel (Acts 22:3) and thus indirectly influenced by Hillel (**2.140**).

The other pharisaic school was led by Shammai, whose intolerance of contact with Gentiles led him to advocate a stricter interpretation of the Mosaic Law and opposition to the Roman government. Combining with the more radical anti-Roman factions who did not hesitate to use violence, his party won control of the Sanhedrin during Jesus' lifetime. Not until after the destruction of the temple in 70 did the moderate views of Hillel become dominant (**2.138**; **2.162**).

After 70, the terms "Pharisee" and "scribe" drop out of common usage, to be replaced by "rabbi," and we find less emphasis on parties or factions in Judaism (**2.133**). Once the center of their worship had been removed, all Jews became concerned with the problem of ensuring the survival of their faith. It is possible to see the whole pharisaic movement as an attempt to free Judaism from the domineering priesthood and the restrictive temple cultus, themes not entirely alien to Jesus' own ministry (**2.158**; **2.161**). To the extent that was true, the destruction of the temple was less a disaster than an opportunity to promote an alternative mode of Judaism.

The spiritual leaders who survived the fall of Jerusalem gathered at the little town of Yavneh (or Jamnia) in western Judea and set themselves to studying the Torah (**2.143**). The exact role of this "council" in the development of post-destruction Judaism is still not clear (**2.127**). The synagogue, a familiar feature of Jewish life since the Babylonian exile, now became its very foundation (**2.142**). By the end of the century, the rabbis had resolved the problem of which books were sacred, a discussion in process for at least a century or two (**2.130**; **2.145–146**). After 70, the Jews were not troubled by splits like those between the Sadducees and Pharisees. But Yavneh should be seen as the formation of a coalition, not a pharisaic triumph. The rabbis, looking back on the disastrous consequences of strife between parties, "saw themselves as members of the same philosophical school who could debate in friendly fashion the tenets of the school" (**2.132**:51).

The Herodians

The groups discussed so far were essentially religious, although the Sadducees did have considerable political influence. But other Jewish factions mentioned in the New Testament had predominantly political overtones. The Herodians (Matt. 22:16; Mark 3:6; 8:15; 12:13) apparently were a party favoring the restoration of one of Herod's descendants to the throne (**2.164–165**). Herod's son Antipas was tetrarch of Galilee during Jesus' lifetime, while another son, Philip, ruled Ituraea and Trachonitis (east of Galilee). In the Gospels the Herodians are always mentioned in connection with the Pharisees, but it seems to have been the Pharisees who initiated the contact (Mark 3:6), perhaps in an effort to gain political allies in their campaign against Jesus. Herod Antipas, however, was deeply concerned about Jesus because of his connection with John the Baptist, whom Antipas had beheaded (Mark 6:16), so he may have been willing to cooperate with the Pharisees in their opposition to Jesus.

Luke's Gospel never mentions the Herodians, even in passages which parallel Mark's account (Luke 6:1–11; cf. Mark 3:1–6). Luke is the only evangelist to relate that Pilate sent Jesus to Herod Antipas during the deliberations over his fate. Since Jesus was a Galilean, Pilate hoped to evade a decision on a technicality. Antipas questioned Jesus, then allowed his soldiers to mock and abuse him before sending him back to Pilate (Luke 23:6–12). Luke reports that this led to a reconciliation between Antipas and Pilate. The point of the story is obscure, as is Luke's motive for omitting any reference to the Herodians' opposition to Jesus. One possibility is that, by absolving Herod and his party (Rome's allies) from blame, he fixes the heavier fault for Jesus' execution on the Jewish populace and the Pharisees.

The Herodians must have been pleased when Herod's grandson Agrippa I was made king of Judea in 41 by his friend, the new emperor Claudius (3.83). But Agrippa died in 44 (Acts 12:20–23), and the province reverted to being governed by a Roman prefect. Agrippa II eventually ruled over various northern territories, including Galilee, but Judea remained under direct Roman control. We hear no more of the Herodian party. A couple of the church fathers thought the Herodians believed that Herod was the Messiah, but this mistaken assumption was an attempt to fill a void when they lacked solid information (cf. also the section on The Herodian Family in chapter 3).

Zealots

One of Jesus' lesser-known disciples, Simon, is referred to in Luke 6:15 and Acts 1:13 as "the Zealot." This also happens to be the name of the radical party which led the defense of Jerusalem, fighting the Romans almost as vehemently as they fought among themselves. Before we assume that one of Jesus' followers was a revolutionary, note three things: first, in Mark 3:18 and Matthew 10:4, Simon is called "the Cananaean;" second, there is no evidence in any other source, including Josephus, that the Zealots, as a political party, existed before the outbreak of the revolt against Rome in 66 (2.176); third, Luke, with his purpose to make a strong case for Christianity (see chapter 3), would hardly have described one of Jesus' disciples as a member of the group which had led the fanatical resistance to the Roman conquest of Jerusalem. As with the Pharisees, confusion is rife when we try to determine who the Zealots were, when they arose, and what they stood for (2.170).

Some scholars trace the origins of the faction to the revolt of Judas of Gamala, founder of what Josephus calls the "fourth philosophy"—"philosophy" being a term he uses for the sects such as the Pharisees, Sadducees, and Essenes. Judas led a revolt in 6 A.D. in opposition to the census of Quirinius. His followers "agree completely with the views of the Pharisees, except that their desire for freedom is almost unconquerable, since they believe God to be their only leader and master" (*Ant.* 18.23–24). Josephus, however, does not call this group Zealots. They were zealous for the Law,[4] as were many Jews in the first century, but they seem to have been a splinter group among the Pharisees, rather than a separate group with their own name (2.174). The Aramaic word *qanna'im,* the origin of Cananaean, corresponds to the

Greek *zelotes*. Simon's name, in either language, simply means "Simon, the zealous one" (**2.166**). Why that title was thought more appropriate for this Simon than for Simon Peter, we cannot say.

As tensions with Rome heightened, various groups of zealous Jews resorted to violence. The Sicarii, or Assassins, are first mentioned in 54 A.D., mingling in crowds with daggers concealed under their cloaks, striking down someone thought to be collaborating with the Romans, then melting back into the throng (**2.172**; **2.178**). For Josephus, they are nothing but bandits (**2.168**; **2.171**). It was once thought that Judas' nickname, Iscariot, might be a corrupted form of that group's name, but the chronology is wrong and the word Iscariot seems to have another derivation, from an Aramaic word meaning "false" (**2.177**).

Finally, as the war broke out in 66, a party or faction labeling itself "the Zealous Ones" or "the Zealots" took the lead, perhaps inspired by the example of the Maccabean resistance to the Seleucids (**2.169**). Fortified with apocalyptic notions of the imminent arrival of a Davidic messiah, they were eager to fight the Romans (**2.167**:59). They seized control of Jerusalem early in the war, defending it with a fanaticism which made any solution except destruction of the city impossible. Josephus blames them for the bitter factional strife which split the population even while they were besieged by the Romans. The Pharisees actually left Jerusalem once the Zealots took control. In a sense, then, the defense of the city hardly represented mainstream Judaism. It was the work of one of its most radical wings (**2.173**; **2.179**). (For more on Rome's relationships with Judea, see chapter 3.)

Essenes

A group not mentioned by name in the New Testament, but which influenced Jewish thought heavily at that time, was the Essenes. These devout individuals lived either in sequestered groups in towns (**2.206**) or in communities in the desert, such as the one discovered in the late 1940s at Qumran (**2.181**). If the Dead Sea Scrolls are an accurate indication, their theology was heavily apocalyptic and their lifestyle was self-disciplined and ascetic. John the Baptist had strong overtones of Essene thought in his preaching and appearance (**2.180**; **2.183**). Some also think that Jesus' forty days in the wilderness (Mark 1:12–13) might have been spent at an Essene community or that he had been in previous contact with such a group and was accustomed to spending time alone in the desert. But if Josephus' description of the Essenes is accurate (*War* 2.119–161), it seems unlikely that Jesus could have had anything to do with the group (**2.179**; **2.194**). Some points of contact between Paul and the Essenes have also been noted (**2.203**).

There are, however, problems with virtually everything that was said in the preceding paragraph. The "classic" identification of the Qumran community with the Essenes and the Dead Sea Scrolls as their product is summarized in **2.184** and at greater length in **2.197**. Challenges to that picture are easy to find (**2.185**). It is quite possible that the scrolls

Many ancient documents, such as this commentary on Habakkuk, were included among the Dead Sea Scrolls. (Photo by Howard Vos)

have nothing to do with the Qumran community. The room identified as a scriptorium at Qumran may not be that (**2.195**). Some scholars argue that the Dead Sea Scrolls were hidden in A.D. 70 by Jews fleeing from Jerusalem (**2.196**). Others go so far as to maintain that the scrolls were produced in the fifth or sixth century A.D. (**2.191**).

One difficulty in determining what the authors of the scrolls believed is the diversity and even contradictions in thought among the scrolls (**2.204**). Some of the documents seem to teach a bodily resurrection, while others assert the immortality of the soul. If they are the product of a small, unified community, one would expect them to be less ambiguous on such an important matter. J. A. Sanders expresses the longing of most scholars who investigate these materials: "One could easily wish the scrolls were clearer on this as on many other points" (**2.209**:129).

This diversity of thought suggests that the scrolls may be a random collection, the sort of thing someone leaving a place in a hurry might gather up, rather than the organized library of a community. The apocalyptic imagery—war between the sons of light and the sons of darkness—sounds more appropriate to the Zealots than to an ascetic community of hermits, as the Essenes are described by

Josephus, by Philo (*That Every Good Man Is Free*), and by Pliny the Elder (*Nat. Hist.* 5.15.73). These sources have been analyzed by M. Smith (**2.214**) and S. Zeitlin (**2.225**). Information about other Jewish ascetic groups of this time can be found in **2.188**.

If we concede that the scrolls belong to the Qumran community, we still must ask if the community was a group of Essenes (**2.189**; **2.205**; **2.208**; **2.222**). Nowhere in the literary or archaeological remains of Qumran has the name "Essene" been found. We are by no means certain what the word means (**2.199**; **2.201**) nor when or where the Essenes originated. Do they go all the way back to the Babylonian exile (**2.188**), the Maccabean period (**2.217**), or the early Christian era (**2.216**)?

Further complicating the study of these scrolls is the tight security under which they have been held since their discovery. This situation has caused much controversy and even bitterness among scholars denied access to them (**2.186**; **2.198**; **2.212–213**). Half a century after their discovery, many of the scrolls remain unpublished and untranslated (**2.218**). Those which have been translated are available in a one-volume edition (**2.223**).

In the face of so much uncertainty, we must leave many questions about the scrolls and their significance unanswered (**2.210**). Further discussion of them would take us beyond the bounds set for this study and would not be likely to add measurably to our understanding of the world of the New Testament. For all the excitement they engendered at the time of their discovery, the scrolls have added only tangentially to our understanding of the New Testament, in the view of some scholars (**2.207**; **2.211**; **2.220–221**). In the view of one scholar, the scrolls and the New Testament are "two bodies of material . . . moving in different orbits," orbits which "simply do not intersect" (**2.200**:254).

Apocalypticism

The Dead Sea Scrolls do give us a new perspective from which to study the apocalyptic literature that circulated widely in Palestine during the first century A.D. (**2.233**; **2.239**). The intense interest in the "end times" is shown in Jewish prophecies written after the return from Babylon (**2.238**) and was fomented by the Maccabean revolt. Many of the more devout Jews were not satisfied with the corrupt Hasmonean priestly government of the post-Maccabean period and began to anticipate the coming of a deliverer who would restore Judaism to a purity it had never actually achieved. This would entail a three-step process: first, purging from Israel the wicked, non-observant Jews called the *'am ha-'aretz*, the "people of the land" (**2.236**); second, return of devout Jews from the Diaspora; third, liberation of the land of Israel from foreign domination (**2.228**:193–202).

Details of this process vary from one document to another. Some think of the Messiah as ruling only Israel, others as a world ruler.

Some see him as angelic or of a divine nature, others as a divinely anointed human. Some even expect two messiahs, a presiding priestly one and a lay royal one. No one knew precisely when the deliverance would occur, but expectations ran high in the first century A.D. The calendars used to keep track of major festivals of the Jewish year were also pointing to great things in the heavens, an astrological turning point in history (**2.232**), not unlike the intense interest in the turning of the millennium in our own day. Dealing with disappointed millennial hopes was one of Paul's primary tasks in 1 Thessalonians (**1.26**). Appearances of two comets, Halley's and one other, during this time served to heighten expectations of some epoch-making event (**2.230**).

Changes in Palestine's political fortunes often raised apocalyptic expectations, though some would argue that apocalyptic literature need not come from periods of crisis (**2.229**). Upon Herod's death in 4 B.C. and when Archelaus was removed from power in A.D. 6, "messianic" revolts broke out. Some of the leaders were anointed kings and controlled limited portions of Palestine for short periods of time (**2.231**). The movement was relatively dormant during Jesus' lifetime, but broke out again in the A.D. 60s and erupted one last time with Bar Kochba's revolt in the mid-130s.

We can only speculate on how much Jesus was influenced by apocalyptic thought (**2.226**). Since the movement was not as vital in his lifetime as at certain other times during the century, we might suggest that its impact on him was minimal. Yet Jesus does say that "the kingdom of God has come near" in his preaching and "has come to you" through the mighty deliverance he brings (Mark 1:15; Luke 11:20). This fulfillment curtails extravagant apocalyptic expectations. When the evangelists began to compose their Gospels later in the century, apocalyptic fervor had broken out again. As they wrote about Jesus, they may have seen him in a somewhat different light and emphasized aspects of his teaching which were not major themes in his own view.

Jesus and Judaism

The Gospels show that Jesus behaved like a rabbi, expounding Scripture and applying it to daily life (**2.243**). As biblical critic Julius Wellhausen observed a century ago, "Jesus was not a Christian; he was a Jew. He did not preach a new faith, but taught men to do the will of God; and in his opinion, shared by the Jews of his day, the will of God was to be found in the Law of Moses and in the other books of Scripture" (cited in **2.81**:363; cf. **2.240**). In his own words, he "was sent only to the lost sheep of the house of Israel" (Matt. 15:24).

Jesus disavowed any intention of doing away with the Law (Matt. 5:17). Nor did he advocate overthrowing the authorities of his day (Matt. 23:2–3). What he objected to was the narrow-minded legalism of their teaching and their failure to live up to the higher ethical standards of the Law (Matt. 23:23). One must be careful, some scholars argue, not to read too much anti-Jewishness into Matthew's Gospel (**2.244**). It may be a critique of hierarchy more than of the religion of Judaism.

Numerous articles and books have been written on the Jewishness of Jesus, so it is a topic too complex to discuss at length here. G. Vermes (**2.249**) provides one of the most dispassionate surveys of the subject. A convenient summary of the whole problem can be found in Mark 12 (with parallels in Matthew 21 and Luke 20).

These incidents are so neatly arranged that we may wonder if they actually happened one right after the other. It in no way affects their historical veracity if they did occur separately. None of the Gospels claims to be a precise chronological account of Jesus' life. They relate incidents, known as *pericopes*, in whatever order the writer feels is most effective in presenting a picture of Jesus. A Christian writer named Papias, of the early second century (cited by Eusebius, *Eccl. Hist.* 3.39.15), even says that Mark wrote down the teachings of Peter, "not in any particular order but as he remembered them." Whoever wrote the story first (probably Mark) seems to have recognized that these pericopes illustrated Jesus' attitude toward Judaism as a whole and toward the various factions within it, so he put them together at this point in the narrative.

The scene is the last week of his life. Jesus first tells the parable of the vineyard, suggesting that God had intended to work through the Jews but now must look for others to accomplish his purpose. The Pharisees and Herodians approach him with a trick question about paying taxes to Rome. Then the Sadducees try to trap him with a question about the resurrection. Next comes a scribe (sage, wise man) who asks his insightful question about the greatest commandment. Jesus approves of him individually, and he is not called a Pharisee, a term which almost always expresses disapproval in the Gospels and in the Talmud. The next two pericopes, however, condemn the *soferim* (scribes) as a group because they "like to walk around in long robes, and to be greeted with respect in the marketplaces, and to have the best seats in the synagogues."[5]

One has no difficulty perceiving Jesus' disgust with those who play games with the Law, rather than trying to probe its ultimate meaning. In his view, Judaism itself is not at fault. He wants to reform what he sees as the distorted version of it prevalent in his day. He preaches a new covenant, a Judaism which is to be written on the heart (Jer. 31:31–33). But, perhaps influenced by the Hellenized environment in which he grew up, he goes beyond the boundaries of Judaism (**2.248**). His approach, especially as depicted in Mark's Gospel, is that of a rabbi who differs in his teaching technique from other rabbis but who has no doubt that devotion to Torah—properly interpreted—is the way to eternal communion with God (Luke 10:25–28). The Pharisees did not have him arrested because they allowed room for diverse opinions among their schools. The chief priests, Sadducees, arrested him because of their fears that his popularity with the people and the messianic overtones of his teaching would bring Roman force down on their heads.

Judaism and the Early Church

While Jesus was comfortable within the limits of Judaism, his followers found it hard to reconcile their new understanding of things with the traditional forms. Jesus' warning about new wine and old wineskins proved all too true (Mark 2:22). They tried to remain faithful Jews. The early chapters of Acts show the disciples attending services in the temple (**2.276**; **2.291**), and scholars speak of "Jewish Christianity" in this early period, though they differ widely in what exactly is meant by that term (e. g., **2.270**; **2.273**; **2.277**). But tensions inevitably crept in as Hellenistic converts joined the group and the Jewish authorities rejected its message. The Christian denial of the need for circumcision may have been the crucial factor (**2.272**), or it may have been Christian claims about the incarnation (**288**).

By the time the first three Gospels and Acts were written (probably between A.D. 65 and 85), the Jews and the Christians saw themselves as distinct groups, even if the Romans did not (**2.281**; **2.289**). The Christians were concerned to make it clear that their faith was not a danger to the state, for that was the only basis on which the Romans would persecute them (**2.257**). The Gospels and Acts thus portray the Romans as recognizing the innocence of the Christians, as with Pilate and the centurion at the cross; or even accepting the new faith, as done by the centurion Cornelius and the proconsul Sergius Paulus (**2.253**). In the Gospels it is the Jews who plot against Jesus, seize him in the garden of Gethsemane, and demand his death (**2.261**). In Acts it is the Jews, in particular the Sadducean chief priests, who seize Peter and John, beat them, and admonish them to keep silent. It is the Jews who drag Paul before Gallio and follow him from town to town, contradicting the things he preaches (**2.265**). And in the early chapters of the book of Revelation, it is the Jews, the "synagogue of Satan," and not the Romans who are bringing persecution on the church (**2.278**).

When the Romans besieged Jerusalem in A.D. 69, the Christians left. But so did the majority of the priests and rabbis. The city was defended by political fanatics such as the Zealots, not by religious leaders. Later Christians saw the disastrous siege of Jerusalem as clear evidence that God was rejecting the Jews (see box).

As noted earlier, the rabbis gathered in the village of Yavneh and concentrated on pulling together the essential elements which would enable Judaism to survive without the temple. They defined their canon of Scripture and eventually added to the benedictions regularly pronounced in the synagogue services a malediction or cursing of "the heretics," the Christians (**2.264**). According to Justin Martyr, Eusebius, and Jerome, the rabbis at Yavneh also sent a letter to the Diaspora synagogues denouncing Christian teaching and warning devout Jews to separate themselves from the Christians. The criticisms passed between the two groups can, however, be seen as no more severe than the barbs which ancient philosophical schools hurled at one another (**2.266**).

By the early second century, the breach between Jews and Christians was complete, in the eyes of those outside the faith as well as within it (**2.267**). Tacitus makes no connection between the two, neither in *Annals* 15.44, where he describes Nero's punishment of the Christians after the great fire in Rome, nor in *History* 5, when he gives a comically inaccurate version of the origins of Judaism. His friend Pliny never raised the issue of a connection with Judaism when he was investigating the spread of Christianity in Bithynia (see chapter 4).

The Christian writers of that era, known as Apologists, argued that Christianity was the true Judaism, and that pre-Mosaic figures like Noah and Abraham had not been justified by the Law but by their faith (**2.282**). The Gospel of John depicts Jesus as rejected by "the Jews" and rejecting them in turn. Yet Jesus and the twelve and their challengers are themselves all Jewish, so the conflict during Jesus' ministry is among Jews, intra-Jewish. The Gospel of John reflects conditions prevalent in the 90s and serves as a testimony to the finality of the split between church and synagogue (**2.263; 2.268; 2.271; 2.287**), though at least one scholar sees John as addressed to Jews (**2.252**). Recent studies show that "the Jews" in the Gospel of John means "a group of Jewish leaders who exercise great authority among their compatriots and are especially hostile to Jesus and

> ## A Christian View of the Fall of Jerusalem
>
> The people of the church in Jerusalem were warned by an oracle, revealed before the war to those who were worthy, to leave the city and to settle in Pella, a city of Perea. Those who believed in Christ moved there, so that when holy men had completely deserted the royal capital of the Jews and the entire land of Judea, God's judgment might overtake them as retribution for their crimes against the Christ and his apostles and all that evil generation would be completely eradicated from the earth. Those who want more details can read in Josephus' history what great evils then engulfed the entire nation and how the inhabitants of Judea were driven to the ultimate degree of suffering, with thousands of young men, women, and children dying by the sword, by starvation, and by other horrible forms of death . . . . It was fitting that, on the very day [the Passover] when they had contrived the death of the Savior and benefactor of the world, they should be confined as if in a prison and receive the punishment handed down to them by the judgment of God.
>
> Eusebius, *Eccl. Hist.* 3.5

his disciples," certain religious authorities (Sadducean priests controlling the temple) rather than the Jewish people in general (**2.284**). Yet many readers have mistaken "the Jews" to mean "Jews in general," and the intervening centuries have, unfortunately, not erased the bitterness or healed the split which the controversies of the first century engendered between Jews and Christians (**2.254**; **2.275**; **2.279**).

Notes

1. An analogy might give us another way to think about this situation, though no analogy is ever perfect. I have lived for a number of years in a community founded in the 1840s by Dutch immigrants. Though the Dutch kept to their traditions and language as much as possible, they were surrounded by other ethnic groups and (being on a lake) annual swarms of visitors in the summer. The last church services in Dutch were conducted in the mid-1950s. People from here who visit the Netherlands are usually shocked to see how different the European Dutch are from themselves. But this is inevitable. Whenever a group of people is separated from their roots, they will cling to their heritage as much as possible, but they will develop in their own ways, while the original group back in the homeland will continue to develop along a different path.

2. Vivano and Taylor (**2.126**) give the sense of Acts 23:8 as follows: "The Sadducees say that there is no resurrection, either (in the form of) an angel or (in the form of) a spirit; but the Pharisees acknowledge both." This retains the usual meaning of *amphotera*, "both," rather than the NRSV wording, "all three."

3. Babylonian Talmud Shabbath 31a; cf. Tobit 4:15; Matthew 7:12.

4. Cf. Numbers 25:6–15; 1 Maccabees 2:23–27.

5. Mark 12 also records the condemnation of the rich who make a show of giving to the temple and praise for the poor widow who gives all that she has. This inclusion in the chapter is a medieval editorial decision and not part of the author's original design. Chapter and verse divisions were first put into the text in the Middle Ages.

BIBLIOGRAPHY

Judaism: Hellenistic and Judean

2.1. Bourquin, D. R. *First Century Palestinian Judaism: A Bibliography of Works in English.* San Bernardino, CA: Borgo Press, 1990.

2.2. Bruce, F. F. "Tacitus on Jewish History." *JSemStud* 29(1984): 33–44.

2.3. Cohen, S. J. D. "The Significance of Yavneh: Pharisees, Rabbis, and the End of Jewish Sectarianism." *HUCA* 55(1984): 27–53.

2.4. Feldman, L. H. "How Much Hellenism in Jewish Palestine?" *HUCA* 57 (1986): 83–111.

2.5. Ferguson, E. *Backgrounds of Early Christianity.* Grand Rapids: Eerdmans, 1993.

2.6. Kraabel, A. T. "The Roman Diaspora: Six Questionable Assumptions." *JJewSt* 33(1982): 445–464.

2.7. Lieberman, S. *Hellenism in Jewish Palestine.* New York: Jewish Theological Seminary of America, 1950.

2.8. Murphy, F. J. *The Religious World of Jesus: An Introduction to Second Temple Palestinian Judaism.* Nashville: Abingdon Press, 1991.

2.9. Otzen, B. *Judaism in Antiquity: Political Development and Religious Currents from Alexander to Hadrian.* Sheffield, UK: JSOT Press, 1990.

2.10. Riches, J. *The World of Jesus: First-Century Judaism in Crisis.* New York: Cambridge University Press, 1990.

2.11. Rokeah, D. "Tacitus and Ancient Antisemitism." *REJ* 154(1995): 281–294.

2.12. Schiffman, L. H. *From Text to Tradition: A History of Second Temple and Rabbinic Judaism.* Hoboken, NJ: Ktav, 1991.

2.13. Tcherikover, V. A. "The Decline of the Jewish Diaspora in Egypt in the Roman Period." *JJewSt* 14(1963): 1–32.

The Diaspora

2.14. Amir, Y. "Philo and the Bible." *StPhilon* 2(1973): 1–8.

2.15. Argyle, A. W. "Philo: The Man and His Work." *ExposT* 85(1974): 115–117.

2.16. Bell, B. "The Language of Classical Latin Poets as an Indication of Familiarity with Jewish Institutions." *AClass* 35(1992): 61–71.

2.17. Borgen, P. "The Early Church and the Hellenistic Synagogue." *StudTh* 37(1983): 55–78.

2.18. Clarke, W. "Jewish Table Manners in the *Cena Trimalchionis.*" *CJ* 87(1992): 257–263.

2.19. Cohen, S. J. D. "Conversion to Judaism in Historical Perspective: From Biblical Israel to Postbiblical Judaism." *Conservative Judaism* 36(1983): 31–45.

2.20. ———. "Crossing the Boundary and Becoming a Jew." *HThR* 82(1989): 13–33.

2.21. ———. "The Origins of the Matrilineal Principle in Rabbinic Law." *Assoc. for Jew. Stud. Rev.* 10(1985): 19–53.

2.22. Collins, A. Y. "The Origins of Christian Baptism." *StudLiturg* 19(1989): 28–46.

2.23. Collins, J. J. *Between Athens and Jerusalem: Jewish Identity in the Hellenistic Diaspora.* New York: Crossroad, 1983.

2.24. Delia, D. "The Population of Roman Alexandria." *TAPhA* 118(1988): 275–292.

2.25. Droge, A. J. *Homer or Moses? Early Christian Interpretations of the History of Culture.* Tübingen: Mohr-Siebeck, 1989.

2.26. Every, E. "Jews and God-Fearers in the New Testament Period." *Immanuel* 5(1975): 46–50.

2.27. Feldman, L. H. "Jewish 'Sympathizers' in Classical Literature and Inscriptions." *TAPhA* 81(1950): 200–208.

2.28. ———. *Jew and Gentile in the Ancient World: Attitudes and Interactions from Alexander to Justinian.* Princeton, NJ: Princeton University Press, 1993.

2.29. ———. "The Orthodoxy of the Jews in Hellenistic Egypt." *Jewish Social Studies* 22(1960): 215–237.

2.30. Finn, T. M. "The God-Fearers Reconsidered." *CBQ* 47(1985): 75–84.

2.31. Fredricksen, P. "Judaism, the Circumcision of Gentiles, and Apocalyptic Hope: Another Look at Galatians 1 and 2." *JThS* 42(1991): 532–564.

2.32. Gager, J. G. *Moses in Greco-Roman Paganism.* Nashville: Abingdon Press, 1972.

2.33. Goodman, M. "Nerva, the Fiscus Judaicus and Jewish Identity." *JRS* 79(1989): 26–39.

2.34. Jaeger, W. "Greeks and Jews." *JRel* 18(1938): 127–139.

2.35. Kraabel, A. T. "The Disappearance of the God-Fearers." *Numen* 28(1981): 113–126.

2.36. LaSor, W. S. "Discovering What Jewish Miqva'ot Can Tell Us About Christian Baptism." *BAR* 13, no. 1, (1987): 52–59.

2.37. Lieu, J., et al., eds. *The Jews Among Pagans and Christians in the Roman Empire.* London: Routledge, 1992.

2.38. Meyers, E. M. "The Challenge of Hellenism for Early Judaism and Christianity." *BiblArch* 55(1992): 84–91.

2.39. Neary, M. "Philo of Alexandria." *IrTheolQ* 54(1988): 41–49.

2.40. Nolland, J. "Proselytism or Politics in Horace Satires 1.4.138–43?" *VigChr* 33(1979): 347–355.

2.41. Paget, J. C. "Jewish Proselytism at the Time of Christian Origins: Chimera or Reality?" *JStudNT* 62(June, 1996): 65–103.

2.42. Pusey, K. "Jewish Proselyte Baptism." *ExposT* 95(1984): 141–145.

2.43. Rowley, H. H. "Jewish Proselyte Baptism and the Baptism of John." *HUCA* 15(1940): 313–334.

2.44. Runia, D. T. *Studies in Hellenistic Judaism.* Atlanta: Scholars Press, 1989.

2.45. Sandmel, S. *Philo of Alexandria: An Introduction.* New York: Oxford University Press, 1979.

2.46. Smith, D. "Jewish Proselyte Baptism and the Baptism of John." *RestorQ* 25(1982): 13–32.

2.47. Stark, R. "Christianizing the Urban Empire: An Analysis Based on 22 Greco-Roman Cities." *Sociological Analysis* 52(1991): 77–88.

2.48. White, L. M. "Synagogue and Society in Imperial Ostia: Archaeological and Epigraphic Evidence." *HThR* 90(1997), 23–58.

2.49. Wilcox, M. "The 'God-Fearers' in Acts – A Reconsideration." *JStudNT* 13(1981): 102–122.

2.50. Williamson, R. *Jews in the Hellenistic World: Philo.* New York: Cambridge University Press, 1989.

2.51. Wilson, S. G. "Gentile Judaizers." *NTS* 38(1992): 605–616.

The Septuagint

2.52. Feldman, L. H. "Torah and Secular Culture: Challenge and Response in the Hellenistic Period." *Tradition* 23, no.2, (1988): 26–40.

2.53. Greenspoon, L. J. "Mission to Alexandria: Truth and Legend About the Creation of the Septuagint, the First Bible Translation." *BibRev* 5, no. 4, (1989): 34–37, 40–41.

2.54. Howard, G. "The Letter of Aristeas and Diaspora Judaism." *JThS* 22(1971): 337–348.

2.55. Olofsson, S. *The LXX Version: A Guide to the Translation Technique of the Septuagint.* Stockholm: Almquist & Wiksell, 1990.

2.56. Radin, M. "Roman Knowledge of Jewish Literature." *CJ* 13(1917): 149–176.

Judaism and Hellenism in Judea

2.57. Balsdon, J. P. V. D. *Romans and Aliens.* Chapel Hill: University of North Carolina Press, 1979.

2.58. Batey, R. A. *Jesus and the Forgotten City.* Grand Rapids: Baker, 1991.

2.59. ———. "Jesus and the Theater." *NTS* 30(1984): 563–574.

2.60. Berlin, A. M. "Between Large Forces: Palestine in the Hellenistic Period." *BiblArch* 60(1997), 2–51.

2.61. Bickermann, E. "The Warning Inscription of Herod's Temple." *JQR* 37(1946–49): 387–405.

2.62. Borgen, P. "The Early Church and the Hellenistic Synagogue." *StudTh* 37(1983): 55–78.

2.63. Caragounis, C. C. "Greek Culture and Jewish Piety: The Clash and the Fourth Beast of Daniel 7." *EphThL* 65(1989): 280–308.

2.64. Case, S. J. "Jesus and Sepphoris." *JBL* 45(1926), 14–22.

2.65. Cotton, H. M., et al. "A Greek Ostracon from Masada." *IsrExplJ* 45(1995): 274–277.

2.66. Feldman, L. H. "Hengel's *Judaism and Hellenism* in Retrospect." *JBL* 96(1977): 371–382.

2.67. ———. "How Much Hellenism in Jewish Palestine?" *HUCA* 57(1986): 83–111.

2.68. Freyne, S. "Galilean Religion of the First Century C. E. Against Its Social Background." *Proceedings of the Irish Biblical Association* 5(1981): 98–114.

2.69. ———. *Galilee, Jesus and the Gospels: Literary Approaches and Historical Investigations.* Philadelphia: Fortress Press, 1988.

2.70. Greenhut, Z. "Discovery of the Caiaphas Family Tomb." *JerPer* 4, nos. 4–5, (1991): 6–12.

2.71. Guenther, H. O. "Greek: Home of Primitive Christianity." *TorJTheol* 5(1989): 247–279.

2.72. Hall, R. G. "Epispasm: Circumcision in Reverse." *BibRev* 8, no.4, (1992): 52–57.

2.73. Harris, H. A. *Greek Athletics and the Jews.* Cardiff: University of Wales Press, 1971.

2.74. Harrison, R. "Hellenization in Syria-Palestine: The Case of Judea in the Third Century BCE." *BiblArch* 57(1994): 98–108.

2.75. Hengel, M. *The "Hellenization" of Judaea in the First Century After Christ.* Trans. by J. Bowden. London: SCM, 1989.

2.76. ———. *Judaism and Hellenism: Studies in Their Encounter in Palestine During the Early Hellenistic Period.* Philadelphia: Fortress Press, 1974.

2.77. Hill, C. C. *Hellenists and Hebrews: Reappraising Division Within the Earliest Church.* Minneapolis: Fortress Press, 1992.

2.78. Hoppe, L. J. "Synagogue and Church in Palestine." *BibT* 27(1989): 278–284.

2.79. Ilan, T. "The Greek Names of the Hasmoneans." *JQR* 78(1987): 1–20.

2.80. Kasher, A. *Jews and Hellenistic Cities in Eretz-Israel.* Tübingen: Mohr, 1990.

2.81. Klausner, J. *Jesus of Nazareth: His Life, Times, and Teaching.* Reprint of the 1925 first ed. New York: Macmillan, 1964.

2.82. Lee, B. J. *The Galilean Jewishness of Jesus: Retrieving the Jewish Origins of Christianity.* Mahwah, NJ: Paulist Press, 1988.

2.83. Levine, L. I. "The Nature and Origin of the Palestinian Synagogue Reconsidered." *JBL* 115(1996): 425–448.

2.84. Longstaff, T. R. W. "Nazareth and Sepphoris: Insights into Christian Origins." *AngThRSuppl.* 11(1990): 8–15.

2.85. McNamara, M. "Half a Century of Targum Study." *IrBibSt* 1(1979): 157–168.

2.86. Meyers, E. M. "Early Judaism and Christianity in the Light of Archaeology." *BiblArch* 51, no. 2, (1989): 69–79.

2.87. ——— and J. F. Strange. *Archeology, the Rabbis and Early Christianity.* Nashville: Abingdon Press, 1981.

2.88. ———. "Artistry in Stone: The Mosaics of Ancient Sepphoris." *BiblArch* 50(1987): 223–231.

2.89. ——— et al. "Sepphoris, 'Ornament of All Galilee.'" *BiblArch* 49(1986): 4–19.

2.90. Mussies, G. "Greek as the Vehicle of Early Christianity." *NTS* 29(1983): 356–369.

2.91. Riches, J. K. "The Social World of Jesus." *Interpretation* 50(1996): 383–393.

2.92. Ross, J. M. "Jesus' Knowledge of Greek." *IrBibStud* 12(1990): 41–47.

2.93. Rubin, J. P. "Celsus' Decircumcision Operation: Medical and Historical Implications." *Urology* 16(1980): 121–124.

2.94. Safrai, S. "Spoken Languages in the Time of Jesus." *JerPer* 4, no. 1, (1991): 3–8, 13.

2.95. Sandmel, S. "Palestinian and Hellenistic Judaism and Christianity: The Question of the Comfortable Theory." *HUCA* 50(1979): 137–148.

2.96. Schürer, E. *A History of the Jewish People in the Time of Jesus.* Ed. by N. N. Glatzer. New York: Schocken Books, 1961.

2.97. Segal, P. "The Penalty of the Warning Inscription from the Temple of Jerusalem." *IsrExplJ* 39(1989): 79–84.

2.98. Selby, G. R. *Jesus, Aramaic and Greek.* Doncaster, UK: Brynmill, 1989.

2.99. Shimoff, S. R. "Banquets: The Limits of Hellenization." *JSJ* 27(1996): 440–452.

2.100. Simon, M. *St. Stephen and the Hellenists in the Primitive Christian Church.* London: Longmans Green, 1958.

2.101. Steinhauser, M. G. "The Targums and the New Testament." *TorJTheol* 2(1986): 262–278.

2.102. Tcherikover, V. A. *Hellenistic Civilization and the Jews.* New York: Jewish Publication Society of America, 1959.

2.103. Wright, A. "The Sermon on the Mount: A Jewish View." *NewBlackfr* 70(1989): 182–189.

Oral Tradition in Judaism

2.104. Bowker, J. *The Targums and Rabbinic Literature: An Introduction to Jewish Interpretation of Scripture.* Cambridge University Press, 1969.

2.105. Corré, A. *Understanding the Talmud.* New York: Ktav, 1975.

2.106. Forestell, J. T. *Targumic Traditions and the New Testament: An Annotated Bibliography with a New Testament Index.* Chico, CA: Scholars Pr., 1979.

2.107. Gianotti, C. R. *The New Testament and the Mishnah: A Cross-Reference Index.* Grand Rapids: Baker, 1983.

2.108. Grelot, P. *What are the Targums? Selected Texts.* Collegeville, MN: Liturgical Press, 1992.

2.109. Lipman, E. J. *The Mishnah: Oral Traditions of Judaism.* New York: Schocken, 1974.

2.110. Miller, M. P. "Targum, Midrash and the Use of the Old Testament in the New Testament." *JSJ* 2(1971): 29–82.

2.111. Neusner, J. *The Mishnah: A New Translation.* New Haven, CT: Yale University Press, 1988.

2.112. ———. *The Talmud: A Close Encounter.* Minneapolis: Fortress Press, 1991.

2.113. Tomson, P. J. *Paul and the Jewish Law: Halakah in the Letters of the Apostle to the Gentiles.* Minneapolis: Fortress Press, 1990.

Jewish Factions

2.114. Aune, D. E. "Orthodoxy in First-Century Judaism? A Response to N. J. McEleney." *JSJ* 7(1976): 1–10.

2.115. Boccaccini, G. "Multiple Judaisms." *BibRev* 11, no. 1, (1995): 38–41.

2.116. Grabbe, L. L. "Orthodoxy in First-Century Judaism? What Are the Issues?" *JSJ* 8(1977): 149–153.

2.117. Luke, K. "Society Divided by Religion: The Jewish World of Jesus' Time." *Biblebhashyam* 1(1975): 195–209.

2.118. Mantel, H. "The Dichotomy of Judaism During the Second Temple." *HUCA* 44(1973): 55–87.

2.119. McEleney, N. J. "Orthodoxy in Judaism of the First Christian Century." *JSJ* 4(1973): 19–42.

2.120. Pfeiffer, R. H. *History of New Testament Times: With an Introduction to the Apocrypha.* New York: Harper & Row, 1949.

2.121. Saldarini, A. J. *Pharisees, Scribes and Sadducees in Palestinian Society: A Sociological Approach.* Wilmington, DE: Glazier, 1988.

2.122. Sanders, E. P. *Judaism: Practice and Belief, 63 B.C.E.–66 C.E.* Philadelphia: Trinity, 1992.

Sadduccees

2.123. Horsley, R. A. "High Priests and the Politics of Roman Palestine: A Contextual Analysis of the Evidence in Josephus." *JSJ* 17(1986): 23–55.

2.124. Manson, T. W. "Sadducee and Pharisee: The Original Significance of the Names." *BJRL* 22(1938): 153–158.

2.125. Rosenbloom, J. R. "Jewish Response to Crisis: Success and Failure." *RevQum* 12(1985): 89–94.

2.126. Vivano, B. T., and J. Taylor. "Sadducees, Angels, and Resurrection (Acts 23:8–9)." *JBL* 111(1992): 496–498.

Pharisees/Scribes

2.127. Aune, D. E. "On the Origins of the 'Council of Yavneh' Myth." *JBL* 110(1991): 491–493.

2.128. Baumgarten, A.I. "The Name of the Pharisees." *JBL* 102(1983): 411–428.

2.129. ———. "The Pharisaic Paradosis." *HThR* 80(1987): 63–77.

2.130. Beattie, D. R. G. "Baba Bathra and the Bible, or 'I Don't Know Why Ezekiel Didn't Write Ezekiel.'" *IrBibStud* 6(1984): 177–190.

2.131. Carroll, J. T. "Luke's Portrayal of the Pharisees." *CBQ* 50(1988): 604–621.

2.132. Cohen, S. J. D. "The Significance of Yavneh: Pharisees, Rabbis, and the End of Jewish Sectarianism." *HUCA* 55(1984): 27–53.

2.133. Cook, M. J. "Rabbinic Judaism and Early Christianity: From the Pharisees to the Rabbis." *Rev&Expos* 84(1987): 201–220.

2.134. Culbertson, P. "Changing Christian Images of the Pharisees." *AngThR* 64(1982): 539–561.

2.135. Finkelstein, L. "The Pharisees: Their Origin and Their Philosophy." *HThR* 22(1929): 186–261.

2.136. ———. *The Pharisees: The Sociological Background of Their Faith.* 2 vols. Philadelphia: Jewish Publication Society of America, 1939.

2.137. Goodblatt, D. "The Place of the Pharisees in First Century Judaism: The State of the Debate." *JSJ* 20(1989): 12–30.

2.138. Guttmann, A. "Hillelites and Shammaites – a Clarification." *HUCA* 28(1957): 115–126.

2.139. Hartin, P. J. "The Pharisaic Roots of Jesus and the Early Church." *Neotest* 21(1987): 113–124.

2.140. Jospe, R. "Hillel's Rule." *JQR* 81(1990): 45–57.

2.141. Kampen, J. *The Hasideans and the Origin of Pharisaism: A Study in 1 and 2 Maccabees.* Atlanta: Scholars Press, 1988.

2.142. Kee, H. C. "The Transformation of the Synagogue After 70 C.E.: Its Import for Early Christianity." *NTS* 36(1990): 1–24.

2.143. Kirschner, R. "Apocalyptic and Rabbinic Responses to the Destruction of 70." *HThR* 78(1985): 27–46.

2.144. Lauterbach, J. Z. "The Pharisees and Their Teachings." *HUCA* 6(1929): 69–139.

2.145. Leiman, S. Z. *The Canonization of Hebrew Scripture: The Talmudic and Midrashic Evidence.* Hamden, CT: Archon Books, 1976.

2.146. Lightstone, J. N. "The Formation of the Biblical Canon in Judaism of Late Antiquity: Prolegomenon to a General Reassessment." *SR* 8(1979): 135–142.

2.147. Marcus, R. "The Pharisees in the Light of Modern Scholarship." *JRel* 32(1952): 153–164.

2.148. Mason, S. N. "Was Josephus a Pharisee? A Re-Examination of *Life* 10-12." *JJewSt* 40(1989): 31–45.

2.149. Moore, G. F. *Judaism in the First Centuries of the Christian Era.* 3 vols. Cambridge, MA: Harvard University Press, 1927–1930; rpt. 1971.

2.150. Morgenstern, J. "The Hasidim – Who Were They?" *HUCA* 38(1967): 59–73.

2.151. Neusner, J. "The Rabbinic Traditions About the Pharisees Before 70 A.D.: The Problem of Oral Tradition." *Kairos* 14(1972): 57–70.

2.152. ———. *From Politics to Piety: The Emergence of Pharisaic Judaism.* Englewood Cliffs, NJ: Prentice-Hall, 1973.

2.153. Newport, K. G. C. "The Pharisees in Judaism Prior to A.D. 70" *AndUnivSemStud* 29(1991): 127–137.

2.154. Rankin, A. S. *The Origins of the Festival of Hanukkah.* Edinburgh: Clark, 1930.

2.155. Rivkin, E. "Defining the Pharisees: The Tannaitic Sources." *HUCA* 40(1969): 205–249.

2.156. ———. "Pharisaism and the Crisis of the Individual in the Greco-Roman World." *JQR* 61(1970–71): 27–53.

2.157. ———. "Scribes, Pharisees, Lawyers, Hypocrites: A Study in Synonymity." *HUCA* 49(1978): 135–142.

2.158. Ruether, R. R. "The Pharisees in First-Century Judaism." *Ecumenist* 11(1972): 1–7.

2.159. Saldarini, A. J. *Pharisees, Scribes, and Sadducees in Palestinian Society: A Sociological Approach.* Wilmington: Glazier, 1988.

2.160. Schiffman, L. H. "New Light on the Pharisees: Insights from the Dead Sea Scrolls" *BibRev* 8, no. 3, (1992): 30–33, 54.

2.161. Schwartz, G. D. "As If Jesus and the Pharisees Were Developing Similarly and Simultaneously." *New Theology Review* 4(1991): 63–77.

2.162. Sonne, I. "The Schools of Shammai and Hillel Seen from Within." In *Louis Ginzberg Jubilee Volume, on the Occasion of His 70th Birthday.* New York: American Academy for Jewish Research, 1945: 275–291.

2.163. Zeitlin, S. "The Pharisees: A Historical Guide." *JQR* 52(1961–62): 97–129.

The Herodians

2.164. Perowne, S. *The Later Herods: The Political Background of the New Testament.* London: Hodder & Stoughton, 1958.

2.165. Rowley, H. H. "The Herodians in the Gospels." *JThS* 41(1940): 14–27.

Zealots

2.166. Borg, M. "The Currency of the Term 'Zealot.'" *JThS* 22(1971): 504–512.

2.167. Brandon, S. G. F. *Jesus and the Zealots: A Study of the Political Factor in Primitive Christianity.* New York: Scribners, 1967.

2.168. Donaldson, T. L. "Rural Bandits, City Mobs and the Zealots." *JSJ* 21(1990): 19–40.

2.169. Farmer, W. R. *Maccabees, Zealots and Josephus.* New York: Columbia University Press, 1957.

2.170. Hengel, M. *The Zealots: Investigations into the Jewish Freedom Movement in the Period from Herod I Until 70 A.D.* Trans. by D. Smith. Edinburgh: Clark, 1989.

2.171. Horsley, R. A. "Josephus and the Bandits." *JSJ* 10(1979): 37–63.

2.172. ———. "The Sicarii: Ancient Jewish 'Terrorists.'" *JRel* 59(1979): 435–458.

2.173. ———. "The Zealots: Their Origin, Relationships and Importance in the Jewish Revolt." *NovT* 28(1986): 159–192.

2.174. Kennard, J. S., Jr. "Judas of Galilee and His Clan." *JQR* 36(1945–46): 281–286.

2.175. Kingdon, H. P. "The Origin of the Zealots." *NTS* 19(1972): 74–81.

2.176. Smith, M. "Zealots and Sicarii: Their Origins and Relation." *HThR* 64(1971): 1–19.

2.177. Torrey, C. C. "The Name 'Iscariot.'" *HThR* 36(1943): 51–62.

2.178. Zeitlin, S. "Zealots and Sicarii." *JBL* 81(1962): 395–398.

Essenes

2.179. Beall, T. S. *Josephus' Description of the Essenes Illustrated by the Dead Sea Scrolls.* New York: Cambridge University Press, 1988.

2.180. Betz, O. "Was John the Baptist an Essene?" *BibRev* 6, no. 6, (1990): 18–25.

2.181. Callaway, P. R. *The History of the Qumran Community: An Investigation.* Sheffield, UK: JSOT Press, 1988.

2.182. Cansdale, L. "The Qumran Scrolls: A 2,000-Year-Old Apple of Discord." *AncHist* 21(1991): 90–104.

2.183. Charlesworth, J. H., ed. *John and the Dead Sea Scrolls.* Rev. ed. New York: Crossroad, 1990.

2.184. Cross, F. M., Jr. "The Dead Sea Scrolls and the People Who Wrote Them." *BAR* 3, no. l, (1977): 1, 23–32, 51.

2.185. Crotty, R. B. "Qumran Studies – Challenge to Consensus." *RelTrad* 7–9 (1984–86): 41–51.

2.186. "Dead Sea Scrolls Update." *BAR* 17, no. 1, (1991): 64–71; 17, no. 6, (1991): 62–65.

2.187. DeSilva, D. A. "The Dead Sea Scrolls and Early Christianity." *Sewanee Theological Review* 39(1996): 285–302.

2.188. Desprez, V. "Jewish Ascetical Groups at the Time of Christ: Qumran and the Therapeuts." *AmBenRev* 41(1990): 291–311.

2.189. Dupont-Sommer, A. *The Jewish Sect of Qumran and the Essenes.* New York: Macmillan, 1954.

2.190. Eisenman, R. H. *James, the Brother of Jesus: The Key to Unlocking the Secrets of Early Christianity and the Dead Sea Scrolls.* New York: Viking, 1997

2.191. Fitzmyer, J. A. *The Dead Sea Scrolls: Major Publications and Tools for Study;* rev. ed. Atlanta: Scholars Press, 1990.

2.192. ———. "The Qumran Community: Essene or Sadducean?" *HeyJ* 36(1995): 467–476.

2.193. ———. *Responses to 101 Questions on the Dead Sea Scrolls.* Mahwah, NJ: Paulist Press, 1992.

2.194. Flusser, D. "Jesus and the Essenes." *JerPer 3,* no. 3, (1990): 3–5, 13; no. 4, (1990): 6–8.

2.195. Golb, N. "The Problem of Origin and Identification of the Dead Sea Scrolls." *PAPhS* 124(1980): 1–24.

2.196. ———. "Who Hid the Dead Sea Scrolls?" *BiblArch* 48(1985): 68–82.

2.197. Howlett, D. *The Essenes and Christianity: An Interpretation of the Dead Sea Scrolls.* New York: Harper, 1957.

2.198. Isaac, E. "The Dead Sea Scrolls Controversy." *Mediterranean Quarterly* 1, no. 3, (1990): 75–86.

2.199. Kampen, J. "A Reconsideration of the Name 'Essene' in Greco-Jewish Literature in Light of Recent Perceptions of the Qumran Sect." *HUCA* 57(1986): 61–81.

2.200. LaSor, W. S. *The Dead Sea Scrolls and the New Testament.* Grand Rapids: Eerdmans, 1972.

2.201. Muraoka, T. "'Essene' in the Septuagint." *RevQum* 8(1973): 267–268.

2.202. Murphy-O'Connor, J. "The Essenes and Their History." *Revbib* 81(1974): 215–244.

2.203. ——— and J. H. Charlesworth, eds. *Paul and the Dead Sea Scrolls.* Rev. ed. New York: Crossroad, 1990.

2.204. Pileggi, D. "The Library at Qumran." *JerPer* 3, no. 5, (1990): 7–9.

2.205. ———. "Who Were the Essenes?" *JerPer* 3, no. 4, (1990): 9–10, 15.

2.206. Pixner, B. "Jerusalem's Essene Gateway: Where the Community Lived in Jesus' Time." *BAR* 23, no. 3, (1997): 22–31, 64–66.

2.207. Roberts, B. J. "The Qumran Scrolls and the Essenes." *NTS* 3(1956–57): 58–65.

2.208. Roth, C. "Were the Qumran Sectaries Essenes? A Re-examination of Some Evidence." *JThS* 10(1959): 87–93.

2.209. Sanders, J. A. "The Dead Sea Scrolls – A Quarter Century of Study." *BiblArch* 36(1973): 110–148.

2.210. Schiffman, L. H. "The Significance of the Scrolls." *BibRev* 6, no. 5, (1990): 18–27, 52.

2.211. Schuller, E. "The Dead Sea Scrolls and the Bible." *BibT* 21(1983): 102–109.

2.212. Shanks, H. "The Difference Between Scholarly Mistakes and Scholarly Concealment: The Case of MMT." *BAR* 16, no. 5, (1990): 64–65.

2.213. ———. "Is the Vatican Suppressing the Dead Sea Scrolls?" *BAR* 17, no. 6, (1991): 66–71.

2.214. Smith, M. "The Descriptions of the Essenes in Josephus and the Philosophumena." *HUCA* 29(1958): 273–313.

2.215. Taylor, J. E. "John the Baptist and the Essenes." *JJewSt* 47(1996): 256–285.
2.216. Thiering, B. E. *The Qumran Origins of the Christian Church.* Sidney, Australia: Theological Explorations, 1983.
2.217. Trever, J. C. "The Book of Daniel and the Origin of the Qumran Community." *BiblArch* 48(1985): 89–102.
2.218. Ulrich, E. "The Biblical Scrolls from Qumran Cave 4: An Overview and Progress Report on Their Publication." *RevQum* 14(1989): 207–228.
2.219. Vanderkam, J. C. "The Dead Sea Scrolls and Early Christianity, I: How Are They Related?" *BibRev* 7, no. 2, (1991): 14–21, 46–47.
2.220. ———. "The Dead Sea Scrolls and Early Christianity, II: What They Share." *BibRev* 8, no. 1, (1992): 16–22, 40.
2.221. ———. *The Dead Sea Scrolls Today.* Grand Rapids: Eerdmans, 1994.
2.222. ———. "The People of the Dead Sea Scrolls: Essenes or Sadducees?" *BibRev* 7, no.2, (1991): 42–47.
2.223. Vermes, G. *The Dead Sea Scrolls in English.* Sheffield, UK: JSOT Press, 1987.
2.224. ———. "The Impact of the Dead Sea Scrolls on the Study of the New Testament." *JJewSt* 27(1976): 107–116.
2.225. Zeitlin, S. "The Account of the Essenes in Josephus and the Philosophumena." *JQR* 49(1958–59): 292–300.

Apocalypticism
2.226. Allison, D. "The Eschatological Jesus: Did He Believe the End Was Near?" *BibRev* 12, no. 5, (1996): 34–41, 54–55.
2.227. Cohn, N. R. C. *Cosmos, Chaos, and the World to Come: The Ancient Roots of Apocalyptic Faith.* New Haven, CT: Yale University Press, 1993.
2.228. Foerster, W. *From The Exile to Christ: A Historical Introduction to Palestinian Judaism.* Philadelphia: Fortress Press, 1964.
2.229. Grabbe, L. L. "The Social Setting of Early Jewish Apocalypticism." *JStudPseud* 4(1989): 24–47.
2.230. Horowitz, W. "Halley's Comet and Judean Revolts Revisited." *CBQ* 58(1996): 456–459.
2.231. Horsley, R. A. "Popular Messianic Movements Around the Time of Jesus." *CBQ* 46(1984): 471–495.
2.232. Isenberg, S. R. "Millennarism in Greco-Roman Palestine." *Religion* 4(1974): 26–46.
2.233. Koch, K. *The Rediscovery of Apocalyptic.* London: SCM, 1972.
2.234. Morris, L. *Apocalyptic.* Grand Rapids: Eerdmans, 1972.
2.235. Navone, J. J. "Characteristics of the Apocalyptic." *BibT* 60(1972): 741–745.
2.236. Oppenheimer, A. *The 'Am ha-Aretz: A Study of the Social History of the Jewish People in the Hellenistic-Roman Period.* Leiden: Brill, 1977.
2.237. Reddish, M. G., ed. *Apocalyptic Literature: A Reader.* Nashville: Abingdon Press, 1990.
2.238. Redditt, P. L. "Postexilic Eschatological Prophecy and the Rise of Apocalyptic Literature." *Ohio Journal of Religious Studies* 2(1974): 25–39.
2.239. Zeitlin, S. "The Essenes and Messianic Expectations: A Historical Study of the Sects and Ideas During the Second Jewish Commonwealth." *JQR* 45(1954): 83–119.

Jesus and Judaism
2.240. Betz, H. D. "Wellhausen's Dictum 'Jesus Was Not a Christian, but a Jew' in Light of Present Scholarship." *ScandJTH* 45(1991): 83–110.
2.241. Charlesworth, J. H. *Jesus Within Judaism: New Light from Exciting Archaeological Discoveries.* New York: Doubleday, 1988.
2.242. ———. ed. *Jesus' Jewishness: Exploring the Place of Jesus Within Early Judaism.* New York: Crossroad, 1991.
2.243. Chilton, B. "Jesus and Judaism." New *Blackfr* 63(1982): 237–244.
2.244. Harrington, D. J. "A Dangerous Text: Matthew and Judaism." *Canadian Catholic Review* 7(1989): 135–142.

2.245. Hunter, A. "Rite of Passage: The Implications of Matthew 4:1–11 for an Understanding of the Jewishness of Jesus." *Christian-Jewish Relations* 19, no. 4, (1986): 7–22.

2.246. Lee, B. J. *The Galilean Jewishness of Jesus: Retrieving the Jewish Origins of Christianity.* Mahwah, NJ: Paulist Press, 1988.

2.247. Loader, W. "Hellenism and the Abandonment of Particularism in Jesus and Paul." *Pacifica* 4(1991): 245–256.

2.248. Mills, M. E. "Jesus of Nazareth in His Jewish Background." *Month* 22(1989): 378–383.

2.249. Vermes, G. *Jesus the Jew: A Historian's Reading of the Gospels.* London: Collins, 1973.

2.250. Zeitlin, I. M. *Jesus and the Judaism of His Time.* Cambridge, UK: Polity Press, 1988.

Judaism and the Early Church

2.251. Borgen, P. *Philo, John and Paul: New Perspectives on Judaism and Early Christianity.* Atlanta: Scholars Press, 1987.

2.252. Braine, D. D. C. "The Inner Jewishness of St. John's Gospel as the Clue to the Inner Jewishness of Jesus." *Studien zum Neues Testament und seiner Umwelt* 13(1988): 101–155.

2.253. Brawley, R. L. *Luke-Acts and the Jews: Conflict, Apology and Conciliation.* Atlanta: Scholars Press, 1987.

2.254. Callan, T. *Forgetting the Root: The Emergence of Christianity from Judaism.* Mahwah, NJ: Paulist Press, 1986.

2.255. Campbell, W. S. *Paul's Gospel in an Intercultural Context: Jew and Gentile in the Letter to the Romans.* Frankfurt/Main: Lang, 1991.

2.256. Conzelmann, H. *Gentiles, Jews and Christians: Polemics and Apologetics in the Greco-Roman Era.* Minneapolis: Fortress Press, 1992.

2.257. de Ste Croix, G. E. M. "Why Were the Early Christians Persecuted?" *P&P* 26(1963): 6–38.

2.258. Dunn, J. D. G. *The Parting of the Ways: Between Christianity and Judaism and Their Significance for the Character of Christianity.* London: SCM, 1991.

2.259. Evans, C. A., and D. A. Hagner, eds. *Anti-Semitism and Early Christianity: Issues of Polemic and Faith.* Minneapolis: Fortress Press, 1993.

2.260. Flusser, D. *Judaism and the Origins of Christianity.* Jerusalem: Magnes Press, 1988.

2.261. Freyne, S. "Oppression from the Jews: Matthew's Gospel as an Early Christian Response." *Concilium* 200(1988): 47–54.

2.262. Hare, D. R. A. "The Rejection of the Jews in the Synoptic Gospels and Acts." *Anti-Semitism and the Foundations of Christianity.* Ed. by A. T. Davies. Ramsey, NJ: Paulist Press, 1979: 27–47.

2.263. Harrington, D. J. "'The Jews' in John's Gospel." *BibT* 27(1989): 203–209.

2.264. Horbury, W. "The Benediction of the Minim and Early Jewish-Christian Controversy." *JThS* 33(1982): 19–61.

2.265. Johnson, E. E. "Jews and Christians in the New Testament: John, Matthew, and Paul." *RefRev* 42(1988): 113–128.

2.266. Johnson, L. T. "The New Testament's Anti-Jewish Slander and the Conventions of Ancient Polemic." *JBL* 108(1989): 419–441.

2.267. Katz, S. T. "Issues in the Separation of Judaism and Christianity After 70 C.E.: A Reconsideration." *JBL* 103(1984): 43–76.

2.268. Kaufman, P. S. "Anti-Semitism in the New Testament: The Witness of the Beloved Disciple." *Worship* 63(1989): 386–401.

2.269. Klijn, A. F. J. "The Study of Jewish Christianity." *NTS* 20(1974): 419–431.

2.270. Malina, B. J. "Jewish Christianity or Christian Judaism?" *JSJ* 7(1976): 46–57.

2.271. Manns, F. *John and Jamnia: How the Break Occurred Between Jews and Christians c. 80–100 A.D.* Jerusalem: Franciscan Printing Press, 1988.

2.272. McEleney, N. J. "Conversion, Circumcision, and the Law." *NTS* 20(1973–74): 319–340.

2.273. Murray, R. "Defining Judaeo-Christianity." *HeyJ* 15(1974): 303–310.

2.274. Neusner, J. "The Jewish-Christian Argument in the First Century: Different People Talking About Different Things to Different People." *Cross Currents* 35(1985): 148–158.

2.275. Parkes, J. *The Conflict of the Church and the Synagogue: A Study in the Origins of Antisemitism.* London: Soncino Press, 1934; New York: Atheneum, 1969.

2.276. Perelmuter, H. G. *Siblings: Rabbinic Judaism and Early Christianity at Their Beginnings.* Mahwah, NJ: Paulist Press, 1989.

2.277. Riegel, S. K. "Jewish Christianity: Definitions and Terminology." *NTS* 24(1978): 410–415.

2.278. Rokeah, D. "Anti-Judaism in Early Christianity." *Immanuel* 16(1983): 50 64.

2.279. Ruether, R. R. *Faith and Fratricide: The Theological Roots of Anti-Semitism.* New York: Seabury, 1974.

2.280. Sandmel, S. *Judaism and Christian Beginnings.* New York: Oxford University Press, 1978.

2.281. Segal, A. G. *Rebecca's Children: Judaism and Christianity in the Roman World.* Cambridge, MA: Harvard University Press, 1986.

2.282. Siker, J. S. "From Gentile Inclusion to Jewish Exclusion: Abraham in Early Christian Controversy with Jews." *BTB* 19(1989): 30–36.

2.283. Smiga, G. M. *Pain and Polemic: Anti-Judaism in the Gospels.* Mahwah, NJ: Paulist Press, 1992.

2.284. Smith, D. M. "Judaism and the Gospel of John." In *Jews and Christians: Exploring the Past, Present, and Future.* Ed. by James H. Charlesworth. New York: Crossroad, 1990: 76–99.

2.285. Stegner, W. "Breaking Away: The Conflict with Formative Judaism." *BibRes* 40(1995): 7–36.

2.286. Taylor, J. E. "The Phenomenon of Early Jewish-Christianity: Reality or Scholarly Invention?" *VigChr* 44(1990): 313–334.

2.287. Townsend, J. T. "The Gospel of John and the Jews." In *Anti-Semitism and the Foundations of Christianity.* Ed. by A. T. Davies. Ramsey, NJ: Paulist Press, 1979: 72–97.

2.288. Velasco, J. M., and L. Sabourin. "Jewish Christianity of the First Centuries." *BTB* 6(1976): 5–26.

2.289. Whittaker, M. *Jews and Christians: Graeco-Roman Views.* New York: Cambridge University Press, 1984.

2.290. Wortham, R. A. "The Problem of Anti-Judaism in 1 Thess. 2:14–16 and Related Pauline Texts." *BTB* 25(1995): 37–44.

2.291. Young, F. M. "Temple Cult and Law in Early Christianity: A Study in the Relationship Between Jews and Christians in the Early Centuries." *NTS* 19(1973): 325–338.

2.292. Zeitlin, S. *Studies in the Early History of Judaism.* Vol. 2. New York: Ktav, 1974.

CHAPTER 3

"THE POWERS THAT BE"

Introduction

THE NEW TESTAMENT is anchored firmly in the political processes of the first century A.D. Jesus sanctioned obedience to the government, in certain spheres at least (Mark 12:17; cf. **3.4**; **3.6**), and con-
fronted Agrippa and Pilate during his trial. Paul, a Roman citizen,
argued that the Roman government existed with the approval of God
(Rom. 13:1–4; cf. **3.1–2**) and that Christians should be submissive to it
(Titus 3:1). In the course of his brushes with the government, he stood
before governors such as Gallio, Felix, and Festus, or client kings such
as Herod Agrippa II. He was awaiting a hearing before a court in Rome
when last we hear of him. Other New Testament authors ran afoul of
the Roman government as well. Peter speaks of being imprisoned in
"Babylon" (a Christian code name for Rome: Rev. 17–18), and the
author of the Revelation had been exiled by the government to a small
Mediterranean island when he saw his vision. Luke's primary purpose
in writing was to convince one Theophilus, apparently a Roman official, that the new faith was no threat to the established order (**3.174**).
It would seem, then, that to understand the New Testament world, we
must know, at least in outline, how its government worked and something about the people who ran it.

Imperium Romanum

We could speak of a Roman Empire as early as 240 B.C., when Rome
defeated Carthage in the First Punic War and acquired Sicily, its first

overseas territory. Historians, however, usually reserve the term for the period after Augustus was given certain powers in 27 B.C. Before then, Rome was still officially a republic, though one which was outgrowing the form of government that had allowed it to develop such strength. The city was still ruled by two consuls and various lesser magistrates, but by the late third century B.C., it was well on its way to domination of the Mediterranean basin. After defeating Carthage again in 202 B.C., it turned its attention to the Greek kingdoms at the eastern end of the Mediterranean.

These kingdoms, ruled by Antigonus in Greece and Macedon, Seleucus in Syria, and Ptolemy in Egypt—along with a few smaller territories like Pergamum in western Turkey—had been carved out of Alexander the Great's conquests by several of his most ambitious generals. They combined elements of oriental despotism with Greek culture to produce what is called the Hellenistic culture of the last few centuries B.C. Peoples of various ethnic backgrounds adopted the Greek language and lived in cities modeled after the classical city-states (**3.13**). But, intellectually and politically, they were as far removed from classical Greece as we are from the America of the Revolutionary War era.

The foundation of Rome and other obscure points of the past were of no real relevance to the people of the New Testament era, nor did they have the resources to study them as extensively as we do today. Even the early Empire's greatest historian, Livy, had to admit in the preface to his work that the stories of Rome's foundation were more akin to "poetic fables" than to genuine historical narrative. Since these things had so little impact on the intellectual development of the New Testament world, we won't use space discussing them, as some surveys of this sort do.

Nor is it necessary for an understanding of the New Testament world to delve deeply into the dynastic struggles of the Hellenistic monarchies. Palestine was affected because it sat on the border between Syria and Egypt. For most of the third century B.C., the Ptolemies (the kings of the south in the book of Daniel) were strong enough to control Palestine. About 200 B.C. the Seleucids (Daniel's kings of the north) grew strong enough to push them back. But this struggle, which eventually led to the Maccabean revolt of 167–164 B.C., is of more interest to students of the inter-testamental period. Its most lasting effect on Palestine can be found in the rise of several Jewish sects, notably the Essenes and Pharisees, during the second century B.C., as noted in chapter 2 (**3.8**). By New Testament times the Ptolemies and Seleucids were ancient history. Rome had conquered all of the Hellenistic kingdoms and adopted their Greek culture (**3.10**). That culture then transformed Rome, as will be noted in later chapters of this book, but the political history of this era need not be a primary concern for the reader of the New Testament. Its primary effect may have been that the Romans' experience with Eastern monarchs stiffened their resolve not to have a king themselves (**3.19**). Eventually, however, Octavian's successors acquired more and more of the traits of Oriental despots.

Hail, Caesar!

The first Roman emperor, Augustus, was the survivor of a long, bloody, and exhausting series of civil wars that began in 133 B.C. In succession, Marius and Sulla (80s B.C.), Caesar and Pompey (50s B.C.), and Octavian and Antony (30s B.C.) battled for control of a republic grown into an empire without effective central rule, a republic which had simply failed. The Romans had rejected every suggestion of monarchy since the over-throw of their last king, Tarquin the Proud, ca. 500 B.C. A form of govern-ment suitable for the small, newly inde-pendent city-state was not capable of running a great metropolis with provinces stretched from France to Egypt and completely encircling the Mediterranean Sea (**3.30**). Julius Caesar perceived that Rome needed a king (**3.18**), but certain elements in the Senate were so averse to the idea that they assassinated him in 44 B.C., when his designs became too obvious (**3.17**; **3.20**).

Julius Caesar
(Photo copyright Ewing Galloway, Inc.)

In his will, Caesar adopted his grandnephew, Gaius Octavius, and named him heir. In Roman fashion the eighteen-year-old youth took on his adoptive father's name, with a form of his original name added on, becoming G. Julius Caesar Octavianus. Historians call him Octavian when referring to his activities before 27 B.C. He first gov-erned jointly with Marc Antony and another general, Lepidus, under an arrangement called the second triumvirate (**3.37**). Octavian con-trolled the Latin-speaking western half of the empire, Antony the Greek-speaking eastern part; Lepidus, with no troops, was named *pon-tifex maximus* ("high priest") and given control of what is roughly mod-ern Tunisia. But Antony, urged on by his mistress, the notorious Egyptian queen Cleopatra VII, who had also been Caesar's lover, formed plans for creating his own eastern Mediterranean empire (**3.23**; **3.25**; **3.32**). Octavian could not take action against a fellow Roman official without starting another civil war. Egypt, however, was a "client kingdom," still technically independent of Rome, so he declared war on Cleopatra and defeated her and Antony in the fall of 31 B.C. at the battle of Actium (**3.24**; **3.26–28**; **3.31**). Antony and Cleopatra committed suicide a few months later to escape Octavian's vengeance.

This conflict between Octavian and Antony had repercussions for the New Testament. One step in Antony's plan for an eastern empire was to secure the throne of Judea for Herod, thus planting a friend in

a strategic place. Roman troops under Antony's command helped capture Jerusalem in 37 B.C. and imposed this outsider on the Jews (**3.21**). His position was that of a "client king," dependent on Rome's favor to retain his throne. When Antony was defeated, Herod did some fancy footwork to shift his allegiance to Octavian. Josephus (*War* 1.388) records a speech in which Herod lays most of the blame for the situation on Cleopatra and promises that he will be as loyal to Octavian as he was to Antony.

Pax Romana: Augustus

After Antony's defeat had removed his last opponent, Octavian tried for several years to rule under the antiquated republican system. Finally he imposed his own settlement on the Roman Senate, which was so worn out by civil war that it would agree to anything but a king (Tacitus, *Ann.* 1.1). In 27 B.C. the Senate gave Octavian the honorific title Augustus along with the

Caesar Augustus, portrayed as imperator *(general)*

powers of proconsul (control of the army). In 23 B.C. he was granted the powers of a tribune, especially the power to veto the action of any other magistrate. Other minor adjustments in this arrangement were made at this time (**3.43**). These powers gave him absolute control of the state while preserving the fiction of a republican form of government (**3.34**). He was supposedly just the "chief man" of the Senate, though that body declined in importance throughout the following century (**3.44–45**).

Though we speak of him from that point as emperor, Augustus was never called king or emperor (**3.46**). The only titles he took were *princeps* ("chief man" or "leading citizen"), *imperator* (general of the army), and *pontifex maximus* (a title assumed in the fourth century by the bishop of Rome). Those titles had existed since the early days of Rome. What was vital for Augustus was to show that he did not create any new political position for himself. He was simply acting as a republican magistrate. The most visible change was that the Senate, instead of the people, elected the consuls and other magistrates, but at least there were elections. Augustus had absolute veto power over the actions of any official, but he tried to let the government run on its own as much as possible. The gradual evolution of the principate is a testimony to Augustus' political genius, aided by the fact that he survived several illnesses and lived far longer than anyone—especially his second wife, Livia—could have anticipated (**3.36**).

The potentially fatal flaw in Augustus' position was that, since he was not a king, he could not name a successor. He knew that, to prevent another round of civil war, someone had to be ready to step in immediately upon his death, but his only child was a daughter, Julia, by his first wife.[1] His second wife had two sons by a previous marriage, but Augustus at first refused to consider them as successors. He tried to procure a male descendant by marrying his daughter off to a succession of husbands: first his nephew Marcellus, then his commander-in-chief Agrippa (**3.33**; **3.42**; **3.48**), and—finally yielding to Livia's supplications—to his stepson Tiberius.

But the man who had shaped the destiny of the Roman world—indeed, of western Europe—could not achieve this one goal of securing an heir. Marcellus died in 22 B.C. Julia and Agrippa produced (in addition to several daughters) three sons, but two of them died while in their teens and the other was deemed mentally unfit to rule. Historians from that period drop broad hints about Livia possibly dispensing strategic doses of poison to clear the way for her favorite son. It has even been suggested that she eliminated her popular younger son so that Augustus would have no choice about a successor. Preparing someone to assume power remained a problem for this imperial family until the dynasty came to an end with the childless Nero (**3.39**).

The marriage of Augustus' granddaughter Agrippina to Livia's grandson Germanicus eventually blended the two families into what we call the Julio-Claudian dynasty. The term is usually applied to all the emperors from Tiberius to Nero (**3.47**). Their family relations can best be understood with the aid of a chart like the one in Appendix 2. The machinations of the imperial household have caught the imagination of several writers. Much of what Suetonius and Tacitus record was retold by Robert Graves in his novels *I, Claudius* and *Claudius the God*. The family provides a case study in what can go wrong in the accumulation and exercise of absolute power (**3.38**).

Late in his reign Augustus bowed to the inevitable, adopted Tiberius, and began to share power with him, thus making clear to the Senate and the army his choice for a successor. When he died in A.D. 14, he concluded the longest reign that any Roman emperor would ever enjoy. Tiberius' first act as emperor was to execute Augustus' surviving grandson, so there could be no rallying point for any opposition. This housecleaning technique remained standard in imperial successions, even well into the era of the Christian emperors.

Tiberius (14–37)

Tiberius, whose image was on the denarius handed to Jesus (Mark 12:16), has been much criticized as a ruler. By all accounts except one, he was a dour, antisocial man, stingy, given to sexual perversions, and deeply suspicious of those around him. He believed in astrology and displayed considerable antagonism to Judaism (**3.49**; **3.52**; **3.57**). The minor historian Velleius Paterculus, who served under Tiberius in the army, has only extravagant praise for him. Of course, he was writing while Tiberius was emperor. Tiberius' record as a military commander was outstanding, with victories over tribes in Germany and the upper Balkan peninsula.

Tiberius, the emperor when Jesus was crucified (Photo by Howard Vos)

Tiberius preferred to leave the running of the government to the commander of his bodyguard, the Praetorians. Augustus had lived like a typical Roman aristocrat, walking through the streets with only a few slaves or friends to accompany him, running the state much as a senator would run his far-flung business and agricultural interests. Tiberius' approach to government was to keep his intentions unclear—even to the extent of deliberately making misleading statements—and to seclude himself as much as possible from the people he ruled (**3.51**; **3.55**). Finally he retired to a villa on the isle of Capri, in the Bay of Naples, allegedly passing his time in various sorts of sexual depravity. He did not return to Rome during the last ten years of his reign (**3.63**).

Tiberius had little choice of a successor. His own son died in A.D. 23. His nephew Claudius had a nervous facial tic, stuttered, limped, and in general was considered unfit to rule. Another nephew, Germanicus, the husband of Augustus' granddaughter Agrippina the Elder, had proved too popular with the people, so Tiberius had him murdered. Most of Germanicus' children had also been executed or exiled. As a possible successor, that left only Germanicus' son Gaius, known by the nickname Caligula (Little Boots), which his father's soldiers had given him. Suetonius claims that Tiberius chose his grandnephew Caligula to succeed him because he wanted the Romans to look back on his own reign as a golden age and he suspected what sort of ruler Caligula would become. He chortled that he was "nursing a viper in the bosom of Rome" (Suetonius, *Calig.* 11).[2]

Caligula (37–41)

Caligula did not disappoint Tiberius' low expectations of him. He displayed every evidence of a sociopathic personality, a person who has no sense whatsoever of right or wrong and simply does what pleases him, regardless of the consequences for others. He apparently committed incest with all three of his sisters while still in his teens (**3.66**). He eventually commemorated them on his coinage.

Caligula ruled in an erratic and despotic manner, spending in the first year of his reign all the money that the thrifty Tiberius had amassed over twenty-three years. After eight months in power, he fell ill with a prolonged high fever, which seems to have left him even more unbalanced than he had been up until then. He apparently thought he was the incarnation of Zeus, even marrying one of his sisters as Zeus had married his sister Hera. Various explanations have been offered for the exact nature of this illness (**3.61–62**; **3.67–70**). For the rest of his crazed reign his actions were unpredictable, even sadistic. Wealthy people were often arrested on the slightest charges so their property could be confiscated. According to some stories, he led troops in Gaul in an attack on the sea, ordering the men to stab the water with their spears and collect seashells as booty from their "victory" over Neptune, god of the sea (**3.63**). He named his favorite racehorse a member of the senate and was about to make the animal a consul when he was murdered by a few Praetorians.

At the time of his death, Roman soldiers were on their way to Jerusalem with a statue of the emperor which was to be placed in the temple. Most Roman officials tolerated the Jewish peculiarity about not having images in the city, but Caligula had decided to insist on the divine rights which he felt were his. The commander of the troops was sensitive enough to the situation in the province that he delayed enforcing the order, hoping that Caligula would change his mind. News of Caligula's death reached the province shortly before a new order from Caligula demanding that the commander be removed and the image put in place (**3.58**; **3.64**; **3.72–74**). This was one of the incidents which heightened tensions in the area and led ultimately to the outbreak of war in 66 (**3.71**).

"The Secret of Empire:" Claudius (41–54)

With Caligula dead, the Senate had visions of restoring the old Republic. But the Praetorian Guards realized that without an emperor, there would be no need for an imperial bodyguard, so they saluted as *imperator* Caligula's uncle Claudius, whom they found cowering behind a drapery in the palace. The Senate, too long accustomed to acquiescing to the demands of the emperors and the army, granted him the powers and titles enjoyed by his predecessors. As Tacitus observed, the military basis of this "benevolent" dictatorship was at last revealed. The secret was out: the army made the emperor; in return, the emperor had to keep the army happy.

Claudius, who drove the Jews from Rome over "Chrestus"

Claudius proved, however, to be a competent administrator (**3.78**; **3.81**). During his reign the Romans conquered Britain, a systematic civil service was instituted to replace the old practice of having the emperor's slaves run the various departments of the government, and certain legal rights were granted to women in the area of owning and inheriting property. In his biography of Claudius, Suetonius quotes a letter written by Augustus to Livia in which he expresses his surprise that the young Claudius, who appeared so confused much of the time, could speak so clearly and logically at other times (*Claud.* 4). Historians speculated about whether Claudius feigned stupidity (as Suetonius says he did: *Claud.* 38) so that he would not appear to be a rival for the throne, or whether he was simply slow in maturing. Whatever the case, he surprised everyone else as much as he had puzzled Augustus (**3.80**).

Claudius' fatal weakness was for beautiful women. We know little about his first two wives. His third wife, Messalina, was fourteen and Claudius forty-nine when they were married in A.D. 39. She soon betrayed him and tried to remove him from the throne and marry another man. Claudius had her executed. His next wife was his niece Agrippina the Younger (Caligula's sister), whom he married after forcing the Senate to rewrite the law on incest to exclude a relationship between uncle and niece. Agrippina's son by a prior marriage was adopted by Claudius and became known as Nero. Agrippina persuaded Claudius to prefer Nero over his own son, Britannicus (who was several months younger than Nero), and nominate him as his successor. Shortly after Nero reached sixteen—the age of manhood in Rome—Agrippina apparently poisoned Claudius to set her son on the throne (**3.76**; **3.78**).

Claudius' impact on the New Testament can hardly be overestimated. He put Agrippa I on the throne once occupied by his grandfather Herod (**3.83**). This was the king who "laid violent hands upon some who belonged to the church" (Acts 12:1).[3] Claudius also banished the Jews from Rome in 49, because of a disturbance over someone named "Chrestus," according to Suetonius (*Claud.* 25).[4] This was almost certainly the Roman author's misunderstanding of the name Christus. That expulsion of the Jews (and the Christians, whom the Romans could not distinguish from the Jews) brought Aquila and Priscilla to Corinth, where they met Paul (Acts 18:1–4).

Nero (54–68)

One of Nero's first acts was to poison Britannicus. He ruled for five years with the advice of his mother and the philosopher Seneca. Ancient historians agree that for this brief period, his rule was almost exemplary. But in 59 Nero tired of Agrippina's interference in political affairs and had her murdered. If the ancient accounts can be trusted, it wasn't easy. Poison wouldn't work because she had been taking antidotes for years. She survived his attempt to drown her in a collapsible boat. Tiring of subtlety, he finally sent a squadron of soldiers to kill her (**3.86**). Seneca was soon sent into exile.

The remaining years of Nero's reign saw him indulge his lascivious bent, urged on by sycophantic advisers and checked by no one. As Suetonius says, "Gradually Nero's vices gained the upper hand; he no longer tried to laugh them off, or hide or deny them" (*Nero* 27). He offended all Rome by building his hedonistic Golden House in the center of the city after the great fire in A.D. 64. Most people suspected him of resorting to arson to

> ### Nero and the Christians
>
> Nothing that the emperor did—neither gifts to the crowds nor sacrifices to the gods—could overcome the popular belief that he had ordered the fire to be set. To squelch the rumor, he accused a class of people called Christians, who were despised by the people for their crimes, and inflicted the most elaborate tortures on them. Christus, the origin of the name, was crucified by the procurator Pontius Pilate during the reign of Tiberius. Though checked for a time, this deadly superstition erupted again not only in Judea, where the evil originated, but even in Rome, where everything hideous and shameful flows together and is relished.
>
> First those who pleaded guilty were arrested. Then, on their testimony, a huge crowd of people was convicted, not so much of arson as of hatred of mankind. Disgrace was heaped on their deaths. Covered in the pelts of wild animals, they were torn to death by dogs, or were crucified, or were set on fire as torches when the daylight had faded. . . . However, people began to feel sympathy for them, even though they were criminals deserving extreme punishment as an example. It seemed that they were being destroyed not for the public good but to satisfy one man's cruelty.
>
> Tacitus, *Annals* 15.44

clear the ground for his building project (**3.85**). He tried to fasten the blame on the Christians, but his persecution of them was so brutal that he alienated the populace of Rome (**3.89**; **3.91**; **3.95**; see box).

Nero's mistress, Poppaea Sabina, may have set him against the Christians. Josephus describes how she intervened to have some Jewish priests released from prison (*Ant.* 20.195). He even calls her "god-fearing," indicating that she may have been one of those Gentiles on the fringe of Judaism, like the centurion Cornelius in the book of Acts, though one must be careful not to overstate this case (**3.94**; **3.98**).

For several years Nero indulged his love of the arts and games by participating in various competitions in Greece and establishing his own games in Italy. He may actually have had some poetic or musical talents, but our sources are all biased against him on this score. By 68 he had lost the confidence of the legions on several of Rome's frontiers. Commanders in Spain, Germany, and Syria were hailed as *imperator* by their troops. The Senate declared Nero an outlaw, and he took his own life to escape the painful and degrading death which his enemies would have inflicted on him. Upon Nero's death, civil war broke out for the first time in a century, with troops loyal to three different generals advancing upon Rome. Galba, Otho, and Vitellius ruled for a few months each during the year 69 before Vespasian seized control in the fall of that year (known as the Year of the Four Emperors). Barbarians, encouraged by the chaos, attacked on the frontiers while Roman troops were fighting each other in Italy. Part of the capital itself was burned, and the Romans feared that "the end of the Empire was at hand" (Tacitus, *Hist.* 4.54).

It may have been at this point and not in 96, as many scholars maintain, that the book of Revelation was written (**3.84**; **3.93**; **3.99**). The heads of the beast in that strange book are clearly the Roman emperors (Rev. 13:1–3; 17:8–11). The fifth head is Nero, whose suicide occurred away from Rome. Since no one saw the body, rumors that he was still alive were circulating even in March of 69 (Tacitus, *Hist.* 2.1). This caused great consternation, especially in the province of Asia, the location of the seven churches addressed in the early chapters of Revelation. Stories about the return of Nero persisted into the early second century (**3.90**; **3.96**).

The Flavians (69–96)

The victor in the melee of 69 was Vespasian, a member of the Flavian family who had worked his way up from lower-middle-class beginnings to become commander of the legions in Syria. At the time the civil war began, he was trying to suppress a Jewish revolt. The Jews, provoked by a couple of particularly insensitive Roman governors, had taken advantage of Nero's distraction from politics in the last years of his reign to try to throw off the Roman yoke. They had not counted on the military skill and tenacity of Vespasian and his son Titus (**3.105**).

The success of these two generals compelled some Jews to abandon their cause. The most notable among them was Josephus, who surrendered his position in Galilee, took the Flavian family name as part of his own, and became an apologist for the Romans. (His life and works are described in Appendix 1.)

Leaving Titus in charge of operations in Judea, Vespasian returned to Italy in the fall of 69 to consolidate his power. In A.D. 70, Titus destroyed Jerusalem; three years later the last contingent of rebels were trapped in the hill fortress of Masada, built by Herod the Great. After enduring a prolonged siege, they committed mass suicide on the night before the Romans finally breached the walls (**3.106**).

Vespasian ruled for ten years, restoring the army's confidence in the government, destroying Nero's Golden House, and beginning work on the amphitheater now known as the Colosseum. His son Titus succeeded him (A.D. 79–81) only long enough to preside over another fire in Rome, an epidemic, and the eruption of Vesuvius which destroyed Pompeii. He seems to have respected Judaism and to have been reluctant to destroy the temple. His mistress was Ber(e)nice, the sister of Agrippa II (**3.104**; cf. Appendix 2).

Vespasian's younger son Domitian, who may have murdered Titus, was emperor almost until the end of the century (A.D. 81–96) and may not have been as bad a ruler as the next generation made him out to be. His accomplishments pale beside those of his father, and he seems to have had an autocratic temper. Toward the end of his reign, he became increasingly paranoid and arrested large numbers of senators and other members of the aristocracy whom he suspected of plotting against him (**3.109**). During this purge, he may have come across some Christians and begun a persecution of the church in Rome, but it does not seem to have spread to other parts of the Empire (**3.107**). His opinion of Judaism also seems to have been unfavorable (**3.110**).

The Emperors and the New Testament

These first-century rulers of the Roman Empire set its policies and appointed men such as Pontius Pilate, Felix, and Gallio to their posts. In turn, these officials interacted in one way or another with the early Christians. Although the emperors are rarely mentioned by name in the New Testament, their decisions and actions lie behind almost every page. As one scholar puts it:

> Each New Testament document was also written at a certain time in the reign of one of these emperors. The chronology reveals an evolution of the theological tradition, and many times this tradition is created because of imperial policy. . . . Depending on who was in charge of the empire, the Christian could see the emperor as an agent of God or of the devil (**3.117**:71).

Luke 2:1 credits Augustus with ordering a census which brought Mary and Joseph to Bethlehem (ca. 6–5 B.C.). When Herod the Great died (early in 4 B.C.), as stated in Matthew 2:1–23, Mary and Joseph felt they could safely return from Egypt. But they went to Nazareth to avoid Archelaus (4 B.C.–A.D. 6), whom Augustus confirmed as king over Judea and Samaria. Tiberius appointed Pilate to govern as prefect[5] of Judea and left him there to stew for ten years, 26–36/37, ruling during the time of Jesus' public ministry (Luke 3:1). Caligula's demand for divine honors heightened the tensions that led to the war of 66–73, which in turn completed the split between Christianity and Judaism. Claudius drove the Jews out of Rome in 49, sending Aquila and Priscilla to Corinth, where they met Paul. Nero banished the author of Revelation (1:9) to that tiny island where he saw his vision; he probably ordered the executions of Peter and Paul as well.

The emperors after Augustus were rather isolated from the people they ruled, and their impact on the daily lives of their subjects was more often indirect, through the policies they set and the people they appointed to carry them out. For the vast majority of the people in the Roman Empire, the "government" meant their town council or the governor of their province. To understand how this system worked, we must look briefly at the structure of the Empire. Then we will consider some of the people mentioned in the New Testament who were part of that structure.

Provinces and Governors

The Roman Empire was divided into territories called provinces. Most of these had been acquired by conquest after 240 B.C. A few had dropped into the Romans' laps. The province of Asia, covering the northwestern portion of modern Turkey, had been willed to the Romans by its last king, who died without an heir in 133 B.C. A few others were technically client kingdoms (**3.118**). The emperors retained direct control of the frontier provinces (such as Gaul and Syria), where troops were stationed, but let the Senate choose the governors of certain interior provinces, such as Asia and Sicily, which had long been pacified (**3.121**). A territory's status could change, as Judea's did, if the Romans became dissatisfied with the behavior of its populace or its ruler. As Suetonius says (*Aug.* 47),

> Augustus kept under his own control all the stronger provinces, which could not be safely or easily governed by annual magistrates. The rest he left to proconsuls chosen by lot. However, from time to time he changed some provinces from the imperial category to senatorial, or vice versa.

This might be the place to define a few terms that cause some confusion. A proconsul is a man who had held the highest office in Rome, the consulship. Each year, beginning around 200 B.C., the Senate assigned governorships, by lot, to the available pool of former consuls. By allowing the Senate to select governors of the quieter provinces, the emperors maintained the fiction of a republic and rewarded men who had made their way up the bureaucratic ladder. Most aristocratic Romans regarded this task as a necessary evil, with some degree of prestige attached. Some, like Cicero, actively resented it because it took them away from Rome for a year or more. Occasionally a man who had held the second highest office in the state, the praetorship, would be sent to one of the smaller provinces if a proconsul was not available. He would be called a *propraetor* and would have all the powers of a governor. Those powers are discussed in detail in chapter 4.

Pompey the Great, who brought Judea under Roman control
(Photo copyright Ewing Galloway, Inc.)

Under the principate the provinces on the frontiers, where armies were stationed, were controlled by the emperor. He governed them all as proconsul and sent out deputies known as *legates* or *procurators* (sometimes called *prefects* in smaller provinces) to administer them for him.[6] The term *governor* is a general one that can be applied to any head of a province. As the supreme proconsul, the emperor retained the right to intervene in the affairs of any province. This system of provincial administration, devised by Augustus, remained in effect with only minor refinements until the Empire began to break up in the third century (**3.122–123**).

The provinces did benefit from the peacefulness of Roman rule, but they paid a price. The Romans collected tribute from all their provinces, usually through a method called tax-farming. Wealthy men in Rome (*publicani*, people engaged in public business) bought contracts giving them the right to collect taxes in an area, the amount to be equal to what they had paid the government plus interest, usually about 25 percent. This system allowed the government to collect its operating expenses each year without effort. The original contractors then subcontracted the collection rights, dividing them into smaller segments of territory. Subcontractors could collect their investment plus interest. Obviously this pyramid scheme soon becomes enormously expensive to the provinces, and it explains why Matthew and Zacchaeus were despised by their compatriots. Not only were they Jews working for the conquerors; they were extorting large sums of money, with Rome's power to back them up. The government had to back the *publicani* if they expected them to bid for contracts in later years.

Rome and Judea

The earliest formal contact between Rome and the Jews occurred during the Maccabean revolt (ca. 165 B.C.). According to 1 Maccabees 8, Judas Maccabeus formed an alliance with Rome to give him some leverage against the Seleucid kings of Syria (**3.126**). The Romans had been trying for a generation before that to maintain a balance of power in the eastern Mediterranean between the Ptolemies (Egypt) and the Seleucids, so this effort to weaken Syria fits with what we know of their policy in the region. The Romans sent no troops to the area at that time.

In 63 B.C. Pompey arrived in Judea, toward the end of a campaign during which he conquered new territories in the east and reasserted Roman control over several recalcitrant areas. Judea at that time was ruled by the last of the Hasmonean dynasty, the descendants of the Maccabees. Two brothers, Hyrcanus II and Aristobulus II, were engaged in a civil war which Pompey settled by siding with Hyrcanus. He allowed Hyrcanus to retain the title of high priest but stripped him of the title of king and limited his jurisdiction to Judea and Idumea, with the title of ethnarch ("ruler of a people"). While in Jerusalem, Pompey entered the Holy of Holies in the temple, laying the groundwork for enmity and misunderstanding between Romans and Jews which persisted for centuries. He was surprised to find it empty; a persistent legend held that the Jews worshiped the head of a donkey, because that animal had supposedly led them to water during their expulsion from Egypt. The story may reflect some awareness among literate Romans of stories such as the one about

---

A Roman View of Judaism

Many sources agree that a plague which disfigured the body broke out in Egypt. King Bocchoris consulted the oracle of Ammon to find a remedy and was ordered to cleanse his kingdom by carrying this race, so hated by the gods, into another land. The people, hunted out and herded together, were dumped in a desert. As the others sat, stunned and weeping, one of the exiles, Moyses, advised them not to look for help from the gods or from men, for they had been abandoned by both. They should take as their divine leader the one who would first help them overcome their present misery. . . . After a journey of six consecutive days, on the seventh day they took over a country, driving out the inhabitants, and founded a city and a temple.

In order to strengthen his control over this nation for posterity, Moyses established new rituals, contrary to those of all other peoples. They consider profane those things which we hold sacred, yet they allow things which are forbidden among us. . . . This form of worship, however it originated, is supported by its antiquity. Their other traditions, which are perverse and debased, gain their strength from their very badness.

Tacitus, *Histories* 5.3–5

Moses striking a rock with his staff and causing water to flow out of it (Ex. 17:1–7; see box).

Aristobulus and his sons continued to foment trouble, with the result that, between 57 and 55 B.C. the Romans deprived Hyrcanus entirely of his civil powers and put Judea under the control of the governor of Syria. The civil wars raging in Rome made it difficult for the Romans to devote much attention to one minor province at the edge of their empire. There was an opportunity for an ambitious man to carve out a place for himself. One of Hyrcanus' strongest backers was Antipater, governor of Idumea. He and his two sons, Phasael and Herod, displayed an uncanny knack for sensing which way the political winds were blowing. In 48 B.C. Antipater sent assistance to Julius Caesar, who was besieged in Alexandria. With Antipater's troops, Caesar was able to break out of the trap. In return for that favor Caesar restored the title of ethnarch to Hyrcanus and appointed Herod and Phasael tetrarchs. But, a few years later, when Caesar's assassin, Cassius, who had command of several eastern provinces at that time, demanded tribute from Judea, Antipater paid.

The late 40s B.C. saw considerable turmoil in Judea. Antipater was murdered in 43. A Parthian invasion in 40 resulted in Aristobulus' son being proclaimed ruler of Jerusalem, with Hyrcanus taken captive to Mesopotamia. Antipater's sons reacted to the crisis quite differently. Phasael committed suicide, while Herod escaped to Rome. A few years later he returned to Judea as king, appointed by Marc Antony, Caesar's former lieutenant.

Few of their territories gave the Romans as much trouble, or as little benefit, as Judea. A. H. M. Jones calls it "the classic instance of an intractable area" (**3.36**:108). Many Jews were excused from paying taxes because of favors (mainly loans) done for Julius Caesar and because of the military assistance which Antipater, Herod's father, had given Caesar in Alexandria. Jews across the Empire—at least those strictly observant—had their taxes reduced by the amount they sent to Jerusalem each year for the maintenance of the temple (**3.127**). Judea produced nothing of any particular economic value and was constantly on the verge of revolt. In trying to govern it, the Romans changed its status from kingdom to province and back to kingdom, divided it several different ways, and alternately gave in to or opposed Jewish demands. Nothing they did seemed to make much difference.

The Herodian Family

At the time of Jesus' birth, Judea was a client kingdom, ruled by Herod the Great. After leaping the political fence from Antony's to Octavian's side in 31 B.C., Herod managed to retain his kingdom, perhaps because there was no strong candidate to replace him or because Octavian knew that Herod would be so grateful to escape with his life that he would forever be under the Romans' thumb. He remained loyal to Rome for the rest of his reign, even sending members of his family to the capital as hostages. They were probably safer there than in Judea, considering how many of his wives and children Herod murdered. Augustus supposedly observed that it would be better to be Herod's pig than a member of his family, since, as a Jew, Herod would not kill and eat a pig. Josephus discusses Herod's family (*Ant.* 18.127–140), and the chart in Appendix 2 attempts to make some sense of the genealogy (**3.133**).

Herod tried all his life to gain acceptance in the eyes of the Jews. He was an Idumaean by birth, one of those allegedly descended from Ishmael, Abraham's son by Hagar. To orthodox Jews, Idumaeans were half-breeds, and their resentment was fueled by having one of them appointed by outsiders as their king. Even his marriage to Mariamne, daughter of Hyrcanus, did little to legitimize his position in the eyes of his subjects. They gave him little credit for his considerable achievements, such as rebuilding the harbor at Caesarea (named in honor of the ruling Roman family) and expanding and refurbishing the temple at Jerusalem.[7] They seemed much more aware of his savagery toward his family and shed no tears at his death (4 B.C.).

Herod's kingdom was divided among his three surviving sons, Antipas, Archelaus, and Philip, who each received the title ethnarch. Philip's domain consisted of several obscure territories east of the Jordan River (Luke 3:1). Antipas was given Galilee and Peraea (Mark 3:8, "beyond the Jordan"), while Archelaus was to govern Judea, Samaria, and Idumea. But Archelaus ruled so brutally that his subjects finally begged Augustus to rescue them from his tyranny. This situation was behind Joseph's decision to avoid Judea while Archelaus was in power (Matt. 2:22). Archelaus was deposed from office and banished to Gaul in A.D. 6. The territory he had ruled was converted into a Roman province under a prefect appointed directly by the emperor. The Herodian family continued to have its supporters, however, who worked for the restoration of one of its descendants to the throne and may even have seen messianic implications in their efforts (see chapter 2).

Pilate

Under Augustus and Tiberius, relations between Rome and the Jews were stable, if not friendly. Jesus' advice to "Give to the emperor the things that are the emperor's" (Mark 12:17) reflects an attitude that could have been prevalent only in the early part of the first century A.D., when Rome seldom interfered directly in Judean affairs. Tacitus (*Hist.* 5.9) says of the province that "under Tiberius all was quiet," which isn't exactly the picture one gets from the Gospels (**3.137**). Augustus believed in changing governors every couple of years. Tiberius, on the other hand, left governors in office for long terms. Various motives were attributed for his decision to do this (Tacitus,

Ann. 1.80). Pilate was prefect of Judea from 26–36/37. Throughout his tenure, he was a source of irritation to the Jews. He typifies the Roman approach to dealing with foreign peoples: He understood virtually nothing about the Jews' faith or their devotion to it and simply forged ahead doing things the Roman way (**3.140**).

Josephus (*War* 2.169–177; *Ant.* 18.3.1) tells us that Pilate arrived in Jerusalem at night and sneaked his soldiers' legionary standards into the city under cover of darkness. This outraged the Jews because the standards had animal figures or images of the emperor on them and were worshiped as minor divinities by the soldiers (in violation of Ex. 20:4–6). The people protested for several days, demanding that Pilate remove the standards. When he threatened to have his soldiers lop their heads off, they bared their necks, declaring that they would rather die than live with pagan idols polluting their city. The Romans were polytheists, worshipers of as many gods as they chose. No Roman had such strong religious beliefs that he would die for them. Rather than risk a bloodbath in his first week as governor, the astonished Pilate yielded to the Jews' demands and removed the standards (**3.143**).

In another controversy, though, Pilate stood his ground. He had used Jewish temple funds (the Corban; cf. Mark 7:11) to finance the construction of an aqueduct (**3.138**). When a mob arrived before his residence to protest, Pilate had his soldiers beat them with clubs. A number of people died in the ensuing panic. It's little wonder that the Jews complained of Pilate as "inflexible, merciless, obstinate" (Philo, *Embassy to Gaius* 38).

Seeing the problems that Pilate had already encountered with the Jews enables us to appreciate the dread with which he must have heard their request that he put Jesus to death. Here was another difficult situation for him, and he seems to have caved in to avoid offending the Jews any further (**3.139**; **3.141–142**; **3.145**; **3.148**). There is a persistent legend in the early church that he informed Tiberius about Jesus. (A document which purports to be Pilate's report to the emperor does exist, but it is recognized now as a concoction of the fourth or fifth century.) His reluctance to condemn Jesus gave rise to the story that he was, as Tertullian claims (ca. 190), "a Christian in his heart" (*Apol.* 21.24; see **3.146**). He drops out of sight about the time of Tiberius' death, but stories about his suicide seem unfounded (Eusebius, *Eccl. Hist.* 2.7; see **3.144**).

Paul and the Romans

Other Roman officials of varying ranks appear in the pages of the New Testament, mostly as they cross Paul's path. Some scholars question whether high-ranking Romans had any contact with Christianity. Luke, they argue, was trying to present the new religion as acceptable to the "right" people. But Pliny the Younger, in his letter about the

Christians of Bithynia (*Ep.* 10.96), reports that "many people of every age, rank, both men and women" were members of the group. Pliny was certainly not trying to make this "wretched superstition" appear respectable in the emperor's eyes, so we ought to give credence to his account and be more willing to believe Luke as well.

Sergius Paulus

In Acts 13, Paul and Barnabas are invited by the governor of Cyprus, Sergius Paulus, to present their message to him. An inscription found on Cyprus and dating from the mid-first century mentions a Paulus who was proconsul there. After Paul's word came true that the Lord would strike blind the false prophet Bar-Jesus (or Elymas), Sergius Paulus "believed" (Acts 13:12). A word of caution should be inserted here. The term which Luke uses to mean "believe" may not imply a full conversion; it could merely suggest that Paulus was impressed by the display of this new god's power (**6.103**). Proconsuls were automatically members of the Senate, so when this man returned to Rome there was at least one person in that body who, if not a full-fledged Christian, at least had some first-hand experience with the movement (**3.152**:150–169). A bit of indirect evidence for the full conversion of Sergius Paulus is the later existence of a house church (ca. 100) in the home of a Roman named Sergia Paulina. None of the (scanty) literature on this subject is in English.

Since it is at this point in the narrative of Acts that Saul's name is changed to Paul (**3.149**), some, even as far back as Jerome in the early fifth century (*De vir. ill.* 5), have thought that he took that name in honor of his first non-Jewish convert. For a number of reasons, that explanation appears unlikely. To mention only one objection, an individual's name would have been changed in that manner only if he were a slave being emancipated and taking on his former master's family name (cf. the case of Felix, below) or if a man was being adopted (cf. the case of Gallio, below). But Paul was a Roman citizen from birth, so some other explanation of his change of name must be sought.

Origen, in the mid-third century, noted that name changes in Scripture are always of divine origin and result from some religious or life-changing event, as in Jacob-Israel or Simon-Peter. A similar phenomenon is observable in non-Christian literature from antiquity (**3.150**). That is not the case here. Origen concluded that Paul always had a double name, as did many Romans of non-Italian background (cf. John Mark, Acts 16:37). Thus Saul was his Jewish name, and Paul his Roman name. Another possibility is that the Hebrew name *Saulos* closely resembles a Greek word with some unfortunate connotations (**3.151**).

Gallio and Seneca

The next Roman official named in Acts is Gallio (Acts 18:12–17). He was born Lucius Annaeus Novatus, brother of the philosopher L. Annaeus Seneca, Nero's tutor. Childless aristocrats would sometimes adopt one of the children of their more prolific friends to insure the survival of their own family names. Novatus, one of three brothers, was adopted by L. Junius Gallio, taking his name and becoming in every legal sense of the word his son. Under Roman law such adoptions were irreversible, even if all the remaining children of the biological family were to die unexpectedly.

Gallio was consul at an unknown date, then became proconsul of Achaea (lower Greece) in ca. A.D. 52 (**3.157**). A couple of inscriptions have been found confirming that he held the office, although they do not establish the year precisely. His tribunal in Corinth has also been excavated. Gallio's refusal to hear charges against Paul (Acts 18:14–15) conforms to Roman policy. Roman bureaucrats tried to leave as much to local governance as possible. They were reluctant to get enmeshed in the internal affairs of local cults as long as they posed no threat to the general social order. They did attempt to squelch the worshipers of Bacchus and of Isis in Rome itself because of the disruptive character of their festivals, but such measures were a last resort. Gallio's "see to it yourselves" was the more typical response.

> ### The God Within Us
>
> We need not lift our hands to heaven or beg the keeper of a temple to allow us to get close to the ear of the idol, as though we could be better heard in that way. God is near you, with you, inside of you. A holy spirit dwells within us, who notices our deeds—good and bad—and is our guardian. As we treat this spirit, so he treats us. Truly no one is good without god. Can anyone rise above fortune unless he is aided by god? It is he who gives grand and upright counsel. As Virgil says, "an unknown god dwells" in each good man.
>
> Seneca, *Ep.* 41.1

The imagination of some Christians has run rampant in trying to explain why Gallio refused to hear charges against Paul. It has been suggested that perhaps he already knew Paul and secretly sided with him. The connection might have been made through his brother Seneca, whose humane Stoic philosophy is close to the Christian ethic at many points (**3.154**).

A body of forged correspondence, the *Letters of Seneca and Paul*, was composed in the fourth century, borrowing phrases from the actual letters of Paul and the works of Seneca. Apparently someone, perhaps acting on Paul's reference to Christians among "those of the emperor's household" (Phil. 4:22), created these letters to suggest that Seneca had been a "closet Christian." Tertullian held that opinion in the late second century (*De anima* 20), as did Jerome in about 400 (*De vir. ill.* 12). J. B. Lightfoot pointed out a number of parallels between the thought of Paul and Seneca in his commentary on Philippians (**3.155**). Seneca talks about god dwelling in man and about a holy spirit (*sacer spiritus*; see box). But, Lightfoot concluded, the source of Seneca's thought is not Paul but earlier Stoicism (see chapter 6).

There is more, however. The nephew of Seneca and Gallio, the poet Lucan, bears an unusual name for a Roman. Its meaning would be "of or pertaining to Luke" (*Loukas* in Greek). Lucius is a common name, Lucian is also known, but Lucan is apparently unique. Could it have been given to him in honor of the physician Luke, who, the argument runs, might have attended his birth? This conveniently overlooks the fact that midwives normally attended births in Rome and Greece (**8.122**). Ancient doctors knew little about gynecological care, as the poor woman in the Gospels who had been bleeding for twelve years would probably testify (Mark 5:25–26; see chapter 8).

This highly placed family, the Annaei, came to grief in A.D. 65. Seneca, by then shunted aside by Nero, was implicated in a plot on the emperor's life. In good Roman fashion, he was allowed to commit suicide rather than suffer the degradation of an execution, a peculiarity of the Roman penal system (discussed in chapter 4). Gallio and Lucan, also suspected of complicity in the plot, killed themselves as well. In his *Life of Lucan*, Suetonius reports that the poet tried to implicate his mother in the plot in order to save himself.

There might seem to be several connections between Paul and the family of Seneca, but when we examine the evidence thoroughly, it has no substance (**3.158**). Gallio acted as any Roman provincial governor would have in Paul's case. Seneca's humanistic philosophy is representative of a finer side of Roman thought, often overlooked because of the orgies and the bloody games in the arena. The oddity of Lucan's name may have a perfectly reasonable explanation which has been lost to us, like so much other information about antiquity. We have no evidence to connect Luke with Seneca's family in any way (**3.159**).

The stories that have grown up around this family and their supposed connection to Christianity arose out of an understandable impulse. Early Christians wanted to know as much as they possibly could about their own origins and to claim as distinguished a background for their faith as they could get away with. These were people accustomed to explaining things with stories. The same process of elaboration can be seen at work in the stories of the wise men who honored Jesus at his birth (see chapter 9).

All this should be a lesson to us in evaluating evidence. We cannot make the evidence say what we want it to if that is not its natural meaning. Nor can we manufacture material to fill the gaps created by the loss of documents or the silence on certain points in those documents which survive. Reasonable deductions can sometimes be made at points where the evidence is incomplete or ambiguous. We must remember, however, that they are only conjectures and not use them as though they were sound evidence to build a further case, as occasionally happens. It is better to live honestly with uncertainty than to create some imposing edifice of interpretation which rests only on the sandy foundation of suppositions.

Felix

The next highly placed Roman official named in Acts is Felix, governor of Judea from about 53–60. If we were looking for possible links between the Christians and the Roman hierarchy, we could note that Felix is described as being "rather well informed about the Way" (Acts 24:22). He was a former slave of Antonia, mother of the emperor Claudius, and took the name Marcus Antonius Felix (or perhaps Marcus Claudius Felix; see **3.160**) when he was freed. He rose spectacularly in social standing, even marrying Drusilla, sister of King Herod Agrippa II. His brother Pallas was one of Claudius' closest advisers and remained influential in Nero's reign until about the year 60 (**3.161**).

Felix's knowledge of the Way is intriguing in light of Nero's use of the Christians as a scapegoat for the great fire which ravaged Rome in A.D. 64. Most scholars have felt that Nero had no knowledge of the Christians before he began casting around for someone on whom to fix the blame (cf. p. 66). But if Felix knew a good deal about them, and if Felix's brother Pallas had been close to Nero for several years, is it mere speculation to suggest that the emperor had received some information about this group? Judea was a trouble spot for the Romans, and Nero no doubt received regular briefings on the situation there. The Christians could hardly have escaped his notice, though his information probably would not have extended to names and details of their beliefs.

Felix may have been a man of some conscience. When he heard Paul preach, he was "frightened" and sent him away. But we shouldn't read too much into that. He was also hoping for a bribe to release Paul, which says something about the social status of Paul and his friends, as well as about Felix's character (Acts 24:25–26). Tacitus (*Hist.* 5.9) describes Felix as "sampling every kind of cruelty and lust, exercising a king's power with a slave's heart." Felix was removed from office in 60, probably as part of a purge which Nero undertook—after murdering his mother—to rid himself of persons, such as Seneca and Pallas, whom she had put into positions of power.

Festus

Felix's successor, Porcius Festus, served only two years before dying in office, but he earned Josephus' praise for his efforts to put down the terrorists called the *sicarii* (*Ant.* 20.185–188). Festus found himself faced with a case left over from the previous administration which he wanted to clear up as quickly as possible. He tried to ingratiate himself with the Jews by offering to try Paul's case in Jerusalem (Acts 25:9). Paul was astute enough to know how that would turn out, so he appealed to Caesar, a right reserved to Roman citizens, as we'll see in chapter 4 (**3.163**).

Whatever would happen to the prisoner in Rome, Festus was probably relieved by Paul's appeal for it took the responsibility for the case off the prefect and passed it on to a higher authority. The workings of bureaucracies have changed little over the centuries.

Some Minor Characters

In addition to these major individuals mentioned by name in the New Testament who have some connection with the Roman government, there are some other minor figures about whom we can say little with any certainty.

Quirinius

One whose name causes considerable difficulties is Quirinius (wrongly called Cyrenius in some late Latin manuscripts and thus in some translations). According to Luke, he was governor of Syria when Jesus was born. But Quirinius' governorship—associated with the census of Judea mentioned in Luke 2:2—can be firmly dated from Roman sources to A.D. 6. In that year Archelaus was removed from the kingship of Judea and the area became a Roman province. Quirinius then supervised the taking of a census with the imposition of new taxes, which triggered a revolt led by Judas the Galilean (Acts 5:37). The relation of that census to the registration recorded in Luke has been a matter of dispute for the past century (**3.167–168**).

The question revolves around how Luke, so accurate in most details, could make such a mistake in chronology. If he was writing for a Roman official, the pseudonymous Theophilus (God-lover), he would have to be careful with his facts. Some scholars have tried to discover an earlier governorship for Quirinius, but the names of the governors of Syria from 9–4 B.C., when Jesus was most likely born (see chapter 9), are known from inscriptions. The governor in 6 B.C. was Sentius Saturninus, mentioned by Tertullian (*Against Marcion* 4.19,10) as the one under whom Jesus' birth occurred. One possibility is confusion between Quirinius and Quinctilius Varus, governor of Syria between 9 and 6 B.C. In 5/4 B.C., Quirinius conducted campaigns in the Taurus mountain area against a rebellious tribe, the Homonadenses, thus exercising some military rule near the Syrian frontier, and perhaps having some extraordinary command in the East. It has been suggested that Luke "erroneously attached the name of the Roman official responsible for the later, much more notorious, census" of A.D. 6–7 to an earlier one (**3.130**:571). Would such confusion have been possible? It seems so. In one passage the church historian Eusebius admits that there is a contradiction in names between two of his sources. He concludes that "either the name has been changed by some scribal mistake or there were two names for the same man, as often happens" (*Eccl. Hist.* 2.9, 10).

Another possible explanation is that the Greek phrase which Luke uses should be translated "*before* Quirinius was governor of Syria." It is, admittedly, not the most natural translation, but the standard New Testament Greek dictionaries do list that usage under *protos*. Josephus (*Ant.* 17.42) does mention that Herod required all his subjects to take an oath of allegiance to Augustus in 7 B.C., something which client kings or provincial governors occasionally did to impress the emperor with their loyalty (**3.166**). Everyone had to appear before local magistrates, register, and take the oath. Herod's loyalty oath may well have been the "registration" to which Luke refers. We must remember that he begins his birth narrative with the phrase "in the days of Herod, king of Judea," so whatever registration Luke has in mind must have taken place before 4 B.C., when Herod died.

Augustus took several censuses, the last in 8–4 B.C. But that would not have covered Judea, a client kingdom and not part of the Roman Empire at that time. It is possible that Luke, writing seventy or more years later, could not distinguish between Augustus' and Herod's "registrations," since they produced essentially the same results. Luke may have thought that Herod's oath of allegiance was part of Augustus' empire-wide census—perhaps begun in the East under another governor of Syria and completed by Quirinius. The decree may have been Augustus' effort to obtain accurate citizenship lists, for purposes of taxation (**3.172**). The debate seems to have reached what one scholar calls "a condition of agnostic stalemate" (**4.60**:163). This is another case where, however much we may want precise, irrefutable answers, we must be careful not to assert more than the evidence warrants.[8] (The question of the date of Jesus' birth will be discussed at further length in chapter 9.)

The Soldiers

Several of the minor figures mentioned in the New Testament are soldiers. The centurion Cornelius (Acts 10) became a convert, but we know nothing else about him. Not even Eusebius, who rarely passed up a good story, has any apocryphal tales about him (*Eccl. Hist.* 2.3). The tribune Claudius Lysias (Acts 23:26ff.), who found nothing blameworthy in Paul, is otherwise unknown to us.

The nameless centurion who stood by the cross is an example of an individual "baptized" by the early Christians because they felt that such persons must have believed in Christ, even if the New Testament does not specifically say so. Such "testimonies" were considered important evidence in Christian disputes with pagans. The centurion becomes

Longinus ("Longspear") in some third-century stories. His awe-struck admiration for Christ was understood as a profession of faith. This story, which appears in somewhat different versions in the synoptic Gospels (Matt. 27:45–56; Mark 15:33–39; Luke 23:47), does not appear in John at all. Its interpretation (discussed in chapter 10) will be easier after we've finished this survey and gained some insight into several aspects of Greco-Roman social history and thought.

Theophilus

Though he does not appear as a character in the New Testament narrative, the person to whom Luke was writing ought to be mentioned briefly. He is identified only as Theophilus (God-lover). This is a title, not a name, the sort of honorific applied to persons out of respect or a desire to flatter. Sometimes such a title could be a self-designation. Ignatius, an early second-century bishop and martyr, refers to himself in the opening of his letter to the Ephesians as "Ignatius, who is also called Theophorus [God-bearer]."

Who was Theophilus? Because he is called "most excellent" (Luke 1:3), we are probably safe in thinking he was a Roman official. The Greek word used (*kratiste*) is typically addressed to persons in authority. "God-lover" indicates that he was at least an inquirer, if not a member of the Christian fellowship. But some scholars argue that he might have been a hostile Roman official. Beyond that we cannot go, though this has not prevented speculation. It has been suggested that he might have been Flavius Clemens, a cousin of the emperor Domitian, who was executed around 95 for treason (**3.174**:539). The emperor distrusted Clemens because of his interest in Judaism, but there is nothing to connect him indisputably with Christianity (**3.84**:95–96). Depending on the date of Luke-Acts, it might be possible to suggest that Sergius Paulus was the person to whom the work was dedicated, but there are too many unknowns in that equation—his age and later career, the date and place of the composition of Luke-Acts. We cannot solve it at the present time.

Dionysius the Areopagite

We might wonder about the reliabilty of ancient historical sources when we see the confusion that arises over similarly named persons, even when several centuries separate them. Dionysius the Areopagite is such a figure. His conversion by Paul is mentioned in Acts 17:34, along with "a woman named Damaris, and others" (**3.177**). His title means that he was a member of the Areopagus, the aristocratic "supreme court" of ancient Athens, and thus a person of some stature in the city. By the late second century, he was reckoned as the first bishop of the church at Corinth, though he was sometimes confused with a later bishop of the same name. In the sixth century, he was confused with another Dionysius who (ca. 250) went as a missionary to the Gauls. His name was also attached to some mystical writings of the early sixth century which profoundly influenced contemplative thought in the Middle Ages.

Erastus inscription in Corinth
(Photo by Gustav Jeeninga)

"And Others"

Sometimes we are tantalized by connections which it appears we might be able to make between persons mentioned in the New Testament and those known from other sources. In Romans 16:23 Paul sends greetings from "Erastus the city treasurer" of Corinth. Now an inscription has been found in Corinth which says that a man named Erastus, holding the office of aedile, paid to pave a portion of a street. He would obviously have been a person of some wealth and standing in the community (**3.181**). Dare we identify this aedile with Paul's "city treasurer"? Is Paul really saying that Erastus is a Christian (**3.179**)?

Later generations of Christians were not satisfied to leave some persons referred to in the New Testament without names. Traditions arose about the names of the seventy-two disciples sent out by Jesus (Luke 10:1), about the names of the shepherds who came to see Jesus at his birth (Luke 2), or about characters such as the Philippian jailer (Acts 16:27–33). Even minor players, such as the bridegroom at the wedding in Cana for whom Jesus created an extra supply of wine or Mary's mother, were given names as the stories were passed down through the centuries.

The most famous example of this process of naming anonymous individuals occurs with the Magi of Matthew's nativity account (Matt. 2). They have no individual names to begin with, nor do we know from Matthew how many there were. No number is mentioned in the first

Gospel, though even well-established scholars sometimes speak as though there were a figure (**3.176**). Some lists created by early commentators mention as many as twelve. The tradition of three wise men arose when the church began decorating buildings after the emperor Constantine legalized Christianity early in the fourth century. When

The marketplace at Corinth, where Paul appeared before Gallio
(Photo by Howard Vos)

nativity scenes were painted or shown in mosaics, it was natural to depict one man holding the gold, another the frankincense, and a third the myrrh. Ancient Christians saw these pictures far more regularly than they read the texts (or heard them read).

At some point before the sixth century, the natural human tendency to fill in gaps in knowledge supplied names. By the time the emperor Justinian built a cathedral in Ravenna (in northern Italy) in the mid-sixth century, the anonymous, unnumbered Magi had become the three wise men: Balthasar, Melchior, and Gaspar. But taking all the sources in which they are mentioned together, there are several dozen names by which they were known in various parts of the world (**3.182**). The number three was also thought to symbolize the three continents (Europe, Asia, and Africa), and the three magi are usually shown as men of approximately twenty, forty, and sixty, to cover all the stages of human life.

Names were never created for some important figures in the New Testament. Acts refers several times (17:4; 17:12) to "not a few of the leading women" of some Greek towns who converted to the faith (see **3.178**). Women appear to figure prominently in the church at Rome itself (**3.178**). One woman's name—Junia (Rom.16:7)—may have been misunderstand as a man's name (Junias) by later copyists (**3.184**). In

Acts 19:31, some of the Asiarchs of the province of Asia (modern western Turkey) persuaded Paul not to try to address the crowd of irate worshipers of Artemis. The Asiarchs were a council of the wealthiest men in the province, who oversaw public works programs such as aqueducts, roads, and games or shows. They are not described as Christians but as "friendly to" Paul (**3.180**). This suggests that Paul moved in rather influential circles. Or at least Luke is making such a claim to show that the Christians weren't all seditious riffraff. He could not make entirely unsubstantiated claims, of course, since many of the people he was writing about were still alive and his story could be checked out.

From even this quick survey, we can see that persons of all social ranks were interested in Christianity. It has long been fashionable among scholars to assume that the early church consisted of slaves and freedmen, what Edward Gibbon in the late eighteenth century called "the dregs of the populace," gathering in their occasional free hours to worship. But, even allowing for a tendency to promote their own cause, the writers of the New Testament clearly show another picture. Individuals of even the highest ranks were familiar with Christianity and, if we can accept that Sergius Paulus was converted, even became adherents of the new faith. Working against a powerful, efficient, political system that controlled every aspect of its subjects' lives, Christianity spread both laterally across the Empire and vertically to all social classes much more rapidly than has generally been recognized. Though some have still argued for the old view (**1.26**), other modern scholars have begun to see the church of the first century in a new light sociologically (**1.30**; **3.183**).

Conclusion

The church in the mid-first century A.D. faced two external problems simultaneously: first, how to define its relationship with Judaism; and second, how to gain legal standing in the eyes of the Roman government. We looked at the first of these in chapter 2. We will examine the second in the next chapter.

Notes

1. For discussion of the formation of women's names, see chapter 7 under "Women."

2. Perhaps an allusion to the method by which Cleopatra had committed suicide. Cleopatra's lover Marc Antony was the great-grand-father of Caligula through his daughter Antonia.

3. He belongs to Herod's family, but only in Acts is he called "Herod." His full name was Marcus Julius Agrippa.

4. The apparently common confusion between these two words plays an important part in Tertullian's defense of the faith in his *Apology*.

5. Josephus anachronistically calls Pilate a *procurator*, but an inscription on a stone found in Caesarea Maritima in 1961 clarifies that he was a *prefect* (*The Anchor Bible Dictionary*, 5:397). The term *procurator* is appropriate in Judea after A.D. 70, when these governors had enlarged powers to procure/collect taxes.

6. See note 5.

7. One Talmudic tractate does concede that "he who has not seen Herod's temple has not seen beauty" (b. Baba Bathra 4a).

8. For an accessible analysis of this question, see I. H. Marshall, *The Gospel of Luke*, The New International Greek Testament Commentary (Grand Rapids: Eerdmans, 1978), 97–104: "The census . . . serves to place the birth of Jesus in the context of world history and to show that the fiat of an earthly ruler can be utilized in the will of God to bring his more important purposes to fruition."

BIBLIOGRAPHY

Introduction

3.1. Abineno, J. L. C. "The State, According to Romans Thirteen." *SEAJTh* 14(1972): 23–27.

3.2. Bruce, F. F. "Paul and 'the Powers That Be.'" *BJRL* 66(1984): 78–96.

3.3. Cullmann, O. *The State in the New Testament*. New York: Scribners, 1956.

3.4. Kennard, S. *Render to God: A Study of the Tribute Passage*. New York: Oxford University Press, 1950.

3.5. Kik, J. M. *Church and State in the New Testament*. Philadelphia: Presbyterian and Reformed Publishing Company, 1962.

3.6. Rowland, C. "Render to God What Belongs to God." *NewBlackfr* 70(1989): 365–371.

Imperium Romanum

3.7. Badian, E. *Roman Imperialism in the Late Republic*. 2nd ed. Ithaca, NY: Cornell University Press, 1968.

3.8. Beckwith, R. T. "The Pre-History and Relationships of the Pharisees, Sadducees and Essenes: A Tentative Reconstruction." *RevQum* 11(1982): 3–46.

3.9. Bowersock, G. W. *Augustus and the Greek World*. Oxford: Clarendon Press, 1965.

3.10. Branigan, K. "Hellenistic Influence on the Roman World." In *The Roman World*. Ed. by J. Wacher. London: Routledge and Kegan Paul, 1987: 38–54.

3.11. Ferguson, J. *The Heritage of Hellenism: The Greek World from 323 B.C. to 31 B.C.* New York: Science History Publications, 1973.

3.12. Grant, M. *The World of Rome*. New York: New American Library, 1960.

3.13. Green, P. *Alexander to Actium: The Historical Evolution of the Hellenistic Age*. Berkeley: University of California Press, 1990.

3.14. Isager, J. "The Hellenization of Rome: Luxuria or Libertas?" in *Aspects of Hellenism in Italy: Towards a Cultural Unity?*. Ed. by P. Guldager Bilde, et al. Copenhagen: Museum Tusculanun Press, 1993: 257–275.

3.15. Lintott, A. "What Was the 'Imperium Romanum'?" *G&R* 28(1981): 53–67.

3.16. Peters, F. E. *The Harvest of Hellenism: A History of the Near East from Alexander the Great to the Triumph of Christianity*. New York: Simon & Schuster, 1970.

Hail, Caesar!

3.17. Balsdon, J. P. V. D. "The Ides of March." *Historia* 7(1958): 80–94.

3.18. Carson, R. A. G. "Caesar and the Monarchy." *G&R* 4(1957): 46–53.

3.19. Erskine, A. "Hellenistic Monarchy and Roman Political Invective." *CQ* 41(1991): 106–120.

3.20. Fuller, J. F. C. *Julius Caesar: Man, Soldier and Tyrant*. New Brunswick, NJ: Rutgers University Press, 1965.

3.21. Grant, M. *Herod the Great*. London: Weidenfeld & Nicolson, 1971.

3.22. ———. *The Roman Emperors: A Biographical Guide to the Rulers of Imperial Rome 31 B.C.–A.D. 476*. New York: Scribners, 1985.

3.23. Huzar, E. G. *Mark Antony: A Biography*. Minneapolis: University of Minnesota Press, 1978.

3.24. Korfmacher, W. C. "Actium – and After." *CB* 49(1973): 40–44.

3.25. Rawson, B. "Antony and Cleopatra: Fact and Fiction." *AncSoc* 12(1982): 34–46.

3.26. Reinhold, M. "The Declaration of War Against Cleopatra." *CJ* 77(1981–82): 97–103.

3.27. Richardson, G. W. "Actium." *JRS* 27(1937): 153–164.

3.28. Skeat, T. C. "The Last Days of Cleopatra." *JRS* 42(1953): 98–100.

3.29. Smith, R. E. *The Failure of the Roman Republic*. New York: Cambridge University Press, 1955.

3.30. Syme, R. *The Roman Revolution*. Oxford: Clarendon Press, 1939.

3.31. Tarn, W. W. "The Battle of Actium." *JRS* 21(1931): 173–199.

3.32. von Wertheimer, O. *Cleopatra: A Royal Voluptuary*. Philadelphia: Lippincott, 1931.

Pax Romana: Augustus

3.33. Bell, A. A., Jr. "Marcus Vipsanius Agrippa." In *Great Lives from History: Ancient and Medieval.* Ed. by F. N. Magill. Pasadena, CA: Salem Press, 1989: 65–69.

3.34. Chilver, G. E. F. "Augustus and the Roman Constitution." *Historia* 8(1950): 408–435.

3.35. Dirckx, J. H. "Julius Caesar and the Julian Emperors: A Family Cluster with Hartnup Disease?" *American Journal of Dermatopathology* 8(1986): 351–357.

3.36. Jones, A. H. M. *Augustus.* New York: Norton, 1970.

3.37. Millar, F. "Triumvirate and Principate." *JRS* 63(1973): 50–67.

3.38. Moss, G. C. "The Mentality and Personality of the Julio-Claudian Emperors." *MedHist* 7(l963): 165–175.

3.39. Parker, E. R. "The Education of Heirs in the Julio-Claudian Family." *AJPh* 67(1946): 29–50.

3.40. Powell, G. "The Praetorian Guard." *HT* 18(1968): 858–866.

3.41. Raaflaub, K. A., and M. Toher, eds. *Between Republic and Empire: Interpretations of Augustus and His Principate.* Berkeley: University of California Press, 1990.

3.42. Reinhold, M. *Marcus Agrippa: A Biography.* Geneva, NY: W. F. Humphrey Press, 1933.

3.43. Salmon, E. T. "The Evolution of Augustus' Principate." *Historia* 5(1956): 456–478.

3.44. Talbert, R. J. A. "Augustus and the Senate." *G&R* 31(1984): 55–62.

3.45. ———. *The Senate of Imperial Rome.* Princeton, NJ: Princeton University Press, 1984.

3.46. Wallace-Hadrill, A. "*Civilis Princeps:* Between Citizen and King." *JRS* 72(1982): 32–48.

3.47. Wiedeman, T. *The Julio-Claudian Emperors, A.D. 14–70.* Bristol, UK: Bristol Classical Press, 1989.

3.48. Wright, F. *Marcus Agrippa, Organizer of Victory.* London: Routledge, 1937.

Tiberius

3.49. Allen, W. "The Political Atmosphere of the Reign of Tiberius." *TAPhA* 72(1941): 1–25

3.50. Houston, G. W. "Tiberius on Capri." *G&R* 32(1985): 179–196.

3.51. Levick, B. *Tiberius the Politician.* London: Thames & Hudson, 1976.

3.52. Maranon, G. *Tiberius: A Study in Resentment.* London: Hollis & Carter, 1956.

3.53. Marsh, F. B. *The Reign of Tiberius.* New York: Oxford University Press, 1931.

3.54. Mason, E. *Tiberius.* New York: Ballantine Books, 1960.

3.55. Millar, F. "Emperors at Work." *JRS* 87(1967): 9–19.

3.56. Rutgers, L. V. "Roman Policy Towards the Jews: Expulsions from the City of Rome During the First Century C.E." *ClassAnt* 13, no. 1, (1994): 56–74.

3.57. Williams, M. H. "The Expulsion of the Jews from Rome in A.D. 19." *Latomus* 48(1989): 765–784.

Caligula

3.58. Balsdon, J. P. V. D. "The Chronology of Gaius' Dealings with the Jews." *JRS* 24(1934): 13–24.

3.59. ———. *The Emperor Gaius (Caligula).* Oxford: Clarendon Press, 1934.

3.60. Barrett, A. A. *Caligula: The Corruption of Power.* New Haven, CT: Yale University Press, 1990.

3.61. Benediktson, D. T. "Caligula's Madness: Madness or Interictal Temporal Lobe Epilepsy?" *CW* 82(1989): 370–375.

3.62. ———. "Caligula's Phobias and Philias: Fear of Seizure?" *CJ* 87(1992): 159–163.

3.63. Bicknell, P. "Gaius and the Sea Shells." *AClass* 5(1962): 72–74.

3.64. Bilde, P. "The Roman Emperor Gaius (Caligula)'s Attempt to Erect His Statue in the Temple of Jerusalem." *StudTh* 32(1978): 67–93.

3.65. Ferril, A. *Caligula, Emperor of Rome.* London: Thames & Hudson, 1991.

3.66. Humphrey, J. W. "The Three Daughters of Agrippina Major." *AJAH* 4(1979): 125–143.

3.67. Katz, R. S. "The Illness of Caligula." *CW* 65(1972): 223–225.

3.68. Massaro, V., and I. Montgomery. "Gaius – Mad, Bad, Ill or All Three?" *Latomus* 37(1978): 894–909.

3.69. Morgan, M. G. "Caligula's Illness Again." *CW* 66(1973): 327–329.

3.70. Sandison, A. T. "The Madness of the Emperor Caligula." *MedHist* 2(1958): 202–209.

3.71. Smallwood, E. M. "The Chronology of Gaius' Attempt to Decorate the Temple." *Latomus* 16(1957): 3–17.

3.72. Swain, J. W. "Gamaliel's Speech and Caligula's Statue." *HThR* 37(1944): 341–349.

3.73. Taylor, N. H. "Palestinian Christianity and the Caligula Crisis. Part I: Social and Historical Reconstruction." *JStudNT* 61(1996): 101–124.

3.74. ———. "Palestinian Christianity and the Caligula Crisis. Part II: The Markan Eschatological Discourse." *JStudNT* 62(1996): 13–41.

3.75. Wood, S. "Diva Drusilla Panthea and the Sisters of Caligula." *AJA* 99(1995): 457–482.

"The Secret of Empire:" Claudius

3.76. Bagnani, G. "The Case of the Poisoned Mushroom." *Phoenix* 1, no. 2, (1946): 14–20.

3.77. Carney, T. F. "The Changing Picture of Claudius." *AClass* 3(1960): 99–104.

3.78. Grimm-Samuel, V. "On the Mushroom that Deified the Emperor Claudius." *CQ* 41(1991): 178–182.

3.79. Levick, B. *Claudius*. New Haven, CT: Yale University Press, 1990.

3.80. Major, A. "Was He Pushed or Did He Leap? Claudius' Ascent to Power." *AncHist* 22(1992): 25–31.

3.81. Momigliano, A. *Claudius: The Emperor and His Achievement*. Oxford: Clarendon Press, 1934.

3.82. Scramuzza, V. M. *The Emperor Claudius*. Cambridge: Harvard University Press, 1910.

3.83. Schwartz, D. R. *Agrippa I, the Last King of Judea*. Tübingen: Mohr-Siebeck, 1990.

Nero

3.84. Bell, A. A., Jr. "The Date of John's Apocalypse: The Evidence of Some Roman Historians Reconsidered." *NTS* 25(1978): 93–102.

3.85. Bohm, R. K. "Nero as Incendiary." *CW* 79(1985–86): 400–401.

3.86. Dawson, A. "Whatever Happened to Lady Agrippina?" *CJ* 64(1969): 253–267.

3.87. Grant, M. *Nero, Emperor in Revolt*. New York: American Heritage Press, 1970.

3.88. Griffin, M. T. *Nero: The End of a Dynasty*. Oxford: Clarendon Press, 1976.

3.89. Keresztes, P. "Nero, the Christians and the Jews in Tacitus and Clement of Rome." *Latomus* 43(1984): 404–413.

3.90. Kreitzer, L. "Hadrian and the Nero Redivivus Myth." *ZNTW* 79(1988): 92–115.

3.91. Mans, M. J. "The *Tunica Molesta* and the Neronian Persecution of the Christians." *Akroterion* 29(1984): 53–59.

3.92. Morford, M. "The Age of Nero." *CO* 62(1984–85): 1–5.

3.93. Robinson, J. A. T. *Redating the New Testament*. Philadelphia: Westminster Press, 1976.

3.94. Smallwood, E. M. "The Alleged Jewish Tendencies of Poppaea Sabina." *JThS* 10(1959): 329–335.

3.95. Taylor, J. "The Love of Many Will Grow Cold: Matthew 24:9–13 and the Neronian Persecution," *Revbib* 96(1989): 352–357.

3.96. Tuplin, C. J. "The False Neros of the First Century A.D." In *Studies in Latin Literature and Roman History*, V. Ed. by C. Derricks. Brussels: Soc. Latomus, 1989: 364–404.

3.97. Warmington, B. H. *Nero: Reality and Legend*. New York: Norton, 1969.

3.98. Williams, M. H. "'Theosebes gar en'–The Jewish Tendencies of Poppaea Sabina." *JThS* 39(1988): 97–111.

3.99. Wilson, J. C. "The Problem of the Domitianic Date of Revelation." *NTS* 39(1993): 587– 605.

The Flavians

3.100. Barnard, L. W. "Clement of Rome and the Persecution of Domitian." *NTS* 19(1964): 251–260.

3.101. Botha, P. J. J. "The Historical Domitian – Illustrating Some Problems of Historiography." *Neotest* 23(1989): 45–59.

3.102. Jones, B. W. *The Emperor Domitian.* New York: Routledge, 1992.

3.103. ———. *The Emperor Titus.* London: Croom Helm, 1984.

3.104. ———. "Titus: His Reign and Its Significance." *AncHist* 19(1989): 21–25.

3.105. ———. "Titus in Judea, A.D. 67." *Latomus* 48(1989): 127–134.

3.106. Magness, J. "Masada – Arms and the Man." *BAR* 18, no.4, (1992): 58–67.

3.107. Milburn, R. L. "The Persecution of Domitian." *Church Quarterly Review* 139(1944–45): 154–164.

3.108. Sullivan, P. B. "A Note on the Flavian Accession." *CJ* 49(1953–54): 67–70.

3.109. Syme, R. "Domitian: The Last Years." *Chiron* 13(1983): 121–146.

3.110. Williams, M. H. "Domitian, the Jews and the 'Judaizers' – a Simple Matter of *Cupiditas and Maiestas?*" *Historia* 39(1990): 196–211.

3.111. Yavetz, Z. "Reflections on Titus and Josephus." *GRBS* 16(1975): 411–432.

The Emperors and the New Testament

3.112. Baldwin, B. *The Roman Emperors.* Montreal: Harvest House, 1980.

3.113. Burn, A. R. *The Government of the Roman Empire from Augustus to the Antonines.* London: Philip, 1952.

3.114. Grant, M. *The Twelve Caesars.* New York: Scribners, 1975.

3.115. Lissner, I. *Power and Folly: The Story of the Caesars.* London: Jonathan Cape, 1958.

3.116. Millar, F. *The Emperor in the Roman World (131 B.C.–A.D. 337).* Ithaca, NY: Cornell Univ. Press, 1977.

3.117. Sarno, R. A. "Caesar in the New Testament." *CB* 51(1975): 71–75.

Provinces and Governors

3.118. Braund, D. *Rome and the Friendly Kings: The Character of the Client Kingship.* New York: St. Martin's, 1984.

3.119. Burton, G. P. "Provincial Procurators and the Public Provinces." *Chiron* 23(1993): 13–28.

3.120. Duncan-Jones, R. *The Economy of the Roman Empire.* New York: Cambridge University Press, 1982.

3.121. Millar, F. "The Emperor, the Senate and the Provinces." *JRS* 56(1966): 156–166.

3.122. Richardson, J. *Roman Provincial Administration: 227 B.C. to A.D. 117.* Basingstoke, UK: Macmillan, 1976.

3.123. Stevenson, G. H. *Roman Provincial Administration Till the Age of the Antonines.* Oxford: Blackwell, 1939.

Rome and Judea

3.124. Feldman, L. H. "Pro-Jewish Intimations in Tacitus' Account of Jewish Origins." *REJ* 150(1991): 331–360.

3.125. Grant, M. *The Jews in the Roman World.* New York: Scribners, 1973.

3.126. Mandell, S. R. "Did the Maccabees Believe that They Had a Valid Treaty with Rome?" *CBQ* 53(1991): 202–220.

3.127. ———. "Who Paid the Temple Tax When the Jews Were Under Roman Rule?" *HThR* 77(1984): 223–232.

3.128. McLaren, J. *Power and Politics in Palestine: The Jews and the Governing of Their Land, 100 B.C.–A.D. 70.* Sheffield, UK: JSOT Press, 1991.

3.129. Price, J. J. *Jerusalem Under Siege: The Collapse of the Jewish State, 66–70 C.E.* Leiden: Brill, 1992.

3.130. Smallwood, E. M. *The Jews Under Roman Rule.* Leiden: Brill, 1976.

3.131. Tamm, D. "Roman Anti-Jewish Legislation and Adversus-Judaeos Literature." *RHD* 60(1992): 177–184.

The Herodian Family

3.132. Grant, M. *Herod the Great.* London: Weidenfeld & Nicolson, 1971.

3.133. Hanson, K. C. "The Herodians and Mediterranean Kinship, Part 2: Marriage and Divorce." *BTB* 19(1989): 142–151.

3.134. Hoehner, H. W. *Herod Antipas.* New York: Cambridge University Press, 1972.

3.135. Holum, K., et al. *King Herod's Dream: Caesarea on the Sea.* New York: Norton, 1988.

3.136. Jones, A. H. M. *The Herods of Judea.* Oxford: Clarendon Press, 1938.

Pilate

3.137. Barnett, P. W. "Under Tiberius All was Quiet." *NTS* 21(1975): 564–571.

3.138. Bond, H. K. "The Coins of Pontius Pilate: Part of an Attempt to Provoke the People or to Integrate Them into the Empire?" *JSJ* 27(1996): 241–262.

3.139. Brandon, S. G. F. "The Trial of Jesus." *Horizon* 9, no. 1, (1967): 4–13.

3.140. Corbishley, T. "Pontius Pilate." *Clergy Review* 12(1936): 368–381.

3.141. Foreman, D. *Crucify Him: A Lawyer Looks at the Trial of Jesus.* Grand Rapids: Zondervan, 1990.

3.142. Fricke, W. *The Court-Martial of Jesus: A Christian Defends the Jews Against the Charge of Deicide.* Trans. by S. Attanasio. New York: Grove Weidenfeld, 1990.

3.143. Hedly, P. L. "Pilate's Arrival in Judea." *JThS* 35(1934): 56–67.

3.144. Maier, P. L. "The Fate of Pontius Pilate." *Hermes* 99(1971): 362–371.

3.145. ———. "Who Killed Jesus?" *ChrT* 34, no. 6, (1990): 16–19.

3.146. McGing, B. C. "Pontius Pilate and the Sources." *CBQ* 53 (1991): 416–438.

3.147. Morison, F. *And Pilate Said: A New Study of the Roman Procurator.* London: Rich & Cowan, 1939.

3.148. Reid, B. "The Trial of Jesus – Or Pilate?" *BibT* 26(1988): 277–282.

Paul and the Romans

Sergius Paulus

3.149. Harrer, G. A. "Saul Who Is Also Called Paul." *HThR* 33(1940): 19–34.

3.150. Horsley, G. H. R. "Name Change as an Indication of Religious Conversion in Antiquity." *Numen* 34(1987): 1–17.

3.151. Leary, T. J. "Paul's Improper Name." *NTS* 38(1992): 467–469.

3.152. Ramsay, W. M. *The Bearing of Recent Discoveries on the Trustworthiness of the New Testament.* London: Hodder & Stoughton, 1915.

Gallio and Seneca

3.153. Bacchiocchi, S. "Rome and Christianity Until A.D. 62." *AndUnivSemStud* 21(1983): 3–25.

3.154. Larson, V. T. "Seneca and the Schools of Philosophy in Early Imperial Rome." *ICS* 17(1992): 49–56.

3.155. Lightfoot, J. B. *Commentary on Philippians.* Grand Rapids: Baker Books, 1970 reprint.

3.156. Murphy-O'Connor, J. "Paul and Gallio." *JBL* 112(1993): 315–317.

3.157. Rees, W. "Gallio the Proconsul of Achaia." *Scripture* (1951): 11–20.

3.158. Sevenster, J. N. *Paul and Seneca.* Leiden: Brill, 1961.

3.159. Wenham, J. "The Identification of Luke." *EvangQ* 63(1991): 3–44.

Felix

3.160. Kokkinos, N. "A Fresh Look at the *Gentilicum* of Felix, Procurator of Judea." *Latomus* 49(1990): 126–141.

3.161. Oost, S. I. "The Career of M. Antonius Pallas." *AJPh* 79(1958): 113–139.

3.162. Saddington, D. B. "Felix in Samaria: A Note on Tac. *Ann.* 12.54.1 and Suet. *Claud.* 28.1." *AClass* 35(1992): 161–163.

Some Minor Characters

Festus

3.163. Tajra, H. W. *The Trial of St. Paul: A Juridical Exegesis of the Second Half of the Acts of the Apostles.* Tübingen: Mohr, 1989.

Quirinius
3.164. Barnett, P. W. *"Apographé* and *Apographesthai* in Luke 2:1–5." *ExposT* 85(1974): 377–380.
3.165. Corbishley, T. "Quirinius and the Census: A Re-Study of the Evidence." *Klio* 11(1936): 81–93.
3.166. Harris, B. F. "Oaths of Allegiance to Caesar." *Prudentia* 14(1982): 109–122.
3.167. Ogg, G. "The Quirinius Question Today." *ExposT* 79(1968): 231–236.
3.168. Ramsay, W. M. "The Census of Quirinius." *Expositor* 1(1897): 274–286, 425–435.
3.169. Taylor, L. R. "Quirinius and the Census of Judea." *AJPh* 54(1933): 120–133.
3.170. Thorley, J. "The Nativity Census: What Does Luke Actually Say?" *G&R* 26(1979): 81–84.
3.171. ———. "When Was Jesus Born?" *G&R* 28(1981): 81–89.
3.172. Wiseman, T. P. "There Went Out a Decree from Caesar Augustus . . . ." *NTS* 33(1987): 479–480.

Theophilus
3.173. Cadbury, H. J. "The Purpose Expressed in Luke's Preface." *Expositor* 21(1921): 431–441.
3.174. Streeter, B. H. *The Four Gospels: A Study of Origins.* London: Macmillan, 1924, 1964 reprint.

Dionysius the Areopagite
3.175. Rist, J. M. "In Search of the Divine Denis." In *The Seed of Wisdom: Essays in Honour of T. J. Meek.* Ed. by W. S. McCullough. Toronto: University of Toronto Press, 1964: 118–139.

"And Others"
3.176. Bell, A. A., Jr. "Three Again." *CJ* 70(Feb.–Mar.1975): 40–41.
3.177. Bremmer, J. "Why Did Early Christianity Attract Upper-Class Women?" In *Fructus centesimus: Mélanges offerts à Gerard J. M Bartelink à l'occasion de son soix-ante-cinquieme anniversaire.* Ed. by A. A. R. Bastiaensen, et al. Dordrecht: Kluwer, 1989: 37–47.
3.178. Cooper, K. "Insinuations of Womanly Influence: An Aspect of the Christianization of the Roman Aristocracy." *JRS* 82(1992): 150–164.
3.179. Gill, D. W. J. "Erastus the Aedile." *TynBull* 40(1989): 293–301.
3.180. Kearsley, R. A. "Asiarchs, *Archiereis,* and the *Archiereiai* of Asia." *GRBS* 27(1986): 183–192.
3.181. Meggitt, J. J. "The Social Status of Erastus (Rom. 16:23)." *NovT* 38(1996): 218–223.
3.182. Metzger, B. M. "Names for the Nameless in the New Testament: A Study in the Growth of Christian Tradition." In *Kyriakon: Festschrift Johannes Quasten.* Ed. by P. Granfield and J. Jungman. Münster: Aschendorff, 1970: 79–99.
3.183. Smith, R. H. "Were the Early Christians Middle-Class? A Sociological Analysis of the New Testament." *CTM* 7(1980): 260–276.
3.184. Thorley, J. "Junia, a Woman Apostle." *NovT* 38(1996): 18–29.

CHAPTER 4

ROMAN LAW
AND THE
NEW
TESTAMENT

"Church and State" in Rome

WHILE THE DISPUTE between the Christians and the Jews was theological, that between the Christians and Romans was legal. Yet when we say that, we must remember that the ancient mind did not distinguish as clearly as we try to do between religion and politics (**2.257**). Pilate did not interrogate Jesus about his doctrine. That was what the Sanhedrin had focused on, especially the issue of blasphemy. Pilate's questions to Jesus reflect the governor's concern with the possibility of a revolt. If Jesus was claiming to be the king of the Jews, there was a basis for a charge of treason against him, but it would be politically and not religiously motivated. After Pilate determined that the charge was groundless, he was willing to release Jesus, with perhaps a beating to warn him to keep his mouth shut (**4.2**). His need to appease the Jews was the only thing that made him give in to their clamor and order Jesus to be crucified (Mark 15:15; see p. 72).

The Romans had no genuine religious convictions, as we'll see in chapter 5. When they encountered a new cult or form of worship, they were interested only in its origins and behavior patterns and the effect which those aspects of it would have on the larger community. That's where the line between religion and politics becomes blurred. Persecution of a cult would be undertaken if the government deemed the group dangerous to the life of the state, revolutionary, or disruptive of social order. The cult of Dionysus, for example, encouraged its devotees—mostly women—to drink to excess and run through the countryside shrieking and chasing small animals, which would be torn apart and eaten raw. The Romans banned it soon after its first appearance in the city in the early second century B.C., "out of their fear that such secretive nightly assemblies might give rise to some plot or unseen threat" (Livy 39.14).

Religious groups suspected of engaging in criminal activities could also draw the government's wrath. Josephus (*Ant.* 18.65–70) records that a man named Mundus bribed the priests of Isis to connive in the seduction of a Roman matron who had resisted all his overtures. When the plot was uncovered, the emperor Tiberius tore down the temple, dumped the cult's idol into the Tiber River, and ran the priests and Mundus out of town. Religious doctrine was not the issue; criminal behavior was. The Jews, perhaps deemed guilty by association because of their eastern origins, were expelled at the same time (cf. **3.57**).

Trajan, whose rescript defined Rome's policy toward Christians

(Photo from Alinari/Art Resource, NY)

It was an open question to the Romans whether some religious groups were by nature criminal or whether commission of specific crimes had to be proved against their members. The most serious charge brought against the Christians, however, was simply that they refused to be loyal citizens and to prove their loyalty by performing ritual acts, whether they believed in them or not. Many philosophers of the time belittled the gods as outmoded superstitions, but they engaged in the sacrifices and offerings which their communities made periodically to those gods (Tertullian, *Apol.* 46.4). They were, in modern terms, willing to salute the flag. The Christians were not. Christians appeared, to the general public and to the government, as a deviant and dangerous group. That was why the Romans took action against them, sometimes in the form of spontaneous and violent mob action, at other times in an official government persecution (**2.257; 4.1**).

The Romans insisted on state regulation of, and interference in, the affairs of religious groups because for them religion was a function of civic life, not a private matter. Any religious group needed state approval to operate legally, just as any union or guild of tradesmen did. No unlicensed group could incorporate itself, maintain a treasury, or carry on its activities in public. Christianity's problem in the first century was to obtain this sort of legal recognition without losing the benefits which it enjoyed as a sect of Judaism, a cult which had long since come to hold a privileged status among the religions of the Empire.

Christians and the Law: A Case Study

Sometimes the easiest way to approach a complex issue is to find an example which can be analyzed. The smaller parts of the question become visible and can be discussed in more manageable portions. We can then move from the particular to the more general. Social scientists call this the case study approach. Pliny's letter (*Ep*. 10.96) to the emperor Trajan describing his treatment of Christians in the province of Bithynia, along with Trajan's reply (*Ep*. 10.97), provides a case study that illustrates virtually every point of the question of Christians and the law under the Roman Empire. Along with a passage in Tacitus, it is our most valuable non-Christian source of information about early Christianity (**4.4**). The letter was written in A.D. 112 from an area that is now north-central Turkey. This document is important enough that the text is given in its entirety, along with the emperor's brief reply, known as a rescript (**4.3**).

Pliny to the Emperor Trajan:

It is my custom, my lord, to refer to you all things about which I am uncertain. For who is better able to settle my doubts or to instruct me when I am ignorant?

I have never attended a trial of Christians. Therefore I do not know what sort of punishments are usually handed out to them or their severity; nor do I know for what reasons, or to what extent, an inquiry should be made. I am very unsure whether those of different ages should be treated differently, or if the young should be treated the same as the adults. Should forgiveness be granted for repentance, or do people who have been Christians at any time gain nothing if they renounce it? Is it the very name "Christian" which is to be punished, even if no crime is associated with it, or is it the crimes connected with the name?

For the time being I have taken this approach with those who have been accused before me of being Christians. First I ask them whether they are Christians. Those who confess I question a second and third time, threatening them with punishment. Those

who persist I order to be led away [i. e., for execution]. I have no
doubt that, whatever it is they're professing, their stubbornness
and inflexible obstinacy deserve punishment. Others afflicted with
similar madness I have put on the list to be sent to Rome [i. e., for
trial], because they are Roman citizens.

As a result of my handling of the situation, as usually happens,
I have encountered a greater variety of charges and the problem
has spread. An unsigned pamphlet has been posted, containing
the names of many people. The ones who denied that they were
Christians, or ever had been, I decided to excuse, once they had
called upon the gods, reciting after me, and had made offerings
with wine and incense to your statue (which I had ordered to be
set up for this reason alongside the images of the gods). In addition, they cursed Christ. I'm told that true Christians cannot be
forced to do any of those things.

Others, who had been named by an informer, first said they
were Christians but soon denied it. Some of them claimed that
they had ceased to be Christians two or three years ago, others
several years previously, and a few of them as long as twenty years
ago. They all worshiped your statue and those of the gods and
cursed Christ.

They asserted, moreover, that their only guilt or mistake consisted of the following:

• they were accustomed to assemble on a certain day before
dawn;

• they would sing to Christ as if he were a god, alternating verses among themselves;

• they would put themselves under an oath, not to commit any
sort of crime, but not to commit theft, robbery or adultery,
not to betray a trust, and not to deny a deposit to one who
calls for it;

• having completed these rituals, they were in the habit of
breaking up and then convening again to partake of
food—common, harmless food.

They had ceased to do these things after my edict in which,
according to your orders, I forbade the existence of political
clubs. This convinced me all the more of the necessity of determining the truth by torturing two slave-women, who are called
deaconesses. I found nothing other than a depraved and extravagant superstition.

Therefore I have deferred my investigation and hurried to
consult you. The matter seems to me worthy of your attention,

especially because of the number of persons in danger. Many people of every age, every rank, both men and women, are being summoned to trial and will be summoned. The contamination of this superstition has permeated not only the towns, but also the villages and rural areas. It still seems that it can be stopped and corrected. It is clear enough that the temples, which had been almost desolate for a long time, have begun to be crowded once more, and the sacred rites which had been interrupted are being performed again, and flesh of sacrificial victims is being sold everywhere, which until recently found only the rarest buyer. It is easy to conclude from this what a throng of people could be corrected if there is an opportunity for repentance.

Trajan to Pliny:
    You have done what you ought to, my dear Pliny, in trying the cases of those who had been brought to you as Christians. For it is impossible for something universally applicable to be established, as if there were a fixed rule. These people must not be sought out; if they are brought before you and convicted, they must be punished. However, anyone who denies that he is a Christian, and gives evidence of this by offering prayers to our gods, should be pardoned because of his repentance, no matter how suspect he may have been in the past. But pamphlets posted anonymously ought not to have any place in an accusation. They are very bad examples and not characteristic of our age.

Powers of Governors

Unless a resident of the Empire lived in Rome itself, he encountered the power of the Empire only in its local embodiment, the provincial governor. As noted in chapter 3, the Romans began sending out governors to their overseas provinces in the third century B.C. These men had absolute power over the inhabitants of their provinces and command of any troops that might be stationed there. They could emend or abolish the laws of a province, or do whatever suited their purposes or whims (**4.10**). It cannot be stressed too strongly that they, and the people on their staffs, were answerable to no one, except insofar as provincials could bring charges before courts in Rome—a lengthy and expensive process. Only under the Empire was some check imposed by the fact that most governors were appointed by the emperor and served at his pleasure. Even those chosen by the senate could be overruled by the emperor.

Perhaps the worst example of a provincial official's abuse of his powers can be found in the career of Verres. In 70 B.C. Cicero successfully prosecuted him for extortion while he was governor of Sicily, but even earlier, while on the staff of the governor of another province, he had attempted to kidnap and rape the daughter of a provincial family. When the young woman's father and brother, with the help of some townspeople, put up a fight, one of the men with Verres was killed. The

Senate Building (Curia) in Rome
(Photo by Howard Vos)

father and brother were arrested, tried, and convicted of killing the man. Verres was a member of the jury that passed judgment, and he helped the prosecutors present their case. The father and brother were executed (Cicero, *Oration II vs. Verres* 1.24, 63–83).

In spite of improvements in treatment of provincials under the Empire, "it would be wrong to assume that abuses were infrequent or redress easy to secure" (**4.5**:189). In general, the governors were left alone to do as they pleased as long as they did not turn their troops against the government in Rome or allow the provincials to revolt. They could be "as harsh as they liked as long as they did not take money or property from . . . the ordinary provincial subject" (**4.54**:139).

The primary ground for complaints about the governors was their tendency to take bribes or extort money in return for favorable judgments in legal cases, as Felix hoped to do with Paul (Acts 24:26). Under the late Republic, the problem of extortion became so severe that special courts had to be set up in Rome to allow provincials to take legal action against the worst of the governors. The Romans, recognizing the importance of maintaining calm in the provinces, made a reasonable effort to deal fairly with their subjects. A number of governors were convicted and forced to make reparations to the provincials. In one case the governor died, but the disgruntled people of his province were allowed to bring legal action against his heirs (Pliny, *Ep.* 3.9). Imperial oversight of the provincial administration improved conditions somewhat, but cases of extortion and mismanagement still came up in the early second century (Pliny, *Epp.* 5.20; 7.6).

Maintenance of public order was a top priority of the governors, and they or their subordinates would move quickly to squelch trouble before it got out of hand, as the town clerk of Ephesus reminded his fellow citizens in Acts 19:40 (**4.7; 4.9; 4.14**). The tribune Claudius Lysias reacted to a report that "all Jerusalem was in an uproar" by bringing in soldiers to break up the mob attacking Paul (Acts 21:31–32). He had no interest in the merits of either side of the argument and was simply trying to stop a riot. Sometimes a governor had to restore order by giving in to provincial demands, as Pilate did in consenting to Jesus' crucifixion when he saw "that a riot was beginning" (Matt. 27:24).

It is the governor's function as judge, however, which most concerns the student of the New Testament, and that role is clearly delineated in Pliny's letter. The governor normally traveled around to the larger towns in his province (**4.6; 4.11–12**), hearing cases that might have been waiting for him for several weeks or months. Paul had been under house arrest in Caesarea for two years, waiting for the governor to act (Acts 24:23–27). Persons brought before the governor were accused of something; he must determine the charges and whether there was basis for a trial.

Not all governors were legal experts. They had lists of various crimes and the penalties normally associated with them, a troubleshooter's guide to legal procedure. Such a list was called an *ordo*. In addition, the governor's power allowed him to deal with cases not on the list (*extra ordinem*) if he felt there was good reason to pursue some matter. He was not obliged to do so, as we see when Gallio refused to hear the charges against Paul. But Pliny was a meticulous man and a cautious bureaucrat, whose correspondence shows him to be concerned about whether he is doing the wrong thing or not doing something needed, and then being called to account by the emperor. If this new cult was getting strong enough to draw people away from the worship of the traditional gods—which was an important measure of their political loyalty, as we will see in chapter 5—Pliny knew he had to take some action.

Underlying all of Pliny's actions in this case is his *imperium*, or general grant of power, and in particular his *ius gladii*, "power of the sword," the power to put people to death (**4.8**). That was the authority by which Pilate condemned Jesus to death. It was the one power which could not be delegated to the governor's underlings. If an execution was ordered, it had to be ordered by the governor himself. This fact throws light on Revelation 2:13, addressed to the church at Pergamum which "did not deny my faith even in the days of Antipas my witness, my faithful one, who was killed among you" (RSV). The first three chapters of Revelation talk about persecution and trials, but this is the only reference to a specific person being put to death. And it happened in the capital city of the province of Asia, where the governor had his residence.

Criminal Procedures

The first two paragraphs of Pliny's letter show how uncertain he was of his ground. He had not been present at trials of Christians in Rome, a statement which indicates clearly that such things had taken place there by that time (**4.26**), and he does not find anything about Christianity in the *ordo*. Getting messages back and forth between Bithynia and Rome would take several weeks (see chapter 9), so Pliny acts on his own authority, hoping the emperor will back him up. His method conforms to everything we know of Roman legal procedures (**4.25**).

A case was initiated when someone brought a person physically to the magistrate and set out the charges against him. Except in the case of highway bandits and revolutionaries (**4.24**), the Roman government did not go out and arrest people. The law was explicit on this point (**4.28**, vol. 1:102):

> If plaintiff summons defendant to court, he shall go. If he does not go, plaintiff shall call witness thereto. Then only shall he take the defendant by force. If defendant shirks or takes to his heels, plaintiff shall lay hands on him. If disease or age is an impediment, plaintiff shall grant defendant a team; he shall not spread the covered carriage with cushions if he does not so desire.

We must, therefore, discard the image of Roman soldiers knocking down doors in the middle of the night to arrest Christians (or anybody else). Lodging charges against someone and seeing that the defendant appeared before the magistrate were the plaintiff's responsibilities. As the Ephesian town clerk noted in Acts 19:38, "If therefore Demetrius and the artisans with him have a complaint against anyone, the courts are open, and there are proconsuls; let them bring charges there against one another." Any time Paul was tried, he was physically "brought before" the magistrates by his accusers. Jesus urged his followers to settle with an accuser on the way to court, "or you may be dragged before the judge" (Luke 12:58). That was what Jesus' own enemies knew they had to do. That's why it was important for them to be able to locate and identify him.

Accusations in a Roman court were supposed to follow the pattern of a named accuser stepping forth to present charges against another person. As Festus said, "It was not the custom of the Romans to hand over anyone before the accused had met the accusers face to face and had been given an opportunity to make a defense against the charge" (Acts 25:16). But sometimes, especially in the provinces, a magistrate might hear rumors of a problem that needed to be investigated before it got out of hand. Legal papyri from Egypt give us insight into how criminal investigations were handled in at least one other province (**4.19**). Pliny is doing nothing out of the ordinary. Like every governor, he had the power of *inquisitio,* the right to inquire into something, whether formal charges had been brought or not (see box). Such action was usually taken as a means of checking on the activities of the lower classes. In the case of the Christians in Bithynia, "it was Pliny's duty to see that the sources of trouble were identified and brought under control" (**4.20**:440).

Part of Pliny's procedure in this case is based on this power. Wanting more information than had been revealed by the plaintiffs or defendants, he tortured two members of the group. Those who think that only men should hold positions of authority in the church might note that in A.D. 112 there were two deaconesses (the Latin word used is *ministrae*) in this particular church (**4.18**). The tortures to which they were subjected would be limited only by the ingenuity of the magistrate. Apuleius describes a slave being whipped, burned, stretched on the rack, and forced to sit on a wooden sawhorse with weights on his feet (*Golden Ass* 10.10). The fact that these unfortunate women were slaves and yet held positions of authority says something important about the mixing of social classes as well as genders in the early church. They are certainly not the only women known to have held important posts in the church in its formative years (**4.32**; cf. Rom. 16:1–15).

A Christian Reaction to Roman Justice

Trajan wrote back that this group was not to be sought after, but if brought in they must be punished. What an inevitably confused decision! He says not to look for them, as if they are innocent, and he orders them to be punished, as though they are guilty. He lets them alone and rages against them. He overlooks them but punishes them. Why circumvent your own judgment? If you condemn them, why not look for them? If you don't look for them, why not also absolve them? The job of tracking down bandits is assigned to the soldiers in all the provinces. Everyone is a soldier against those guilty of treason and against public enemies; the investigation is extended to their co-conspirators, even to accomplices. Christians only may not be hunted down, but they can be brought to trial, as if hunting down led to anything but a trial. So you condemn someone brought into court, someone whom nobody wanted to be sought out, someone who (I suppose) really has not merited punishment because of his guilt, but because he was found when nobody was supposed to be looking for him!

Tertullian, *Apology* 2.8–9

Once the magistrate had decided to accept a case, he would proceed in the manner Pliny followed. Wishing to show that he had observed proper procedures in this uncertain business, Pliny reports that he interrogated the defendants and decided how they could demonstrate their innocence. A simple denial of the charge was not sufficient. The Romans rarely used physical evidence or third-party testimony in a trial. It was hard to insure the authenticity of documents or other physical evidence. In one case Pliny could not even be sure an imperial decree was genuine (*Epp.* 10.58, 10.65). Testimony was considered reliable primarily if it was obtained under torture, but Roman citizens could not be tortured. Only noncitizens and slaves were subject to such cruelty (**4.16**).

An important aside to this inquisition is the question of how Pliny communicated with the provincials, for it might throw some light on Jesus' confrontation with Pilate. Pliny mentions no interpreters. He himself spoke Greek, as any educated Roman of the time did, and a simplified version of Greek, known as Koiné, had long been the universal language of the eastern Mediterranean world. The Greeks invented the word "barbarian" to describe anyone, no matter how cultured, who did not speak Greek. The Romans likewise had little patience with provincials who did not know either Greek or Latin (**4.21**). In uncivilized Gaul, Caesar found it necessary to use interpreters (*Gallic Wars* 5.36), but it seems that if the provincials could manage Greek, the Romans could communicate with them. On the eastern frontier of the empire Ovid found that some of his neighbors spoke a very uncultured sort of Greek, but "I must make myself understood by gestures. Here I am the barbarian, unintelligible to anyone" (*Tristia* 5.10, 36–37). He did eventually master enough of the Getic (Gothic, i. e., German) language to write poetry in it.

The trial itself consisted of statements first by the accusers and then by the defendants or their lawyers (cf. Acts 24:1–21). The speeches could be quite lengthy, several hours at times, and often brought in historical analogies and other material that would be considered irrelevant in a modern court. In one poem (6.19) Martial complains that his lawyer is spending too much time making comparisons with events from history when the case concerns the theft of three of his goats. The point of all the rhetoric, though, was not to establish facts, but to sway the jury or magistrate to one side or the other. Trials were often held out in the open, with bystanders listening in. Lawyers tried to stir up the feelings of the crowds to convince the jury or magistrate that popular opinion was on one side or the other. Stephen's speech in Acts 7 follows this pattern.

A person who refused to respond to his accusers was tossing away his only chance to defend himself. Such behavior was almost unheard of. That's why Pilate was so puzzled by Jesus' silence: "The chief priests accused him of many things. Pilate asked him again, 'Have you no answer? See how many charges they bring against you.' But Jesus made no further reply, so that Pilate was amazed" (Mark 15:3–5). The defendant was not supposed to present any philosophical rationale or justification for his actions but to address the question of his guilt or innocence. In their defense speeches, Christians may have tried to preach too much to suit the Romans. Tertullian says that by the late second century, they were denied the right to speak at their trials (*Apol.* 2.2).

Because evidence and testimony could not establish innocence in the case before Pliny, the accused had to do certain things to prove that they did not belong to the cult. A governor could impose such requirements under his power of *coercitio*, the right to compel or force someone to submit to his authority. In a letter describing a case which he helped try in Rome, Pliny tells how the provincials based their defense on the fact that "they were provincials and were compelled by fear to obey every order of the governor" (*Ep.* 3.9, 15).

Pliny could thus force the persons on trial before him in this case to do whatever he felt necessary to establish their innocence. Since atheism was one of the charges associated with the name of Christian, the defendants had to pay homage to the images of the gods, including the emperor, and pronounce a curse on the name of Christ (**4.23**; **4.29–30**). From what Pliny had learned of the group, no sincere member of it would do or say such things (cf. 1 Cor. 12:3).

Those who refused to perform these rituals were deemed guilty of refusal to obey a governor's order, if nothing else. The Christian position that "we must obey God rather than any human authority" (Acts 5:29) was completely antithetical to the Romans' understanding of the proper order. If the governor (or any other magistrate) gave an order, people were expected to obey it or be guilty of *contumacia*, stubbornness (**2.257**; **4.33**).

The Christians on trial here do not seem to have been given an opportunity to explain what Christianity was or why it was not criminal to be a Christian. The government associated certain illegal activities with the group; therefore, confessing membership in the group was admitting to those activities. The debate about guilt "for the name" continued into the late second century. Tertullian protested that other defendants were tried on the basis of what they had done, Christians on the basis of who they were (*Apol.* 6). Modern scholars are by no means in agreement on whether the Romans were persecuting the name itself or crimes believed to be inherent in the profession of the name. No law known to us specifically prohibited the existence of Christianity (**4.15**; **4.17**).

In this case a procedure was outlined by which the accused could disprove the charge, and the penalty for their "crime" was explained to them. Pliny states that their stubbornness, if nothing else, deserves punishment. This is a remarkable contrast to the attitude he shows in his treatment of his own slaves, to whom he was quite humane (**1.55**).

But in the provinces, the Romans expected unquestioning obedience to their orders. The Jews, and then the Christians, gave them more trouble on this point than all their other subjects combined.

As Pliny interrogated people accused of being Christians, he began to get a picture of what the cult did, largely from information supplied by people who had withdrawn from it. He was surprised to learn that they did nothing shockingly evil. Their "guilt" consisted in meeting before dawn (which was against Roman law), worshiping Christ as though he were some sort of god, then taking an oath of some sort.

This letter is of inestimable importance as an objective source of information about the Christians, free of the polemics often generated by groups within the church who read their divergent theologies back into their accounts of the first-century church (**4.27**; **4.36**). The "oath" or *sacramentum* which the Christians took sounds like the Ten Commandments or a summary of the Law, perhaps taken from Mark 10:19, where Jesus inserts "you shall not defraud" into his summary of the Torah. The christological motif in the hymn corresponds well with what we know of early Christian hymns from fragments preserved in Colossians 1:15–20 and Philippians 2:5–11 (**4.1**; **4.35**).

Roman Regulation of Groups

Pliny's eyes must have widened when he heard that the Christians met before it was light and took some sort of oath. This was the heart of the new faith's problems with the government, because the Romans strictly regulated the activities of all sorts of groups or associations, known as *collegia*. Roman officials seem to have been deeply suspicious of any group meetings. The earliest collection of Roman laws, the Twelve Tables (written ca. 450 B.C.), prohibits groups from meeting at night and allows them to make rules governing themselves only so long as these do not promote public disorder.

The Roman government's attitude toward group meetings is summed up by one of the speakers in Livy's account of the persecution of the cult of Dionysus (39.15):

> Your ancestors did not allow even citizens to assemble for whatever reason they chose. . . . Whenever a crowd gathered, they decreed that someone in authority should preside. What kind of assemblies do you think these are? To begin with, they are assembling at night, and, secondly, men and women are gathering in mixed groups, without supervision!

The Christians would have been guilty of the same "crimes." This suspicion of the motives of people who wanted to congregate continued into imperial times. After a major fire in one of the towns in his province, Pliny suggested to Trajan that the townspeople be allowed to start a fire brigade to lessen the danger of another disaster. The number of people involved would be kept small, he promised, and "I will take care that no one except firefighters is admitted and that the privilege granted is not used for some other purpose" (*Ep.* 10.33).

Trajan's reaction (*Ep.* 10.34) was emphatically negative: "Let us bear in mind that that province, and especially the cities, has been troubled by groups of this sort. Whatever name we give them and whatever the reason for their meetings, people who gather for some purpose soon become a political club." In another case the emperor only reluctantly allowed the formation of a charitable society, provided "the collections are not spent on riotous and unlawful gatherings, but to relieve the destitute condition of the poor" (*Ep.* 10.93).

The government's attitude may help to explain why Luke was especially careful to emphasize that when Paul and a group of Christians prolonged a meeting until after midnight "there were many lights in the upper chamber" where they had "gathered together to break bread" (Acts 20:7–8 RSV). In other words, it was simply a dinner party that went on longer than anticipated because they were enjoying the conversation so much. The room was well lighted and not some dark, conspiratorial den. People can plot sedition in the daytime, of course, but the Romans felt that groups gathering at night had no purpose other than something illicit. Why else were they reluctant to be seen by their neighbors?

One way in which criminals or political dissidents of that time strengthened their resolution was to swear an oath binding themselves together until the deed was committed. The term normally used for such an oath was *sacramentum,* and that is the term Pliny uses in his letter. An example of what the Romans dreaded can be seen in Acts 23:12–13: "In the morning the Jews joined in a conspiracy and bound themselves by an oath neither to eat nor drink until they had killed Paul. There were more than forty who joined in this conspiracy." Since Paul was rescued from their ambush, those men might have starved. But the rabbis provided an interpretation to release people from rash vows which could not be fulfilled due to unavoidable constraints (Mishnah Nedarim 3.3).

As a Roman governor, Pliny would now have had a lot to worry about. Here was an unlicensed collegium, meeting regularly under cover of darkness, taking an oath. An oath to do what? That was probably Pliny's next question. He must have been relieved—and puzzled—to discover that it was "not to commit any sort of crime, but not to commit theft, robbery or adultery, not to betray a trust, and not to deny a deposit to one who calls for it." Obviously he had suspected the Christians of criminal intent, but he could find nothing more sinister than a *superstitio.* This word was used for cults like that of Dionysus, which the Romans tried to keep in check because they exalted the individual against the community. Having categorized it, he knew how to proceed against it (**4.39**).

In addition to their illegal pre-dawn gathering, this group also held an assembly to eat together (**4.40**). Notice that they had given up that practice when Pliny, acting upon Trajan's instructions, had banned all *collegia*. He is quick to point out that they ate "common, harmless food." This is certainly a reaction to the charge of cannibalism frequently leveled against the early Christians (Tertullian, *Apol.* 7.1; 9.11–15).

The idea that Christians were cannibals may have become current from half-understood references to the words of institution in the Lord's Supper: "Take, eat; this is my body. . . . Drink . . . for this is my blood" (Matt. 26:26–28). If one member of a family became a Christian and the others had only limited knowledge of what was going on, or if someone listened through a wall while Christians met in his neighbor's apartment, such slanders of an unpopular group could get started easily enough. Stories of cannibalism do occur in Greco-Roman myths, so the charge would not be totally unbelievable in this instance. Pliny doesn't spell out all of that, but he seems relieved to lay the rumor to rest. The charge continued, however, to be brought against the Christians on into the late second century (**4.38**; cf. Tertullian, *Apol.* 6).

Informers

Pliny mentions that he questioned some people who had been named by an informer. That word has a traitorous sound to the modern ear, but such people played an important part in helping the government keep tabs on the populace in New Testament times. They were necessary because the government lacked police to enforce laws (**4.44**). In early Rome it had been considered the duty of every citizen to report wrongdoing and to turn the perpetrators in to the magistrates. These informers (*delatores*) acted as prosecutors in court cases, since the government had no one to carry out that duty (**4.43**). The government encouraged such efforts by awarding the informer a fourth of any property or money taken from a convicted person. Before we condemn that system, we should recall that if someone today turns in a tax-cheater to the U.S. Internal Revenue Service, the informer gets 10 percent of whatever the IRS recovers. The modern informer, however, can perform this "service" only once.

Under the emperors this system of informers became a network of spies (**4.45**). Slaves in aristocratic households knew they could report bits of gossip or conversation overheard while serving dinner, and a suspicious emperor like Tiberius or Caligula could distort them into a plot. The most trivial actions could lead to a charge of treason: changing clothes beside a statue of the emperor; going into a latrine or brothel while carrying the emperor's likeness (which was on almost all coins); beating a slave who held in his hand a coin bearing the emperor's image (**4.41–42**). People were actually arrested for these and lesser offenses to the imperial dignity (Suetonius, *Tib.* 58; Dio Cassius 58, frag. 2). Suetonius says that Tiberius especially encouraged informers, and the senate followed his lead: "Special awards were decreed for those who brought accusations. . . . Whatever an informer said was always believed. Every crime was treated as a capital offense, even speaking a few words off-hand" (*Tib.* 61).

This is the role Judas played in Jesus' arrest. It's easy for us to condemn Judas, but we should recognize that he was acting in a manner not considered altogether reprehensible in his day. Informers made the government aware of people who posed some threat to society and assisted in their removal. It seemed only reasonable that they should be rewarded. That, at least, was the theory. In actual fact, people informed on their personal enemies or those whom they wanted out of the way to gain some financial or social advantage. Well-to-do people in particular lived in daily fear of falling victim to an informer. They never knew when some disgruntled slave or political rival might whisper a few malicious words into a magistrate's ear.

Citizenship

Some of those accused before Pliny were Roman citizens. They were treated differently from the provincials, a clear lesson in the value of being able to say *civis Romanus sum* (I am a Roman citizen). The only protection an individual might have against the arbitrary powers of a Roman governor, or any other magistrate, was to be a Roman citizen. This status conferred three primary benefits (**4.48**).

Benefits of Citizenship

First, citizenship exempted a person from being subjected to torture or corporal punishment without a trial (**4.49**; **5.53**). That was the basis of Paul's objection to his treatment in Acts 16:37: "They have beaten us in public, uncondemned, men who are Roman citizens." That experience seems to have taught Paul a lesson. In Acts 22:25 he asks *before* the lash begins to fly, "Is it legal for you to flog a Roman citizen who is uncondemned?" (**4.54**).

Second, possession of Roman citizenship meant that one was not subject to the laws of the individual cities and towns of the empire (**4.51**). These could vary tremendously from place to place because the Romans left internal matters to the discretion of each municipality (**4.52**). Travelers could find themselves at the mercy of unknown statutes, as did two poor fellows in Petronius' *Satyricon* 14–15 in a dispute over a stolen cloak. Two of Pliny's letters mention problems which arose from the freedom of towns in his province to administer their own laws (*Epp.* 10.47; 10.92).

This privilege was also extended to occasional groups, such as the Jews, with a recognized tradition of their own, even though they were scattered among the Roman population. The Jews in Alexandria lived in a certain quarter of the city, elected their own officials, and judged their own legal cases. In other towns as well, though they were less numerous, they still had the right to decide matters among themselves, as Gallio reminded them in Acts 18. In the event of a dispute between a Roman citizen and the officials of some town, the Roman citizen was entitled to have his case heard by a Roman magistrate under Roman law.

The third benefit of Roman citizenship was that it entitled those who possessed it to have their legal business conducted in Rome. This did not mean, however, that each citizen could have his case heard personally by the emperor. Suetonius (*Aug.* 33) mentions that Augustus began a policy of referring citizens' appeal cases to the city praetor. Tacitus (*Ann.* 13.4) records Nero's promise that cases from the provinces would be heard by a "tribunal of consuls." Pliny dutifully ships the Roman citizens in this case off to Rome, just as Festus did Paul (Acts 25). It's highly unlikely that any of these people were ever tried by the emperor personally, but their cases would have been reviewed by some highly placed official or panel (**4.50**).

Obtaining Citizenship

Roman citizenship could be obtained in several ways. A child born to citizen parents was automatically a citizen. A slave emancipated by a citizen master received citizenship. Some conservatives, like Juvenal, objected to the "mongrelization" of the Roman population which resulted from this practice, as Syrians, Germans, Egyptians, and others were freed and enrolled on the lists of citizens.

For the student of the New Testament, Paul's statement that he was born a citizen simply moves the question back one generation. How did his father become a citizen? No one knows, nor can we know, but that has not stopped speculation (**4.61**). Some early Christian writers, like Jerome in his commentary on Philemon, thought Paul's father had done some service to Marc Antony in his effort to put Herod on the throne of Judea, but then had moved his family from Judea to Tarsus after a war destroyed their hometown.

Citizenship could be granted by the emperor for services rendered to the state or at the request of influential friends. In one letter Pliny asks Trajan to extend citizenship to a doctor whose treatment had healed Pliny of a serious ailment (*Ep.* 10.5). At the same time, he requests citizenship for two "freedwomen." Could women be Roman citizens? Yes, they could. Although it did not entitle them to vote or hold office, they could enjoy the same protection against prosecution under the laws of another town or district. In *Ep.* 10.106, Pliny asks for the same status to be granted to the daughter of a soldier. To judge from the form of his name, the soldier is already a citizen; any legitimate children of his would not need a special grant of citizenship. This girl may have been his daughter by a common-law marriage with a provincial woman. Trajan replies, "I have granted his daughter Roman citizenship. I have sent you a copy of the order, which you should give to him."

That last statement provides a possible answer to an oft-asked question: How did Paul prove he was a Roman citizen? There is no evidence that every citizen carried a passport. We do know that soldiers who were not citizens when they joined the army were granted that status upon retirement and were given a "diploma," a small bronze plaque identifying them and attesting to their citizenship status (**4.56**).

For civilians, registration and census lists, of the sort referred to in the nativity story in Luke, would indicate the citizenship of the people on them. Because these lists were also the basis of their tax collections, the Roman bureaucrats worked hard to keep them up to date. From the time of Augustus, all Roman citizens were required to register their legitimate children. Non-citizens usually registered theirs, too, to forestall disputes over inheritances. A child not on a registration list would have a difficult time establishing a claim to his parents' property. Fragmentary copies of such lists still exist today (**4.59**). If any question arose about an individual's legal status, a magistrate from another town could write to his hometown and inquire about his citizenship.

Obviously such a procedure would take time. As A. N. Sherwin-White says, "There may have been a certain awkwardness in asserting one's Roman status on alien territory" (**4.60**:149). Paul makes no mention of his citizenship except in emergencies. An individual facing a beating, such as Paul was, might make a claim of Roman citizenship to forestall his punishment. The magistrate (or military officer, in this case) could not risk inflicting a beating on a citizen, so he would have to check. If the claim proved to be false, the penalties were the same as those for forgery, which were severe (**4.58**). In one instance, Claudius executed some men who falsely claimed Roman citizenship (Suetonius, *Claud.* 25.3). Paul would not have gained much by making a claim he could not substantiate. Knowing that, the tribune accepted his word.

The tribune's question to Paul reveals another means by which Roman citizenship might be obtained. The standard English translation, "It cost me a large sum of money to get my citizenship" (Acts 22:28), is somewhat misleading. The money which exchanged hands was actually a bribe to persuade some imperial secretary or provincial governor to put one's name on the lists of persons to be granted citizenship. These were presented to the emperor periodically for his approval.

Normally the fees involved in this transaction were fairly small but according to Dio Cassius (ca. A.D. 200) during Claudius' reign his wife, Messalina, who exercised considerable influence over the emperor, demanded exorbitant sums from persons who wished to become citizens. This tribune's name, Claudius Lysias, indicates that he became a citizen under Claudius, since it was the custom for new citizens to take the name of the reigning emperor as part of their own. Nero put a stop to the practice of extorting money from new citizens and dismissed one functionary still attempting to enrich himself this way (Tacitus, *Ann.* 14.50).

Pliny's letter and Paul's experience make clear the benefit of obtaining citizenship through whatever means (**4.55; 4.57**). It protected individuals from a governor's death sentence and from torture inflicted to gain information or beatings administered as punishment. Roman citizens could be punished, but for them the judicial process moved much slower and they had an opportunity to have their cases heard on several levels before action was taken. Citizenship was in fact an individual's only defense against an omnipotent government, which could behead people merely for being stubborn.

Roman Penal Practices

There were, in either theory or practice, no checks on the government's power to inflict punishment on persons convicted of crimes. As noted in chapter 1, imprisonment was not considered a punishment, though people might be detained for a time to await their fate. Fines might be levied for minor misdeeds; for most offenses an individual could be exiled or put to work in the mines or quarries (**4.77**). The death penalty was meted out for a variety of crimes, from libel to murder.

For an aristocrat to be arrested and put to death would bring disgrace on the whole clan. This was an especially important consideration in a society where reputation loomed so large. Upper-class Roman citizens were entitled to a non-public execution, usually by beheading. They were also offered the option of committing suicide, and many of them—such as Seneca, Lucan, and Petronius, as we've already seen—availed themselves of the opportunity. We may ask ourselves, why would they acquiesce so meekly? Why not run away, or stand and fight? In fact, they had nowhere to run, unless they were willing to live among the Germans or the Parthians. And they probably could not get that far before they were caught.

On the other hand, if they killed themselves, the emperor would let their wills stand—as long as he was mentioned as an heir of at least some small sum—and would not confiscate all their property (**4.80**). Thus they could leave something to take care of their families. Augustus took particular interest in what people said about him in their wills (Suetonius, *Aug.* 66.4). Such statements were regarded as somehow truer than things said in life (**4.66**). Suicide was also considered an honorable way out of an unmanageable situation, a notion which Christians found difficult to eradicate (**4.70**). When a friend of his starved himself to death to escape the effects of a lingering, painful illness, Pliny (*Ep.* 1.12, 3) consoled himself that "the highest form of reasoning had led [him] to this decision. . . . He had been suffering for so long from such a serious illness that the rewards of living, as great as they are, were outweighed by his reasons for dying." This concept of the nobility of suicide may have become a factor in the Christian glorification of martyrdom (**4.71**; see box).

The lower classes were not so fortunate in the manner of their death. "Cruel and unusual" punishments were not only permitted, they were deliberately contrived (**4.62**; **4.65**). Some scholars do caution that the ancient accounts not be taken too literally. Writers opposed to certain emperors often exaggerated their cruelty (**4.63**). But so much of the literature certainly does reveal the Romans' joy in watching victims suffer. Martial's first work, the short book *On the Spectacles*, describes some of the inhuman treatment inflicted on people sentenced to die in the arena. One man was tied up in a net and thrown in front of a bull, which tossed him around like a toy. Another was hung on a cross and had his abdomen ripped open by a bear.

Sometimes the victims were forced to reenact mythological stories or legends in which a person was killed (**4.67**). One woman, Martial says, was forced to play the part of Pasiphae, the queen who had intercourse with a bull and gave birth to the Minotaur (half bull/half human). "Whatever fame sings about," he boasts, "the Arena puts on display." He is referring to the Colosseum in Rome, the largest amphitheater in the Empire, but smaller arenas existed all over the

---

A Stoic on Suicide

When some external power has decreed your death, you cannot formulate a universally valid rule about whether you should await the sentence or anticipate it. Valid arguments can be made on both sides. If one type of death involves torture, while the other is quick and easy, why not opt for the latter? When I'm getting ready to sail I choose a ship, or if I'm looking for a place to live, I choose one house or another. In the same way, when I am about to die, I should choose the manner of my death. Just as a longer life is not necessarily better, thus a longer death is not necessarily worse. In death, more than at any other time, we ought to indulge the soul. Let it depart in whatever way it chooses, whether it prefers the sword or the noose or some poisonous potion. Let it go ahead and break the chains of servitude. We ought to live our life so that it meets other people's approval, but our death is for us alone. The best form of death is the one that satisfies us. . . . Reason teaches us to die as we choose, if at all possible. If not, we should die as best we can, and use whatever means presents itself to do away with ourselves.

Seneca, *Ep.* 70

Colosseum exterior (above)—brackets around the top supported posts for the awning
(Photo by Gustav Jeeninga)

*Colosseum interior (below)—a wooden floor covered the cells where prisoners and animals
awaited their deaths* (Photo by Ben Chapman)

Mediterranean world. Apuleius describes a woman being similarly debased before her execution in the arena in Corinth (*Golden Ass* 10.29).

In addition to the combats of gladiators and fights between people and animals, the Romans staged group executions designed to amuse spectators during the breaks in the heavy fighting. A favorite spectacle was to have thirty or forty condemned people with leather helmets which covered their eyes brought into the arena. They would be armed and turned loose to attack each other in a lethal game of blindman's bluff. The last one standing was freed. Such sights worked the crowds into what Augustine called "a frenzy of delight" and a "lust for blood" (*Conf.* 6.8). Pagan writers also complained of the spectators' savagery (see box).

The crowds at these spectacles could be quite large. Pompeii's amphitheater seated 20,000, typical for a provincial arena; the Colosseum in Rome held about 50,000, and the Circus Maximus, over 200,000. A matter of special concern was the safety of the spectators and their comfort (**4.81**).

Before the Colosseum was built in A.D. 80, games and shows were held in the Circus Maximus. It was not the ideal site for such spectacles because of its long, bullet-like shape and the presence of the *spina,* a divider that ran the length of the race course. This would block the spectators' view of some of the action. Amphitheaters (the word means "seeing from both sides") offered everyone an unobstructed view of the slaughter.

Awnings, hauled into place by sailors, were stretched over the amphitheaters on hot days; advertisements for the games in Pompeii mention whether an awning will be provided. Caligula expressed his contempt for his subjects by having soldiers block the entrances to an amphitheater he was visiting and ordering the awning pulled back, forcing the crowd to swelter in the heat for a while (Suetonius, *Calig.* 26).

What actually went on in the arenas would be highly offensive to modern sensibilities, except perhaps for fans of certain TV talk shows. Caligula liked to stage fights between elderly combatants or between

---

A Roman Aristocrat Views the Games

I happened to see the noon-time show. I expected a bit of fun, some wit, something relaxing, which would give people's eyes rest from human slaughter. It was quite the contrary. The fighting that had gone on before was merciful by comparison. With all the trifling put aside, this was murder, pure and simple. The men had nothing to protect themselves; they were exposed to blows on every part of their bodies. No blow fell without effect. Many people prefer this to the usual pairs of gladiators and to the "specially requested" bouts. Why wouldn't they? In this case there is no helmet or shield to ward off the sword. What is the point of defensive armor? Why bother with skill? Such things just delay death. In the morning men are thrown to the lions and bears; at noon they're thrown to the spectators.

Seneca, *Epistle* 7.3–4

people with various sorts of physical disabilities (*Calig.* 26). Apuleius (*Golden Ass* 10.29–32) provides the only connected description we have of a day in the amphitheater.

The entertainment begins with a preliminary diversion, as a troop of young men and women in elaborate costumes perform what is called the Pyrrhic dance, consisting of intricate weaving of lines and formation of complicated shapes by the dancers.

After the dance comes a mythological reenactment. A stage has been constructed in the middle of the amphitheater representing a mountain, complete with sod and trees and a stream bubbling down the side. A herd of goats is cropping the grass, tended by an actor costumed as Paris, the Trojan prince. The audience would have known the whole story, so their only pleasure would come from how it was staged.

A lad representing Hermes, messenger of the gods, delivers a golden apple to Paris. By his gestures he indicates that Paris is to decide which of the three chief goddesses—Hera, Athena, and Aphrodite—is the fairest and the winner of the apple. The women playing the goddesses each make their entry, dancing to a type of music appropriate to their nature and accompanied by various attendants. Naked little boys representing Cupid escort Aphrodite. Each goddess promises Paris some desirable bribe if he will name her the fairest. Aphrodite, as the goddess of love, is nude except for a diaphanous scarf; she dances very suggestively, to the great delight of the audience. Paris decides in her favor. In return she promises him the most beautiful woman in the world as his bride. (This proves to be Helen, who was, inconveniently, already married to Menelaus, king of Sparta. According to the myth, Paris's kidnapping of Helen led to the Trojan War.)

Upon the end of this spectacle the crowd is more than ready for the main event of the show. In this case the main feature would be the execution of a woman convicted of poisoning her husband, daughter, sister-in-law, and two others. She would be put in a cage in the center of the arena and forced to have intercourse with a donkey. A hungry lion would then be put into the cage with them. It mattered little which one the lion ate first, although this might be an occasion for wagering.

Not all victims in the arenas were criminals. Some gladiators and chariot drivers were slaves or professional athletes, who earned enormous sums of money and enjoyed a popular following similar to that of modern celebrities (**4.74**; **4.79**). Their banquets before the games were legendary (Apuleius *Golden Ass* 2.15). Some Christians claimed that since some fighters performed willingly, this justified their continued attendance at the spectacles after their conversion to the faith. They enjoyed, almost to the point of addiction, the chariot races, mock naval battles, obscene plays, and other entertainments which the government or wealthy individuals regularly sponsored. In the late second century, Tertullian criticized Christians who persisted in their love of these shows because they could find no explicit scriptural prohibition of them. One will not find a commandment "thou shalt not attend the spectacles," but their sinful nature, he argues, and their association with the worship of the pagan gods should be enough to make them unacceptable to believers (*On the Spectacles* 3). Thoughtful Jews also expressed reservations about the morality of the games (**4.64**).

But habit was hard to break, and the games' function as a means of executing condemned criminals was not easy to dispense with. Even after the emperor Constantine's conversion to Christianity in the early fourth century, the spectacles continued. In the late fourth century Augustine admitted his own attraction to plays (*Conf.* 3.2) and with some difficulty cured a friend of his "special madness" for gladiatorial shows (*Conf.* 6.7–8). Constantine tried to ban gladiatorial games in A.D. 325, but popular demand kept them going. In A.D. 404 a monk named Telemachus jumped into the arena in Rome and broke up a fight between two gladiators. The spectators were so annoyed by the interruption of their sport that they tore Telemachus to bits. The emperor Theodosius, a Christian, was disturbed by the crowd's blood lust and outlawed any further combats. Other forms of public entertainment did not survive long after that in the West because of the Germanic invasions of the Empire.

> ### Christian Eagerness for Martyrdom
>
> I long for the wild beasts that are waiting for me, and I pray that they will be eager to attack me. If not, I will incite them to devour me quickly. Sometimes they have left people untouched from fear [perhaps from crowd noise]. Even if they are reluctant to attack of their own accord, I will compel them to do it. Do this favor for me. I know what I need, for I am just beginning to be a disciple. I pray that nothing on heaven or earth will prevent me from attaining the goal of Jesus Christ. Let me be subjected to fire, the cross, fights with wild beasts, having my body cut and torn apart on the rack, my limbs mangled, my whole body crushed—any of the devil's cruel tortures—just as long as I attain the goal of Jesus Christ!
>
> Ignatius, *To the Romans* 5

Nothing in Pliny's letter suggests what fate awaited the Roman citizens whom he sent back to Rome for trial but we can assume they ended up in the arena. A Christian source from Trajan's reign lets us see this process from the other side. Ignatius, bishop of Antioch, was sent to Rome around A.D. 108 During his journey he wrote letters to various churches, including one to Rome, in which he explained his eagerness for martyrdom (see box). This eagerness for martyrdom characterized many of the early Christian victims of persecution and befuddled their captors (**4.73**; **4.75**).

The violence which people witnessed in the arenas typified first-century life. In large cities criminals ruled the streets after dark. Even "law-abiding" citizens were given to settling disputes out of court with their fists. Abuse of wives and slaves appears to have been commonplace. Christians—if they took Jesus' teachings about nonviolence seriously (Matt. 5:38–39)—placed themselves at odds with their society and could leave themselves defenseless.

Christian writers objected not only to the mayhem of the arenas but also to the violence inherent in military service, though in the first century the latter was not a major concern. At that time citizens seldom served in the army; soldiers were mercenaries, often from the frontier provinces. Paul could use military analogies (Eph. 6:10–17) without embarrassment. In the second and third centuries, as the Empire declined, more citizens turned to military service and Christians began to wrestle more earnestly with the ethical issues involved (**4.68**; **4.71**).

Trajan's Reply and Imperial Policy

Though there is some evidence to suggest that the Romans condemned criminals to the arena rather hastily to meet public demand for the spectacles, Trajan's approach to the problem of the Christians was not heavy-handed (**4.96–97**). In his reply he makes it clear that the Romans followed a case-by-case approach to dealing with the group, "for it is impossible for something universally applicable to be established, as if there were a fixed rule." That's how Trajan approached most problems (Pliny, *Ep.* 10.69). He forbids Pliny to pursue the sect. The Romans simply did not have the manpower to bother with ferreting out people devoted to some "wretched cult" (*superstitio* is Pliny's Latin word for it).

The emperor makes it clear, however, that conviction of being a Christian, without any crime associated with that name, is sufficient grounds for punishment. That became the guiding principle in the Romans' dealings with the Christians. They may not have been certain what Christians were or what they did, but they knew that the very name itself deserved official condemnation. There need not be proof of a crime committed; confession of the name itself became a crime (**4.90–91**; **4.93**; **4.95**). The only way to establish one's innocence was to engage in a ritual like the one prescribed by Pliny.

Such an imperial reply, known as a rescript, became a precedent for later governors in that province. The rescripts of one emperor carried over into the next reign (Pliny, *Ep.* 10.65). If the circumstances were similar, a rescript might be used as a guideline in other provinces as well but that principle was slow in developing. Trajan specifically says in one letter to Pliny that two of Domitian's rescripts, "which probably ought to be followed," did not specifically cover Bithynia (*Ep.* 10.66). In effect, Rome had no legislation that applied across the Empire. One reason for that was their basic theory of law, which saw it as a tool for protecting the interests of the upper classes. While they developed private law to a level it did not regain until the nineteenth century (**4.89**), they did little to promote criminal law. Decisions in that realm always remained in the hands of magistrates and thus continued to be *ad hoc* and arbitrary (**4.105**; **8.23**).

The Roman Theory of Law

Underlying Pliny's letter and the legal questions in the New Testament is the Roman view that each group of people, each nation, had its own law. The term *ius gentium* (law of the nations) expresses this concept that the influence of a set of laws extends to the boundaries of the people who enacted them.

Each nation made its own laws by its own methods. The Jews had their laws clearly set down by Moses, with the Pharisees as interpreters. For the Romans, laws were made first by the popular assembly, by decrees of the senate, or by magistrates' edicts. Under the Empire the people's legislative powers passed to the senate, and the senate issued only decrees which the emperors approved. The emperors' decisions in judicial matters and their rescripts to provincial governors came to have the effect of law, though slowly and always with some uncertainty as to how widely they applied. The result was that "Rome did not . . . impose a unitary system of legal institutions like a giant dishcover upon all these diverse sets of people. Their legal relationships inside their own communities went on in most ways as before" (**8.23**:11).

Because of the notion of laws as limited to the nation or ethnic group which originated them, two groups of people could live in the same area under two sets of laws (**4.101**). The Jews of Alexandria decided their own legal cases without reference to the laws of the Greeks who surrounded them. Gallio extended the same privilege to the Jews in Corinth (Acts 18:15). In Rome during its republican days, as larger numbers of foreigners were attracted to the commercial opportunities of the city, they brought their ways of doing things with them. The Romans set up a new office, the *praetor peregrinus* (judge for foreigners), who handled cases in which the *ius gentium* came into conflict with Rome's law. Roman law always prevailed, of course, but some cases, especially those involving contracts between Romans and foreigners, required careful scrutiny to avoid alienating a growing sector of the city's population.[1]

As they became better acquainted with laws of other nations, the Romans adapted some of them to their own needs, especially from the Greeks. This led them to see that certain common characteristics underlay the laws of most civilized peoples (**4.98**). By the mid-first century A.D., some Roman jurists were talking about a "natural law," of which the laws of the various nations were but imperfect manifestations (**4.100**). The Stoic philosophy so popular in Rome propagated the idea of natural law existing in each person like a seed or a spark which must be nurtured (**4.99**). Paul is close to this notion when he says (Rom. 2:14–15), "When Gentiles, who do not possess the law, do instinctively what the law requires . . . they show that what the law requires is written on their hearts." Nor is James' reference to the "perfect law, the law of liberty" (1:25) too far removed from what Roman philosophers and legal theorists of that day were saying about law in general.

Rome Versus the Christians

A major part of the Christians' problems with the government stemmed from Rome's theory and administration of law. An overworked bureaucracy was reluctant to tackle yet another problem but unwilling to let a potentially dangerous group grow unchecked. The legal measures by which the government regulated groups and controlled the provinces favored Roman citizens, and not many early Christians held that privileged status. During the first century of the church's existence, decisions about its status were made on a case-by-case basis, so the Christians were never quite sure how they would be treated if brought to trial. One governor might dismiss the whole matter, while another would choose to inflict heavy damage on the Christian community in his province (**4.94**). This arbitrary treatment led to understandable resentment on the part of the Christians and a view of the government as evil (**4.102–103**).

Once established in their own minds and in the public perception as distinct from the Jews, the Christians, except for those individuals who possessed Roman citizenship, were defenseless against Roman law. Their only hope lay in convincing the government that they were not some cannibalistic, treasonous society but were a new expression of religious faith, deserving of a legal place among the dozens of other groups active in the Empire at that time (**2.289**). They continued to be regarded, however, as a group of people who stubbornly refused to see the light of reason (**4.105; 4.107**).

In the early second century, the Christians took a more aggressive stance in defending themselves against mob violence and government persecution and began to argue publicly for the superiority of their faith (**4.106**). Athenagoras maintained that Old Testament worthies such as Noah and Abraham, who lived before the Mosaic covenant was established, were proto-Christians. Christianity therefore could claim legitimacy because of its antiquity, a crucial positive point in the Greco-Roman understanding of a religion.

The Epistle to Diognetus, another second-century defense of the new faith, portrays Christians as sober citizens (5.10–17). Its anonymous author claims that Christians

> obey the established laws, and in their personal lives even surpass the laws. They love everyone and are persecuted by everyone. They are unknown and yet they are condemned. . . . They are attacked

as foreigners by the Jews and are persecuted by the Greeks, and those who hate them cannot give a reason for their hostility.

But, in spite of such arguments, the Christians did not fit the Roman definition of a religion (**4.104**), which we'll discuss further in the next chapter. On the contrary, they appeared to be a dangerous political society, so they could not gain legal standing before the law as a group. Their only hope for protection under the law lay in whatever rights individual Christians may have been able to claim as citizens.

Notes

1. This principle is not entirely ancient. I recently saw a newspaper article describing how a lawyer in Los Angeles had proposed that his client, a Laotian, be tried under the laws of his tribe from the hills of Laos. The man had acted, his lawyer claimed, as he should have under those laws, if not under U.S. law.

BIBLIOGRAPHY

"Church and State" in Rome

4.1.   Eastwood, B. S. "Causes of the Early Persecutions." *HT* 16(1966): 555–563.

4.2.   Horvath, T. "Why Was Jesus Brought to Pilate?" *NovT* 11(1969): 174–184.

Christians and the Law: A Case Study

4.3.   Sherwin-White, A. N. "Trajan's Replies to Pliny: Authorship and Necessity." *JRS* 52(1962): 114–125.

4.4.   Winter, P. "Tacitus and Pliny on Christianity." *Klio* 52(1970): 498–502.

Powers of Governors

4.5.   Brunt, P. A. "Charges of Provincial Maladministration Under the Early Principate." *Historia* 10(1961): 189–227.

4.6.   Burton, G. P. "Proconsuls, Assizes and the Administration of Justice Under the Empire." *JRS* 65(1975): 92–106.

4.7.   Crocker, P. T. "Ephesus: Its Silversmiths, Its Tradesmen, and Its Riots." *BurHist* 23, no. 4, (1987): 76–78.

4.8.   Garnsey, P. "The Criminal Jurisdiction of Governors." *JRS* 58(1968): 51–59.

4.9.   Hoff, M. C. "Civil Disobedience and Unrest in Augustan Athens." *Hesperia* 58(1989): 267–276.

4.10.   Hoyos, B. D. "*Lex Provinciae* and Governors' Edicts." *Antichthon* 7(1973): 47–53.

4.11.   Kinman, B. "Pilate's Assize and the Timing of Jesus' Trial." *TynBull* 42(1991): 282–295.

4.12.   Lewis, N. "The Prefect's Conventus: Proceedings and Procedures." *Bulletin of the American Society of Papyrologists* 18(1981): 119–129.

4.13.   Marshall, A. J. "Governors on the Move." *Phoenix* 20(1986): 231–246.

4.14.   Stoops, R. F. "Riot and Assembly: The Social Context of Acts 19:23–41." *JBL* 108(1989): 73–91.

Criminal Procedures

4.15.   Barnes, T. D. "Legislation vs. the Christians." *JRS* 58(1968): 32–50.

4.16.   Brunt, P. A. "Evidence Given Under Torture in the Principate." *Zeitschrift der Savigny-Stiftung für Rechtsgeschichte* 97(1980): 256–265.

4.17.   Crake, J. E. A. "Early Christians and Roman Law." *Phoenix* 19(1965): 61–70.

4.18.   Davies, J. G. "Deacons, Deaconesses, and the Minor Orders in the Patristic Period." *JEH* 14(1963): 1–15.

4.19.   Davies, R. W. "The Investigation of Some Crimes in Roman Egypt." *AncSoc* 4(1973): 199–212.

4.20.   Downey, G. "'Un-Roman Activities': The Ruling Race and The Minorities." *AngThR* 58(1976): 432–443.

4.21.   Dubuisson, M. "Some Aspects of Graeco-Roman Relations: The Attitude of Roman Administration Toward Language Use. Xenophobia and Disparaging Words in Greek and Latin." *Prudentia* 15(1983): 35–47.

4.22.   Ferguson, J. "Hymns in the Early Church." *Bulletin of the Hymn Society of Great Britain and Ireland* 12(1989): 114–123.

4.23.   Fishwick, D. "Pliny and the Christians: The Rites *ad imaginem principis*." *AJAH* 9(1984): 123–130.

4.24.   Isaac, B. "Bandits in Judaea and Arabia." *HSCP* 88(1984): 171–203.

4.25.   Jones, A. H. M. *The Criminal Courts of the Roman Republic and Principate.* Ed. by J. A. Crook. Oxford: Blackwell, 1972.

4.26.   Keresztes, P. "The Jews, the Christians, and Emperor Domitian." *VigChr* 27(1973): 1–28.

4.27.   Kraemer, C. J. "Pliny and the Early Church Services: Fresh Light from an Old Source." *CPh* 29 (1934): 293–300.

4.28.   Lewis, N., and M. Reinhold, eds. *Roman Civilization: Sourcebook.* 2 vols. New York: Harper & Row, 1966; 3d ed., New York: Columbia University Press, 1990.

4.29. Millar, F. "The Imperial Cult and the Persecutions." In *Le culte des souverains dans l'empire romain.* Ed. by W. den Boer. Geneva: Fondation Hart, 1973: 143–175.

4.30. Price, S. R. F. "Between Man and God: Sacrifice in the Roman Imperial Cult." *JRS* 70(1980): 28–43.

4.31. Salzmann, J. C. "Pliny (*Ep.* 10.96) and Christian Liturgy: A Reconsideration." *StudPatr* 20 (1989): 389–395.

4.32. Schulz, R. R. "A Case for 'President' Phoebe in Romans 16:2." *LuthTheolJ* 24(1990): 124–127.

4.33. Sherwin-White, A. N. "Early Persecutions and Roman Law Again." *JThS* 3(1952): 199–213.

4.34. ———. "Why Were the Early Christians Persecuted? An Amendment." *P&P* 27(1964): 23–27.

4.35. Thompson, L. "Hymns in Early Christian Worship." *AngThR* 55(1973): 458–472.

4.36. van Beeck, F. J. "The Worship of Christians in Pliny's Letters." *StudLiturg* 18(1988): 121–131.

Roman Regulation of Groups

4.37. Downing, F. G. "Cynics and Christians, Oedipus and Thyestes." *JEH* 44(1993): 1–10.

4.38. Gooch, P. D. *Dangerous Food: I Corinthians 8–10 in its Context.* Waterloo, Ont.: Wilfred Laurier University Press, 1993.

4.39. Janssen, L. F. "'Superstitio' and the Persecution of the Christians." *VigChr* 33(1979): 131–159.

4.40. Kilmartin, E. J. *The Eucharist in the Primitive Church.* Englewood Cliffs, NJ: Prentice Hall, 1965.

Informers

4.41. Bauman, R. A. *The* Crimen Maiestatis *in the Roman Republic and Augustan Principate.* Johannesburg: Witwatesrand University Press, 1967.

4.42. ———. Impietas in Principem: *A Study of Treason Against the Roman Emperor with Special Reference to the First Century A. D.* Munich: Beck, 1974.

4.43. Johnson, G. J. "*De conspiratione delatorum*: Pliny and the Christians Revisited." *Latomus* 47(1988): 417–422.

4.44. Nippel, W. "Policing Rome." *JRS* 74(1984): 20–29.

4.45. O'Neal, W. J. "Delation in the Early Empire." *CB* 55(1978): 24–28.

Citizenship

4.46. Brewer, E. "Roman Citizenship and Its Bearing on the Book of Acts." *RestorQ* 3(1961): 205–219.

4.47. Gardner, J. *Being a Roman Citizen.* London: Routledge, 1993.

4.48. Sherwin-White, A. N. *The Roman Citizenship.* Oxford: Clarendon Press, 1973.

Benefits of Citizenship

4.49. Black, M. "Paul and Roman Law in Acts." *RestorQ* 24(1981): 209–218.

4.50. Garnsey, P. "The Lex Iulia and Appeal Under the Empire." *JRS* 56(1966): 167–189.

4.51. ———. *Social Status and Legal Privilege in the Roman Empire.* Oxford: Clarendon Press, 1970.

4.52. Jones, A. H. M. "Rome and the Provincial Cities." *RHD* 39(1971): 513–551.

4.53. Lyall, F. "Roman Law in the Writings of Paul—Aliens and Citizens." *EvangQ* 48(1976): 3–14.

4.54. Reese, B. "The Apostle Paul's Exercise of His Rights as a Roman Citizen." *EvangQ* 47(1975): 138–145.

Obtaining Citizenship

4.55. Cadbury, H. J. "Roman Law and the Trial of Paul." In *The Beginnings of Christianity.* Ed. by F. J. Foakes Jackson and K. Lake. London: Macmillan, 1920, 5: 297–338.

4.56. Dusanic, S. "The Issue of Military Diplomata Under Claudius and Nero." *ZPE* 47(1982): 149–171.

4.57. Goodfellow, C. E. *Roman Citizenship: A Study of Its Territorial and Numerical Expansion from the Earliest Times to the Death of Augustus.* Lancaster, PA.: Lancaster Press, 1935.

4.58. Reinhold, M. "Usurpation of Status and Status Symbols." *Historia* 20(1971): 275–302.

4.59. Schulz, E. "Roman Registers and Birth Certificates." *JRS* 32(1942): 78–91; 33(1943): 55–64.

4.60. Sherwin-White, A. N. *Roman Society and Roman Law in the New Testament.* Oxford: Clarendon Press, 1963.

4.61. Woloch, M. "St. Paul's Two Citizenships." *Cahiers des études anciennes* 2(1973): 135–138.

Roman Penal Practices

4.62. Auguet, R. *Cruelty and Civilization: The Roman Games.* London: Allen & Unwin, 1972.

4.63. Baldwin, B. "Executions, Trials, and Punishment in the Reign of Nero." *P&P* 22(1967): 425–439.

4.64. Brettler, M. Z., and M. Poliakoff. "Rabbi Simeon ben Lakish at the Gladiator's Banquet: Rabbinic Observations on the Roman Arena." *HThR* 83(1990): 93–98.

4.65. Buchanan, D. *Roman Sports and Entertainment.* London: Longman, 1976.

4.66. Champlin, E. "*Creditur vulgo testamenta hominum speculum esse morum*: Why the Romans Made Wills." *CPh* 84(1989): 198–215

4.67. Coleman, K. M. "Fatal Charades: Roman Executions Staged as Mythological Enactments." *JRS* 80(1990): 44–73.

4.68. Driver, J. *How Christians Made Peace with War: Early Christian Understandings of War.* Scottdale, PA: Herald Press, 1988.

4.69. Droge, A. J. "Did Paul Commit Suicide?" *BibRev* 5, no. 12, (1989): 14–21.

4.70. ———. "*Mori lucrum*: Paul and Ancient Theories of Suicide." *NovT* 30(1988): 263–286.

4.71. ———, and J. D. Tabor. *A Noble Death: Suicide and Martyrdom Among Christians and Jews in Antiquity.* San Francisco: Harper & Row, 1992.

4.72. Hunter, D. G. "A Decade of Research on Early Christians and Military Service." *RelStudRev* 18(1992): 87–94.

4.73. Frend, W. H. C. *Martyrdom and Persecution in the Early Church: A Study of a Conflict from the Maccabees to Donatus.* Oxford: Blackwell, 1965.

4.74. Grant, M. *Gladiators.* London: Weidenfeld & Nicolson, 1967.

4.75. Lesbaupin, I. *Blessed Are the Persecuted: Christian Life in the Roman Empire A. D. 64–313.* Maryknoll: Orbis Books, 1987.

4.76. Mannix, D. P. *Those About to Die.* New York: Ballantine, 1958.

4.77. Millar, F. "Condemnation to Hard Labour in the Roman Empire, from the Julio-Claudians to Constantine." *PBSR* 52(1984): 124–147.

4.78. Pilch, J. J. "Death with Honor: The Mediterranean Style Death of Jesus in Mark." *BTB* 25(1995): 65–70.

4.79. Poliakoff, M. B. *Combat Sports in the Ancient World: Competition, Violence and Culture.* New Haven, CT: Yale University Press, 1987.

4.80. Rogers, R. S. "The Roman Emperors as Heirs and Legatees." *TAPhA* 78(1947): 140–158.

4.81. Scobie, A. "Spectator Security and Comfort at Gladiatorial Games." *Nikephoros* 1(1988): 191–243.

4.82. Seeley, D. *The Noble Death: Graeco-Roman Martyrology and Paul's Concept of Salvation.* Sheffield, UK: Academic Press, 1990.

4.83. Thome, G. "Crime and Punishment, Guilt and Expiation: Roman Thought and Vocabulary." *AClass* 35(1992): 73–98.

4.84. van Hooff, A. J. L. *From Autothanasia to Suicide: Self-Killing in Classical Antiquity.* New York: Routledge & Kegan Paul, 1990.

4.85. Wheelan, C. F. "Suicide in the Ancient World: A Re-Examination of Matthew 27:3–10." *LThPh* 49(1993): 505–522.

4.86. Wiedemann, T. *Emperors and Gladiators.* London: Routledge, 1992.

4.87. Wistrand, M. *Entertainment and Violence in Ancient Rome: The Attitudes of Roman Writers of the First Century* A.D. Göteborg: Acta Universitatis Gothoburgensis, 1992.

4.88. ———. "Violence and Entertainment in Seneca the Younger." *Eranos* 88(1990): 31–46.

Trajan's Reply and Imperial Policy

4.89. Buckland, W. W. *The Main Institutions of Roman Private Law.* New York: Cambridge University Press, 1931.

4.90. Frend, W. H. C. "The Failure of the Persecutions in the Roman Empire." *P&P* 16(1959): 10–30

4.91. Gilchrist, J. M. "On What Charge was St. Paul Brought to Rome?" *ExpT* 78(1966–67): 264–266.

4.92. Green, E. "Law and the Legal System in the Principate." In *The Roman World.* Ed. by J. Wacher. London: Routledge & Kegan Paul, 1987: 440–454.

4.93. Henrichs, A. "Pagan Ritual and the Alleged Crimes of the Early Christians." In *Kyriakon: Festschrift Johannes Quasten.* Ed. by P. Granfield and J. A. Jungmann. Münster: Aschendorff, 1970: 18–35.

4.94. Keresztes, P. "Law and Arbitrariness in the Persecution of the Christians and Justin's First Apology." *VigChr* 18(1964): 204–214.

4.95. Last, H. "The Study of the Persecutions." *JRS* 27(1937): 80–92.

4.96. Plescia, J. "On the Persecution of the Christians in the Roman Empire." *Latomus* 30(1971): 120–132.

4.97. Sordi, M. *The Christians and the Roman Empire.* Norman: University of Oklahoma Press, 1986.

The Roman Theory of Law

4.98. Daube, D. *Roman Law: Linguistic, Social and Philosophical Aspects.* Edinburgh University Press, 1969.

4.99. Horowitz, M. C. "The Stoic Synthesis of the Idea of Natural Law in Man: Four Themes." *JHI* 35(1974): 3–16.

4.100. Levy, E. "Natural Law in Roman Thought." *SDHI* 15(1949): 1–23.

4.101. van den Bergh, G. C. J. J. "Legal Pluralism in Roman Law." *IrJur* 4(1969): 338–350.

Rome Versus the Christians

4.102. Collins, A. Y. "Oppression from Without: The Symbolization of Rome as Evil in Early Christianity." *Concilium* 200(1988): 66–74.

4.103. Downing, F. G. "Pliny's Prosecutions of Christians: Revelation and I Peter." *JStudNT* 34(1988): 105–123.

4.104. Grant, F. C. "Religio Licita." *StudPatr* 3–4(1961): 84–89.

4.105. Keresztes, P. *Imperial Rome and the Christians From Herod the Great to About 200* A.D. Lanham, MD: University Press of America, 1989.

4.106. Pagels, E. "Christian Apologists and 'the Fall of the Angels': An Attack on Roman Imperial Power?" *HThR* 78(1985): 301–325.

4.107. van Stekelenburg, A. V. "*Lucifugax natio*: The Pagan view of Early Christianity." *Akroterion* 29(1983): 157–171.

CHAPTER 5

GRECO-
ROMAN
RELIGION

Introduction

THE NEW TESTAMENT, except for Luke-Acts, was written by Jews—
however Hellenized they may have been—but its audience was primarily Greco-Roman. The gospel it proclaimed competed with the many
religious cults and philosophical schools which flourished during the
first century A.D. As Paul discovered in Athens (Acts 17:18), the people
who heard the gospel often understood it in terms of their own religious experience (**5.1**). Jesus and the resurrection seemed to them to
be two divinities, one male and one female.[1] This pattern of a goddess
and her consort was familiar to Paul's audience from the mystery cults
which featured gods who died and rose again, often with the help of a
goddess (**5.10**; **5.13**). A big challenge for the early church was to maintain the integrity of its message while making it intelligible to people
whose religious and philosophical ideas had been centuries in the making and often offered stiff resistance (**5.2**).

In dealing with both religion and philosophy (see chapter 6), it is
appropriate to discuss the systems of the Greeks and Romans together
because the Romans borrowed most of their religious practices from
the Greeks and never had a philosophical system other than what was
taken over wholesale from Greece. This was part of a larger process of
Greek influence on all facets of Roman culture, which some Romans
welcomed heartily but which others saw as evidence of decline.

However, in what appears to us a curious reversal of roles, the
Greco-Roman religions tolerated one another while the philosophical

schools nurtured long and bitter disputes. Such arguments arose because "philosophers maintained various factual propositions about the world—that it was made of 'breath' or atoms, that it was finite or infinite, and so on—whereas ancient religions only presupposed the existence of forces capable of being persuaded by prayer and sacrifice" (**5.8**:3). These religions had no systematic doctrines but only engaged in certain rituals designed to put the gods in a favorable mood. Thus there was no basis for disagreement among them. The philosophers, however, defended their well-defined positions tenaciously. In fact, the word *heresy* originally meant a difference of opinion among philosophers.

In religion and philosophy, as in most other fields, the Romans stood in awe of the Greeks' achievements (**5.7**). As H. J. Rose says, the Romans' "theology and philosophy, when they had such things at all, were simplified adaptations of Greek thought" (**5.11**:157). The Romans identified their native divinities with Greek gods which served similar functions. In their early days, the Romans seem not to have created images of their gods (**5.11**:169), but their love of Greek art soon led them to adopt the practice of representing their gods in sculpture and painting (**5.9**). The religious impulses of the Greeks and Romans manifested themselves in several different types of cults, some of which crossed socio-economic classes. Philosophy remained largely the indulgence of an intellectual elite.

> ### A Roman Rationalist's View of the Gods
>
> The philosophers' opinions of the gods are little more than the ravings of madmen. No less absurd are the spoutings of the poets, which are insidious because of their charm. The poets depict the gods as inflamed by anger and raging with lust and have crafted, for us to see, their wars, battles, and wounds, as well as their hatreds, their feuds, their quarrels, their mourning, their license, their adultery, their bondage, their couplings with humans, and the mortals born from immortals—all poured out in utter lack of restraint. With these mistakes of the poets can be linked the monstrosities of the Magi and the demented myths of the Egyptians, as well as the opinions of the crowd, which are a mass of inconsistencies based on ignorance.
>
> Cicero, *On the Nature of the Gods* 1.16

The Olympian Deities

By the first century A.D., Greco-Roman religion had developed far beyond the fanciful anthropomorphic myths of Homer's day (ca. 750 B.C.), about twelve gods with human characteristics living on Mount Olympus. Even Plato, in the fourth century B.C., had objected to the lack of positive moral values in those tales, which featured petulant gods and goddesses seducing mortals, deceiving one another, and behaving like children when they were offended by mankind. Few educated people took the old Olympian religion seriously by Plato's period, and open skepticism prevailed among the upper classes by Roman times (**5.15**; **5.24**; **5.28**; **5.35– 36**; **5.38**; see box). Plutarch could advise his readers "not to believe that any of these stories actually happened" (*Isis and Osiris* 355b). The Olympians may have originally been associated with gods of the twelve months of the year, but no one remembered that by Roman times (**5.26**).

The notion of the gods as having human form seems to have been one of the last vestiges of the Olympian cults to be discarded. Just a generation before the birth of Christ, Cicero could still assert that "the

An altar to an unknown god
(Photo by Howard Vos)

notion of a god without a body is incomprehensible, for a bodyless deity would of necessity lack sensation, and also wisdom and pleasure; all of these things are comprised in our conception of deity" (*The Nature of the Gods* 1.12). Even among Christians of the first few centuries A.D. this notion of a corporeal deity seems not to have entirely disappeared (**5.29**).

Among the populace at large, belief in the old gods seems to have lingered into the last few centuries before Christ (**5.18**; **5.27**), although mixed with elements of magic, ruler cult, consciousness of the individual, and the syncretism of philosophy and religion which characterized the Hellenistic period (**5.21**). Some maintain that it was still a vital force (**5.41**). Evidence for that contention is found in the New Testament. When Paul and Barnabas healed a lame man in Lystra, they were hailed as Zeus and Hermes and could scarcely restrain the people from offering sacrifices to them (Acts 14:8–18). For most people, though, the worship of the Olympians was merely the official state cult, and conformity to it served as a test of an individual's patriotism. That was precisely the use that Pliny as governor made of it in the trials of the Christians in Bithynia, as we saw in chapter 4.

The Olympian deities (Jupiter/Zeus, Juno/Hera, Minerva/Athena, Apollo, et al.) did not relate to their worshipers on a personal level. They were the gods and goddesses of a clan, tribe, or eventually a city. Their concern was for the group, and their worship was a function of the state. Temples were built and maintained by the state, priests were appointed or elected by the state, and the festivals were public holidays (**5.32**; **5.34**). An individual was not expected to "believe in" a divinity in order to worship him or her (**5.31**; **5.37**). Participation in the cult was expected because it demonstrated one's loyalty to the state. Nor were the gods exclusive. A city could worship Jupiter alongside Apollo with no conflict. The more gods a city worshiped, the better its chances of divine favor. Paul even says that Athens had an altar "to an unknown god," just to cover all bases (Acts 17:16–23). Similar ancient references in the plural have been found, to unknown gods.

Temple to Jupiter, in Baalbek, from the Roman era (Photo by Gustav Jeeninga)

Given that mind-set, it's little wonder that the Romans had difficulty understanding the Christian position. The Christians were making a religious profession by refusing to worship the gods and the image of the emperor; the Romans perceived it as an unpatriotic withdrawal from a civic duty. An analogy can be made to the current attitude toward the Jehovah's Witnesses. Children of this sect are sometimes ridiculed by their schoolmates for their refusal to recite the pledge of allegiance to the flag. They refuse to do this because they believe their only loyalty is to

God. But what they intend as a religious act is often interpreted as a lack of patriotism.

If the Olympian gods were concerned only with the prosperity of the group as a whole, what benefit did the individual worshiper derive from this religion? Very little, actually. He or she would presumably benefit from the protection which the god accorded the state, but the influence of the god on the daily life of an individual was negligible. In times of distress, people made extra offerings to secure healing or financial blessings, but such things could be obtained only through bargaining with the god. If what was asked for was not granted, the worshiper could only assume that the offerings were insufficient or that some detail of the ritual had not been properly observed, thus invalidating the whole process.

Sometimes it was dangerous to pray to these gods, for they could be spiteful, even malicious. Some myths tell of them granting a petitioner's wishes when they knew the gift would have disastrous results. Or they could conceive an implacable hatred of a person who had, even inadvertently, offended them in some way. They objected to *hybris*, excess or lack of moderation in anything, whether something like wealth or power which a person had accumulated, or innate physical attributes. There is, sad to say, no Greco-Roman myth which emphasizes the mercy of the gods. Over them was a Fate (*Moira*) from which not even the gods could escape.

The Olympian gods did not hold out to the individual any hope of a pleasant afterlife either. In book 11 of the *Odyssey*, Homer describes the gray, semiconscious souls (*psyché* in Greek) of the dead drifting around in the underworld (**5.30**). Achilles tells the visiting Odysseus that it's better to be a humble farmer's slave on the surface of the earth than to be the king of the underworld (**5.39**).

Most Greeks and Romans hoped to gain immortality by leaving sons (daughters didn't count) to carry on their names or by achieving glory in their military, political, or artistic endeavors so their fame would live after them. The Stoic philosophy so popular among upper-class Romans denied any conscious existence after death (**5.14**). As Pliny said when reflecting on the death of a friend, "Because a long life is denied us, we should leave something behind to testify that we have lived" (*Ep.* 3.7). In other letters he denies that there is any immortality except that achieved by fame during this lifetime (*Epp.* 5.8; 9.3). His uncle and adoptive father, the elder Pliny, also denied any existence after death (*Nat. Hist.* 7.55.188–190). Many tombstones express this apparently widespread pessimism, though one must use such evidence cautiously (**5.17**; **5.23**; **5.25**).

Emperor Cult

Next below the gods in status and power in the Roman world were the emperors. One ancient interpretation of the Greek myths even held that the gods were only magnified memories of early kings. If, by the first century A.D., the gods were seen as powerless, the adoration of the emperors seemed to shore up religious faith (**5.55**).

The Greeks did not worship their rulers, but many eastern cultures did, such as the Persians and Egyptians. When Alexander the Great conquered those countries around 330 B.C., he took on the trappings of the defeated monarchies to make it easier for his new subjects to comprehend who he was. Even though not all the Greek city-states were democratic, none of them had a place for kings in their systems. Being a "god-man" enabled Alexander to assert his authority over them, too. Aristotle, Alexander's tutor, even argued that a man who brought order to a state and demonstrated his authority over it "should be considered a god among men" (*Pol.* 1284a). By the time the Romans conquered the Greeks in the mid-second century B.C., the idea of the divine ruler was widely accepted in the eastern Mediterranean (**5.62**).

Julius Caesar was the first Roman accorded such an honor, and then it was posthumous. At the request of Augustus, his adoptive father was "deified," declared by the Roman Senate to be divine, and a temple was built in his honor. Later Augustus allowed his own "genius" or protective spirit to be worshiped along with the goddess Roma, but only in the eastern provinces (**5.54**). He knew the people of the western Empire were not yet ready to accept such a status for a living person, though they did eventually participate in the cult (**5.49**).

Part of the problem of acceptance centered on the words used. The Greeks applied the word *theios* (godlike) to living and dead persons. It suggested someone of higher than mortal status but not fully equal to a god. The nearest Latin equivalent, *divus* (deified), could be applied only to the dead (**5.61**). Augustus had the political savvy to allow his subjects to render him this homage if they were comfortable with it but not to insist on it if it was alien to their world view. Tiberius followed the same policy.

The mentally unbalanced Caligula, however, decided that he was a god and demanded that he be addressed as *dominus et deus* ("master and god"), two words which came to have enormous implications for Christians (**5.65**). Their reluctance to use the title *deus* for anyone other than God is easily understood. *Dominus* was the Latin term normally used by slaves for their owners. Christians chose it to translate the Greek *kyrios* (Lord) of the Septuagint, and it was a term they did not like to use in any other context (**5.46**). Fortunately for the Christians, no other emperor insisted on being addressed by those terms until Domitian at the end of the first century (**5.42; 5.58**). After his reign, they became common forms of flattery as the Roman principate grew increasingly dictatorial. The emperor cult was particularly strong in Asia Minor, where Christianity also experienced its first rapid growth (**5.56; 5.62**).

Upper-class Romans did not really "believe in" the emperors as gods, any more than they believed in the gods (**5.45**). Vespasian's dying words were a joke about this process of deification: "Oh my, I think I'm becoming a god" (Suetonius, *Vesp.* 23). Emperor worship was largely a means of impressing the masses. Some evidence suggests that less educated people may have taken the divinity of the emperors more seriously than we would expect (**5.66**). Stories of miracles performed by the emperors were circulated, even when known to be untrue (**5.64**). Vespasian was alleged to have healed a blind man and a lame man, and he did nothing to squelch the rumors (Suetonius, *Vesp.* 7). In some places the emperors were worshiped as part of mystery rites, which will be discussed below (**5.59**). But, even if it was not a genuine religious observance, emperor worship was taken seriously as a test of political loyalty (**5.52**; **5.63**). It was that facet of it which caused such problems for the early church and which is reflected in some New Testament documents (**5.43–44**). Some scholars feel that the accounts of the deification of the emperor, also known as an *apotheosis*, may have influenced early Christology (**5.53**).

Miracles, Magic, and Holy Men

Stories such as Vespasian's healing of the blind and lame may have been conscious public relations ploys, but they succeeded because the popular mentality of the time accepted the possibility of such things happening. Serious writers such as Tacitus and Suetonius regularly report supernatural occurrences and omens. They express no reservations about the authenticity of such accounts, out of a desire to appeal to their readers, out of fear of censorship, or out of genuine belief on their own part (**5.87**). Some of the stories told by pagan historians bear more than passing resemblances to the miracles in the Gospels. The Christians also attempted to turn some of the pagans' terminology back on them (**5.68**).

Miracles were considered plausible because good and evil spirits were believed to be everywhere. One of Petronius' characters cautions another that "our region is so filled with spirits that it's easier to trip over a god than a man" (*Satyr.* 17). Nor were these watchful powers merely neutral observers. They caused strange things to happen and sometimes dwelt in the bodies of men and women. The Greek word *daimon* was originally applied to any such spirit; only in the hands of the Christians did it acquire a negative connotation (**5.80**).

Most people preferred to keep these spirits at arm's length, because they were not always predictable. One that appeared friendly and manageable could prove to be disastrous. Magic provided the surest means of warding off the evil spirits and obtaining help from the good ones (**5.81**), but it could be used only by skilled practitioners, as Lucius found out in Apuleius' *Golden Ass*, when he was turned into a donkey while meddling with magic potions. In the popular mind the Jews were linked with magic, perhaps because so much remained unknown about their religion and because their language, written with different characters, seemed so arcane, just as Nordic runes do today.

Early Christians made use of such secret symbols. A fish, drawn over a doorpost perhaps, could mark a Christian home or meeting place. The Greek word for fish, *ichthus*, was spelled with the Greek letters iota, chi, theta, upsilon, and sigma, which Christians used as an acrostic for the phrase Iesus Christos Theou Uios Soter, "Jesus Christ, God's Son, Savior." Another symbol possibly used by Christians was the ROTAS-SATOR square. It was written in the following form:

```
R O T A S
O P E R A
T E N E T
A R E P O
S A T O R
```

This pattern has been found in various places around the Roman world, including two occurrences in Pompeii, where it must have been inscribed before the eruption of Vesuvius in A.D. 79 It appears to spell out a nonsense phrase, but the letters can be rearranged to spell out "Pater noster," the beginning of the Lord's prayer in Latin, in a cross shape with the single N forming the point of intersection. Two A's and two O's are left over, suggesting Alpha and Omega in Greek:

Some scholars hold it as a Christian symbol, but others attribute it to coincidence, or to Jewish, or even Mithraic, origins (**5.74**; **5.89**).

Ancient magic spells often contain garbled versions of Hebrew words.[2] Such spells invoked the aid of divine powers to obtain some material good or punish an enemy. The deity most frequently called upon was Hecate, called the "triform goddess" because she was thought to have power in the air, on earth, and in the sea. Books of magic spells were enormously popular in the first century A.D. (**5.88**). They were sometimes called "Ephesian writings" because so many of them were produced in Ephesus. In that very city, Paul won one of Christianity's most impressive early victories over this demonic mind-set (Acts 19:11–21). He was able to cast out evil spirits and heal the sick, even indirectly by the use of handkerchiefs which he had touched (**5.72; 5.95**). Other exorcists who tried to use the name of Jesus were rebuffed by the spirits. News of Paul's superior power inspired fear among the superstitious Ephesians. Many of them divulged the secrets of their mysterious practices and burned their books. This was the beginning of a long and important Christian presence in Ephesus (**5.93**).

In this story Paul plays the role of a holy man, filled with a good spirit which enables him to discern the presence of evil and overcome it, as in his encounter with the magician Bar-Jesus on Cyprus (Acts 13:6–12). This notion was not alien to the Greco-Roman mind. Apollonius of Tyana, a philosopher and mystic whose life spanned almost the entire first century, was believed to be possessed by a benign spirit (**5.73; 6.169**). According to his biographer, Philostratus, he healed a demoniac boy and various lame, blind, and paralytic people (*Life of Apollonius* 3.38–39), stopped a plague by recognizing a demon disguised as a blind beggar and by urging the Ephesians to stone him (4.10), and raised a girl from the dead (4.45). By the late second century, he was being venerated in many towns, and some pagans made him a cult figure rivaling Jesus, who was also depicted in some circles as more magician than savior (**5.78; 5.92**). Hellenistic Jews like Philo of Alexandria reinterpreted Moses in similar terms during this period, on the basis of Exodus 7:1: "See, I have made you like God to Pharaoh" (**5.94**).

Because their gods were simply exaggerated, immortal humans, the Greeks and Romans did not conceive of a great gulf fixed between gods and men (**5.84**). It was as easy for a god to become a human as for a human to become a god. The divine man (*theios aner* in Greek) was a real possibility in such a world view (**5.71**). Philo used that very phrase to describe Moses, and some elements of the early church's description of Jesus resemble the divine men of pagan stories (**5.69–70; 5.79**). In some cases, such as that of Apollonius, the account of a holy man's life was not committed to writing until after the Gospels had been written. The stories told about Apollonius are at several points obviously influenced by stories about Jesus, not the other way around (**6.164; 6.167**).

The fact remains, however, that the notion of a *theios aner* was part of the intellectual baggage of the first-century world. Whenever an extraordinary individual came along, one like Alexander the Great, who did things beyond normal human ability, the easiest conclusion was that he must have been at least partly a god (**5.85**). Lacking an understanding of the laws of nature, the people of that day had no difficulty believing that gods or divine men could manipulate the physical world to create things that left people amazed. That is the literal definition of a *miraculum*.

Nothing seems to have been too strange for people of the first century to believe. After hearing of an allegedly firsthand experience with a werewolf, Trimalchio swears he believes every word of it, then goes on to tell a ghost story of his own (Petronius, *Satyr.* 62–63). Even an educated person like the younger Pliny could admit that, while he was not absolutely certain, he was "inclined to believe" in the existence of ghosts (*Ep.* 7.27). Many people believed in the "evil eye" and wore amulets—often in the shape of male genitalia—to ward it off (**5.73**).

The temple of Apollo at Delphi
(Photo by Gustav Jeeninga)

Oracles, Astrology, and Dreams

Also important to the general populace, though more difficult to study objectively because of the scarcity of sources, are the matters of oracles, astrology, and the interpretation of dreams. In classical Greece anyone facing a momentous decision or a perplexing problem usually went to an oracle. The chief one was Apollo's at Delphi (**5.100**; **5.104**). The priestess, called the Pythia, chanted answers to visitors' questions in verse form. The responses still extant are ambiguous and capable of several interpretations. The visitor usually went away with an answer that could be right no matter how things turned out.

Herodotus (1.53) provides a memorable example of this process. Croesus, king of Lydia (a sizable territory in western Turkey), was contemplating war against the larger Persian Empire. Upon asking the Delphic oracle whether he should attack, he was told that if he fought Persia, "he would destroy a mighty empire." Croesus rushed into battle, and his own army was routed. The oracle's response had proved correct. In the view of the ancients, if it did not occur to Croesus that the "mighty empire" which was to be destroyed might be his own, that was his problem and did not invalidate the oracular response.

Romans could visit the Sibyl in her grotto at Cumae, near Naples. This allegedly immortal prophetess advised Aeneas when he arrived in Italy on his journey from Troy to a new home in the West (**5.107–108**). But by the first century A.D., oracles had declined in importance. Plutarch (ca. A.D. 100) even wrote an essay, *The Obsolescence of Oracles*, proposing various explanations for why the gods no longer spoke through their oracles. He concluded that the power of the gods had not failed, but the human instruments through whom they had been accustomed to speak were no longer attuned to them. The images were still powerful, though. The rider on the white horse in Revelation 6:2 may represent Apollo (**5.102**).

If the gods no longer spoke directly, they—or the overriding Fate which controlled even them—still were believed to leave messages in the natural order of the universe. Those who wanted to find the divine will could have recourse to astrology (**5.99**; **5.109**). The Roman emperor Tiberius was obsessed with this pseudo-science (**5.101**), but anyone caught inquiring about the imperial horoscope was arrested on charges of desiring the emperor's death. The Jews were not immune to the fascination of astrology, either. Isaiah inveighed against those "who divide the heavens, who gaze at the stars" (47:13 RSV). But in New Testament times and on into the Christian era, Jewish literature is still replete with astrological lore (**5.97**). Some early Christians found authority for this practice in Jesus' words in Luke 21:25: "There will be signs in the sun, the moon, and the stars" (**9.30**). And it was a star that led those Chaldean astrologers to Bethlehem (Matt. 2).

Of enormous interest in the first century was the interpretation of dreams and portents (**5.96**; **5.103**). The Jews had long believed in such things. The Old Testament records that God appeared in dreams to a variety of people (Gen. 20:3; 31:24; 1 Kings 3:5). Their meaning was not always clear and required the help of expert interpreters, such as Joseph (Gen. 37) and Daniel (Dan. 2; 4). In the New Testament Joseph was advised in a dream to take Mary as his wife and in another dream to flee to Egypt (Matt. 1:20; 2:13). Paul does not specifically mention a dream when he advises the ship's captain not to sail, but it is clear that he has had a divine warning of some sort (Acts 27:10). Such things were usually taken seriously and required modification of an individual's plans. Paul undertook his first missionary journey to Europe as a result of a vision (Acts 16:9).

Animism

The fear and propitiation of spirits is technically known as animism, from a Latin word for spirit. It was a common form of worship among the *pagani*, the country folk. Divinities were thought to dwell in trees, caves, rivers, boundary stones, and other natural objects. Even some of the greatest intellects of the time, however, felt the same impulse (see box). Crossroads were even regarded with religious awe (**5.111**). There were multiple divinities for various natural acts or functions. One watched over the seed as it was sown, another over the seed in the ground, still another over the sprouts, and yet another over the mature plants. There was even a god of the manure pile (**5.11**). It's not far from worshiping an individual spirit in every natural object to worshiping a god who indwells everything (pantheism).

Some of these nature divinities were visualized as nymphs or half-human, half-goat satyrs, representing the powerful sexual urge which many Greeks and Romans believed to be the creative force of the universe. That force itself was often worshiped, with graphic representations of human genital organs or of people engaging in intercourse. The satyr Pan (Greek for "all" or "everything") became the most commonly worshiped of these minor divinities, and he is often depicted with oversized genitalia (**5.110**). Augustine reported that the Romans worshiped a "multitude of false gods," including these animistic spirits (*City of God* 4.23). Some counts put the total number of Roman gods and spirits in the thousands.

On the Divine in Nature

If you've ever wandered into a grove crowded with ancient trees which have grown to a remarkable height, blocking the view of the sky with their intertwined branches, the very height of the forest along with the seclusion of the place and your awe at such dense shade in an open spot will convince you of a divine presence. If some cave, created by crumbled rocks, supports a mountain, a place not fashioned by hands but dug out into such roominess by natural causes, your soul will be struck by a certain suggestion of reverence. We venerate the sources of great rivers; we build altars where great streams suddenly break out from their hidden sources; we worship the sources of hot springs, and we consider certain pools sacred because of their dark waters or great depth.

Seneca, *Ep.* 41,3-4

Mystery Cults

A more sophisticated and emotional type of religion was found in the mystery cults. The earliest of these, the cults of Demeter and Dionysus, seem to go back to the time of the Mycenaeans, the early Greeks who fought the Trojan War (1200 B.C. and earlier). The names of both deities occur in clay tablets from that era, though they appear even then to have been popular with the lower classes more than with the aristocracy (**5.113**). Homer (ca. 750 B.C.) knows their names but does not regard them as major divinities.

These and later mystery cults were characterized by initiation ceremonies during which certain secret knowledge (*musterion* in Greek) was revealed to the initiates. This *musterion* would enable them to overcome the dreariness of the underworld and live happily there, united with their god. The cults had no fixed doctrine but emphasized rituals which could evoke varied responses from the initiates. The members of the groups apparently enjoyed a sense of fellowship with the other members which they could not experience in the formal state religion (**5.112**; **5.114**).

We know much less about these mystery cults than we would like. The initiates were sworn to secrecy, with severe punishments—from both civil and heavenly powers—invoked against anyone who broke the oath. Even though some of these initiates eventually became Christians, no one, as far as we know, ever revealed what happened during the secret parts of the initiation rites. We have only "hints in numerous sources" (**5.124**:36). As late as the end of the second century Tertullian could say that the mysteries still "remain unspoken" (*Apology* 7.6).

One Christian writer, Clement of Alexandria (ca. 200), threatened to "tell the mysteries openly and not be afraid to speak about what you are not ashamed to worship" (*Exhort. to the Greeks* 2.13). What he actually does, though, is to ridicule the myths of the gods in common circulation. The closest he comes to unveiling a *musterion* is when he reveals a formula recited by the initiates of the Eleusinian mysteries: "I fasted; I drank the draught; I took from the chest; having done my task, I placed in the basket, and from the basket into the chest" (*Exhort.* 2.18). That doesn't clear things up quite as much as Clement might have thought. Since he provides no context, no description of the action—if any—which accompanied the recitation of this formula, we cannot gauge its significance. It is likely that he knew nothing really "secret" about these cults.

In the following sections we will examine several of these cults in more detail.

Eleusinian Mysteries

Most of the gods associated with mystery cults had some connection with a cycle of death and rebirth or with going into the underworld and coming out alive. Demeter (identified with the Roman Ceres; **5.123**) was a grain goddess whose main sanctuary was a few miles outside Athens at Eleusis, from which her cult is usually called the Eleusinian mysteries (**5.118**; **5.122**). The association of grain or vegetation of any type with death and rebirth is not difficult to make. Each year the seed is put into the ground (buried) and comes up again (rebirth, resurrection). This was a familiar symbol to an agrarian society, so familiar that Paul even used it in his discussion of the resurrection in 1 Corinthians 15:35–44 (**5.116**; **5.179**).

Demeter had a second connection with victory over the underworld. Her daughter Persephone/Proserpina had been kidnapped by Hades/Pluto, the king of the underworld (**5.120**). The story is derived from a seventh-century B.C. hymn to Demeter and appears in its most developed literary form in Ovid (*Meta.* 5.341–550; cf. **5.115**). Zeus eventually permitted Persephone to live part of the year with her mother and part in the underworld. During the time when Persephone was in the underworld, Demeter mourned and neglected her duties as the goddess of crops. The earth fell barren. When her daughter returned to her each spring, the earth rejoiced by bringing forth new plant life (**5.119**).

The temple of Dionysus at Baalbek
(Photo by Ben Chapman)

We do not know the exact content of the Eleusinian ritual. There were three stages of initiation, which took at least six months to complete. The actual initiation ceremony began with the initiates bathing in the sea and then joining a public procession to Eleusis. This bathing process has been linked to the Christian practice of baptism. Large numbers of initiates were crowded into the temple at Eleusis and experienced something which we can only guess at. Those in the highest stage of initiation were called the *epoptai*, or those who had seen, probably indicating that some object was revealed in the private portion of the ritual (**5.121**; cf. Col. 2:18). Wasson and his colleagues suggest that hallucinogenic fungi were consumed during the final stages of the initiation and that the "seeing" may have been heightened by that means. The entire myth of Persephone's abduction, they believe, symbolizes "a drug-induced seizure" (**5.124**:38).

Dionysus

Dionysus, also known as Bacchus or Father Liber, was another god of vegetation, especially of the grape (**5.130**). He may have originated in Thrace, north of Greece, or in Phrygia (central Turkey). In its original form, his cult was open only to women and may reflect a primitive society dominated by women (**5.131**). The only men associated with the cult are elderly or pre-adolescent, i. e., those who would not make sexual demands on the women. The worship of the god took on an ecstatic character as the women drank and engaged in a wild kind of dancing (**5.125–126**). The Greek historian Herodotus (450 B.C.) describes Dionysus as the god "who drives people to madness" (4.79).

His worshipers left their homes and families for several days and roamed over the countryside, working themselves into a frenzy (cf. 1 Cor. 12:2–3). At this point they were said to be "enthused," or filled with the god, for that is the literal meaning of the Greek word *enthusiasmos.* Their ecstasy (meaning "standing outside oneself," beyond reason) was so complete that they could catch small animals, rip them apart, and eat the raw flesh. The catching and eating of these animals may have been a substitute for the cult's original practice of human sacrifice. Euripides' play *The Bacchae* tells how the women of Thebes pursued the king of their city (who opposed the introduction of the cult), caught him, and tore him limb from limb. In their ecstasy he appeared to them to be a deer. Only after they had killed him did Dionysus clear their minds to allow them to see what they had done while in the god's power.

The Greeks feared this cult at first and took steps to ban it, but to no avail. Euripides' play shows how the irrational power of Dionysus swept over all rational opposition. The cult's practices became more subdued as time passed, with a communal meal sometimes taking the place of animal sacrifices; a temple of Dionysus was built next to the larger temple of Apollo in Delphi, symbolic of the subjugation of madness to reason. The Romans, however, persecuted the cult soon after its arrival in Italy ca. 200 B.C. It was practiced there in a perverted form, with men being initiated and sexual orgies being the ultimate expression of the worshipers' "enthusiasm." The government executed hundreds of its adherents, but the cult soon flourished again (**5.129**). Archaeological artifacts give us some gauge of how powerful and widespread this cult was (**5.128**).

The Orphic Cult

Another mystery cult, originating in the sixth century B.C., centered around Orpheus, the poet who went into the underworld to retrieve his dead wife. By the charm of his music and poems, he convinced Pluto and Persephone to let his wife go, but he lost her again when he glanced around to check on her before they were safely back in the upper world. Initiates into this cult were given the words to his songs so they too could overcome the dark powers awaiting them in the afterlife. This pattern of descent into the underworld and return may be reflected in the idea that Christ "preached to the spirits in prison" during his time in the tomb (1 Peter 3:19 RSV). Some Jews of the early Christian period identified Orpheus with David in his role as poet and musician. So little

Orphic literature survives that it's difficult to summarize the group's doctrines. It does seem to have had a more exalted notion of the soul than most other cults and to have been dualistic. Its members were inclined to asceticism and believed in the possibility of reincarnation. For that reason they were vegetarians. Orphic ideas were picked up by the Pythagoreans and came to have a close association with that cult (see chapter 6).

"Great is Artemis of the Ephesians"
(Acts 19:28)
(Photo by Gustav Jeeninga)

The Great Mother

Resurrection was the promise of the cult of Cybele or the Great Mother, from Asia Minor (**5.139**), who restored her consort Attis to life after he had been cut up by an enemy (**5.146–147**). But she was unable to find one crucial part of his anatomy. In his honor the priests of this cult emasculated themselves, which horrified Roman officials but did not stop the spread of the cult. It was brought to Rome around 205 B.C., when the Romans were locked in a titanic struggle with Hannibal and Carthage. A passage in the prophetic Sibylline Books said that if the stone (a meteorite[3]) of the Great Mother were brought to Rome and enshrined, the Romans would defeat Carthage. Shortly after the process was carried out, the Romans' fortunes in the war began to improve.

Though they disapproved of some aspects of the cult's worship, it was hard for the Romans to oppose it officially when it appeared to have saved Rome. Each spring devotees reenacted the murder and restoration of Attis in a tearful public spectacle before the private initiation took place (**5.145**). This cult was active all over the eastern Mediterranean world from very early times (**5.138**). The Old Testament prophet Ezekiel berated the women of Jerusalem because they took part each spring in the wailing for Attis, also called Adonis and Tammuz (Ezek. 8:14). Astarte/Ishtar, other names for the Great Mother, are the origin of the term Easter.

Cybele is but one manifestation of this Great Mother, a symbol of the vegetation cycle and the fertility of the earth, worshiped all over the ancient world (**5.136**; **5.144**). Another, more familiar from the New Testament, is Artemis/Diana, whose most important temple was in Ephesus (**5.133**; **5.142**). The Roman *Bona Dea* (Good Goddess) may be another (**5.134**; **5.148**). Temples of some of these mother goddesses eventually were converted into churches dedicated to Mary, as was the Parthenon, temple of the virgin goddess Athena (**5.141**; **5.143**). Among the lower classes, Mary replaced the mother goddess as an object of devotion. One can trace the attention to her and even adoration of her from the second century, especially in Ephesus (**5.135**; **5.137**; **5.149**).

Isis

Like Cybele, the Egyptian goddess Isis also restored her consort Osiris to life and thus became the center of a popular mystery cult (**5.151**; **5.155**). She is virtually the only ancient divinity who displays any

The Parthenon in Athens
(Photo by Howard Vos)

love or concern for her devotees (**5.150**). Her temple in Pompeii has been excavated, and we have a description of part of the rites associated with her worship in book 11 of Apuleius' *Golden Ass*. The prayer which he addresses to her as "Queen of Heaven" finds echoes in medieval devotion to Mary. Apuleius' book was quite popular in the Middle Ages, so it is not hard to explain the similarities (**5.154**). The modern phenomenon of apparitions of Mary can also be linked to features of the Great Mother cult (**5.152**), of which Isis is another manifestation.

Apuleius (*Golden Ass* 11.22–28) also explains certain public parts of the ritual of Isis, including washing and putting on a clean white robe. His account is all the more remarkable because he comes so close to breaking the oath of secrecy to which initiates were sworn. He takes us up to the point where he enters "the inner chambers of the sanctuary itself," then stops. If he tells any more, he says, "My tongue and your ears would suffer equal punishment for their reckless curiosity." In order not to leave us totally mystified, he reveals "as much as can be explained for the uninitiated without any penalty":

> I approached the borders of death, Persephone's well-trod threshold; having been borne through all the elements, I returned. At midnight I saw the sun blazing with a bright light; I stood near the gods of the underworld and the gods of the upper world, and worshiped them from nearby.

Figures from the temple of Artemis in Ephesus

Mithraism (and Christmas)

Another eastern mystery cult which proved enormously popular in Rome, especially among the army, was that of the Persian Mithra (or Mithras). It is difficult to trace his evolution from a Zoroastrian god of light to Roman warrior and bullslayer (**5.175**). His cult first appeared in the eastern Mediterranean in the early first century B.C., when Rome was consolidating its control over that area (**5.171**). There is evidence that it reached Rome by about A.D. 80. The cult centers, though usually lavishly decorated, were small. The one in Ostia occupies less of the ground floor of an apartment building than does a typical tavern. Archaeologists have confirmed what literary sources tell us, that the cult was for men only and that the initiates engaged in a form of baptism in a bull's blood and shared a ceremonial meal (**5.163**; **5.172**).

The appeal of this cult was apparently twofold. First, it satisfied a yearning for immortality and happiness after death. These promises were more explicitly expressed than in many of the other mystery cults. Then, too, its rituals attracted a number of people, just as the Masons and other secret societies do today, with their color, their vivid imagery, and the impressive stages—from raven to courier of the sun—through which the initiate progressed (**5.160**; **5.162**; **5.173**). Mithra even began to take on the attributes and functions of other gods, particularly the sun god, Sol Invictus (**5.157**; **5.168**).

The cult grew so popular by the fourth century that it seriously rivaled Christianity, especially among the business classes and the army, two segments of the population that the church had to win over if it was to consolidate its control of the empire (**5.159**; **5.169**). The mystery religions were nonexclusive. Initiates of one cult could join another, as long as they paid the fees and went through the rites. To judge from sermons that survive from this time, some Christians were also taking part in other cults, especially Mithra's.

One of the most popular aspects of Mithraic worship was the feast day of the god, which fell on December 25, the day of his birth from a rock. According to Mithraic legend, shepherds brought gifts to the newborn god (cf. Luke 2). It's worth noting also that the priests of this cult were called magi (cf. Matt. 2). But, since the Romans used that term to mean astrologers and priests of any Mesopotamian cult, it is not always possible to determine its specific meaning in a text (**1.37**, vol. 1:373).

Because of miscalculations in ancient calendars, the winter solstice was also celebrated on December 25. Candles were lit in people's homes, to help the sun fight off the darkness of the longest night of the year. The riotous Roman festival called the Saturnalia came to a climax on the same day. Among the laws of that festival were these: "Let no one conduct business, personal or public, during the festival, except what pertains to sports, luxurious living, and entertainment" (Lucian, *Saturnalia* 13). During the Saturnalia greenery was hung and presents exchanged.

The church had no festival to draw its members' attention away from these joyous, colorful occasions, so in the mid-fourth century, the bishops of Rome began celebrating the birth of Christ on December 25 (**5.161**). The New Testament gives no clue to the actual date, except that shepherds were in the field (customarily April through November).[4] Until the fourth century, most Christians had not observed any kind of holiday in honor of the event. Easter was the high moment of the church year. Clement of Alexandria says that among Christians who did take note of Christ's birth, the date varied from April to September (*Stromata* 1.21). He himself prefers May 20. A fourth-century document called the Apostolic Constitutions (5.3,13), which originated in Syria, calls for the birth of Christ to be celebrated "on the twenty-fifth day of the ninth month."

January 6 was kept as the day of Jesus' baptism, his spiritual birth, and the Eastern churches also began to refer to his physical birth as occurring on that day. When the Western churches began celebrating the nativity on December 25, the Eastern churches were horrified that they

Ruins of initiation hall at Eleusis
(Photo by Howard Vos)

had succumbed to pressure from their pagan environment. To this day the Eastern Orthodox Church still observes Christmas on January 6.

Christianity and the Mysteries

From what we have seen of these various mystery cults, we might draw up a general description of them. A mystery cult was one which focused on a god (or human, in the case of Orpheus) who had overcome death. The initiates underwent a ritual washing and partook of a common meal at which the god was either present or was thought to be consumed. Then they received secret knowledge which enabled them to share in the god's victory over the underworld. When they died, they would live in a special portion of the underworld where they would enjoy the company of the god. The closest we can come to a description of the promise held out to the initiates is a choral ode in Aristophanes' play *The Frogs* (345ff), which mentions that the stiffness and aches of old age will vanish as Dionysus leads the initiates in a torch-lit dance across the dewy fields of the underworld.

If the general pattern of the mystery cults strikes us as uncomfortably close to a description of Christianity, we aren't alone. Early pagan critics of the church pointed out that its rituals marked it as another mystery cult. Christian apologists replied that Satan had known what Christianity was going to look like and so had fashioned the mystery cults along the same lines in advance to discredit Christianity. Justin Martyr, for example, in the mid-second century, admitted that some

The temple of Hephaestus in Athens
(Photo by Howard Vos)

Christians "used to worship Bacchus. . . . We pity anyone who gives credence to such things, and their inventors we recognize as devils" (*First Apology* 25). In chapter 66 of the same work he describes Christian communion, then adds:

> The demonic powers have imitated this rite in the mysteries of Mithras, commanding the very same thing to be observed. For they partake of bread and a cup of water with certain incantations in their initiation ceremonies.

The similarities between Christianity, as Paul proclaimed it to the Greco-Roman world, and the mysteries are too obvious to be missed (**5.182**). Even the usually conservative *Zondervan Pictorial Bible Dictionary*[5] admits that "Paul adapted some of the vocabulary of the mystery cults to a Christian purpose, and his use of the word 'mystery' for a truth revealed, but comprehended only by the 'initiated,' is a clear reference to them."

Paul does in fact use the term *musterion* some twenty times:

Rom.	11:25	1 Cor.	15:51	Col.	1:26-27
	16:25	Eph.	1:9		2:2
1Cor..	2:1,7		3:3, 4-5		4:3
	4:1		3:9	2 Thess.	2:7
	13:2		5:32	1 Tim.	3:9
	14:2		6:19		3:16

This term appears in the Gospels in only one passage, paralleled in the Synoptics. In explaining why he uses parables, Jesus says that it is given only to his disciples to know the "mystery of the kingdom of God" (Mark 4:11 NKJV; Matt. 13:11; Luke 8:10). This was not a major theme of Jesus' teaching, but Paul found it useful in addressing a Greco-Roman audience which undoubtedly included people who had been initiated into such cults. As one who prided himself on being "all things to all people" (1 Cor. 9:22), he knew he had to express his new message in terms his hearers could comprehend (**5.177**).

When Paul uses the word in Romans 16:25–26, "the revelation of the mystery that was kept secret for long ages," he seems to be using the foil of mystery-cult terminology and secrecy; yet the mystery of God's purpose is now openly disclosed in the proclamation of the gospel (cf. Eph. 3:5). The reference is also obvious in 1 Corinthians 15:51: "Listen, I will tell you a mystery!" And the famous thirteenth chapter of 1 Corinthians takes on new meaning when we realize what Paul meant by "if I have prophetic powers, and understand all mysteries and all knowledge." If he were initiated into *all* the mystery cults, it would do him no good without love (**5.180**).

Others have pointed to similarities in the mystery cults' doctrine of salvation and that of Christianity (**5.178**). Not all scholars agree with this reading, however. Some argue that Paul and the early Christians were using terminology in common circulation at the time and not applying it specifically to communion (**1.45**:29ff.). Kittel's *Theological Dictionary of the New Testament*[6] says that "*musterion* is a rare expression in the New Testament which betrays no relation to the mystery cults."

The Christian practice of baptism and its possible relation to the mysteries has also been the focus of what John Bligh characterizes as "a long and seemingly interminable controversy" (**5.117**:373). He goes on to sum up the problem concisely:

> Devout commentators have, on the whole, shrunk from recognizing any connection at all, and have catalogued numerous differences. But a dozen differences do not take away the several striking resemblances. Whether Paul recognized it or not, the result of

his presenting Baptism as a mystical death-and-resurrection is to make Baptism an impressive mystery-ritual, more mysterious than the Mysteries, a solemn entry into a new way of life through participation in a liturgical re-enactment of the experience of the divinity in question. Even if Paul was unaware of the resemblance, many of his more educated converts must have seen it. . . . Baptism, as explained by Paul, resembles initiation at Eleusis more than it resembles circumcision or passover, or any other Jewish ritual.

To say that Paul and other early Christians were influenced by what was happening around them is not to say that their work was corrupted or is invalid for us today. In every age the church has tried to frame its proclamation of the gospel in vocabulary intelligible to its hearers. The medieval church depicted God as a feudal lord and interpreted the Scriptures allegorically. In the eighteenth century, under the influence of the birth of modern science, theologians talked about God as a cosmic clock maker, setting up the laws by which the universe operated. These were valid ways to help the people of those eras understand God. The problem arises when we fail to see the contexts of those interpretations. If we try to insist that one generation's interpretation of the gospel is universally valid in all later time periods, we risk freezing God's truth into terms that may not speak to our generation.

Gnosticism

When Paul links mysteries and knowledge in 1 Corinthians 13, he raises a difficult subject for us to consider, but it is appropriate to attempt it here, for it provides a convenient bridge between religion and philosophy in the Greco-Roman world and introduces a concept that provides the background for some of the vocabulary of the earliest Christians. The term he uses is *gnosis*, usually translated "knowledge," but which Elaine Pagels (**5.210**) has suggested might better be understood as "insight." Her point is supported by Paul's distinction between wisdom (*sophia*) and knowledge (*gnosis*) in 1 Corinthians 12:8. Also important for Paul is his "knowledge (*gnosis*) of Christ Jesus" (Phil. 3:8 KJV), likely meaning his personal relationship with Christ (**5.219**).

In one New Testament passage the term seems to be used to denote a religio-philosophical system much like what we now call Gnosticism (**5.231**). In 1 Timothy 6:20, Paul[7] cautions Timothy to avoid the "contradictions of what is falsely called knowledge; by professing it some have missed the mark as regards the faith." The King James Version translates *gnosis* in this verse as "science," because the word *science* in 1611 merely meant knowledge, coming as it does from the Latin verb *scio* (I know). Unfortunately, some modern Christians who take the KJV too literally have based their crusade against the teaching of science in the schools on this translation. What the author of the letter meant had nothing to do with what we know as science. This is a prime example of the need to understand the context of the original text as well as the translation.

The origins of Gnosticism are still poorly understood (**5.187**). Some scholars see it as purely a Christian heresy (**5.214**). Others argue that some form of it existed in the pre-Christian era and that its adherents fastened on to Christianity because it was so congenial to their theosophical views (**5.197**; **5.201–202**; **5.233–234**). It is probably safe to say that elements of a gnostic world view existed in the pre-Christian era, and by the late first century A.D., they were becoming twined together. The fascination of Hellenistic Jews with wisdom literature has led some scholars to suggest a Jewish origin for Gnosticism (**5.227–228**). Yet Gnostic redeemers are often modeled upon the Jesus of the Gospels (**5.197**:13–15). Paul and Philo of Alexandria both use the term *gnosis* in a way that suggests they were familiar with a gnostic philosophy, although we cannot identify any Gnostic teachers or literature from that period (**5.220**; **5.230**).

To summarize even inadequately: Gnosticism was a religious philosophy of metaphysical and radical dualism which taught that God was spirit and good, and that matter and the world were hopelessly evil (**5.200**). Therefore, God could not have created the physical world, because good cannot create evil. A lesser divinity, called by the Platonic term Demiurge, committed the mistake of forming the world, in which souls as divine sparks are imprisoned and asleep. The idea of the body (*soma* in Greek) as a prison (*sema*) comes ultimately from Plato (*Cratylus* 400C), as does much Gnostic terminology (**5.218**). Part of its intellectual trapping was also borrowed from Mithraism (see above), a dualistic cult from the East that emphasized the contrast between light (symbol of goodness) and darkness (symbol of evil).

A *moral* dualism within the context of Judaism is found in the Old Testament doctrine of the two ways (Ps. 1; Prov.). One of the Dead Sea Scrolls, *The War of the Sons of Light with the Sons of Darkness*, uses the light-dark symbolism, but counts on the mighty hand of God to deal an everlasting blow to Satan and his kingdom. The light-dark contrast recurs in New Testament passages, notably in John 1, but also in Matthew 6:23; Luke 1:79; John 3:19; Acts 26:18; 2 Corinthians 6:14; 1 Peter 2:9; and 1 John 1:5–7 (**5.213**; **5.216**; **5.221**). God's good creation is threatened but not overcome by darkness/evil. Thus some common imagery made itself at home in different religious traditions. Some scholars distinguish between a general *gnosis*, a sort of underlying, pessimistic world view current in the early Christian era, and Gnosticism in particular (**5.184**; **5.218**; **5.231**).

Gnostics thought the world was bad and without remedy. For them, knowledge was seen as the key to freeing one's true divine self from this evil fleshly prison. Some Gnostics, called Ophites, saw the serpent in

Genesis 3 as the hero of that story because he offered Eve wisdom, the ability to know good and evil. In their view the evil Demiurge had thwarted mankind's opportunity to escape (**5.193**). Since then, the human race had been awaiting a redeemer, someone who would bring the knowledge of mankind's true state and the way out of it (**5.223**). The longing for such a redeemer/mediator characterized much ancient religious thought. By Hellenistic times, under the influence of philosophical monotheism and the existence of powerful kings and emperors, the notion of the exaltedness of the highest god had grown to the point that he was believed to be inaccessible to mere mortals (**5.209**).

For that reason the Gnostics found Jesus an attractive figure. He could be seen as the redeemer, sent by the true God to awaken sleeping, imprisoned souls and offer them the knowledge that would enable them to break out.[8] Jesus had said that he was the way, the truth, and that knowing the truth would make people free (John 8:32; 14:6). He even thanked God that he had "hidden these things from the wise and the intelligent and have revealed them to infants" (Matt. 11:25). A particularly important passage, in the view of Gnostics, was Luke 23:49, which says that Jesus' acquaintances stood watching the crucifixion from a distance. The Greek word *gnostoi* is translated "acquaintances" or "friends" in modern versions. It simply means "those who knew him," but to the Gnostics it suggested that at least some of those who followed Jesus recognized him as the redeemer in the Gnostic sense (**5.203**).

Whatever its origins, in the last half of the first century A.D., Gnosticism began to flourish within the context of Christianity, like a cowbird's egg laid in another bird's nest (**5.190**; **5.196**). We have documentary evidence that by the early second century it had developed elaborate myths[9] and threatened to push orthodox Christian teaching out of the nest.[10] Even Christian writers such as Clement of Alexandria propounded ideas heavily tinged with Gnosticism (**5.206**). They maintained that Jesus had imparted secret knowledge to his disciples which had not been recorded in the Gospels. Mark 4:11 was their justification: "To you has been given the secret of the kingdom of God, but for those outside, everything comes in parables." The church at Alexandria even claimed to have a "secret gospel of Mark," in which Jesus' true message was preserved (**5.222**). Some scholars claim to find strong Gnostic tendencies in John's Gospel (**5.226**), but others trace its thought patterns to Old Testament speculation about personified Wisdom.

The names of Valentinus, Basilides, and Marcion head the list of Gnostics condemned by more orthodox Christian writers. Marcion is perhaps the best known and had a wider impact (**5.194**; **5.208**). He was the son of a Christian bishop but was excommunicated from the church at Rome in A.D. 144 for his unorthodox teaching. He held that God was a God of love, not of law. The Old Testament God was obviously not the true God, but the Demiurge. Only Paul had understood this, Marcion thought. Jesus and his disciples had been too blinded by their Jewish background to grasp the truth. Therefore Marcion rejected the entire Old Testament and accepted as Scripture only ten of Paul's letters and an edited version of Luke's Gospel (stripping out some Jewish elements), because of Luke's association with Paul. Some Gnostic phraseology is close to that of Paul and his writings appealed to them, as Elaine Pagels has shown (**5.210**). Christians complained that the "ignorant . . . twist [Paul's letters and other Scriptures] to their own destruction" (2 Peter 3:15–17).

Marcion has been characterized as a radical Paulinist, one who intended to carry Paul's message to its logical conclusion (**5.204–205**). His influence was widespread. We know of his opponents in cities all over the Roman Empire. His establishment of a collection of Scriptures forced the orthodox church to begin thinking about its own canon and defining which books were and were not authoritative (**5.207**).

Gnosticism posed a real danger to the fledgling church because it threatened to turn Jesus into a myth with its insistence that, as the true spiritual God, he could not have been truly human. He appeared[11] to be human, but his body, they maintained, was not a real human body. The fact that he could walk on water and materialize in a locked room seemed to them to support this contention. Orthodox Christians countered by insisting on the reality of Jesus' human nature. Paul, in Galatians 4:4, emphasizes that Jesus was "born of a woman." The original purpose of the virgin birth story was to stress not so much the divinity as the full humanity of Jesus (**1.8**; **5.183**; **5.185**; **5.188**; **5.215**; **5.225**). In Jesus "the Word became flesh" (John 1:14), "heard, . . . seen, . . . looked at and touched" (1 John 1:1–2).

The full extent of this Gnostic threat to the church was not grasped until recently because our only documentary evidence came from refutations by orthodox authors, who destroyed all the Gnostic writings they could get their hands on when Christianity came to dominate the Empire in the fourth century (**5.211**). In the 1940s, however, a body of Gnostic writings was found at Nag Hammadi in Egypt, and our knowledge of the teachings of the sect has grown rapidly since then (**5.189**; **5.191–192**; **5.212**; **5.217**; **5.229**).

The basic assumption of Gnosticism, that matter was evil and spirit good, led to two different lifestyles. Some Gnostics "denied the flesh," shunning worldly goods and trying to overcome physical desires[12] in an effort to purify their spirits and hasten their release from the prison of the body. Others concluded that since they were spiritual beings imprisoned in physical bodies, it made no difference what they did with their bodies as long as they kept themselves spiritually pure.[13] Such Gnostics often engaged in lascivious behavior for which they took no responsibility. Some of the charges of indecency leveled at the early church may have been a reaction against the activities of such people, who identified themselves as Christians but would have been con-demned by the majority of orthodox believers. In contrast to Gnosticism, Judaism and Christianity hold that God's creation is "good" and that it should be "received with thanksgiving" (Gen.1—2; 1 Tim. 4:4).

Although Gnosticism by that name had been suppressed by the fourth century, the dualistic philosophy which underlies it has never entirely died out. The Manichees, whom Augustine followed for a while, survived until the thirteenth century in the Near East. A Manichean offshoot, the Bogomils, flourished in the Balkans in the Middle Ages and spread to France and Italy. The Cathars or Albigensians, active in southern France in the twelfth and thirteenth centuries, taught many of the same doctrines as the ancient Gnostics and may have developed from the Bogomils. In present-day Iraq there is still a sect, the Mandaeans, which teaches a mishmash of Christian and Gnostic ideas (**5.186**). Gnostic ideas are even surfacing today in New Age teachings, such as those maintaining that human beings are essentially divine.

"How Extremely Religious!"

We should now be able to see that the New Testament was written against a complex background of religious views, some of them fairly sophisticated and intellectual, others appealing more to popular emo-tions and superstitions (**5.237**; **5.239**). The Athenians were typical in being "extremely religious" (Acts 17:22). The descriptive labels of Jewish, pagan, and Christian can be applied only in general terms (**5.241**; **5.243**). Each of those groups consisted of numerous subcate-gories, and people moved easily from one group to another, taking their intellectual and spiritual traditions with them. It is not always easy to say that a certain idea is Jewish, while another is pagan, and anoth-er Christian. The three groups borrowed from one another and react-ed against one another (**5.242**).

If we are looking for some essential difference between Christianity and the other expressions of religious faith which surrounded it, we might find it in the Christian insistence that knowing God is a matter of a relationship, not a contract dependent on sacrifice or a quest for knowledge (**5.235**; **5.238**; **5.240**). Because of this relation between God and those who worshiped him, it was possible for his believers to grow in their faith (1 Cor. 3:2–3; Heb. 5:12–14). The Greco-Roman gods lacked this ability to change the lives of their followers (**5.236**). They could offer protection for a clan or city or immortality for the individ-ual but they provided no guidance for living from day to day. For that, one had to turn to the philosophical schools, as we are ready to do in the next chapter.

Notes

1. Greek grammar assigns a gender—either masculine, feminine, or neuter—to all nouns, even abstract words or qualities. The gender bears no relation to the nature of the thing itself. The word for "hand," for example, is feminine, while the word for "finger" is masculine.

2. By way of analogy, the phrase "hocus-pocus" came into being in the early Middle Ages as a corruption of a phrase from the Latin mass, "hoc est corpus meum" ("this is my body"). People who did not know Latin but knew that it was used in religious rituals tried to appropriate some of its presumed power for themselves.

3. Cybele wasn't the only divinity whose shrine was associated with a meteorite. A rock falling out of the sky could be guaranteed to get the attention of ancient people. Clement of Alexandria (A.D. 200) mentions that the Arabs venerated a "sacred stone" (*Exhort. to the Greeks* 4.40). This shrine, in Mecca, was taken over by Mohammed and incorporated into his new religion some four hundred years later, since he was unable to eradicate the devotion which it inspired. The black stone, a meteorite, is now the center of the Ka'ba. Every Muslim is supposed to visit Mecca at least once during his life and walk around the Ka'ba.

4. I. H. Marshall, *The Gospel of Luke*, The New International Greek Testament Commentary (Grand Rapids: Eerdmans, 1978), 108.

5. Ed. by M. C. Tenney (Grands Rapids: Zondervan, 1969), 567.

6. Ed. by G. Kittel (Grand Rapids: Eerdmans, 1967), 4:824: "Where there seem to be connections (e. g., in sacramental passages), the term is not used; where it is used, there are no such connections."

7. There is a possibility that First and Second Timothy and Titus may have been written by someone other than Paul but circulated under the apostle's name. In antiquity people sometimes put the names of famous persons on their works to gain credibility. Such a tactic was considered a tribute of respect rather than forgery.

8. Cf. the language of Ephesians 5:14, likely based on Isaiah 60:1.

9. Cf. 1 Timothy 1:4; Titus 3:9.

10. Cf. 2 Timothy 2:18; 1 Corinthians 4:8–13.

11. The Greek word is *dokeo* (seem, appear), from which comes our word for the heresy of Docetism, denying that Jesus was human and was tempted and suffered and died.

12. Cf. the behavior countered in Colossians 2:18–23.

13. Cf. the slogans and attitudes Paul counters in 1 Corinthians 6:12–20.

BIBLIOGRAPHY

Introduction

5.1.   Arseniev, N. "The Christian Message and the Hellenistic Religious Outlook." *Nuovo Didaskaleion* 14(1964): 29–56.

5.2.   Borkowski, Z. "Local Cults and Resistance to Christianity." *Journal of Juristic Papyrology* 20(1990): 25–30.

5.3.   Finegan, J. *Myth and Mystery: An Introduction to the Pagan Religions of the Biblical World.* Grand Rapids: Baker, 1989.

5.4.   Hamilton, J. D. B. "The Church and the Language of Mystery: The First Four Centuries." *EphThL* 53(1977): 479–494.

5.5.   Kerenyi, K. *The Religion of the Greeks and Romans.* London: Thames & Hudson, 1962.

5.6.   Malina, B. J. "Religion in the World of Paul: A Preliminary Sketch." *BTB* 16(1986): 92–101.

5.7.   Momigliano, A. "Roman Religion of the Imperial Period." In *Religions of Antiquity.* Ed. by R. M. Seltzer. New York: Macmillan, 1989: 218–233.

5.8.   Ogilvie, R. M. *The Romans and Their Gods in the Age of Augustus.* New York: Norton, 1969.

5.9.   Pollitt, J. J. "The Impact of Greek Art on Rome" *TAPhA* 108(1978): 155–174.

5.10.   Robertson, N. "The Ritual Background of the Dying God in Cyprus and Syro-Palestine." *HThR* 75(1982): 313–359.

5.11.   Rose, H. J. *Religion in Greece and Rome.* New York: Harper, 1959.

5.12.   Wardman, A. *Rome's Debt to Greece.* London: Elek, 1976.

5.13.   Wedderburn, A. J. M. "Paul and the Hellenistic Mystery-Cults; on Posing the Right Questions." In *La soteriologia dei culti orientali nell'imperio romano. Atti del Colloquio internazionale, Roma, 24–28 settembre 1979.* Ed. by U. Bianchi and M. J. Vermaseren. Leiden: Brill. 1982: 817–835.

The Olympian Deities

5.14.   Akinpelu, J. A. "Stoicism and a Future Existence." *CB* 45(1969): 76–77.

5.15.   Beard, M. "Decline and Fall? Roman State Religion in the Late Republic." *PCA* 79(1982): 21–22.

5.16.   Caldwell, R. *The Origin of the Gods: A Psychoanalytic Study of Greek Theogonic Myths.* New York: Oxford University Press, 1989.

5.17.   Cumont, F. *Afterlife in Roman Paganism.* New York: Dover Press, 1960 reprint.

5.18.   de Ste Croix, G. E. M. "The Religion of the Roman World." *Didaskalos* 4(1972): 61–74.

5.19.   Festugiere, A. J. *Personal Religion Among the Greeks.* Berkeley: University of California Press, 1954.

5.20.   Grant, M. *Myths of the Greeks and Romans.* New York: New American Library, 1962.

5.21.   Griffiths, J. G. "Hellenistic Religions." In *Religions of Antiquity.* Ed. by R. M. Seltzer. New York: Macmillan, 1989: 237–258.

5.22.   Harrison, J. E. *Basic Greek Mythology.* London: Blackwell, 1957.

5.23.   Hopkins, K. "Graveyards for Historians." In *La mort, les morts et l'au-delà dans le monde romain: Actes du colloque de Caen, 20–22 novembre 1985.* Ed. by F. Hinard. Caen: Centre del Publ. de l'Univ., 1987: 113–126.

5.24.   Jocelyn, H. D. "The Roman Nobility and the Republican State." *JRelHist* 4(1966–67): 89–104.

5.25.   Knight, W. F. J. *Elysion: On Ancient Greek and Roman Beliefs Concerning a Life After Death.* New York: Barnes & Noble, 1970.

5.26.   Long, C. R. *The Twelve Gods of Greece and Rome.* Leiden: Brill, 1987.

5.27.   MacMullen, R. *Paganism in the Roman Empire.* New Haven, CT: Yale University Press, 1981.

5.28. Momigliano, A. "The Theological Efforts of the Roman Upper Classes in the First Century B.C." *CPh* 79(1984): 199–211.

5.29. Paulsen, D. L. "Early Christian Belief in a Corporeal Deity: Origen and Augustine as Reluctant Witnesses." *HThR* 83(1990): 105–116.

5.30. Rohde, E. *Psyche: The Cult of Souls and Belief in Immortality Among the Greeks.* New York: Harper & Row, 1966.

5.31. Sale, W. "The Olympian Faith." *G&R* 19(1972): 81–93.

5.32. Schilling, R. "Roman Festivals and Their Significance." *AClass* 7(1964): 44–56.

5.33. Seltman, C. *The Twelve Olympians.* New York: Crowell, 1960.

5.34. Szemler, G. J. *The Priests of the Roman Republic: A Study of the Interactions Between Priesthoods and Magistracies.* Brussels: Collection Latomus, 1972.

5.35. Thrower, J. *The Alternative Tradition: Religion and the Rejection of Religion in the Ancient World.* The Hague: Mouton, 1980.

5.36. Vernant, J. P. "Greek Religion." In *Religions of Antiquity.* Ed. by R. M. Seltzer. New York: Macmillan, 1989: 163–192.

5.37. Versnel, H. S., ed. *Faith, Hope and Worship: Aspects of Religious Mentality in the Ancient World.* Leiden: Brill, 1981.

5.38. Veyne, P. *Did the Greeks Believe in Their Myths? An Essay on the Constitutive Imagination.* Chicago: University of Chicago Press, 1988.

5.39. Warden, J. "Scenes from the Greco-Roman Underworld." *Crux* 13(1976–77): 23–28.

5.40. Wardman, A. *Religion and Statecraft Among the Romans.* London: Granada, 1982.

5.41. Weiss, H. "The Pagani Among the Contemporaries of the First Christians." *JBL* 86(1967): 42–52.

Emperor Cult

5.42. Aune, D. E. "The Influence of Roman Imperial Court Ceremonial on the Apocalypse of John." *BibRes* 28(1983): 5–26.

5.43. Barrett, P. W. "Revelation in Its Roman Setting." *RefThRev* 50(1991): 59–68.

5.44. Botha, P. J. J. "God, Emperor Worship and Society: Contemporary Experiences and the Book of Revelation." *Neotest* 22(1988): 87–102.

5.45. Bowersock, G. W. "Greek Intellectuals and the Imperial Cult in the Second Century A.D." In *La culte des souverains dans l'empire romain.* Ed. by W. den Boer. Geneva: Fondation Hart, 1973: 177–212.

5.46. Cuss, D. *Imperial Cult and Honorary Terms in the New Testament.* Freiburg: Freiburg University Press, 1974.

5.47. Duff, P. B. "The March of the Divine Warrior and the Advent of the Greco-Roman King: Mark's Account of Jesus' Entry into Jerusalem." *JBL* 111(1992): 55–71.

5.48. Fishwick, D. "Dio and Maecenas: The Emperor and the Ruler Cult." *Phoenix* 94(1990): 267–275.

5.49. ———. *The Imperial Cult in the Latin West: Studies in the Ruler Cult of the Western Provinces of the Roman Empire.* 2 vols. Leiden: Brill, 1987–1991.

5.50. Friesen, S. J. *Twice Neokoros: Ephesus, Asia and the Cult of the Flavian Imperial Family.* Leiden: Brill, 1993.

5.51. Hellman, W. E. "Philo of Alexandria on Deification and Assimilation to God." *StPhilon* 2(1990): 51–71.

5.52. Kee, A. "The Imperial Cult: The Unmasking of an Ideology." *Scottish Journal of Religious Studies* 6(1985): 112–128.

5.53. Kreitzer, L. "Apotheosis of the Roman Emperor." *BiblArch* 53(1990): 210–217.

5.54. Mellor, R. *Thea Rome: The Worship of the Goddess Roma in the Greek World.* Göttingen: Vandenhoeck & Ruprecht, 1975.

5.55. Momigliano, A. "How Roman Emperors Became Gods." *American Scholar* 55(1986): 181–193.

5.56. Oster, R. "Christianity and Emperor Veneration in Ephesus: Iconography of a Conflict." *RestorQ* 25(1982): 143–149.

5.57. Pao, D. W. "The Sebasteion in Aphrodisias: Structure and Meaning of a Temple Complex for the Imperial Cult." *Jian Dao* 6(1996): 55–75.

5.58. Parker, H. M. "Domitian and the Epistle to the Hebrews." *Iliff Review* 36(1979): 31–43.

5.59. Pleket, H. W. "An Aspect of the Emperor Cult: Imperial Mysteries." *HThR* 58(1965): 331-347.

5.60. Price, S. R. F. "From Noble Funerals to Divine Cult: The Consecration of the Roman Emperors." In *Rituals of Royalty: Power and Ceremonial in Traditional Societies.* Ed. by D. Cannadine and S. R. F. Price. New York: Cambridge University Press, 1987: 56–105.

5.61. ———. "Gods and Emperors: The Greek Language of the Roman Imperial Cult." *JHS* 104(1984): 79–95.

5.62. ———. *Rituals and Powers: Roman Imperial Cult in Asia Minor.* New York: Cambridge University Press, 1984.

5.63. Roth, C. "The Debate on the Loyal Sacrifices, A.D. 66." *HThR* 53(1960): 93–97.

5.64. Scherrer, S. J. "Signs and Wonders in the Imperial Cult: A New Look at a Roman Religious Institution in the Light of Revelation 13:13–15." *JBL* 103(1984): 594–610.

5.65. Simpson, C. J. "The Cult of the Emperor Gaius." *Latomus* 40(1981): 489–511.

5.66. ———. "Real Gods." *Britannia* 24(1993): 264–265.

5.67. Talbert, C. H. "The Concept of Immortals in Mediterranean Antiquity." *JBL* 94(1975): 419–436.

Miracles, Magic, and Holy Men

5.68. Aune, D. E. "The Apocalypse of John and Graeco-Roman Magic." *NTS* 33 (1987): 481–501.

5.69. Betz, H. D. "Jesus as Divine Man." In *Jesus and the Historian: Written in Honor of Ernest Cadman Colwell.* Ed. by F. T. Trotter. Philadelphia: Westminster Press, 1968: 114–133.

5.70. Blackburn, B. *Theios Aner and the Markan Miracle Traditions: A Critique of the Theios Aner Concept as an Interpretative Background of the Miracle Traditions Used by Mark.* Tübingen: Mohr-Siebeck, 1990.

5.71. Corrington, G. P. *The 'Divine Man': His Origin and Function in Hellenistic Popular Religion.* Bern: P. Lang, 1986.

5.72. Edwards, M. J. "Three Exorcisms and the New Testament World." *Eranos* 87(1989): 117–126.

5.73. Elliott, J. H. "Paul, Galatians, and the Evil Eye." *CTM* 17(1990): 262–273.

5.74. Fishwick, D. "On the Origin of the Rotas-Sator Square." *HThR* 57(1974): 39–53.

5.75. Fridrischen, A. *The Problem of Miracle in Primitive Christianity.* Minneapolis: Augsburg Press, 1972.

5.76. Gager, J. G. *Curse Tablets and Binding Spells from the Ancient World.* New York: Oxford University Press, 1992.

5.77. Garcia Teijeiro, M. "Religion and Magic." *Kernos* 6(1993): 123–138.

5.78. Grant, R. M. "The Problem of Miraculous Feedings in the Graeco-Roman Period." *Center for Hermeneutical Studies Protocol Series* 42(1982): 1–15.

5.79. Holladay, C. R. *Theios Aner in Hellenistic Judaism: A Critique of the Use of This Category in New Testament Christology.* Missoula, MT: Scholars Press, 1977.

5.80. Hull, J. M. *Hellenistic Magic and the Synoptic Tradition.* London: SCM Press, 1974.

5.81. Kee, H. C. *Medicine, Miracle and Magic in New Testament Times.* New York: Cambridge University Press, 1986.

5.82. ———. *Miracle in the Early Christian World: A Study in Sociohistorical Method.* New Haven, CT: Yale University Press, 1983.

5.83. Kern-Ulmer, B. "The Depiction of Magic in Rabbinic Texts: The Rabbinic and the Greek Concept of Magic." *JSJ* 27(1996): 289–303.

5.84. Koester, H. "The Divine Human Being." *HThR* 78(1985): 243–252.

5.85. Kolenkow, A. B. "Divine Men and Society." *Forum* 2(1986): 85–92.

5.86. Lesses, R. "Speaking with Angels: Jewish and Greco-Egyptian Revelatory Adjurations." *HThR* 89(1996): 41–60.

5.87. Lown, J. W. "The Miraculous in the Greco-Roman Historians." *Forum* 2(1986): 36–42.

5.88. Luck, G. *Arcana Mundi: Magic and the Occult in the Greek and Roman Worlds: A Collection of Ancient Texts Translated, Annotated and Introduced.* Baltimore: Johns Hopkins University Press, 1985.

5.89. Moeller, W. O. *The Mithraic Origin and Meanings of the Rotas-Sator Square.* Leiden: Brill, 1973.

5.90. Oster, R. E. "Ephesus as a Religious Center under the Principate, I: Paganism before Constantine." *ANRW* II, 18, 3 (1990): 1661–1728.

5.91. Remus, H. "Does Terminology Distinguish Early Christian from Pagan Miracles?" *JBL* 101(1982): 531–551.

5.92. ———. *Pagan-Christian Conflict over Miracle in the Second Century.* Cambridge, MA: Philadelphia Patristic Foundation, 1983.

5.93. Trudinger, P. "The Ephesus Milieu." *DownRev* 106(1988): 286–296.

5.94. Wedderburn, A. J. M. "Philo's 'Heavenly Man.'" *NovT* 15(1973): 301–326.

5.95. Yamauchi, E. M. "Magic in the Biblical World." *TynBull* 34(1983): 169–200.

Oracles, Astrology, and Dreams

5.96. Achte, K. "Ancient Greeks and Romans and Their Dreams." In *Ancient and Popular Healing: Symposium on Ancient Medicine, Athens 4–10 October 1986.* Helsinki: Academic Bookstore, 1989: 43–69.

5.97. Charlesworth, J. H. "Jewish Astrology in the Talmud, Pseudepigrapha, the Dead Sea Scrolls, and Early Palestinian Synagogues." *HThR* 70(1977): 183–200.

5.98. Cramer, F. H. *Astrology in Roman Law and Politics.* Philadelphia: Amer. Philos. Soc., 1954.

5.99. Dietrich, B. C. "Oracles and Divine Inspiration." *Kernos* 3(1990): 157–174.

5.100. Fontenrose, J. E. *Didyma: Apollo's Oracles, Cult and Companions.* Berkeley: University of California Press, 1988.

5.101. Hayes, W. M. "Tiberius and the Future." *CJ* 55(1959): 2–8.

5.102. Kerkeslager, A. "Apollo, Greco-Roman Prophecy, and the Rider on the White Horse in Revelation 6:2." *JBL* 112(1993): 116–121.

5.103. Lewis, N. *The Interpretation of Dreams and Portents.* Toronto: Hakkert, 1976.

5.104. Lloyd-Jones, H. "The Delphic Oracle." *G&R* 23(1976): 60–73.

5.105. MacMullen, R. "Social History in Astrology." *AncSoc* 2(1971): 105–116.

5.106. Miller, J. E. "Dreams and Prophetic Visions." *Biblica* 71(1990): 401–404.

5.107. Momigliano, A. "From the Pagan to the Christian Sibyl: Prophecy as History of Religion." In *The Uses of Greek and Latin: Historical Essays.* Ed. by A. C. Dionisotti et al. London: Warburg Institute, 1988: 3–18.

5.108. Parke, H. W. *Sibyls and Sibylline Prophecy in Classical Antiquity.* Ed. by B. C. McGing. London: Routledge, 1988.

5.109. Pines, S., and W. Z. Harvey. "To Behold the Stars and the Heavenly Bodies." *Immanuel* 20(1986): 33–37.

Animism

5.110. Borgeaud, P. *The Cult of Pan in Ancient Greece.* Trans. by K. Atlass and J. Redfield. Chicago: University of Chicago Press, 1988.

5.111. Johnston, S. I. "Crossroads." *ZPE* 88(1991): 217–224.

Mystery Cults

5.112. Godwin, J. *Mystery Religions in the Ancient World.* San Francisco: Harper & Row, 1981.

5.113. Meyer, M. W., ed. *The Ancient Mysteries: A Sourcebook. Sacred Texts of the Mystery Religions of the Ancient Mediterranean World.* San Francisco: Harper & Row, 1987.

5.114. Reitzenstein, R. *Hellenistic Mystery-Religions: Their Basic Ideas and Significance.* Pittsburgh: Pickwick Press, 1978.

Eleusinian Mysteries

5.115. Alderink, L. J. "The Eleusinian Mysteries in Roman Imperial Times." *ANRW* II, 18, 2 (1989): 1457–1498.

5.116. Berg, W. "Eleusinian and Mediterranean Harvest Myths." *Fabula* 15(1974): 202–211.

5.117. Bligh, J. "Baptismal Transformation of the Gentile World." *HeyJ* 37(1996): 371–381.

5.118. D'Alviella, G. *The Mysteries of Eleusis: The Secret Rites and Rituals of the Classical Greek Mystery Tradition.* Wellingborough, UK: Aquarian Press, 1981.

5.119. Gallant, C. "A Jungian Interpretation of the Eleusinian Myth and Mysteries." *ANRW* II 18, no. 2 (1989): 1540–1563.

5.120. Kerenyi, K. *Eleusis: Archetypal Image of Mother and Daughter.* New York: Pantheon Books, 1967.

5.121. Martin, L. H. "Those Elusive Eleusinian Mystery Shows." *Helios* 13(1986): 17–31.

5.122. Mylonas, G. E. *Eleusis and the Eleusinian Mysteries.* Princeton, NJ: Princeton University Press, 1961.

5.123. Spaeth, B. S. *The Roman Goddess Ceres.* Austin: University of Texas, 1996.

5.124. Wasson, R. G., et al. *The Road to Eleusis: Unveiling the Secret of the Mysteries.* New York: Harcourt Brace Jovanovich, 1978.

Dionysus

5.125. Cavander, K. "The Dionysian Frenzy." *Horizon* 14, no. 2, (1972): 10–13.

5.126. Evans, A. *The God of Ecstasy: Sex-Roles and the Madness of Dionysos.* New York: St. Martin's, 1988.

5.127. Graf, F. "Dionysian and Orphic Eschatology: New Texts and Old Questions." In *Masks of Dionysus,* ed. by T. H. Carpenter and C. A. Faraone. Ithaca, NY: Cornell University Press, 1993.

5.128. Hutchinson, V. J. "The Cult of Dionysus/Bacchus in the Graeco-Roman World: New Light from Archaeological Studies." *Journal of Roman Archaeology* 4(1991): 222–230.

5.129. Nilsson, M. P. *The Dionysiac Mysteries of the Hellenistic and Roman Age.* Lund: Gleerup, 1957.

5.130. Otto, W. F. *Dionysus: Myth and Cultus.* Bloomington: Indiana University Press, 1965.

5.131. Zeitlin, F. I. "Cultic Models of the Female: Rites of Dionysus and Demeter." *Arethusa* 15(1982): 129–157.

The Orphic Cult

5.132. Paget, R. F. *In the Footsteps of Orpheus: The Story of the Finding and Identification of the Lost Entrance to Hades, the Oracle of the Dead, the River Styx and the Infernal Regions of the Greeks.* London: Hale, 1967.

The Great Mother

5.133. Abrahamsen, V. A. *Women and Worship at Philippi: Diana/Artemis and Other Cults in the Early Christian Era.* Portland, ME: Astarte Shell, 1995.

5.134. Brouwer, H. H. J. *Bona Dea: The Sources and a Description of the Cult.* Leiden: Brill, 1989.

5.135. Brown, R. E., et al. *Mary in the New Testament: A Collaborative Assessment by Protestant and Roman Catholic Scholars.* Mahwah, NJ: Paulist Press, 1978.

5.136. Corrington, G. P. "The Milk of Salvation: Redemption by the Mother in Late Antiquity and Early Christianity." *HThR* 82(1989): 393–420.

5.137. Gritz, S. H. *Paul, Women Teachers, and the Mother Goddess at Ephesus: A Study of 1 Timothy 2:9–15 in Light of the Religious and Cultural Milieu of the First Century.* Lanham, MD: University Press of America, 1991.

5.138. James, E. O. *The Cult of the Mother-Goddess: An Archaeological and Documentary Study.* New York: Praeger, 1958.

5.139. Jurkic, V. "The Cult of Magna Mater in the Region of Istria." *Ziva Antika* 2(1975): 285–298.

5.140. Kraemer, R. S. *Her Share of the Blessings: Women's Religions Among Pagans, Jews, and Christians in the Greco-Roman World.* New York: Oxford University Press, 1992.

5.141. Nassivera, J. C. "Ancient Temples to Pagan Goddesses and Early Churches to the Virgin in the City of Rome: A Topographical Survey." *EMC* 20(1976): 41–54.

5.142. Oster, R. "The Ephesian Artemis as an Opponent of Early Christianity." *JbAC* 19(1976): 24–44.

5.143. Pelikan, J. *Mary Through the Centuries: Her Place in the History of Culture.* New Haven, CT: Yale University Press, 1996.

5.144. Roller, L. E. "The Great Mother at Gordion: The Hellenization of an Anatolian Cult." *JHS* 111(1991): 128–143.

5.145. Sfameni Gasparro, G. *Soteriology and Mystic Aspects in the Cult of Cybele and Attis.* Leiden: Brill, 1985.

5.146. Thomas, G. "Magna Mater and Attis." *ANRW* II, 17, no.3 (1988): 1500–1535.

5.147. Vermaseren, M. J. *Cybele and Attis: The Myth and the Cult.* London: Thames & Hudson, 1977.

5.148. Versnel, H. S. "The Festival for Bona Dea and the Thesmophoria." *G&R* 39(1992): 31–55.

5.149. Warner, M. *Alone of All Her Sex: The Myth and Cult of the Virgin Mary.* New York: Knopf, 1976.

Isis

5.150. Griffiths, J. G. "Isis and 'the Love of the Gods.'" *JThS* 29(1978): 147–151.

5.151. ———. *The Origins of Osiris and His Cult.* Leiden: Brill, 1980.

5.152. Malina, B. J. "From Isis to Medjugorje: Why Apparitions?" *BTB* 20, no. 2, (1990): 76–84.

5.153. Tobin, V. A. "Isis and Demeter: Symbols of Divine Motherhood." *Journal of the American Research Center in Egypt* 28(1991): 187–200.

5.154. Witt, R. E. "Isis-Hellas." *PCPhS* 12(1966): 48–69.

5.155. ———. *Isis in the Graeco-Roman World.* Ithaca, NY: Cornell University Press, 1971.

Mithraism (and Christmas)

5.156. Beck, R. "The Mithras Cult as Association." *SR* 21(1992): 3–13.

5.157. ———. *Planetary Gods and Planetary Orders in the Mysteries of Mithras.* Leiden: Brill, 1988.

5.158. Betz, H. D. "The Mithras Inscriptions of Santa Prisca and the New Testament." In *Gesammelte Aufsätze, I: Hellenismus und Urchristentum.* Tübingen: Mohr, 1990: 72–91.

5.159. Brandon, S. G. F. "Mithraism and Its Challenge to Christianity." *HibJ* 53(1954–55): 107–114.

5.160. Campbell, L. A. *Mithraic Iconography and Ideology.* Leiden: Brill, 1968.

5.161. Cullmann, O. "The Origin of Christmas," in *The Early Church.* Philadelphia: Westminster Press, 1956: 21–36.

5.162. Cumont, F. *The Mysteries of Mithra.* New York: Dover, 1956 reprint.

5.163. Duthoy, R. *The Taurobolium: Its Evolution and Terminology.* Leiden: Brill, 1969.

5.164. Ferguson, J. "More About Mithras." *HibJ* 53(1954–55): 319–326.

5.165. Geden, A. S. *Mithraic Sources in English.* Hastings, UK: Chthonios, 1990; reprint of 1st ed., 1925.

5.166. Gordon, R. L. "Mithraism and Roman Society: Social Factors in the Explanation of Religious Change in the Roman Empire." *Religion* 2(1972): 92–121.

5.167. ———. "Reality, Evocation and Boundary in the Mysteries of Mithras." *JMS* 3(1980): 19–99.

5.168. Halsberghe, G. H. *The Cult of Sol Invictus.* Leiden: Brill, 1972.

5.169. Martin, L. H. "Roman Mithraism and Christianity." *Numen* 36(1989): 2–15.

5.170. North, J. D. "Astronomical Symbolism in the Mithraic Religion." *Centaurus* 33(1990): 115–148.

5.171. Roll, I. "The Mysteries of Mithras in the Roman Orient." *JMS* 2(1977): 53–68.

5.172. Rutter, J. B. "The Three Phases of the Taurobolium." *Phoenix* 22(1968): 226–249.

5.173. Swerdlow, N. M. "On the Cosmical Mysteries of Mithras." *CPh* 86(1991): 48–63.

5.174. Toynbee, J. M. C. "Still More About Mithras." *HibJ* 54(1955–56): 107–114.

5.175. Ulansey, D. *The Origins of the Mithraic Mysteries: Cosmology and Salvation in the Ancient World.* New York: Oxford University Press, 1989.

5.176. Vermaseren, M. J. *Mithras, the Secret God.* London: Chatto & Windus, 1963.

Christianity and the Mysteries

5.177. Maccoby, H. *Paul and Hellenism.* London: SCM, 1991.

5.178. Nobbs, A. "The Idea of Salvation: The Transition to Christianity as Seen in Some Early Papyri." In *The Idea of Salvation.* Ed. by D. W. Dockrill and R. G. Tanner. Auckland: University of Auckland, 1988: 59–63.

5.179. North, J. L. "Sowing and Reaping (Galatians 6:7B): More Examples of a Classical Maxim." *JThS* 43(1992): 523–527.

5.180. Price, C. P. "Mysteries and Sacraments." *AngThR, Suppl.,* 11(1990): 124–139.

5.181. Smith, J. Z. *Drudgery Divine: on the Comparison of Early Christianities and the Religions of Late Antiquity.* Chicago: University of Chicago Press, 1990.

5.182. Wagner, G. *Pauline Baptism and the Pagan Mysteries: The Problem of the Pauline Doctrine of Baptism in Romans 6:1–11 in the Light of Its Religio-Historical Parallels.* Edinburgh: Oliver & Boyd, 1967.

Gnosticism

5.183. Barrett, J. E. "Can Scholars Take the Virgin Birth Seriously?" *BibRev* 4, no. 5, (1988): 10–15, 29.

5.184. Bianchi, U., ed. *Selected Essays on Gnosticism, Dualism and Mysteriosophy.* Leiden: Brill, 1978.

5.185. Brown, R. E. *The Virginal Conception and Bodily Resurrection of Jesus.* New York: Paulist Press, 1973.

5.186. Brown, S. "Religious Imagination—Then and Now." *BibT* 29(1991): 237–241.

5.187. Churton, T. *The Gnostics.* London: Weidenfeld & Nicolson, 1990.

5.188. Cranfield, C. E. B. "Some Reflections on the Subject of the Virgin Birth." *ScotJTh* 41(1988): 177–189.

5.189. Dart, J. *The Laughing Savior: The Discovery and Significance of the Nag Hammadi Gnostic Library.* New York: Harper & Row, 1976.

5.190. Drummond, R. H. "Studies in Christian Gnosticism." *Religion in Life* 45(1976): 7–21.

5.191. Edwards, M. J. "New Discoveries and Gnosticism: Some Precautions." *Orientalia Christiana Periodica* 55(1989): 257–272.

5.192. Fisher, E. J. "Nag Hammadi and the Bible." *BibT* 20(1982): 226–232.

5.193. Fossum, J. "The Origin of the Gnostic Concept of the Demi-urge." *EphThL* 61(1985): 142–152.

5.194. Gager, J. G. "Marcion and Philosophy." *VigChr* 26(1972): 53–59.

5.195. Grant, M. "The Gods of Light and Darkness." *HT* 18(1968): 268–276.

5.196. Grant, R. M. "Early Christians and Gnostics in Graeco-Roman Society." In *The New Testament and Gnosis: Essays in Honor of Robert McL. Wilson.* Ed. by A. H. B. Logan and A. J. M. Wedderburn. Edinburgh: Clark, 1983: 176–183.

5.197. ———. *Gnosticism and Early Christianity.* New York: Columbia University Press, 1959; New York: Harper & Row, 1966.

5.198. ———. *Gnosticism: A Source Book of Heretical Writings from the Early Christian Period.* New York: Harper & Brothers, 1961.

5.199. Green, H. A. *The Economic and Social Origins of Gnosticism.* Atlanta: Scholars Press, 1985.

5.200. Gunther, J. J. "Syrian Christian Dualism." *VigChr* 25(1971): 81–93.

5.201. Hanratty, G. "The Early Gnostics, I." *IrTheolQ* 51(1985): 208–224.

5.202. ———. "The Early Gnostics, II." *IrTheolQ* 51(1985): 289–299.

5.203. Hartin, P. J. "Gnosticism and the New Testament." *TheolEvang* 9(1976): 131–146.

5.204. Hoffman, R. J. "How Then Know This Troublous Teacher? Further Reflections on Marcion and His Church." *SecCent* 6(1987–88): 173–191.

5.205. ———. *Marcion: On the Restitution of Christianity: An Essay on the Development of Radical Paulinist Theology in the Second Century.* Chico, CA: Scholars Press, 1984.

5.206. Lilla, S. R. C. *Clement of Alexandria: A Study in Christian Platonism and Gnosticism.* New York: Oxford University Press, 1971.

5.207. MacRae, G. W. "Why the Church Rejected Gnosticism." In *Jewish and Christian Self-Definition, 1: The Shaping of Christianity in the Second and Third Centuries.* Ed. by E. P. Sanders. London: SCM, 1980: 126–133.

5.208. May, G. "Marcion in Contemporary Views: Results and Open Questions." *SecCent* 6(1987–88): 129–151.

5.209. Nilsson, M. P. "The High God and the Mediator." *HThR* 56(1963): 101–120.

5.210. Pagels, E. H. *The Gnostic Paul: Gnostic Exegesis of the Pauline Letters.* Philadelphia: Fortress Press, 1975.

5.211. ———. "The Threat of the Gnostics." *New York Review of Books* 26, no. 17, (1979): 37–45.

5.212. Pearson, B. A. "Early Christianity and Gnosticism: A Review Essay." *RelStudRev* 13(1987): 1–8.

5.213. ———. *The Pneumatikos-Psychikos Terminology in 1 Corinthians: A Study in the Theology of the Corinthian Opponents of Paul and Its Relation to Gnosticism.* Missoula, MT: Society of Biblical Literature, 1973.

5.214. Pétrement, S. *A Separate God: The Christian Origins of Gnosticism.* Trans. by C. Harrison. San Francisco: Harper & Row, 1990.

5.215. Piper, O. A. "The Virgin Birth: The Meaning of the Gospel Accounts." *Interpretation* 18(1964): 132–148.

5.216. Quispel, G. "Gnosticism." In *Religions of Antiquity.* Ed. by R. M. Seltzer. New York: Macmillan, 1989: 259–271.

5.217. Robinson, J. M. "The Discovery of the Nag Hammadi Codices." *BiblArch* 42(1979): 206–224.

5.218. Rudolph, K. *Gnosis: The Nature and History of Gnosticism.* San Francisco: Harper & Row, 1983.

5.219. Schenke, H. M. "The Problem of Gnosis." *SecCent* 3(1983): 73–87.

5.220. Schmitals, W. *Paul and the Gnostics.* Nashville: Abingdon Press, 1972.

5.221. Schuessler, F. E. "Apocalyptic and Gnosis in the Book of Revelation and Paul." *JBL* 92(1973): 565–581.

5.222. Smith, M. *Clement of Alexandria and a Secret Gospel of Mark.* Cambridge, MA: Harvard University Press, 1973.

5.223. Talbert, C. H. "The Myth of a Descending-Ascending Redeemer in Mediterranean Antiquity." *NTS* 22(1976): 418–440.

5.224. van den Broek, R. "The Present State of Gnostic Studies." *VigChr* 37(1983): 41–71.

5.225. von Campenhausen, H. *The Virgin Birth in the Theology of the Ancient Church.* London: SCM, 1964.

5.226. Vouga, F. "The Johannine School: A Gnostic Tradition in Primitive Christianity?" *Biblica* 69(1988): 371–385.

5.227. Wilson, R. M. *The Gnostic Problem: A Study of the Relations Between Hellenistic Judaism and the Gnostic Heresy.* London: Benn, 1958.

5.228. ———. "Jewish Christianity and Gnosticism." *Recherches de science religieuse* 60(1972): 261–272.

5.229. ———. "Nag Hammadi and the New Testament." *NTS* 28(1982): 289–301.

5.230. ———. "Philo and Gnosticism." *StPhilon* 5(1993): 84–92.

5.231. ———. "Slippery Words II: Gnosis, Gnostic, Gnosticism." *ExposT* 89(1978): 296–301.

5.232. Wink, W. *Cracking the Gnostic Code: the Powers in Gnosticism.* Atlanta: Scholars Press, 1993.

5.233. Yamauchi, E. M. "Pre-Christian Gnosticism in the Nag Hammadi Texts?" *ChHist* 48(1979): 129–141.

5.234. ———. "Pre-Christian Gnosticism, the New Testament and Nag Hammadi in Recent Debate." *Themelios* 10(1994): 22–27.

"How Extremely Religious!"

5.235. Bleeker, C. J. "The Significance of the Religions of Antiquity." *Jaarbericht van het Voor-Aziatisch-Egyptish Genootschap Ex Oriente Lux* 17(1963): 249–252.

5.236. Colless, B. E. "Divine Education." *Numen* 17(1970): 118–142.

5.237. Ferguson, J. *The Religions of the Roman Empire.* Ithaca, NY: Cornell University Press, 1970.

5.238. Lee, P. "Worship, Ancient and Modern." *ExposT* 102(1991): 105–109.

5.239. MacMullen, R. *Paganism in the Roman Empire.* New Haven, CT: Yale University Press, 1981.

5.240. Nolland, J. "Christian Thought in the Greek World." *Crux* 16(1980): 9–12.

5.241. Rokeah, D. *Jews, Pagans and Christians in Conflict.* Leiden: Brill, 1982.

5.242. Simon, M. "Early Christianity and Pagan Thought: Confluences and Conflicts." *RelStud* 9(1973): 385–399.

5.243. Wiles, M. F. "The Central Concepts of Judaism, Graeco-Roman Paganism, and Christianity." *Didaskalos* 4(1973): 223–226.

GRECO-
ROMAN
PHILOSOPHY

The Greeks and Philosophy

IN THE HISTORY of intellectual achievement it's rare to know the name of the first person to accomplish something or the date when that person began to do it. We don't know who the first painter was, or the first mathematician, or the first person to devise an alphabetic symbol. Ancient people liked to be able to identify an individual who had inaugurated an activity or a custom (Gen. 10:8) because the inception of such a thing was supposed to be accompanied by certain religious rituals. If the origins of a thing were lost, how could they know if it had divine sanction? When they did not know when or by whom something was begun, they exercised their myth-making talents and created a name and a story, often deriving the character's name from his achievement, as Romulus takes his name from the city of Rome. We must, therefore, be wary when reading these foundation myths, whether of places, customs, or crafts.

But we do know with certainty who the first philosopher was. The ancient sources agree that he was Thales, a citizen of the Greek city of Miletus (located on the eastern coast of the Aegean Sea, in modern Turkey), and he began to publicize his ideas around 580 B.C. (**6.3**). His innovation was simply a non-mythic way of trying to explain the way the world around him functioned.

It has been suggested that the Greeks borrowed their basic approach to the discipline of philosophy from one of the older eastern cultures, such as the Egyptians (**6.6**) or the Hebrews (**6.7–8**). This idea was first suggested by Hellenistic Jews, who equated the legendary Greek poet-lawgiver Musaeus with Moses and made a philosopher out of Abraham (**6.4**). But there can be no doubt that the Greeks invented philosophy (**6.9**). Their aptitude for it perhaps arose from their "peculiar gifts . . . in which understanding and imagination, rational and instinctive forces were united in a fruitful combination" (**6.10**:35). The Athenians especially seem to have had an insatiable thirst for knowledge, which by New Testament times had degenerated into an obsession with novelty. The author of Acts ridicules them for their inquisitiveness: "Now all the Athenians and the foreigners living there would spend their time in nothing but telling or hearing something new" (Acts 17:21). Paul's speech was designed to take advantage of this thirst for new ideas (**6.168**).

The more prosaic Romans considered most philosophical debate a waste of time because nothing substantial seemed to come of it. It might be said that the Greeks would theorize endlessly about the perfect form of a bridge while the Romans were building perfectly functional bridges and marching over them to conquer the Mediterranean world. In fact, the Greeks, for all their philosophizing about the perfect state, never advanced beyond the concept of the small independent city-state, with a severely limited definition of citizenship. The Roman Empire was not philosophically perfect; some of its strongest opponents were a group of Stoic philosophers in the mid-first century A.D. But Rome, the "great Babylon," did manage to govern a disparate conglomeration of peoples spread from England to Armenia and back along the northern coast of Africa to Morocco, albeit with many abuses (Rev. 16–18).

The Classical Philosophical Schools

From about the fifth century B.C. on, the Greeks were able to trace schools of philosophy, one teacher attracting students who passed his ideas down to the next generation. Because this orderly progression was the norm in the late classical period, they assumed it must have been the same in the early days of philosophy. They often deduced connections among the earliest philosophers which in fact did not exist. The quotations which survive from the early philosophers may have been selected because they supported the positions of later writers, not because they accurately represent the thought of the person quoted. It is also difficult to assess the role women played in these early philosophical "schools." Several are mentioned, such as Diotima, a teacher of Socrates, but virtually nothing can be known of them with certainty (**6.11–12**). With these precautions in mind, let's look at some of the major philosophers.

The Pre-Socratics

Thales and the early Greek philosophers who came after him were what we would call natural scientists. They attempted to answer questions about the origin and functioning of the world without resorting to divine intervention. These pre-Socratic philosophers sought some basic element which would explain the make-up of the world in a rational, non-mythic way. Some thought the fundamental matter was water, others air, or earth, or fire. Empedocles decided it was a mixture of all four, drawn together by the creative power of *eros*-love, and torn apart by the destructive power of *eris*-strife (**6.20**; **6.24**). Democritus and Leucippus concluded that the answer lay in an even smaller particle of matter, the *atomos* (uncuttable), which combined with other atoms to make all forms of matter and which moved randomly through infinite space (**6.21**). Christian writers from the first through the eighteenth centuries tried to credit Moses with that idea (**6.27**).

In addition to identifying the basic stuff of the universe, the Greek philosophers also sought to answer the question of how and why (or if) things change. To the Greeks, striving for perfection in this as in other areas of life, change implied lack of perfection. Something which changed was either better or worse than it had been; it either had not been perfect or was no longer perfect. Some philosophers, such as Parmenides and Zeno of Elea and their Eleatic school, denied that change or motion (which is another form of change) actually happened. Logic could be used to show that change was an illusion. To do so, one must trust logic against sense perception, a step some Greek thinkers were willing to take, though it led to some paradoxical conclusions.

While their theories and techniques seem naive and nonscientific by modern standards, some of these thinkers came up with some surprisingly modern notions. Many of them thought that the material elements—from heavy earth to ethereal fire—were separated from a primordial mass by the vortex motion of the universe (**6.22**). The current scientific notion of a galaxy is a mass of stars moving in a spiral-vortex. The idea of a basic element of the universe is not too far removed from modern four-field theory in physics. Given the limitations of their outlook and the lack of modern scientific equipment, their accomplishments loom even larger than they might at first glance (**6.17**). Some connections between their thought and that of the early Christians can be established (**6.23**).

Anaximander (ca. 580 B.C.) taught that all forms of life had developed from primitive, fishlike creatures (**6.19**; **6.25**). Pythagoras (ca. 550 B.C.), who tried to express reality in terms of numbers or geometrical forms, believed the earth was a sphere; this idea came to be commonly held by the Greeks and Romans (**6.26**). At least one scholar has found points of contact between the thought of Jesus and that of Pythagoras as it was developed by his followers (**6.29**). Anaxagoras

(500–428 B.C.) suggested that the annual flooding of the Nile River was caused by snow melting on mountains in central Africa—a laughable idea at the time, since everybody thought they knew that the farther south you went in Egypt, the hotter it got. But nobody got to the source of the Nile until the nineteenth century, and they found that Anaxagoras had been right. He also explained the patterns on the moon's surface as caused by mountains and plains (**6.18**), another theory that had to wait until modern times for verification.

Socrates

Socrates (469–399 B.C.) began his career probing questions about nature. He soon became more interested in what we would call problems of ethics or human behavior and transformed philosophy into the study of humankind (**6.34**; **6.38**; **6.41**). To Socrates we also owe the development of the notion of the soul as an immortal part of human beings, something which continues to exist after the body dies (**6.37**). As noted in the last chapter, the Olympian cult paid no attention to the survival of individuals, and the mystery cults promised a pleasant afterlife only to their initiates. Socrates stressed that every person has this divine spark in him and that its survival as an intelligent entity is part of its nature.

Although atheism was one of the crimes for which he was eventually put to death, Socrates' thought has profound religious overtones, closer to monotheism than his contemporaries could appreciate (**6.33**). Most early Christians considered him a proto-Christian, and his asceticism and disdain for material things influenced Christian views on those subjects (**6.40**). This strain of his thought was picked up and exaggerated by the Cynics (see p. 175).

Like Jesus, Socrates wrote nothing that survived and ended his life an apparent failure. He is known to us at all because of the impression he made on his contemporaries, who praised or criticized him in their writings. The peculiar characteristic of his teaching was his insistence on the definition of terms. To judge from the writings of his pupil Plato (who admittedly was not writing a biography), Socrates felt it was of the utmost importance to achieve a precise definition of a term like "neighbor" or "justice" before one could talk about its significance.

Comparisons are sometimes drawn between Socrates and Jesus, but at this point Socrates resembles the Jewish scribes more than he does Jesus. This basic difference in attitudes stands out in Luke 10:25–37, the story of the good Samaritan. When the scribe asks Jesus, "Who is my neighbor?" he is trying to get him trapped into a definition of terms. Whatever definition Jesus might propose, the scribe could raise some objection and try to make the definition more precise or show the impossibility of defining it and thus refute Jesus. Refutation or elenchus (from *elenchos* in Greek) was Socrates' basic technique of argument (**6.42–43**). But by telling a story and then asking, "Who was the neighbor?" Jesus emphasizes that the important part of the commandment is the action prompted by love, not the definition of neighbor.

Love of fellow humans was not a familiar concept to Greco-Roman philosophers, or to the ordinary person in that culture. At best the philosophers strove for justice—Plato's *Republic* is a lengthy and unsuccessful effort to define the term—but even that quality is perceived as something needful for the benefit of the community, not the individual. Neither philosophy nor religion taught philanthropy or charity. What generosity we do find record of is usually self-serving, designed to enhance the donor's reputation or to obligate the recipient (cf Pliny, *Epp.* 1.8; 1.19; 2.4). One of the things about the early believers that most astounded their pagan neighbors was the Christians' willingness to minister to the poor and needy for no ulterior purpose (**6.36**).

Socrates' influence on Western thought should not be undervalued, however, because he did not inspire his society to rise to modern standards in certain areas. His legacy includes the insistence on precise definition of terms, the Socratic method of inquiry which elicits information by asking questions rather than stating things dogmatically (cf. Jesus' questions, "How do you read the Scriptures?" Luke 10:26, and "Who do men say that I am?" Mark 8:27) and the exalted concept of the nature of the soul. To some degree, all of his ideas had an impact on Christian thought in the first few centuries A.D.

Plato and Platonism

As a young man Plato (427–347 B.C.) had set out on a career as a playwright. When he heard Socrates teaching, according to ancient accounts, his eyes filled with tears. He tore up his plays and devoted himself to a life of philosophy. This kind of "conversion" experience is repeated in many biographical stories about the great philosophers. The phenomenon provides another example of the crossover between religion and philosophy from antiquity to modern times. We cannot conceive of a person being a Catholic and a Baptist simultaneously. The two groups teach mutually exclusive doctrines. One must convert wholeheartedly from one to the other. In antiquity that was the requirement with philosophical schools, not religious cults (**1.45**:92).

Plato began writing to set forth Socrates' doctrine, and his earliest dialogues probably reflect his master's teaching technique and his views with reasonable accuracy. Scholars disagree, however, over where Socrates ends and Plato begins (**6.48**). The emphasis in the earliest dialogues is on defining qualities such as holiness, justice, and self-control. Rather than pointing to persons who exemplify these qualities, Socrates/Plato tried to extract from all the examples the essence of the quality. As he matured, Plato developed his own system, which he then put into the mouth of Socrates as the main speaker in most of his dialogues. In the middle period of his life Plato's dialogues presented the concept of the Forms or Ideas, described briefly below. In the last stage of his life Plato turned to mathematics and logic to explain his ideas. The character Socrates no longer asks questions; in the late dialogues he becomes a lecturer. Some Socratic ideas, such as the immortality of the soul, Plato elaborated and passed on to later philosophical schools and to early Christian thinkers (**6.49**); his influence is discernible in Paul's letters (**6.61**).

One difficulty in knowing what Plato thought is that the dialogues may not represent the full exposition of his teaching. In a letter generally believed to come from him, he says that he had never written down the essentials of his doctrine. These were apparently taught orally to students in the Academy. Later generations could claim that almost anything they presented under Plato's name was based on this oral tradition.[1]

Even an introductory survey of Plato's work would require several volumes the size of this one; a number of scholars have provided guides for the nonspecialist (**6.52**; **6.57–58**; **6.62–63**). The essence of it is the notion that the only true knowledge is knowledge of the absolute, the unchanging. One cannot acquire such knowledge by studying the changeable things of the physical world. Each tree, for example, is different from every other tree, and they all change from day to day. How can one learn anything absolute about trees by studying samples which differ and change? The only suitable object of knowledge is the Idea or Form of a tree, or Treeness, which exists in the mind of God. For Plato the search for knowledge of the Forms becomes a search for knowledge of God (**6.55–56**). Philosophy thus becomes the contemplation of transcendent ideas, based on the study of mathematics and music (**6.51**). There is an element of inspiration in the philosopher's method, which can be likened to prophetic inspiration (**6.46**; **6.53–54**).

Plato was not, however, entirely an ivory-tower intellectual. He was invited to Syracuse by the tyrant Dionysius to set up a model state, governed by a philosopher-king. But the experiment ended with his expulsion by Dionysius after a few months (**6.47**; **6.67**). Plato returned to Athens and established his school, the Academy, on the outskirts of the city.

Just as Plato had built upon Socrates' teaching, so his own pupils created variations and modifications of his. The stages are distinct enough that they are referred to as the Middle or Second Academy and the New or Third Academy. By the late third century B.C. several heads of the Academy had turned it onto a path of Skepticism, the view that nothing can be known for certain. We can't even be sure that we don't know. By the first century A.D., Plato's teaching circulated in a form known as Middle Platonism, which combined some of Plato's ideas with Aristotle's logic, the ethics of the Stoics, and the religious mysticism of the Neopythagoreans. Contemplation of the Ideas was the path toward union of the soul with God. Philo, the Alexandrian Jewish philosopher and biblical exegete, is a prime example of this school (**6.73**). In his view, the God of Plato and the God of the Old Testament were the same, if the Old Testament was read in an allegorical sense. He was convinced that Plato had read the Torah and was simply explaining it in terms that Greeks could understand. Philo had little impact on Jewish thought, but he profoundly influenced later Christian writers such as Clement of Alexandria and Origen (**6.44**). By A.D. 200 Platonism had metamorphosed again into Neoplatonism (see p. 175).

Aristotle

Plato's pupil Aristotle (384–322 B.C.) stressed logic and reasoning rather more than Plato did. Aristotle was also more interested in observing animals and plants than his immediate predecessors were. Instead of reasoning from the Forms to the individuals, like Plato, he tried to group things according to similar characteristics and to derive some sense of the world's organization thereby. He wrote books not only on metaphysics, ethics, and political science, but also on the heavens, on the generation of animals, and on the parts of animals. Everything, he taught, had some ultimate reason or goal (*telos*) for its existence. (The brain, he thought, served only to cool the body.) As tutor to Alexander the Great, he might have had an opportunity to shape the conqueror's attitude toward government, but his influence is not discernible from what we know of Alexander.

Aristotle's work was little known in later antiquity, though his rhetorical theories appear to have had some impact (**6.78**). The Muslims "discovered" him when they conquered the eastern Roman Empire after A.D. 640. Aristotle's scientific outlook appealed to them much more than Plato's transcendentalism. They translated and commented upon his works, and those elaborations of his thought were passed on to the West after the Crusades. For Muslims and for medieval Christians Aristotle became "the philosopher."

Hellenistic Philosophy

The Academy and the Lyceum, the schools founded by Plato and Aristotle, continued to exist after the deaths of their masters, but other philosophical systems sprang up which gained greater popular acceptance and influenced the Romans to a far greater degree than either Plato or Aristotle. One measure of the importance of these schools in later antiquity can be found in the biographies of Diogenes Laertius (ca. A.D. 200). The three receiving the longest treatment are Plato, Zeno the Stoic, and Epicurus. And the biographies of Zeno and Epicurus are each half again as long as the account of Plato's life. The two major schools of the Hellenistic era— a term designating the time from Alexander the Great's death (323 B.C.) to the coming of the Roman Empire (31 B.C.)—are mentioned in Acts 17:18, where we read that "some Epicurean and Stoic philosophers" met Paul.

Both of these schools originated in the late fourth century B.C., during Alexander's reign. Both tried to offer some way of dealing with the sense of powerlessness, even despair, that many people felt as the various Greek city-states lost the independence which they had cherished for centuries and were welded into an empire which also encompassed non-Greek peoples from the Near East. The mood of the era was fatalistic, as Alexander's successors encouraged people to believe that they could not change what was happening in the world around them (**6.89–81**; **6.84**).

A sign of the mood of the Hellenistic era can be seen in the rising importance of the goddess Tyche or Fortune, who personified the vagaries of chance to which people of this period felt they were subject. An invading army could come along at any time, it seemed, or political alliances could shift for reasons the average person could not comprehend. As geographical boundaries expanded, so too did people's awareness of other cultures. The old certainty that a particular way of doing things was the only way and thus the right way was challenged by contact with new customs and ethical systems. The sense of insecurity and rootlessness which afflicted many people in this era made them receptive to any teacher who offered an explanation and at least the illusion of stability and inner peace. All the Hellenistic philosophical schools claimed that their adherents would be able to maintain their tranquility in the face of any of the upheavals which characterized the life of that time.

How much Christianity and Judaism were affected by this environment is still an open question. It can be argued that the influence was superficial, limited to vocabulary and imagery, and did not extend to essentials of doctrine (**1.43**). Others see extensive influence of Hellenistic philosophy on Judaism (**6.86–87**) and on various aspects of Christian thought (**6.82**; **6.88–89**).

Though we will examine the schools separately, we should remember that the prevailing tendency among Hellenistic philosophers was eclecticism, i. e., the borrowing of ideas and vocabulary from one another, even across the boundaries of the schools. It's not unusual to find the Stoic Seneca quoting Epicurus to prove a point, or Cicero, a follower of the Academy, citing a grab-bag of philosophical opinions in his dialogues.

Epicureanism

Epicurus (341–270 B.C.) attracted a small group of disciples to the garden of his home in Athens—whence the school is often called the philosophy of the Garden. His school was a close-knit community, secluded from the mainstream of Athens and therefore an object of suspicion. Women, even prostitutes, were accepted into membership. The group's sometimes licentious behavior earned it a reputation which has dogged the name through the centuries. Their devotion to Epicurus himself was as intense as the adoration bestowed on divinities. Numerous statues of Epicurus were created and were used, almost as cult images, in the propagation of the school's ideas. After his death no successor appeared, so his ideas did not undergo the kind of evolutionary development which altered the teachings of other philosophers. The Epicurean school was thus in one way the most conservative of all the philosophical schools.

Epicurean philosophy has been the most "generally and completely misrepresented" of all the ancient schools (Armstrong p. 130). It was not widely popular in its own day and enjoyed only a limited influence. Its avowed atheism made it an easy target for its intellectual opponents—who were numerous and highly vitriolic—and its reclusive, quietistic character aroused suspicion among the common people. One particular point of criticism seems to have been Epicurus' acceptance of women into his circle of friends. We find it difficult to evaluate his thought today because so much of his writing has perished. Diogenes Laertius says that Epicurus "eclipsed all before him in the number of his writings" and that his works contain no quotations from earlier thinkers; "it is Epicurus himself who speaks throughout" (*Epicurus* 26). His thirty-seven volumes *On Nature* formed the basis of his system. All that we have to judge him by are fragmentary quotations preserved in other writers and two letters to disciples of his. A third letter is generally considered the work of a disciple, though one which uses some of Epicurus' own words and accurately reflects his thought.

The basis of Epicurus' system is the idea that all existence is material, made up of atoms which are eternal and always in motion. This motion is not caused by any outside force, but arises from the natural weight of the atoms. Their downward motion is sometimes altered by "the swerve," an unpredictable sideways movement which causes one atom to collide with another. This seems to have been the only way Epicurus could introduce the concept of free will into an otherwise entirely mechanistic system of thought. People's actions are not predetermined because people are capable of swerving. In Epicurus' view, even the gods and the human soul were material. They were immortal simply because all matter is immortal, but this did not mean that they would always exist in their present form.

Epicurus taught that pleasure was the ultimate purpose of life (**6.93**; **6.106**). But by "pleasure" he did not mean self-indulgence. For Epicurus and his followers, pleasure was freedom from pain or disturbance, *ataraxia* (**6.99**; **6.110**). They achieved this by avoiding behavior or situations which might lead to pain or distress. They did not overeat or drink too much, to avoid the unpleasant consequences. Sexual relations were permissible, because of the pleasure they produced, but the emotional involvement of love was to be avoided because it brought with it the lover's agonies of uncertainty and the fear of losing the beloved (**6.90**).

Epicureans also did not involve themselves in political life because of the disappointment that could result from a lost election or the aggravation that went along with serving in an office.

The teachings of the school were spread, as were the tenets of other Hellenistic philosophers, by traveling teachers, who recruited members energetically and may have provided a model for Jewish and Christian missionaries (**6.97**; cf. Matt. 23:15; Acts). Plato's conversion to philosophy became the archetype for the intellectual enlightenment sought by the disciples of these itinerant philosophers (**6.103**).

Epicurus' theology and ethics attracted the most interest and criticism among Jews and Christians (**6.92**). He saw that the single greatest source of pain or disturbance in human life was the fear of what the gods could do to people during this life and the punishments that awaited evildoers in the next life. Basing his doctrine on the atomic theory of Democritus and Leucippus, Epicurus taught that all things, including the gods and the human soul, result from random combinations of atoms (**6.102**). Thus the gods cannot affect a person's life, nor can they punish or reward anyone after death (**6.95–96**). At death the atoms of the soul dissolve and begin their random motion again, along with all other atoms of the body (**6.101**; **6.104**; **6.107**).

His denial of the afterlife finds interesting echoes in the book of Ecclesiastes. Consider these two verses: "I commend enjoyment, for there is nothing better for people under the sun than to eat, and drink, and enjoy themselves" (Eccl. 8:15). "The living know that they will die, but the dead know nothing; they have no more reward, and even the memory of them is lost" (Eccl. 9:5). Some Old Testament scholars date this book to the third century B.C. and have found evidence of the author's awareness of Epicureanism, if not of its direct influence on him (**6.98**).

The Epicurean View of Creation

Granted that I don't know the ultimate origins of things, I would dare to affirm, from the way the world is organized, and to demonstrate from many other arguments, that no divine power created this world for us. So great are the flaws built into it. To begin with, a great part of what the sky covers is taken up by mountains and forests full of wild animals. Rocks and wide marshes cover some of it, and the sea which holds the shores far apart. Almost two-thirds of it is rendered useless for humans by burning heat and bitter cold. Of the land that is left, nature would cover it with weeds and thorns if it weren't for human resistance. We must constantly bend our backs to the hoe and turn over the soil with a heavy plow. Even then the plants which we do encourage to grow with such great labor are either scorched by the heat of the sun or nipped by rains and frost, or the blasts of the wind batter them to the ground.

Lucretius, *On the Nature of Things*
5.195–215

Epicureanism is essentially a passive philosophy. The teachings of its founder survive in a few letters and fragmentary quotations, such as the *Principal Doctrines*, three of which may sum up its basic points:

1. The blessed and immortal is not vexed itself, nor does it vex another. Therefore, it is not sensible to anger or favor, which are characteristic of weakness.

2. Death means nothing to us; something which has been dissolved feels nothing, and what has no sensation is of no concern to us.

3. By removing everything that causes pain we reach the boundary of pleasure. Wherever there is pleasure and for as long as it lasts, there is no suffering or grieving.

Contrary to the modern popular perception of it, his ethical system stressed simplicity and freedom from the desire of material goods (**6.90**). In one fragment Epicurus strikes a curiously New Testament note: "To love money unfairly gained is wrong, and to love money fairly gained is shameful" (cf. 1 Tim. 6:10).

Epicureanism was never as popular among the Romans as among the Greeks. In the last two centuries B.C., the Romans were too politically active and too busy acquiring an empire to be much interested in a philosophy that denied the validity of all they were doing. One Roman attracted to it, though, was the poet Lucretius (ca. 50 B.C.). His long poem *On the Nature of Things* attempted to present the Epicurean viewpoint to Latin readers. It's valuable to us because it preserves more of Epicurus' teaching than the surviving fragments of that philosopher's own writings (see box). Note the (unintended) parallel to the sentence handed down to Adam in Genesis 3:17–19. The church objected to this poem and the works of Epicurus because of their denial of divine providence and their lax morality. Yet many Christians found Epicurean arguments against the existence of the pagan gods to be useful in the defense of their own faith (**6.100**).

Stoicism

Virtually the only branch of Greek philosophy which did appeal to the Romans was Stoicism, perhaps because its austere doctrine exalted some of the virtues the Romans had long venerated, such as Justice and Harmony. Lacking any ethical base in their religion, the Romans had personified some of these qualities and built temples to them (**6.130**). The ground was prepared, in a sense, for the appearance in Rome of the first philosophers, a Platonist and a Stoic, in the early second century B.C. The younger generation received Greek philosophy with enthusiasm, but some xenophobic conservatives attempted to drive the philosophers back to Greece, so that Roman youths could give attention "to Roman laws and magistrates, as they used to" (Plutarch, *Cato the Elder* 22).

The founder of the Stoic school was Zeno, who first followed Crates the Cynic. Zeno's school was known as Stoicism because he originally taught in a stoa[2] (colonnade) in Athens. Zeno himself was a Semite, a native of the town of Citium, on Cyprus, and his doctrine can be compared to certain facets of Old Testament thought (**6.123**). Like Epicureanism, Stoicism took a passive, fatalistic view of life, though it did not counsel withdrawal from public life. The only thing that mattered, in Zeno's view, was virtue. Possessing that made one wise and therefore happy.

Zeno held that the gods, and above them Fate, governed everything that happened in the world (**6.143**). People could not change anything by their actions. The only hope for happiness, then, was to accept whatever happened as coming from the gods and not protest against it, not to "kick against the goads" (Acts 26:14), a phrase which appears in classical literature as well as the New Testament. Do not be too sad when misfortune comes your way, or too happy when you seem to be blessed. Neither state of affairs arises from anything you as an individual have done, and either of them can change in an instant (**6.114**; **6.125**; **6.127**). Just be thankful that "God has . . . given us the ability to bear whatever happens without being crushed or depressed," as Epictetus (A.D. 90) put it (cf. Phil. 4:11–13).

Zeno's writings have not survived, but his followers and critics give us a comprehensive view of Stoic philosophy. The Stoics seem to have been "voluminous writers, with generally speaking a highly unattractive style" (**6.1**:120). Their views on logic and physics are of little concern to one attempting to understand the background of the New Testament (**6.140**). They did hold that everything, even the human soul, is material and that matter is eternal. History is essentially a cycle. The world is periodically consumed in a flaming cataclysm and then regenerated again (cf. Matt. 19:28; 2 Peter 3:10–13), but always in exactly the same pattern. Something which occurs now has happened before and will happen again. Thus the future, either in this life or after it, is nothing to look forward to (**5.14**). Such a view is at odds with biblical salvation history (cf. Acts 13:16–47). It obviously limits the power of any divinity that one may believe in and makes human endeavor futile (**6.121**). Stoics also believed that everything in the universe, even evil, works toward a common goal (cf. Rom. 8:28). Also closely akin to Christian thought is the Stoic idea of natural revelation, the argument that God's existence and activity are evident in the workings of the universe. Paul's Areopagus speech in Acts 17:22–31 contains echoes of this Stoic theme (**6.124**; cf. Rom. 1:20).

Stoic ethics have more appeal to the modern mind, at least on the surface, and a certain kinship with points of Christian doctrine. The Stoics preached an ethic of "the life lived in accordance with nature," downplaying the value of material wealth (**6.116**; **6.132**). Seneca, for example, held that "good does not result from evil. But riches result from greed; therefore, riches are not a good." Believing that, however, did not prompt him to divest himself of his vast wealth, and he has often been accused of being a hypocrite (**6.136**; **6.138**; **6.147**). The true Stoic was to regard such things as "indifferent." Having them or not supposedly made no difference in one's quality of life. The call to pursue philosophy could bear a certain resemblance to Jesus' call to discipleship in Luke 9:59—10:4 or Luke 12:22–30 (see box).

To their credit, the Stoics did treat their slaves more humanely than did most Romans, because they realized that being a slave was an accident of birth or a result of some political or military misfortune over which the individual had no control. Anyone's luck could change, and one might find oneself a slave, or a slave could be freed and become a prominent citizen. Such turns of fortune were to be greeted with *apatheia*, indifference. Since such things were predetermined by the natural order of the universe, the only way to find happiness was not to resist. Stoic influence in this area led to an improvement in legal protection for slaves, who had originally been subject to the life-and-death power of their masters (**6.143**; **6.148**).

The occasional points of contact between Stoic and Christian ethics, especially in the work of Seneca, led to imagined connections between the two groups, as

A Call to the Life of Philosophy

If any obligation holds you back, loosen it, cut it. "Well," you say, "family business delays me. I want to arrange things so that I'll have enough when I become a philosopher, so that my poverty won't be a burden to me, or me to others." When you say this, you don't seem to realize the power and potential of the good which you're considering. . . . Trust me, call wisdom to your side. She will persuade you not to sit at your account books. No doubt, you hope by your delay to amass enough resources so that you won't have to fear poverty. But what if poverty is something to be desired? . . . If you want leisure for your soul, you must either be a pauper or live like one. Study is of no use unless you live simply, and living simply is voluntary poverty. Away with all your excuses. . . . This ideal, which you are deferring and placing after other things, should be sought after before anything else. You should start with it.

Therefore don't go after riches first. You can follow philosophy even without money for the journey. When you have everything else, then do you think you can find wisdom as well? Is philosophy to be the last necessity of life, a supplement, so to speak? No matter what you have now, devote yourself to philosophy. How do you know that what you already have isn't enough? Even if you have nothing, seek knowledge first, before anything else. . . . If the wise man truly has scanty means, he will do the best he can with them, and he won't be concerned or anxious about anything beyond the necessities.

Seneca, *Ep.* 37

noted in chapter 3. The thought of Cornutus, a freed slave of Seneca or his family, also resembles Christian thought at some points (**6.144**). There are subtle similarities to Christianity traceable in the writings of Musonius Rufus, who lived from A.D. 30–100 (**6.145**). Musonius and his son-in-law, also a Stoic sage, were known and much admired by Pliny (*Ep.* 3.11).

Perhaps the most noteworthy Stoic idea in terms of background to the New Testament is the school's concept of the reason or "Logos" which is evident in the orderly arrangement of the world (**6.111**). Just as converts brought trappings from the mystery cults into their new faith, so individuals coming from a Stoic background may have carried this element of the school over into their understanding of Christianity. But we cannot establish direct borrowings in either direction. No Stoic writer mentions the Christians by name. Marcus Aurelius, the philosophical emperor of the mid-second century, seems to allude to them in several passages in his *Meditations*, but never in a positive sense.

While Roman Stoicism produced no particularly original dogmas, it did build on Zeno's thought in two areas: dealing with death and grief, and the philosophy of government. Because it was fatalistic, it taught acceptance of death without fear. The soul does not cease to exist after death; it simply enters another stage of its existence. There is no reason for joy, still less for grief. Acceptance is the key (**6.113**; **6.117**; **6.137**). A popular form of Stoic literature is the *consolatio* written on the occasion of the death of a friend or loved one or some other tragic occurrence. Seneca's *Ad Marciam* and *Ad Helviam* are the two best examples of this genre (**6.132–133**).

The Roman Stoics came closest to originality in their conception of the philosopher's duty to advise and improve the government (**6.126**). Starting from the premise that a ruler is not ensconced in his position from any merit of his own but because inexorable fate has placed him there, they concluded that the ruler is no more important than a slave and has no more right to command or intimidate others than does a slave. It is the duty of subjects to obey and not resist, and it is the duty of rulers to rule justly (cf. Rom. 13:1–7). Not all rulers heard this message gladly. From time to time, especially late in the first century, the Stoics expressed firm opposition to the emperors. In an effort to improve the state, Domitian drove them out of Rome in A.D. 93, exiling some and executing others (**6.120**; **6.135**). In one of his letters, Pliny describes his efforts to stand by the victims (*Ep.* 3.11).

By the late first century, Stoicism had been reshaped by Musonius Rufus and his pupil, the former slave Epictetus (**6.115**). They stressed inner detachment from external problems and concerns and the potential divinity of the human soul. Since all people are assigned their lot by fate, and since they all are part of the world soul, "Epictetus knew only one single obligation: the general love of human beings. All human beings are brothers and sisters, which requires that they be treated with love and respect" (**1.37**, vol. 1:354). At this point in the development of Stoicism, we find the first inklings in any pagan religion or philosophy of the notion of a human conscience, a concern for other people simply because they are fellow beings (**6.134**). The short distance from that philosophy to the Christian ethic is easy to perceive (**6.112**; **6.129**; **6.142**).

The Cynics

Antisthenes is generally reckoned as the founder of this school, but its preeminent early practitioner was Diogenes (ca. 410–324 B.C.), who has been described as "Socrates gone mad" (**6.156**). The Cynics stressed Socrates' disdain for worldly goods, preaching what W. Durant has called the "simple and soapless life." The term Cynic comes from the Greek word for a dog. It may have been applied to the group derisively at first, as the label "Christian" was to Christ's followers. But the Cynics claimed to be the watchdogs of philosophy and turned the name into a source of pride (**6.160**).

For the Cynics happiness consisted in reaching a state of self-sufficiency, *autarkeia* in Greek (**6.149**). This was no easy task in the Hellenistic world, where a person who did not participate in the life of the community and share its values was likely to be despised. The Cynics steeled themselves to live with no more physical comforts than homeless people have today and to be ready to suffer abuse because of their refusal to conform to social conventions (**6.162**). Some of the abuse they drew on themselves by deliberately violating social norms (performing bodily functions in public, etc.). They presented their ideas to the public in what is called a *diatribe*, taking advantage of the Greek citizen's privilege of boldness of speech (**6.159**; cf. 1 Thess. 2:2).

By the first century A.D. a more moderate form of Cynicism had developed. The followers of this branch of the school lived in closer harmony with their communities but still tried to teach the relative unimportance of ephemeral, worldly goods. A few of them were advisors to important political figures of the era. The influence of the Cynics on Christian and Jewish thought is gaining new recognition (**6.152**). The earliest Christian monks may have had Cynic philosophers as their models (**6.153**).

Neopythagoreanism and Neoplatonism

Philosophical ideas associated with Pythagoras and Plato enjoyed a resurgence in the first century A.D. The developments that led to Neoplatonism have already been described briefly. The Pythagorean school had ceased to exist by 300 B.C.; its first-century revival taught many things, including a potpourri of Platonic dualism and demonology that would have astounded Pythagoras himself. It took over a number of ideas and some of its literature from the Orphic cult (p. 137).

Both of these movements lacked the formal organization of schools, and their adherents taught a wide range of ideas. An interest in mathematics, the Platonic doctrine of the Forms, and reincarnation (taught by both Pythagoras and Plato) was about all that linked them with the classical philosophers whose names they bore. They mixed religion, metaphysics, some astrology, and advice for daily living to produce religious movements that presented themselves as eclectic philosophies, not unlike the New Age movement of our day. Paul warns the Colossian church against such a combination of "philosophy and empty deceit" (Col. 2:8).

The prime example of a Neopythagorean teacher in New Testament times was Apollonius of Tyana, mentioned on page 131. He was credited with a miraculous birth, with the ability to exorcise demons and heal the sick, and with a teaching ability that amazed even the Brahmins of India. He traveled all over the Near East, accompanied by a few disciples. As already noted, the written account of his life is later than the Gospels and Acts, so we cannot be sure how much the picture of Apollonius is influenced by stories about Jesus and Paul, which were relatively well known by A.D. 200. Suffice it to say that the traveling philosopher-guru was a familiar figure in the first century (**6.164**; **6.167**; **6.169**).

Pliny records an encounter with one such man, a Syrian. His letter (*Ep.* 1.10) serves to show us how eagerly people received these itinerant teachers. Notice in the second paragraph that Pliny contrasts this man to the usually filthy, deliberately offensive Cynics.

> If our city has ever supported humane studies, they are certainly flourishing there now. I could give many outstanding examples, but one will suffice: the philosopher Euphrates. . . . Just as only an artist has the ability to judge painting, sculpture, and modeling, so no one can understand a philosopher except another philosopher. As much as I am able to judge, Euphrates has many exceptional and outstanding qualities which attract and edify even people who are only modestly educated. He argues subtly, with profundity and eloquence; he often displays a truly Platonic richness and breadth of learning. He can speak at length on a variety of topics and has a particular charm which draws a reluctant audience and persuades them.
>
> In addition he is tall and distinguished in appearance, with long hair and a long white beard. These attributes are his by chance and may seem trivial, but they win him a great deal of respect. There's nothing repulsive about his dress; his manner is austere without being gloomy, so that as soon as you meet him you admire rather than shun him. The sanctity of his life is equalled only by his kindness; he attacks faults, not persons, and does not chastise wrongdoers but corrects them. You would follow him as

he taught, hanging on every word, and you would want him to
continue persuading you after you've been persuaded.

One cannot help but think of Agrippa's reaction to Paul's preaching (in the KJV): "Almost thou persuadest me to be a Christian" (Acts
26:28).[3] Christian missionaries must have appeared to their pagan
audiences as another variety of the traveling philosopher. The message
they brought was not entirely alien, containing elements similar to the
mystery cults and philosophical schools of the day. And the Christians
took advantage of those similarities to make their message intelligible
to their hearers. We've already seen how Paul adapted mystery-cult terminology to fit his needs. He and John also appropriated the Logos
concept from the Stoics and turned it into a designation for Christ. In
his speech to the Athenians in Acts 17:22–31 Paul even quotes the
Phaenomena of Aratus, a poem popular in Stoic circles of the time
(**6.168**; **6.175**).

Christians and Philosophy

Not all Christians welcomed the cross-fertilization that went on
between Christianity and the philosophical schools during the first century (though all of our sources on the matter are second-century).
Tertullian, in the late second century, asked the question that became
the battle cry for those who wanted to keep Christianity free of
Hellenistic "contamination": *Quid ergo Athenis et Hierosolymis?* (What
does Athens have to do with Jerusalem?) He wanted to propound a
Christian theology totally devoid of cultural influences (**6.173**). The
majority of Christian thinkers, though, saw no reason to forfeit the
Greco-Roman tradition in which they had been reared and educated.
Many of these people came to Christianity as adult converts, with many
years of a non-Christian world view behind them. They saw a need for
diplomatic relations, or at least a cultural exchange, between Athens
and Jerusalem. They assimilated the two by interpreting the teaching
of the philosophical schools as early, imperfect versions of Christian
doctrine (**6.174**; **6.177**).

They were aided in this process by the fact that certain terms used
in the philosophical schools had been taken over by the church. As
noted in chapter 5, *heresy* had originally meant a difference of opinion
between philosophers. *Dogma* had also originated in philosophical circles, as had the related term *doxa* (opinion). If the philosophical
schools were using terms familiar in a Christian context and were talking about God (usually in the singular), it was easy for people without
a sense of historical-critical judgment to assume that they were talking
about the same things as the philosophers.

So close was the association between Christianity and the philosophical schools that by the second century some Christians were arguing

that Christianity deserved to be legitimized not as a religion but as a philosophy. It met all the criteria. It had a founder with a coterie of disciples, a code for daily living, and metaphysical and theological overtones. This argument was put forth most cogently by Justin Martyr, also called Justin the Philosopher. He says that he sought out first a Stoic teacher, then a Peripatetic (a follower of Aristotle) who was interested above all in his fee, then a Pythagorean, finally a Platonist, "so that in a short time I believed that I had become wise; such was my ignorance" (*Dialogue with Trypho* 2). Having found all those schools inadequate, he turned to the true philosophy, Christianity. Justin equates baptism to the moment of conversion to a philosophical school: "We call our washing 'enlightenment' because those who learn these things have their minds enlightened" (*First Apology* 61).

Clement of Alexandria summed up the Christian attitude toward philosophy as it had developed by A.D. 200: "By philosophy I don't mean the Stoic or Platonic school, or the Epicurean and Aristotelian, but whatever has been said correctly by any of the schools and whatever teaches righteousness along with wisdom combined with reverence; this eclectic body of learning is what I mean by philosophy" (*Stromata* 1.7; **6.165**).

Notes

1. Cf. what is said about oral traditions in Judaism in chapter 2. The Catholic Church also bases part of its dogma on teachings supposedly given orally to the apostles by Jesus (as in Acts 1:3) and then passed on to the bishops, the successors of the various apostles.

2. In John 5:2 this is the word translated as "porticoes," or covered porches.

3. The exact meaning, and best translation, of this passage is unclear. The RSV and other modern versions translate it in various ways.

BIBLIOGRAPHY

The Greeks and Philosophy

6.1. Armstrong, A. H. *An Introduction to Ancient Philosophy*. 3d ed. Totowa, NJ: Littlefield, Adams, 1981.

6.2. Bell, A. A., Jr., and J. B. Allis. *Resources in Ancient Philosophy: An Annotated Bibliography of Scholarship in English, 1965–1989*. Metuchen, NJ: Scarecrow Press, 1991.

6.3. Davies, C. "Thales of Miletus: The Beginnings of Greek Thought." *HT* 20(1970): 86–93.

6.4. Feldman, L. H. "Abraham the Greek Philosopher in Josephus." *TAPhA* 99(1968): 144–156.

6.5. Irwin, T. *A History of Western Philosophy, I: Classical Thought*. New York: Oxford University Press, 1989.

6.6. James, G. G. M. *Stolen Legacy: The Greeks Were Not the Authors of Greek Philosophy, But the People of North Africa, Commonly Called the Egyptians*. New York: Philos. Library, 1954.

6.7. Moorhead, J. "The Greeks, Pupils of the Hebrews." *Prudentia* 15(1983): 3–12.

6.8. Roth, N. "The 'Theft of Philosophy' by the Greeks from the Jews." *CF* 32(1978): 53–67.

6.9. Snell, B. *The Discovery of the Mind in Greek Philosophy and Literature*. New York: Dover, 1982 reprint.

6.10. Zeller, E. *Outlines of the History of Greek Philosophy*. Trans. by L. R. Palmer. 13th ed., rev. by W. Nestle. Cleveland: World, 1950.

The Classical Philosophical Schools

6.11. Levin, S. "Diotima's Visit and Service to Athens." *Grazer Beiträge* 3(1975): 223–240.

6.12. Menage, G. *The History of Women Philosophers*. Trans. by B. H. Zedler. Lanham, MD: University Press of America, 1984 reprint.

6.13. Waithe, M. E., ed. *A History of Women Philosophers, I: Ancient Women Philosophers, 600 B.C.–500 A.D.* Dordrecht: Nijhoff, 1987.

6.14. Wider, K. "Women Philosophers in the Ancient Greek World: Donning the Mantle." *Hypatia* 1(1986): 21–62.

The Pre-Socratics

6.15. Austin, S. "Parmenides and Ultimate Reality." *Ultimate Reality and Meaning* 7(1984): 220–232.

6.16. Baker, H. "Pythagoras of Samos." *Sewanee Review* 80(1972): 1–38.

6.17. Burnet, J. *Early Greek Philosophy*. New York: Macmillan, 1892.

6.18. Cleve, F. M. *The Philosophy of Anaxagoras*. The Hague: Nijhoff, 1973.

6.19. Davies, C. "Anaximander of Miletus." *HT* 20(1970): 263–269.

6.20. ———. "Empedocles of Acragas." *HT* 21(1971): 708–714.

6.21. de Ley, H. "Democritus and Leucippus: Two Notes on Ancient Atomism." *Antiquité classique* 27(1968): 620–633.

6.22. Ferguson, J. "Dinos." *Phronesis* 16(1971): 97–115.

6.23. Grant, R. M. "Early Christianity and Pre-Socratic Philosophy." in *Harry Austin Wolfson Jubilee Volume*. Jerusalem: American Academy for Jewish Research, 1965: 57–68.

6.24. Hershbell, J. "The Idea of Strife in Early Greek Thought." *Personalist* 55(1974): 205–215.

6.25. Loenen, J. H. "Was Anaximander an Evolutionist?" *Mnemosyne* 7(1954): 215–232.

6.26. Philip, J. A. *Pythagoras and Early Pythagoreanism*. Toronto: University of Toronto Press, 1966.

6.27. Sailor, D. B. "Moses and Atomism." *JHI* 25(1964): 3–16.

6.28. Salmon, W. C. *Zeno's Paradoxes*. Indianapolis: Bobbs-Merrill, 1970.

6.29. Schattenmann, J. "Jesus and Pythagoras." *Kairos* 21(1979): 215–220.

6.30. Smith, J. W. "Zeno's Paradoxes." *Explorations in Knowledge* 2(1985): 1–12.

6.31. Whyte, L. L. *Essay on Atomism: From Democritus to 1960*. London: Nelson, 1961.

Socrates

6.32. Annas, J. "The Heirs of Socrates." *Phronesis* 33(1988): 100–112.

6.33. Beckman, J. *The Religious Dimension of Socrates' Thought*. Waterloo, Ont.: Wilfred Laurier University Press, 1979.

6.34. Berland, K. J. H. "Bringing Philosophy Down from the Heavens: Socrates and the New Science." *JHI* 47(1974), 299–308.

6.35. Davies, C. "Socrates." *HT* 20(1970): 799–805.

6.36. Downey, G. "Who Is My Neighbor? The Greek and Roman Answer." *AngThR* 47(1965): 3–15.

6.37. Ehnmark, E. "Socrates and the Immortality of the Soul." *Eranos* 44(1946): 105–122.

6.38. Guthrie, W. K. C. *Socrates*. New York: Cambridge University Press, 1971.

6.39. Jackson, D. B. "The Prayers of Socrates." *Phronesis* 16(1971): 14–37

6.40. ———. "Socrates and Christianity." *CF* 31(1977): 189–206.

6.41. Taylor, A. E. *Socrates*. London: Macmillan, 1932.

6.42. Tejera, V. "The Socratic Elenchus." *JPh* 84(1982): 711–714.

6.43. Vlastos, G. "The Socratic Elenchus." *Oxford Studies in Ancient Philosophy* 1(1983): 27–58.

Plato and Platonism

6.44. Andresen, C. "The Integration of Platonism into Early Christian Theology." *StudPatr* 15(1984): 399–413.

6.45. Armstrong, A. H. "Greek Philosophy and Christianity." In *The Legacy of Greece: A New Appraisal*. Ed. by M. I. Finley. Oxford: Clarendon Press, 1981: 347–375.

6.46. Avni, A. "Inspiration in Plato and the Hebrew Prophets." *CompLit* 20(1968): 55–63.

6.47. Barker, E. *The Political Thought of Plato*. New York: Dover, 1960 reprint.

6.48. Baron, J. R. "On Separating the Socratic from the Platonic in *Phaedo* 118." *CPh* 70(1975): 268–269.

6.49. Bett, R. "Immortality and the Nature of the Soul in the *Phaedo*." *Phronesis* 31(1986): 1–26.

6.50. Bozonis, G. A. "Platonic Philosophy and Modern Thought." *Diotima* 2(1974): 181–201

6.51. Brumbaugh, R. S. *Plato's Mathematical Imagination: The Mathematical Passages in the Dialogues and Their Interpretation*. Bloomington: Indiana University Press, 1954.

6.52. Carrol, K. M. "Plato for the Uninitiated: An Account for Non-Classical Pupils." *G&R* 5(1958): 144–158.

6.53. Carter, R. E. "Plato and Inspiration." *JHPh* 5(1967): 111–121.

6.54. ———. "Plato and Mysticism." *Idealist Studies* 5(1975): 255–268.

6.55. Chen, C. H. "Plato's Theistic Teleology." *AngThR* 43(1961): 71–87.

6.56. Cicholas, P. "Plato, the Attic Moses? Some Patristic Reactions to Platonic Philosophy." *CW* 72(1978–79): 217–225.

6.57. Clegg, J. S. *The Structure of Plato's Philosophy*. London: Assoc. University Press, 1977.

6.58. Cushman, R. E. *Therapeia: Plato's Conception of Philosophy*. Chapel Hill: University of North Carolina Press, 1958.

6.59. Despland, M. *The Education of Desire: Plato and the Philosophy of Religion*. Toronto: University of Toronto Press, 1985.

6.60. de Vogel, C. J. "Platonism and Christianity: A Mere Antagonism or a Profound Common Ground?" *VigChr* 39(1985): 1–62.

6.61. Dillon, J. "Logos and Trinity: Patterns of Platonist Influence on Early Christianity." In *The Philosophy in Christianity*. Ed. by G. Vesev. New York: Cambridge University Press, 1989: 1–13.

6.62. Drake, H. L. *The People's Plato.* New York: Philosophical Library, 1958.
6.63. Grube, G. M. A. *Plato's Thought.* Boston: Beacon Press, 1958.
6.64. Hare, R. M. *Plato.* New York: Oxford University Press, 1982.
6.65. Havelock, E. A. *A Preface to Plato.* Oxford: Blackwell, 1962.
6.66. Jordan, N. *The Wisdom of Plato: An Attempt at an Outline.* Washington, DC: University Press of America, 1981.
6.67. Levy, G. R. *Plato in Sicily.* London: Faber, 1956.
6.68. Melling, D. J. *Understanding Plato.* New York: Oxford University Press, 1987.
6.69. Novotny, F. *The Posthumous Life of Plato.* The Hague: Nijhoff, 1977.
6.70. Patterson, R. *Plato on Immortality.* University Park: Pennsylvania State University Press, 1965.
6.71. Rist, J. M. *Platonism and Its Christian Heritage.* London: Variorum Reprints, 1985.
6.72. Rowe, C. J. *Plato.* New York: St. Martin's Press, 1984.
6.73. Sterling, G. E. "Platonizing Moses: Philo and Middle Platonism." *StudPhil* 5(1993): 96–111.

Aristotle

6.74. Adler, M. J. *Aristotle for Everybody: Difficult Thought Made Easy.* New York: Macmillan, 1978.
6.75. Edel, A. *Aristotle and His Philosophy.* Chapel Hill: University of North Carolina Press, 1982.
6.76. Ferguson, J. *Aristotle.* Boston: Twayne, 1972.
6.77. Lloyd, G. E. R. *Aristotle: The Growth and Structure of His Thought.* New York: Cambridge University Press, 1968.
6.78. Wallis, E. E. "Aristotelian Echoes in Luke's Discourse Structure." *Occasional Papers in Translation and Textlinguistics* 2(1988): 81–88.

Hellenistic Philosophy

6.79. Croy, N. C. "Hellenistic Philosophies and the Preaching of the Resurrection (Acts 17:18, 32)." *NovT* 39(1997): 21–39.
6.80. Festugiere, A. J. "Nature and Quietism in the Hellenistic Age." *Sileno* 1(1975): 125–141.
6.81. Jones, A. H. M. "The Hellenistic Age" *P&P* 27(1964): 3–22.
6.82. Krentz, E. "Roman Hellenism and Paul's Gospel." *BibT* 26(1988): 328–377.
6.83. Kristeller, P. O. *Greek Philosophers of the Hellenistic Age.* New York: Columbia University Press, 1993.
6.84. Long, A. A. *Hellenistic Philosophy: Stoics. Epicureans, Sceptics.* London: Duckworth, 1973.
6.85. Malherbe, A. J. "Hellenistic Moralists and the New Testament." *ANRW* II, 26,1 (1992): 287–293.
6.86. Neusner, J. *Judaism as Philosophy: The Method and Message of the Mishnah.* Columbia: University of South Carolina Press, 1991.
6.87. ———. "The Mishnah's Philosophical Method: The Judaism of Hierarchical Classification in Greco-Roman Context." *SecCent* 7(1989–90): 193–211.
6.88. Osborn, E. F. *The Beginning of Christian Philosophy.* New York: Cambridge University Press, 1981.
6.89. Seeley, D. *The Noble Death: Graeco-Roman Martyrology and Paul's Concept of Salvation.* Sheffield, UK: JSOT Press, 1990.

Epicureanism

6.90. Arkins, B. "Epicurus and Lucretius on Sex, Love, and Marriage." *Apeiron* 18(1984): 141–143.
6.91. Avotins, I. "Training in Frugality in Epicurus and Seneca." *Phoenix* 31(1977): 214–217.
6.92. Bastomsky, S. J. "The Talmudic View of Epicureanism." *Apeiron* 7(1973): 17–19.
6.93. Dewitt, N. W. *Epicurus and His Philosophy.* Minneapolis: University of Minnesota Press, 1954.

6.94. ———. *St. Paul and Epicurus*. Minneapolis: University of Minnesota Press, 1954.

6.95. Farrington, B. *The Faith of Epicurus*. London: Weidenfeld & Nicolson, 1967.

6.96. Festugiere, A. J. *Epicurus and His Gods*. Oxford: Blackwell, 1955.

6.97. Frischer, B. *The Sculpted Word: Epicureanism and Philosophical Recruitment in Ancient Greece*. Berkeley: University of California Press, 1982.

6.98. Gordis, R. *Koheleth, the Man and His World: A Study of Ecclesiastes*. New York: Schocken Books, 1968.

6.99. Hibler, R. W. *Happiness Through Tranquility: The School of Epicurus*. Lanham, MD: University Press of America, 1984.

6.100. Jungkuntz, R. P. "Christian Approval of Epicureanism." *ChHist* 31(1962): 279–293.

6.101. Kerferd, G. B. "Epicurus' Doctrine of the Soul." *Phronesis* 16(1971): 80–96.

6.102. Long, A. A. "Chance and Natural Law in Epicureanism." *Phronesis* 22(1977): 63–88.

6.103. MacMullen, R. "Two Types of Conversion to Early Christianity." *VigChr* 37(1983): 174–192.

6.104. Miller, F. D. "Epicurus on the Art of Dying." *SJPh* 14(1976): 169–177.

6.105. Obbink, D. "The Atheism of Epicurus." *GRBS* 30(1989): 187–223.

6.106. Panichas, G. A. *Epicurus*. New York: Twayne, 1967.

6.107. Rosenbaum, S. E. "How to Be Dead and Not Care: Defense of Epicurus." *AmPhQ* 23(1986): 217–225.

6.108. Sayers, B. "Death as a Loss." *Faith&Ph* 4(1987): 149–159.

6.109. Sedgwick, H. D. *The Art of Happiness, or the Teachings of Epicurus*. Freeport, NY: Books for Libraries Press, 1970 reprint.

6.110. Tsinorema, V. "The Concept of Pleasure in Epicurus' Moral Philosophy." *Diotima* 13(1985): 147–155.

Stoicism

6.111. Akinpelu, J. A. "'Logos' Doctrine in the Writings of Seneca." *CB* 44(1968): 3336.

6.112. Balch, D. L. "1 Corinthians 7:32–35 and Stoic Debates About Marriage, Anxiety and Distraction." *JBL* 102(1983): 429–439.

6.113. Boal, S. J. "Doing Battle with Grief: Seneca, *Dialogue* 6." *Hermathena* 116(1973): 44–51.

6.114. Bodunrin, P. O. "The Religion of the Ancient Stoics." *N&C* 11(1969): 17–25.

6.115. Bonforte, J. *The Philosophy of Epictetus*. New York: Philosophical Library, 1955.

6.116. Boylan, M. "Seneca and Moral Rights." *New Scholasticism* 53(1979): 362–374.

6.117. Caponigri, A. R. "Reason and Death: The Idea of Wisdom in Seneca." *PACPhA* 47(1968): 144–151.

6.118. Colish, M. L. "Stoicism and the New Testament: An Essay in Historiography." *ANRW* II, 26, 1(1992): 334–379.

6.119. DeSilva, D. A. "Paul and the Stoa: A Comparison." *JEvangThSoc* 38(1995): 549–564.

6.120. Devine, F. E. "Stoicism on the Best Regime." *JHI* 31(1970): 323–336.

6.121. Edelstein, L. *The Meaning of Stoicism*. Cambridge, MA: Harvard University Press, 1966.

6.122. Edwards, M. J. "Quoting Aratus." *ZNTW* 83(1992): 266–269.

6.123. Faj, A. "The Stoic Features of the Book of Jonah." *Apeiron* 12(1978): 34–64.

6.124. Gartner, B. *The Areopagus Speech and Natural Revelation*. Lund: Gleerup, 1955.

6.125. Gould, J. B. "The Stoic Conception of Fate." *JHI* 35(1974): 17–32.

6.126. Griffin, M. T. *Seneca, a Philosopher in Politics*. Oxford: Clarendon Press, 1976.

6.127. Inwood, B. *Ethics and Human Action in Early Stoicism*. Oxford: Clarendon Press, 1985.

6.128. Jaquette, J. L. "Paul, Epictetus, and Others on Indifference to Status." *CBQ* 56(1994): 68–80.

6.129. Lee, P. "'Conscience' in Romans 13:5" *Faith&Mission* 8(1990): 85–93.

6.130. Lind, L. R. "Roman Religious and Ethical Thought, Abstraction and Personification." *CJ* 69(1973): 108–119.

6.131. Long, A. A. "The Logical Basis of Stoic Ethics." *PAS* 71(1970–71): 85–104.

6.132. Manning, C. E. *On Seneca's* Ad Marciam. Leiden: Brill, 1981.

6.133 Mansfield, J. "Resurrection Added: The *Interpretatio Christiana* of a Stoic Doctrine." *VigChr* 37(1983): 218–233.

6.134. Marietta, D. E. "Conscience in Greek Stoicism." *Numen* 17(1970): 176–187.

6.135. Millar, F. "Epictetus and the Imperial Court." *JRS* 55(1965): 141–148.

6.136. Motto, A. L. "Seneca on Trial: The Case of the Opulent Stoic." *CJ* 61(1966): 254–258.

6.137. Nietmann, W. D. "Seneca on Death: The Courage to Be or Not to Be." *IntPhQ* 6(1966): 81–89.

6.138. Photiades, P. J. "A Profile of Seneca." *Orpheus* 9(1962): 53–57.

6.139. Rist, J. M. *Stoic Philosophy*. New York: Cambridge University Press, 1969.

6.140. Sambursky, S. *Physics of the Stoics*. London: Rutledge, 1959.

6.141. Sandbach, F. *The Stoics*. New York: Norton, 1975.

6.142. Sevenster, J. N. "Education or Conversion: Epictetus and the Gospels." *NovT* 8(1966): 247–262.

6.143. Shaw, B. D. "The Divine Economy: Stoicism as Ideology." *Latomus* 44(1985): 16–54.

6.144. van der Horst, P. W. "Cornutus and the New Testament." *NovT* 23(1981): 165–172.

6.145. ———. "Musonius Rufus and the New Testament." *NovT* 16(1974): 306–315.

6.146. Watts, W. "Seneca on Slavery." *DownRev* 90(1972): 183–195.

6.147. Wedeck, H. E. "The Question of Seneca's Wealth." *Latomus* 14(1955): 540–544.

6.148. ———. "Seneca's Humanitarianism: The Testimony of the *Epistulae morales*." *CJ* 50(1955): 319–320.

The Cynics

6.149. Brenk, F. E. "Old Wineskins Recycled: *Autarkeia* in I Timothy 6.5–10." *FNT* 3(1990): 39–52.

6.150. Crossan, J. D. "Open Healing and Open Eating: Jesus as a Jewish Cynic?" *BibRes* 36(1991): 6–18.

6.151. Downing, F. G. *Christ and the Cynics: Jesus and Other Radical Preachers in First-Century Tradition*. Sheffield, UK: JSOT Press, 1988.

6.152. ———. *Cynics and Christian Origins*. Edinburgh: Clark, 1992.

6.153. ———. "Cynics and Christians." *NTS* 30(1984): 584–593.

6.154. ———. *Jesus and the Threat of Freedom*. London: SCM Press, 1987.

6.155. ———. "Quite Like Q. A Genre for 'Q': The 'Lives' of Cynic Philosophers." *Biblica* 69(1988): 196–225.

6.156. Eddy, P. R. "Jesus as Diogenes? Reflections on the Cynic Jesus Thesis." *JBL* 115(1996): 449–469.

6.157. Luz, M. "A Description of the Greek Cynic in the Jerusalem Talmud." *JSJ* 20(1989): 49–60.

6.158. Malherbe, A. J. *The Cynic Epistles*. Missoula, MT: Scholars Press, 1977.

6.159. ———. "'Gentle as a Nurse': The Cynic Background to 1 Thessalonians ii." *NovT* 12(1970): 205–217.

6.160. Rankin, H. D. "Absolute Dog: The Life and Thought of Antisthenes." *PCA* 82(1985), 17–18.

6.161. Steiner, G. "Diogenes' Mouse and the Royal Dog: Conformity in Nonconformity." *CJ* 72(1976), 36–46.

6.162. Xenakis, J. "Hippies and Cynics." *Inquiry* 16(1973), 1–15.

Neopythagoreanism and Neoplatonism

6.163. Balch, D. L. "Neopythagorean Moralists and the New Testament Household Codes." *ANRW* II, 26, 1(1992): 380–411.

6.164. Campbell, F. W. G. *Apollonius of Tyana: A Study of His Life and Times*. Chicago: Argonaut, 1968.

6.165. Grant, R. M. "Early Alexandrian Christianity." *ChHist* 40(1971): 133–144.

6.166. Guthrie, W. K. C. *Orpheus and Greek Religion: A Study of the Orphic Movement*. London: Methuen, 1952; 2nd ed.

6.167. Harris, B. F. "Apollonius of Tyana: Fact and Fiction." *JRelHist* 5(1969): 189–199.

6.168. Marcus, J. "Paul at the Areopagus: Window on the Hellenistic World." *BTB* 18(1988): 143–148.

6.169. Mead, G. R. S. *Apollonius of Tyana: The Philosopher-Reformer of the First Century* A.D. New York: University Books, 1966.

6.170. Nilsson, M. P. "Early Orphism and Kindred Religious Movements." *HThR* 28(1935): 181–230.

6.171. Whittaker, J. "Plutarch, Platonism and Christianity." In *Neoplatonism and Early Christian Thought: Essays in Honour of A. H. Armstrong*. Ed. by H. J. Blumenthal and R. A. Markus. London: Variorum, 1981: 50–63.

Christians and Philosophy

6.172. Admas, M. M. "Philosophy and the Bible: The Areopagus Speech." *Faith&Ph* 9(1992): 135–150.

6.173. Ferguson, J. "Athens and Jerusalem." *RelStud* 8(1972): 1–13.

6.174. ———. "Stoicism, Epicureanism and Christianity." *Phrontisterion* 3(1964): 37–41.

6.175. Malherbe, A. J. "Paul: Hellenistic Philosopher or Christian Pastor?" *Proceedings of the American Theological Library Association* 39(1985): 86–98.

6.176. Timothy, H. B. *The Early Christian Apologists and Greek Philosophy Exemplified by Irenaeus, Tertullian and Clement of Alexandria*. Assen: Van Gorcum, 1973.

6.177. Weltin, E. G. *Athens and Jerusalem: An Interpretive Essay on Christianity and Classical Culture*. Decatur, GA: Scholars Press, 1987.

CHAPTER 7

THE
STRUCTURES
OF
GRECO-
ROMAN
SOCIETY

SOMEONE ONCE COMPLAINED that "historians give us the extraordinary events, and omit just what we want, the everyday life of each particular time and country." That complaint is certainly justified in the study of the New Testament. There's a great deal of scholarly discussion about Greek verb tenses or other such abstruse matters. At the other extreme, there is much preaching about the application of the message of the New Testament to modern life. Both of those facets of the study of the New Testament are important, but neither is a complete approach to the New Testament writings. Both examine the text in great detail, but too often neither pays enough attention to the context (see chapter 1). Both are greatly enhanced by knowing something about how people lived from day to day in New Testament times.

Thus far we've examined some larger issues—powers of government, religious practices, and intellectual outlook. In this chapter we'll look at matters pertaining to social status and family life. Unfortunately the New Testament writers didn't bother to fill us in on such things, any more than a modern novelist stops to explain the functions of a mayor or a senator if one of his characters happens to hold that position. The audience for whom the book is written knows what those positions involve. The original readers of the New Testament books had that kind of knowledge about the social classes and living situations of their day and didn't need commentary. Ovid says that there were poems written about how to play different types of ball games, how to swim, how to play with a hoop, rules for dinner parties, and other day-to-day matters (*Tristia* 2.485–490). None of them survive, largely because they weren't very interesting to people who knew those things and therefore didn't think they needed to make copies of them. Nor did they clutter their other works with explanations of things they could assume their readers knew.

When the author of Acts refers to Asiarchs (19:31), for example, he didn't have to stop and explain in a footnote what that term meant. We modern readers of that passage—and of many others—must look to sources outside the New Testament for information we need to understand many of the assumptions and casual references within its pages. In this chapter we'll examine the more formal aspects of social organization in New Testament times. In the next chapter we'll look at people's behavior and their relations with one another.

Social Classes

Society of the first century A.D. displayed a curious mixture of class consciousness and social mobility (**7.2**; **7.7**). A vast gulf separated the wealthy few from the poor masses, with only a relative handful of what might be called middle-class people, and those largely in the provinces. At the bottom of the social scale, as in any ancient society, were the slaves. We will examine this structure from the top down.

The Free Classes

From the earliest days of Rome, there had been two large classes of people: patricians and plebeians. Patricians were those whose ancestors had been in the senate at the time the Republic was founded (509 B.C.). Anyone not born into that class was a plebeian, no matter how wealthy one might become or what offices one might hold. At first all offices

A Roman food shop, selling poultry and vegetables
(Photo from Fototeca Unione)

were reserved for patricians, but as a result of pressure from the plebeians, the right to hold office and to marry into patrician families was gradually extended. The term *nobiles* came to be used to designate plebeian-born men who rose to hold high office and sit in the senate (**7.13**; **7.30**; **7.34**).

By the time Augustus became emperor, there were legally three groups of Roman citizens, in descending order: first, the senatorial class; second, the equestrians; third, the plebeians. Wealth was the basis on which one was placed into these classes. The magistrates known as censors kept tabs on everyone's financial assets (**7.24**; **7.50**). A total worth of 400,000 sesterces[1] qualified an individual for entry into the equestrians, so called because in Rome's early days they were plebeians wealthy enough to own a horse and ride into battle (**7.32**). Membership in the senatorial class required a million sesterces. The censors didn't care where the money came from. Pliny (*Ep.* 1.19) simply gave one of his friends 300,000 sesterces to qualify him for the equestrian class. A character in one of Martial's epigrams (4.67) had less luck begging an old friend for a loan of 100,000 sesterces to bring him up to the minimum.

The number of people in these top two classes was quite small. One scholar estimates that no more than two-thousandths of one percent of the Empire's population were of senatorial rank, while the equestrians totalled less than one-tenth of one percent (**7.39**). These were privileged classes in every sense of the word. They sat in the front rows in the theaters and arenas, with a wall separating their section from the rest of the seats (**7.16**). They were entitled to wear a purple stripe on their clothing, broad for the senators and narrow for the equestrians (**7.43**). This purple (actually closer to our scarlet) dye was expensive because of the difficulty of extracting it from seashells (**7.55**).

Loss of these ranks was a serious blow in a society where one's *dignitas* mattered almost as much as life itself. Martial, himself promoted to the equestrian class by the emperor Domitian, ridiculed men who tried to retain their seats in the equestrian section of a theater after they had been demoted from that order. The fact that he devoted five poems (5.8, 14, 23, 25, 38) to the subject suggests that it was an important topic for his audience. Paul seems to be suggesting in 2 Corinthians 10 that such concerns with social status need to be set aside (**7.21**).

In spite of what might appear to be a rigid class system, it was possible for a hard-working or unscrupulous person to make his way up the social ladder (**7.36**). In another poem, addressed to a freedman named Callistratus, Martial (5.13) points out that he himself is a famous writer (because of his talent), while Callistratus is inordinately wealthy: "You can't be what I am, but anyone of the common people can become what you are." This ability of lower-class people to rise to the equestrian order, and the order's prominence in business and civil service, may have contributed to the spread of Christianity across social boundaries (**7.27**).

The Romans relied on tribute from the provinces and levied no income taxes on citizens. There was little, if any, government regulation of business practices, beyond providing supervisors of the marketplaces (usually called aediles), whose job was to insure fair weights and measurements and protect against the most outrageous forms of price-gouging. Apuleius parodied the activities of such a magistrate (see box). Free of taxes and close regulation, an individual could acquire vast wealth in a short time. Slaves who were emancipated often used their contacts with their former master's friends and business associates to enrich themselves. Pliny describes a man named Macedo, a member of the senate and a former public magistrate, who was "a haughty and cruel master, who retained little memory—or perhaps too keen a memory—of his own father's status as a slave" (*Ep.* 3.14). Trimalchio, in Petronius' *Satyricon*, is a caricature of a freed slave who became so rich that he counts his own slaves in battalions and throws out a silver dish which a slave dropped. While most Romans were eager to take advantage of this mobility, some aristocrats, like Pliny, felt it was important to preserve distinctions between the classes (*Ep.* 9.15). Juvenal and others echo this snobbery (**7.19**; **7.42**).

In the provinces the wealthier people were called *decurions*, and they made up the councils which had oversight of local matters and collection of taxes. If the province was unable to supply the tax burden assigned it by Rome, the decurions had to make up the difference out of their own personal wealth. The Asiarchs who were friends of Paul (Acts 19:31) were members of this class. Although they were wealthy by local standards, property qualifications for decurions were about a tenth of those for senators and equestrians in Rome. The percentage of those who held such status in each province was not much higher than the percentage of equestrians in the population at large. Inscriptions reveal that some persons

---

Protecting the Consumer in Ancient Rome

[Leaving the marketplace, Lucius ran into Pythias, whom he had not seen in several years. They exchanged greetings.]

Pythias said, "I am in charge of the grain supply and am aedile. If you want anything, I'll be happy to help you."

"You're very kind," Lucius said, "but I've already purchased some fish for my dinner."

Pythias, when he saw the basket, shook it so that he could inspect the fish more carefully. "What did you pay for this garbage?" he demanded.

"I was finally able to bargain the fishmonger down to twenty denarii," Lucius replied.

When he heard that, Pythias grabbed Lucius by the arm and dragged him back into the marketplace. "From which one of these thieves did you buy these scraps?"

(Continued on page 189)

honored for civic benefactions—who had to be quite wealthy to make such donations—were Christians (**7.37**; **7.54**).

The group most conspicuous by its near absence from Greco-Roman society is a middle class of tradesmen and shopkeepers (**7.33**). The growth of such a class was checked by the nobility's reliance on slavery and the tendency of the lower classes to be content with hand-outs from the rich and a fairly low standard of living. The upper classes did not need to hire free laborers or go to shops to buy goods (**7.26**). Much of what they consumed was produced on their estates; services were provided by their numerous slaves, clients, or tenant farmers (**7.52–53**). At certain times, notably harvest or other special occasions, day laborers may have been hired (cf. Matt. 20:1–16), but such employment must have been sporadic and low-paying (**7.17**).

This does not mean that craftsmen and shopkeepers did not exist. In the large cities they certainly did, but they never achieved the kind of economic security or social respectability possible in those positions today (**7.18**; **7.38**). Manual labor was disdained by aristocratic Greeks and Romans and by those with pretensions to aristocracy; it was something that slaves and women did (**7.20**; **7.41**). Theorizing about scientific principles was a genteel, intellectual exercise; inventing something was for mechanics. Someone like Archimedes, who put his ideas to work, was rare (**7.22**; **7.25**; **7.40**). Paul took some risk in terms of social status by engaging in tent-making (**7.35**; cf. Acts 18:3; 20:34; 1 Cor. 4:12; 1 Thess. 2:9). Perhaps that's why he wanted his preaching to support him, but more likely he wanted the extra free time to proclaim the gospel (1 Cor. 9:14).

Roman senators were forbidden by law to engage in business; most dodged the restriction by having their slaves and freedmen run their enterprises (**7.29**). The only socially acceptable way to earn money was to own land, which could be farmed or rented out (**7.28**). Investment in overseas trade was not considered too disreputable as long as the senator did not conduct the business himself and as long as he made a

---

(Continued from page 188)

Lucius pointed at an old man sitting in a corner of the market.

With all the authority of his office, Pythias immediately began berating the old fellow in a very harsh tone of voice. "Is this how you treat visitors to our city, especially a friend of mine? How dare you charge twenty denarii for these wretched little minnows! If you drive food prices up like that, no one will be able to afford to live here, and our fair city will be deserted. You're not going to get off with just a warning, either."

He then dumped Lucius' fish on the ground and ordered one of his servants to trample them. Satisfied with the way he had fulfilled his duties, he turned to Lucius. "You can go along home now," he said. "I think the old scoundrel has been sufficiently punished."

Apuleius *Golden Ass* 1.24–25

lot of money at it. Marriage and inheritance were the preferred ways of passing large sums of money around in Rome.

Such attitudes produced a society which one scholar has described as having at the top "a quite minute but extraordinarily prominent and rich nobility; . . . at the bottom, a large mass of the totally indigent; . . . strung out between the extremes, a variety too heterogeneous to be called in any sense a middle class. . . . Great were the differences between the extremes" (**7.39**:93). Another scholar has calculated that by the first century A.D., the income of a moderately wealthy

Ancient bakery with mills, in Pompeii
(Photo by Howard Vos)

person would have been seven hundred times as great as that of a poor person, and the income of an extremely wealthy person would have been over 17,000 times that of a poor person (**7.14**). Such vast disparity between the rich and the poor created resentment which is reflected in the New Testament (**7.46**).

The poor in the Roman Empire survived by crowding into small apartments, taking advantage of free water available in fountains all over any town, and receiving a subsistence allowance of grain from the government (**7.23**; **7.44–45**). Maintaining the grain supply and the shows which distracted the populace (Juvenal's "bread and circuses") became a cornerstone of imperial policy (**7.15**). The lower classes almost certainly suffered from various kinds of dietary problems (**7.19**). Beggars are rarely mentioned in the literature, perhaps because philanthropy, either individual or corporate, was not part of the Greco-Roman social conscience, as noted earlier. The Romans instituted a system to support orphans only in the early second century A.D. Not even among non-Christian Jews is there clear evidence of organized charity before the destruction of the temple in A.D. 70, despite many prophetic cries

Food from Pompeii (Photo from Alinari/Art Resource, NY)

for justice to the poor and the high value placed on almsgiving.[2] The Talmud describes the collection and distribution of money and food for the poor, but the practice may have started in imitation of the Christians (**7.47**).

In general the Greeks and Romans felt no responsibility or sympathy for the poor. In the second century B.C. Polybius (31.25) summed up the Roman attitude toward charity: "No Roman willingly gives anything to anyone." The poverty of poor people was considered to be the will of the gods or the result of their own folly. As Juvenal put it, "What is worse than the mere fact of being poor is that it makes people the object of ridicule" (*Sat.* 3.151–152; cf. **7.42**). Most Romans would have agreed with Jesus that the poor will always be with us (Matt. 26:11), but they would have missed the poignancy of his observation and his deep-seated concern for the downtrodden (**7.31**; **7.49**). The suffering among this class of people went largely unrecorded but was none the less real (**7.51**).

Patrons and Clients

No society could survive for long with such vast and obvious inequities. The Romans had no thought of government intervention to redistribute the wealth. They contrived a system, however, whereby enough money trickled down from the top to keep the lower classes pacified. Each wealthy man was expected to act as patron/protector to as many lower-class people as he could reasonably support. In the early days of the Republic, this assistance took the form of legal help and financial assistance during illness or when a dowry was needed to marry off a daughter. In return, the client supported his patron in elections, did odd jobs for him, and escorted him through the streets, giving the patron's social standing a healthy boost.

By imperial times electoral support was no longer an issue, since elections took place in the senate. The patron-client system had become hereditary, though, and patrons continued to support clients as a measure of their status. Some nobles supported entire towns (**7.61**). The client was expected to provide noisy support for his patron whenever the latter went to court. Court cases were usually heard outside and, since secret ballots were not commonly used in the courts,[3] the jury could be swayed by a vociferous audience. Anyone who could afford a client or two considered it an investment. Even slaves in wealthy households are known to have had clients, who hoped that the slave would use his influence with his owner to secure favors for the client (**7.64**).

This relationship functioned as an informal welfare system, but it also reinforced the low opinion in which labor was held (**7.63**; **7.65**). An able-bodied man need not work as long as he had a patron. Each day he received from his patron a small sum of money for his daily expenses. On birthdays and other special occasions, he could anticipate a gift (**7.56**). Martial complains in some of his poems that his patron has been stingy with such gifts; he seems to regard them as a right. We also see in Martial's poems (3.36) that a client had little time to work because he was expected to attend his patron on his trips around town, even carrying his sedan chair through the muddy streets. This fundamental feature of Roman society seems to underlie several passages in the New Testament (**7.56–60**; **7.67**).

Slaves

Though at the bottom of the social scale, slaves were a numerous and important part of society in New Testament times. Roman slavery, however, differed in one important way from the institution which existed in the American South before the Civil War. In Rome, slaves and masters were of the same ethnic background and thus indistinguishable from one another (**7.82**). Seneca records that a proposal was once put forward in the senate to have slaves wear distinctive clothing, but when someone pointed out that the slaves could then see how numerous they were in comparison to the free population, the idea was quickly dropped (*De clementia* 1.24.1).

Emancipation, which was common, conferred citizenship (**7.75**). But even freed slaves continued to have obligations to their former masters, who became their patrons (**7.71**; **7.79**). In some ways a man was better off as a slave, since the free man had no one but himself and his family to care for him if he was sick or injured. A slave owner had money invested in his slaves and saw to it that they had medical care and sufficient food and housing. A free man could take none of those things for granted (**7.74**).

How slaves were treated in the first century A.D. varied with the individual master (**7.70**). Pliny claims to treat his slaves humanely, never working them in chains, allowing them to make wills, and sending one to a friend's villa on the French Riviera to recuperate from an illness. Pliny was probably an exception, though. Seneca criticizes the typical Roman master as thoughtless and cruel in his treatment of his slaves (*Ep.* 47), and anecdotes from other writers support the charge (**6.146**). Martial (2.66, 3.13) describes an aristocratic woman striking a slave girl who had not arranged her mistress's hair to suit her, and a man who cut out a slave's tongue and crucified him. The satirist Juvenal also comments on upper-class women who take out their anger at their husbands by beating their slaves (*Sat.* 6.475–485). The problem was common enough that the city of Athens provided a place of refuge where slaves could escape brutal treatment, though not slavery itself (**7.73**). The emperor Claudius passed laws limiting a master's right to punish or kill slaves, but in law the slave always remained a piece of property.

> ### Intercession for a Runaway
>
> You did well to take back into your heart and your home the freedman who was once dear to you, as I asked you to do in my letter. You'll be glad you did; I certainly am, first because I see that you're so ready to listen to advice and that you can be in control of yourself even when angry, and then because you have paid me such a great tribute by yielding to my authority or granting my request. And so I commend you and offer you thanks. At the same time I caution you that in future you stand ready to forgive the faults of your people, even if there's no one like me around to intercede for them.
>
> Pliny, *Ep.* 9.24

By the middle of the first century A.D., Stoic philosophy was widespread enough to bring about improvements in the condition of slaves because of its view that all persons are subject to fate and not responsible for their social status. Seneca (*Ep.* 47) professed to see no difference between the slave and the free person except an accident of birth or political misfortune (cf. Gal. 3:28). Anyone could become a slave if his country was conquered by another. There is thus no inborn inferiority in a slave. Aristotle, by contrast, had taught that some ethnic groups were by nature suited to be slaves (cf. **7.78**). Seneca claimed to allow his slaves to eat dinner with him as equals and to discuss important topics with them. Under the influence of Stoicism—and later of Christianity (**7.68**; **7.77**)—the Romans gradually came to acknowledge the humanness of their slaves (**7.69**; **7.81**). Christians did not advocate the abolition of slavery; such a notion would have been the equivalent of someone today campaigning for the prohibition of automobiles. Slaves were such an essential, fundamental part of society that no one of that day could have stood far enough outside the social structure to talk about doing away with the institution of slavery. What Christians did call for was an enlightened attitude toward slaves as fellow human beings (**7.68**; **7.76**).

Freedmen

However slaves were treated, they could, once freed, blend into the surroundings in a way that blacks were never able to do in the South. Pliny's friend Macedo had been able to rise to the pinnacle of Roman society from humble beginnings, achieving both wealth and status. Roman law provided that any child born to a slave after emancipation was a free person, without any legal stigma deriving from the father's former servitude. The poet Horace, son of a freedman, became a close friend of the emperor Augustus. The freed slave himself, though barred from holding office or advancing into the upper echelons of society, could achieve whatever financial success he was capable of in his own lifetime. If he lived long enough, he might see his children gain social respectability to complement their wealth. By the mid-first century A.D., even the restrictions against freedmen holding positions of power were crumbling, especially if the emperor was interested in advancing an individual's career, as Claudius did with his freedman Antonius Felix (**7.83**; see p. 77).

The freed slave continued to have obligations to his former master, now his patron. In some cases the freedman would still live in the master's house, especially if his wife was still a slave. A freedman might have nowhere else to go and few resources to fall back on. Little would change about his life except his legal status. In two letters that merit comparison with Paul's letter to Philemon, Pliny pleads with a friend to receive back into his fellowship a freedman who had offended his patron in some way (*Epp.* 9.21; 9.24; cf. box, p. 193).

Women

In Rome at this time, it remained true, as always in antiquity, that women did not count for much, quite literally. They were not included in census figures. Not even the New Testament writers were enlightened enough to count them. When describing the feeding of the five thousand, Matthew (14:21) concludes, "Those who ate were about five thousand men, besides women and children" (**7.112**). Roman women did not even bear individual names. Their names were simply feminine forms of their fathers' family name, as with Julia from Julius. If a man had more than one daughter, the second would be designated "Secunda," the third "Tertia," and so on. Or they might be designated as "Major" and "Minor," the elder and the younger.

Under the Empire women enjoyed greater social freedom than at any time before or since until this century. Many women ran businesses left to them when their husbands died (**7.106**), bought and sold property on their own (though this was not strictly legal until the emperor Claudius' reign), remained single because there was no particular pressure on them to marry, and in general lived what could be called a "liberated" life. As noted in chapter 4, women could even obtain Roman citizenship, although it did not allow them to vote or hold office. But, as Michael Grant (**7.105**:38) observes, "Though women could not hold office, they were traditionally influential, and the early empire produced some terrifying autocrats and termagants."

Women figured prominently in the social life of Rome. They enjoyed freedom of movement and socialization which was denied them in other ancient societies, particularly in Greece. Greek men considered women by nature intellectually inferior to men; the primary level of interaction between them was sexual (**7.104**). Greek women of the citizen class were typically excluded from social functions (**7.93**). Roman men shared the Greeks' opinion to a degree, so women never enjoyed political rights in Rome, but their opportunities for education and social activity were greater in Rome than in Greece (**7.87**; **7.92**). Some religious cults, such as those of Dionysus and the Bona Dea, were primarily or exclusively for women (**7.114**); their rituals allowed the women an opportunity to be out from under the domination of men for a few days.

Greco-Roman women lived under the protection of their fathers until they were handed over to their husbands. If the husband and father both

---

The Ideal Roman Wife

[My wife] has the greatest intelligence and just as great skill at running the house. She loves me, which is an indication of her purity. To these qualities she adds a love of literature, which arises from her love of me. She keeps copies of my writings at hand and even memorizes them. When I am arguing a case in court, she is anxious until she learns the verdict. She arranges for messengers to tell her what sort of reception I got and whether I won the case. When I read one of my compositions, she sits nearby, shielded by a curtain, and eagerly drinks in my applause. She sets my poetry to music and sings it, accompanying herself on the lyre. Her only teacher is love, the best of all masters.

For these reasons I have the most certain hope that our harmony will increase each day and will last forever. For she does not love me for my age or physical appearance, which will slowly change, but for my fame.

Pliny, *Ep.* 4.19

died, the closest male relative became the woman's guardian. Throughout their lives, they had the legal status of children (**7.85**; **7.95**; **7.111**). In Cicero's words, "Our ancestors made it a rule that women, because of their weak intellects, should have guardians to take care of them" (*Pro Murena* 12.27). That may have been the legal situation, but in actual fact Roman women were educated, ate and conversed with their husbands and guests, and often ran family businesses when their husbands were unable to do so (**7.103**). Cicero's wife had properties, including an apartment building, which were part of her dowry; in addition she managed her husband's financial affairs while he was in exile. Ovid pays frequent and lengthy tribute to the way his wife handled their affairs and kept pressing his case for recall while he was exiled to Tomis (*Tristia* 4.3).

In spite of women's apparent "liberation," we need to be reminded that men of the first century A.D. never ceased to regard them as second-class persons, always in need of education and toleration and always defined in relation to a man, preferably a husband (see box, p. 195). The considerable difference in age that typically existed between husband and wife helped foster such attitudes as Pliny displays. For a man of the first century A.D., marrying a wife was more like adopting a daughter.

The list of noteworthy Roman women is long, from Lucretia, who inspired the overthrow of Rome's last king; to Cornelia, mother of the Gracchus brothers (reformers of the late Republic); and on to the women of the imperial family, most notably Livia and the two Agrippinas (**7.88**; **7.98**). Nor should one forget Domitilla, the emperor Domitian's cousin, who may have been a Christian and who was sent into exile when her husband was executed. Pliny also mentions several womem whom he admires for their brave deeds or inspiring words (*Epp.* 3.16; 6.24; 7.19, cf. **7.97**). We should also recall those two nameless deaconesses whom Pliny tortured to get information about the Christians in Bithynia (see chapter 4). There must have been large numbers of women who played such active roles in Roman society at that time. Their diminished role in surviving records of the period may be a function, first, of who produced those records (upper-class males) and, secondly, of what has survived.

Because they weren't bound to the house the way Greek women were, Roman women seem not to have been content to play mother and homemaker. They gradually assumed a freer place in society (**7.90**; **7.101**). By Augustus' day, women reclined on couches at dinner beside their husbands instead of sitting by their feet or on chairs. As noted earlier, the emperor Claudius (A.D. 41–54) enacted legislation allowing women to inherit property and own businesses in their own names. The owner of Rome's largest apartment house in the second century was a woman (**7.109**).

Not everyone was comfortable with the freedom which women enjoyed by the mid-first century A.D. To many it appeared license, and there is no denying that Roman women conducted themselves as aggressively as women ever have in any era before our own (**7.84**; **7.100**; **7.117**; **7.119**). Roman men, once the emperors rendered them politically impotent, could only try to salvage a few scraps of power by urging women to be subject to their husbands; "that's the only way woman and man become equals" (Martial 8.12). That sentiment is common in the New Testament epistles, yet with notes of mutuality and the husband owing the wife love and conjugal rights (1 Cor. 7:2–5; 11:3, 11–12; Eph. 5:21–33; Col. 3:18–19; 1 Tim. 2:11–12; 1 Peter 3:1–8; cf. **7.86**; **7.89**; **7.107**; **7.115**; **7.122**). Under Roman law, women outside Palestine could sue for divorce, as shown by Mark 10:12 and 1 Corinthians 7:13 (see chapter 8).

In Domitian's time (A.D. 81–96) it became the custom for men and women to bathe together in the public baths in Rome, and some evidence suggests that this practice was copied in other cities (see chapter 8). By 100, women had cast off almost all the old social conventions and were asserting their equality with men, taking part in court cases (Juvenal, *Sat.* 6.242–245; cf. **7.94**; **7.110**; **7.116**) and composing literary pieces (Pliny, *Ep.* 1.16). Unfortunately, they also rivaled men in less admirable ways, such as gorging themselves at banquets and engaging in athletic contests, even as gladiators in the arena (Juvenal, *Sat.* 6.246–267; Petronius, *Satyr.* 45), though it should be pointed out that some scholars believe these last passages are literary exaggerations (**7.99**).[4]

Daily Schedule

The pattern by which a people organize their daily lives reveals much about their attitudes toward life and their values. Our modern nine-to-five routine stresses the importance of putting in a full day's work. A two-hour lunch is regarded as almost sinful, unless it's a working lunch. Such a schedule also implies that the hours before and after work time are private. Many of us work only five days a week. Anything beyond those hours is "overtime," above and beyond the call of duty and deserving of extra pay. We are always aware of time, seldom away from a clock or watch for more than a few minutes. In the summer we arbitrarily change our timepieces to create more daylight in the evenings.

The ancients did not manipulate the day the way we do. They followed a more primitive—or natural—schedule of rising with the sun, resting in the early afternoon when the day was warmest, then resuming activities in the late afternoon before retiring fairly early at night, a pattern still familiar in most countries around the Mediterranean. David Dinges, a psychologist at the University of Pennsylvania School of Medicine, has concluded from his research that most people experience "a measurable lull in their level of alertness" between 1:00 and 4:00 p.m. The Romans' daily schedule was structured to allow for a break at precisely that time.

By the first century A.D. this pattern of daily life was well established all around the Roman Empire (**7.123–125**). Martial (4.8) describes a typical Roman day:

> The first and second hours wear out clients greeting their patrons; the lawyers are getting hoarse by the third hour; till the end of the fifth hour Rome works at its various tasks; the sixth offers rest to the weary; the seventh will be the end. From the eighth to the ninth hour the oiled wrestlers take the fore; the ninth bids us throw ourselves upon the beautifully adorned couches.

This all becomes clearer when one reckons from about 6:00 a.m. as the first hour. Most lower-class Romans had wealthy patrons on whom they were expected to call at daybreak, when everybody in Rome got up, to pay their respects and receive a small sum of money to help them through the day; this process was known as the *salutatio*. Courts and other public offices were open only in the mornings. Any business not presented by the fifth hour (about 11:00 o'clock) had to be held for the next day. This pattern held true across the Empire. The NRSV note to Acts 19:9 reports from some manuscripts that Paul taught in Ephesus "in the lecture hall of a certain Tyrannus, from the fifth hour [11:00 a.m.] to the tenth [4:00 p.m.]," i. e., during the midday hours after Tyrannus had finished his business for the day.[5] People must have been interested enough in what Paul had to say to skip lunch and the siesta, or perhaps they drifted in and out during that time.

By noon everyone was ready for lunch and a nap. A bit of exercise and a bath in the afternoon preceded dinner, which could begin as early as three. People expected either to entertain guests or to be invited out, but it wasn't safe to be on the streets of Rome long after dark. Dinner parties had to break up early, so they had to start rather early (Pliny, *Ep.* 3.12; Suetonius, *Domitian* 21). On holidays, whether regular or specially decreed by the emperor, games and theatrical shows would fill the day.

The daily schedule might have been different on a farm or in a rural village—especially at planting and harvest time (**7.126–128**; cf. Matt. 20:1–16), but urban life in the provinces would have differed only in degree from Martial's description. The workday began early, the afternoon and early evening were reserved for relaxation, and everyone tried to be safe in their homes shortly after dark. That much was constant across the Empire. The Jews may have eaten dinner a little later than the Romans, perhaps because they didn't have to worry about getting mugged on the way home or because their dinners weren't as elaborate. The late dinner described in Acts 20:7–8 would have struck most Greeks and Romans as out of the ordinary, even suspicious.

Meals

The evening meal was the major event of the day in the Mediterranean world (**7.132**). Breakfast was usually a bit of bread and water, whatever happened to be left from the previous evening's dinner. Grain—wheat, oats, or barley (for the poor)—was the staple of the ancient diet (**7.134**; **7.136**). Government policy often hinged on the necessity of securing an adequate supply (**7.135**; **7.139**). Lunch was also meager. In towns across the Empire there were "taverns," small shops where people could get a bite to eat and a drink. Excavations have shown that there was often no room to sit in these places, so we can assume that people in the first century A.D. were familiar with the notion of "fast food."

By late afternoon, then, the average person of New Testament times was ready for a substantial meal. The Greeks had developed their evening meal into an elegant party called a *symposium*, at which musicians entertained and the guests engaged in conversation on a topic chosen by a master of ceremonies. The Romans refined the preparation and serving of such a meal to an art, and they made a significant social occasion of it.

Securing an invitation to dinner was a prime objective for anyone with any social pretensions. Wealthy men invited to their dinners large numbers of friends, clients, and social parasites, usually sending out invitations like the rich man in Matthew 22:1–14. A few dinner invitations survive among the scraps of papyrus documents discovered over the years in Egypt. They were probably carried by servants and read to the guests (**7.137**). Other guests might be invited on an impulse during the day. Anyone able to do favors for the host or enjoying current celebrity status was assured of free meals (**7.131**). That's probably why Jesus was invited to the home of Simon the Pharisee (Luke 7:36–50).

This process of wangling an invitation to dinner occupied much of a lower-class person's day, to judge from the number of poems Martial devotes to it. Those who issued invitations wanted to show how important they were by the quality of the people who dined with them, or they expected dinner to lead to something else. They also expected their guests to reciprocate (Luke 14:12–14). Martial has unkind things to say about people who repeatedly find excuses for not fulfilling this obligation.

We have a detailed and riotously funny description of a dinner party in Petronius' "Dinner of Trimalchio," the major surviving portion of the *Satyricon*. After some exercise and a bath, the guests take their places on couches in Trimalchio's dining room, have their hands washed and their toenails trimmed by slaves, and enjoy course after course of elaborate dishes, most of them prepared to impress rather than nourish the guests. It was expected that guests would eat everything that was put before them. If necessary, it was socially acceptable to excuse oneself, go to the bathroom and induce vomiting to empty the stomach, then come back to enjoy the rest of the meal.[6]

Gold lamp found in Pompeii
(Photo by Howard Vos)

There is still in existence a Roman recipe book, attributed to Apicius, which tells how to prepare the *garum* sauce[7] that the Romans globbed on most of their meat dishes to cover the salty taste resulting from the way they preserved foods (**7.130**; **7.133**). The gourmet will also find recipes for stuffed sows' udders, baked snails, and other such delicacies. One noteworthy dish is white bread, with the crusts trimmed, dipped in a mixture of eggs and milk, fried, and covered with honey. "French" toast, indeed!

A frequent complaint about the food at these dinners is that distinctions were made among the guests in regard to the quality of food served. Sometimes those reclining near the host, or at his table if several tables were set up, were treated to elegant dishes, while less honored guests at the other tables were served second-rate fare. Much of Juvenal's fifth satire is taken up with a complaint against this kind of stingy patron, e. g.: "He soaks his fish in the best olive oil; you get some pale cabbage reeking of stuff that would smell fine in a lantern." Pliny explains that people sometimes made these distinctions as a sort of false economy. He prefers to keep expenses down by serving the same moderate menu to all his guests (*Ep.* 2.6). Such distinctions among those at the dinner may have been part of the reason for the dissension among the Corinthians (cf. **7.129**).

People who know nothing of the ancient world think they know that Roman dinners were drunken orgies. That popular notion is not entirely inaccurate. Even the potluck dinners at the church in Corinth got a bit rowdy (1 Cor. 11:21; cf. **7.138**). But the fact that most people perceive the Romans to have been engaged in such things regularly is another case of the most extreme examples of behavior drawing all the attention. Most lower-class Romans never got within ogling distance of an orgy, just as the average person in Los Angeles never gets invited to a wild Hollywood party.

Many upper-class Romans abhorred such excesses. The dinner parties of the emperor Titus, "were pleasant rather than elaborate" (Suetonius, *Titus* 7.2). His brother Domitian also took a puritanical approach: "He gave dinners frequently and generously, but almost hurriedly. They never went on past sunset, nor did he hold drinking bouts afterwards" (Suetonius, *Dom.* 21). In reply to a friend who had written complaining of having to attend a riotous dinner, Pliny sanctimoniously pointed out that "I certainly don't give that kind of dinner" (*Ep.* 9.17). He preferred a dinner that was "simple, informal, abounding only in Socratic conversation" (*Ep.* 3.12). But some Romans would have considered Pliny a wet blanket because they found nothing wrong with what we would call an orgy.

One of Ovid's poems (*Amores* 1.4) can serve as an example of what might happen at a dinner party. The poet is addressing his mistress, whose husband has fouled up their plans by deciding to come to the dinner. Ovid says he'll be in agony, reclining on a couch opposite them, watching her husband reclining next to her, fondling her in ways which American couples reserve for their most private moments:

> Don't let him put his arms around your neck; don't lay your sweet head on his rough chest. Don't let his nimble fingers slide under your gown to touch your breasts. Above all, don't let him kiss you. And if you kiss him, I'll reveal myself as your lover, take your hand, and say, "She's mine." I guess I can watch these things, but the acts that your cloak hides so well, those will be a reason for my blind fear.

This last sentence indicates, incredible as it may seem, Ovid's dread that his mistress and her husband would actually make love on the couch during dinner. He goes on to say that he has made love to Corinna under her *pallia*, the long outer cloak which women wore. He begs her not to wear it to this dinner party, so there will be no possibility of her doing the same thing with her husband. We know from other sources that such a thing was not unheard of.

The activities which Ovid describes were made possible, even encouraged, by the fact that the Romans ate while reclining on couches, on the left elbow and reaching for food and drink with the right hand. This was an old custom borrowed from the Greeks, who seem to have picked it up from Asia Minor. It was regarded as a symbol of luxury. Those who

"lounge on their couches" are condemned in Amos 6:4. This manner
of eating required that one have a large enough house to contain a sizable dining room (outdoor eating areas were also fashionable) and servants to bring in the food and clear the tables. The food had to be cut
into bite-sized portions, since the guests could not use knives from this
position and forks had not yet been invented. A Roman dining room
was called a *triclinium* because three people reclined together on a
couch and three couches were normally arranged around a table in the
following manner:

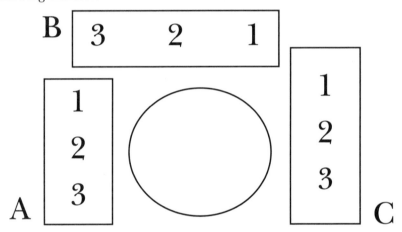

Couch A would be occupied by the host and his wife or any other
family members present; B and C were reserved for guests. Position 3
on couch B was the "head of the table," the place reserved for the most
honored guest (Martial 6.74: "he who reclines lowest on the middle
couch"); position A1 would be taken by the host. In early Rome,
women sat by their husbands' feet or on chairs, but by Jesus' day, they
reclined along with the men. With larger couches, as many as eighteen
people could eat from one table. If there were more guests than could
be accommodated at one table, other tables and couches would be set
up (**7.142**).

Everyone in that day knew which positions were assigned the most
status. One of the guests in Petronius' *Satyricon* (70) was offended when
Trimalchio impetuously invited the cook to join the party, and the
cook—a servant—took a place "above" the guest. It would obviously be
extremely embarrassing to someone to think that he was one of the
more important personages at a dinner and take one of the "higher"
positions, then be asked to move to one that was lower in terms of
social status. His gaffe would be immediately apparent to everyone.
This social practice is what underlies Jesus' advice (Luke 14:7-14) that,
when invited to a dinner, one should not take the seat of honor: "When
you are invited, go and sit down [*recline* in Greek] at the lowest place,
so that when your host comes, he may say to you, 'Friend, move up
higher.'"

What Jesus says in this passage only makes sense if the people to whom he was speaking were accustomed to eating like the Greeks and Romans. There is ample evidence in the New Testament and other sources that at least wealthy Jews of the first century A.D. had adopted the habit of reclining on couches to eat. Even those who did not regularly eat in this manner would have been familiar with the practice.

Another dinner party is depicted in Luke 7:36–50, at the home of Simon the Pharisee. During the meal a woman bathed Jesus' feet with her tears and dried them with her hair. The KJV and RSV both describe Jesus as "sitting at table in the Pharisee's house" and the woman as "standing behind him at his feet." But if Jesus was sitting up in a chair, how could the woman have been standing behind him at his feet? Must one imagine a terribly awkward scene like this one from a children's Bible story book?

But this is nonsense. Jesus was reclining on a couch. That's what is said by the Greek verb used here, and the translators of the NIV are to be commended for translating it accurately. This meant that his feet were protruding behind him, so the woman would have had no difficulty tending to him.

It would have been easy for the woman to slip into the house unnoticed because the other guests had their servants with them. The number of people milling around in the house would have been considerable. Servants normally stood behind their masters, ready to attend to their needs (even bringing them chamberpots during dinner, according to Martial 6.89), to accompany them home, and to carry leftovers from the meal. Guests were expected to bring their own napkins to a meal and were free to take reasonable amounts of food home with them. Martial (2.37) complains about a guest who swept practically everything off the table and passed it back to his servant. "If you have any shame," the poet says, "put it back. I didn't invite you to dinner tomorrow."

We should also envision Jesus and his disciples reclining at the Last Supper. Mark 14:15 and Luke 22:12 specify that the place where they shared the meal was "a large room upstairs," so there would have been space for couches and a table. Several common Greek words used in the New Testament mean "to recline (at table)." The most frequently used (in various compounds) is *keimai*, which means "to lie down":

anakeimai: Matt. 9:10; 22:10–11; 26:7, 20; Mark 6:26; 14:18; 16:14; Luke 22:27 (twice); John 6:11; 12:2; 13:23 (discussed in chapter 1); 13:28

katakeimai: Mark 2:15; 14:3; Luke 5:29; 7:37; 1 Cor. 8:10

sunanakeimai: Matt. 9:10; 14:9; Mark 2:15; 6:22; Luke 7:49; 14:10, 15

The root *pipto* means "to fall," so the verb *anapipto* might be something like "to throw oneself down," or "to flop down." We probably won't see it translated that way in any published version of the New Testament:

anapipto: Matt. 15:35; Mark 6:40; 8:6; Luke 11:37; 14:10; 17:7; 22:14; John 6:10 (twice); 13:12, 25; 21:20; and frequently in pagan literature

A third verb is *klino* and its compounds. This means "to lean" or "to recline" and is used only by Luke:

kataklino: Luke 7:36; 9:14–15; 14:8; 24:30

If someone was reclining next to Jesus, we can conclude that Jesus was not occupying the position of honor. A glance at the diagram on page 202 will show that the person in position B3 could not have had someone reclining "close" to his "breast," as in John 13:23 (RSV). But Jesus was the host for this dinner, acting as head of the family for a traditional Jewish seder meal, and would have taken position A1. John, the beloved disciple (cf. 20:2), would have been in position A2. None of the synoptic Gospels provides much detail, but according to John 13:24 (RSV), Peter "beckoned" to the disciple next to Jesus and urged him to ask Jesus the identity of his betrayer. Was Peter in position A3, able to converse quietly with John? Or was he across the table, on couch C, so that he needed hand signals to get John's attention? Jesus handed the piece of dipped bread to Judas, which he could have done easily only if Judas was in the other spot close to him, B3, the position of honor!

Many Jews, then, reclined at the table, like the Greeks and Romans. Even when they were not in the presence of Romans and were celebrating the most ancient of Jewish rituals, a group of devout Jews like Jesus and his disciples chose that manner of eating instead of the more typical

Near Eastern habit of sitting on the floor. Hellenization affected the serving of the Passover meal and the conversation that went on during it. It came to resemble "to some extent the symposium of the Greeks: it was eaten in a reclining position, and was the setting for important discourses on a set theme" (**7.140**:810).

If the Jews modified things so basic as their eating pattern and the observance of the Passover, we must be safe in concluding that they were also influenced by other facets of the Greco-Roman lifestyle. By the time we get into Acts and Paul's letters, the cultural background is Roman, not Jewish, and much of what we know about the Roman manner of living can be applied directly to the New Testament.

Housing and Urban Life

All over the ancient world, housing varied from simple dwellings for the poor to the elaborate mansions of the wealthier classes. The size and arrangement of dwellings in any ancient city, however, were influenced by the crowding that characterized all urban life of that time (**7.156–157**; **7.160–161**). These cities had originally been confined within defensive walls. Luxuries such as yards and public parks had no place when living space was so severely restricted. Houses and shops were jammed up next to one another, sharing walls, like row houses in modern cities. One would find open space with grass and a few trees only in connection with a temple or public bath, or in a park donated by a civic-minded aristocrat (Pliny, *Ep.* 9.39).

The quality of life in a large city of the time was wretched for all but the very richest inhabitants. The constant noise and the difficulty of sleeping in rooms that were hot in summer and cold in winter seem to have kept people's nerves on edge. Police forces didn't exist, so people had to protect themselves as best they could, though burglars seem not to have been deterred by the inadequte security devices of the day. Violence was epidemic because it was usually the only recourse one had to righting wrongs one had suffered. And if the city was dangerous during the day, it became an absolute no-man's land by night. Juvenal says that only a fool would go out after dark without having his will up-to-date: "This is freedom for a poor man; after being beaten and cut up by an attacker's blows, he begs and pleads to be allowed to go home with a few teeth left" (*Sat.* 3.299–301). The citizens of any ancient city would certainly have been in sympathy with America's "Take Back the Night" movement.

In Rome (as in modern Manhattan), because of the expense of land in the capital city, the average person lived in a large apartment house, usually shabbily built and poorly maintained by a landlord looking for exorbitant profits on his investment (**7.154–155**). Fire was an ever-present and usually lethal threat. Before Augustus' time, Rome had no fire-fighting force. The best Augustus could institute was a system of night watchmen who were supposed to wake people up and form bucket brigades (**7.151**; **7.156**). Juvenal pities the poor man on the top floor of a tenement (see box).

The crowding in the cities made filth a major problem. Large towns of the Roman Empire had the most advanced sewage systems in the ancient world, but most of the homes weren't hooked up to them. Homes of the wealthy usually had stone-lined latrines, emptied periodically. Waste was used as fertilizer. The main purpose of the sewers was to handle the runoff from heavy rains. Public latrines were provided and were cleaned out by leather-tanners and cloth-bleachers, who needed uric acid as a raw material in their processes.[8]

Many people seem to have been unwilling to use the public latrines at inconvenient times. They resorted to chamberpots, which then had to be emptied. Landlords were required to keep slop jars in the halls of their buildings, but few did. Most people disposed of their waste by dumping it out a window. Juvenal says that having a chamberpot emptied on one's head was a minor inconvenience compared to being hit by a brick falling from a decrepit building (*Sat.* 3.270–275). Other types of garbage were also tossed into the streets and alleys of the city, where—theoretically—rain would eventually wash them into the sewers (**7.146**).

Poor Housing for the Poor

We live in a city propped up, for the most part, on slender reeds. The landlord may stand in front of the building, even as it's falling down, and cover up a crack in the ancient wall. Then he'll tell you to sleep soundly, though the building is about to collapse. It's better to live out where there are no fires, no reason to be afraid at night. Here one neighbor is calling for water while another bundles his shabby goods to safety. The third floor – your abode – is already smoking, but you don't know it. If an alarm is sounded on the lower floors, you'll be the last to burn, up there where only the tiles protect you from the rain and where the gentle doves cover their eggs.

Juvenal, *Satire* 3.193–203

Smaller cities, which did not have such luxuries as sewers, had major health problems. Pliny (*Ep.* 10.98) described a town in his province of Bithynia as "elegant and well laid out," but right through the middle of its main street "runs something called a stream, which is actually an extremely foul sewer. It is disgusting to look at and is unhealthy because of the odor which it emits." He proposed, and Trajan approved, covering the stream to make a proper sewer.

We know from census lists that there were only about a thousand private homes in Rome, compared to over 14,000 apartment buildings (**7.158**). Even tradesmen and shopkeepers, like Priscilla and Aquila, could not afford to own a private house. Their "house" (Rom. 16:5) was, in all likelihood, an apartment, perhaps one which took up most or all of one floor of a building. The ground floors of these large apartment buildings were given over to shops. Priscilla and Aquila probably had a shop in the building where they lived, if they did not live in a portion of the shop itself. A typical apartment had three rooms: a large central living room, a dining room, and a bedroom (**7.159**). This, and not some luxurious villa, is likely to have been the sort of "house" in which the earliest Christian groups gathered (**7.145**; **7.147–148**).

In other towns in Italy, like Pompeii and Herculaneum, apartment houses are also found, though none so large as those in Rome. Beginning in the second century B.C., under the influence of Greek city planners, these large apartment houses became common in the Near East, as did luxurious private homes similar to those in Greece and Italy. In the words of archaeologist H. K. Beebe, "The impact of Greek culture upon the people of Palestine was stunning" (**7.169**:91). Remote villages may have escaped Hellenization, but "city life was revolutionized."

Archaeologists in Palestine have traditionally given more attention, Beebe says, to "fortifications of cities, the palaces of kings and governors, the complexities of temples," and other such grandiose edifices (**7.169**:89). Until recently "little attention has been given to how ordinary people lived in biblical days." That situation is changing, and the results show that life in Judea in the first century A.D. was little different from anywhere else in the Roman Empire.

Remains of several apartment buildings have been found in Judea. Many lower-class people, however, continued to live in small, one- or two-room houses, usually with flat roofs because so little rain fell. The roof served some of the functions of the garden in a wealthy person's house, allowing the family to get fresh air and sunshine without standing in the street. On muggy nights people would even sleep on their roofs (cf. Mark 13:15). But there were also large, expensive homes in Judea, with running water, bathrooms, and large dining rooms, as the New Testament clearly shows and as recent archaeological finds confirm (**7.153**; **7.163**). Such houses would require large numbers of servants (Mark 13:34).

The first reference to a house in the New Testament is in the Christmas story as recorded by Matthew. Contrary to the popular image of the wise men (**3.176**; the number three is nowhere mentioned[9]), kneeling before the babe in the manger, surrounded by oxen and sheep, Matthew 2:11 says, "On entering the *house*, they saw the child with Mary his mother."

In Matthew 5:15, Jesus seems to have a small house in mind. He says that no one "after lighting a lamp puts it under the bushel basket, but on the lampstand, and it gives light to all in the house." Many of the people to whom he spoke probably lived in homes which could be lighted by a single lamp. Peter's house in Capernaum—which archaeologists think they have actually found (**7.167**)—seems to have been small, since people had to crowd around the door while they waited on Jesus (Mark 1:33).

Jesus also mingled with people on the other end of the social scale. We've already seen that Simon the Pharisee could accommodate a large dinner party in his home. One day Jesus went to the house of Jairus to heal his daughter and found flute players and mourners (probably hired) making a racket. "When the crowd had been put outside, he went in and took her by the hand, and the girl got up" (Matt. 9:23–26). In both these cases, we should envision rather large houses, not unlike those we can visit today in Pompeii and Herculaneum.

We actually have in the Gospels a couple of clues to the size of Jesus' own house. It's clear in Mark 2:1–2 that the evangelist has Jesus' house in mind. It was large enough that "many" could gather, but eventually the crowd got too numerous even for a house of that size. In Mark 2:15 we see Jesus having dinner "in his house." Whether it was his or Matthew's is not entirely clear from the Greek *his* (see NRSV note), but the inference that it was Jesus' house is more natural, though not all scholars would agree with that conclusion (**7.162**). It must have been a fairly large house since "many tax collectors and sinners were also reclining with Jesus and his disciples" (NRSV note). The disciples by themselves would have made a good-sized dinner party, especially when we recall that the term *disciple* applies to any of his followers, not just the twelve.

The likelihood that Jesus—or at least his family—owned a large home should not surprise us. Joseph had been a builder, likely a general contractor rather than a mere carpenter, and undoubtedly had built his family a comfortable home. The Greek word *tekton*, used in Mark 6:3 to describe Joseph, means someone who builds with wood and stone (**7.143**). Jesus likely followed the same trade, because he knew about planning and financing buildings (Luke 14:28–30). Paul says he was "rich" when he began his ministry, then "became poor" because of it (2 Cor. 8:9). The concept of Jesus as a homeless, itinerant preacher may have been read back too widely into the Gospel texts under the influence of the monastic movement, beginning in the fourth century A.D. Yet according to one tradition (Matt. 8:20; cf. Luke 9:58), Jesus as the Son of Man did experience rejection and homelessness at a later stage of his career.

Most of the other references to houses in the Gospels are too vague to allow us to determine anything about their size. In Acts, however, we find several references to what must have been rather sizable homes. On the day of Pentecost, "They were all together in one place" when a sound like wind "filled the entire house where they were sitting" (2:1–2). If the first *all* refers to the whole company of Christians, then there were a hundred and twenty people in that house (cf. 1:15). If, however, it was just all the apostles, there would have been twelve. The phrase "all the house" or "the entire house" does seem to suggest a dwelling of some size. Yet, since a crowd soon gathers, it might mean a portico of the temple, where they later meet (Acts 3:11; 7:49 calls the temple a "house").

The homes of Cornelius the centurion and Simon the tanner undoubtedly reflected their power or economic prosperity. Simon's must have been built in the Jewish fashion, since Peter could go up onto the roof to pray (Acts 10:9). One other home of the wealthy, that of Mark's mother, is mentioned in Acts 12:12–17. When Peter was miraculously released from prison, he went there, "where many had gathered," and knocked "at the outer gate." This would not have been the front of the house. Houses in ancient cities opened directly onto the sidewalk (if there was one) or the street. A wealthy home had a garden in the rear, almost always with a gate opening onto an alley or back street. Peter was using common sense to go to this back entrance. He was an escaped prisoner and could hardly stand around on the street at the front door waiting for someone to let him in, especially the maid named Rhoda, who in her joy and distraction left Peter standing at the gate (12:14).

Clothing

Because clothing carried implications for social status in antiquity, it is appropriate to examine it here. References to clothing are rare in the New Testament, simply because the writers saw no need to enlighten later generations on such a mundane topic. But there are a few, and we can learn something by looking at general practices in this area. The style of garments in Judea may have differed somewhat from those in Greece and Rome, but the principles on which those styles were based varied little across the Empire.

In addition to literary references, we can see in their artwork how the Greeks and Romans dressed. Representations of Jews are rare in ancient art because of the Old Testament prohibition against representing human figures, though some rabbis did interpret the words "graven image" quite literally to forbid only statues. At least one synagogue (in Dura-Europas in Mesopotamia) has numerous and colorful frescoes on its walls, but it is too far east and a bit too late to provide information for the New Testament period. Mosaics on the floor of the synagogue of Sepphoris may yield more information about the looks of Jews in Palestine in the Roman period, but it has not yet been analyzed. Few artists of other nations depict Jews, except when they are being taken captive.

Greco-Roman clothing fell into two categories (**7.168**; **7.170**). Garments put on by wrapping them around the body, such as the Roman *toga* or the Greek *himation*, were classified as *amictus*. These outer garments were worn on formal occasions or for warmth in winter. They were cumbersome and had to be removed when a person engaged in physical exertion. That's why the men stoning Stephen "laid their coats (*himatia*) at the feet of a young man named Saul" (Acts 7:58). The Roman man's toga was larger and more elaborately draped than the woman's cloak, known as a *pallia*. In haste an individual could sometimes just throw a cloak around himself. The mysterious young man of Mark 14:51—who may have been camping in the garden of Gethsemane, as pilgrims often did—had clothed himself in that careless fashion when he came to see what all the fuss was about (**7.174**). When someone grabbed him, he slipped out of his garment and ran away naked (**7.169**; **7.172**).

Cloaks were expensive, so it was necessary to have someone watch one's clothing in public places like the baths. Or at a public execution. Complaints of stolen clothes are frequent (e. g., Petronius, *Satyr*. 30). Perhaps the cost of the garment was one reason why Paul asked Timothy to bring with him a cloak which Paul had left in Troas (2 Tim. 4:13). Because cloth was expensive and difficult to make at home, few people other than the wealthy owned more than two garments at a time. Martial (5.79) chides an ostentatious host who changed his clothes eleven times during a dinner, on the pretext of being sweaty. Jesus, however, says that his disciples are not to have even two cloaks (Matt. 10:10).

The more casual type of clothing was classified as *indutus*, meaning that it had sleeves and a neck hole and was slipped on over the head. The Romans called this a *tunic*, the Greeks a *chiton*. This two-layer arrangement of clothing is what Jesus had in mind when he advised his disciples that "if anyone wants to sue you and take your coat, give your cloak as well" (Matt. 5:40). Both men and women wore this type of clothing, with women's outfits differing from the men's primarily in length and colors. There was, however, enough difference in the appearance of the garments that it was considered indecent for a man to wear a woman's tunic (Seneca, *Ep*. 122.7). In cold weather extra tunics could be worn. The emperor Augustus, in his old age, usually wore four tunics and a heavy wool cloak in the winter (Suetonius, *Aug*. 82). Elderly people also sometimes wrapped pieces of wool around their legs.

Women typically wore a short tunic under a longer, outer garment. This outer robe, known as a *stola*, could be left unstitched at the shoulders to allow it to be put on or removed without disturbing the elaborate hairstyles popular in New Testament times. In that case it would be fastened at the shoulders with pins or broaches (**7.171**). One of the most captivating pieces of artwork from antiquity, now in the National Museum in Naples, is a life-sized bronze statue showing a young woman with her hands poised on her shoulder. She is either about to unpin her stola, or she has just pinned it.

These types of garments were universal around the Mediterranean basin, though there would have been local variations—just as today someone from New York or Los Angeles wouldn't dress quite like someone from a small Midwestern town. In antiquity only barbarians wore breeches. Jewish clothing varied only slightly from the Greco-Roman; by the first century A.D., it is questionable, according to the *Encyclopedia Judaica* (vol. 6:215), "whether there was a distinctive Jewish dress." It is also significant that "in the Midrash, the Mishnah, and the Talmud the words used to describe dress are almost entirely Greek or Latin terms transliterated into Hebrew and most of the garments are of Greek, Roman or Iranian origin" (**7.173**:21). Another scholar sums it up: "Jews dressed like the rest of the Hellenistic world" (**7.140**:797).

The basis of native Jewish dress was the *ketonet,* a tunic, slightly shorter and closer fitting than the Roman model. Over this was worn a *simlah,* or loose-fitting cloak. Important men in Judea wore a *meil,* a long robe with loose sleeves (Mark 12:38).

People in the first century sometimes also wore an undergarment, a loin-cloth of cotton or wool. This, with the tunic tucked up, was common garb for men engaged in vigorous labor (Luke 12:35; Eph. 6:14). In warm weath-

An aqueduct in France, with arches supporting a water channel and a roadway
(Photo from Fototeca Unione)

er it might be the only clothing worn at work, though Jews were generally more reluctant to exhibit their bodies than were the Greeks and Romans (John 21:7). Women wore such a garment during their menstrual cycles and would also sometimes wear a breast band.

Both sexes wore a belt around the tunic which allowed them to regulate the length of the garment. At times when speed or increased physical activity was necessary, the tunic could be drawn up and held in place by the belt (or "girdle" in older translations; Luke 12:37). The belt was usually cloth. John the Baptist's leather belt struck his contemporaries as worth noting (Mark 1:6). We have no ancient information about the length of the belt, but Paul's was long enough that Agabus could bind the apostle's hands and feet with it in a symbolic gesture (Acts 21:11).

Among the Greeks and Romans, wool was the most common material for both tunics and cloaks. In the early days of Greece and Rome, women were expected to spend a good portion of their time spinning wool and weaving garments. By the first century A.D. clothes were more likely to be purchased, although women's tombstones still claimed of any virtuous woman that "she worked wool." In the Near East, linen and cotton were favored for clothing. Garments intended for summer wear were woven more loosely than winter garments. Seneca (*Epp.* 90.5; 114.21) complains of disreputable men wearing tunics so loosely woven that one could see through them (**7.175**). Men's tunics and cloaks were normally left the natural color of the wool and would be bleached white on special occasions. As noted earlier, the senatorial and equestrian classes were allowed to have a purple stripe along the hem of their garments. Women's dresses could be a variety of colors and have embroidery or designs stitched on the hem or around the throat. For a Roman man to wear a colored tunic or cloak except at a dinner party was considered scandalous (Martial 4.2). In the provinces, however, there seems to have been more latitude in the matter of color. The only restriction was that purple was reserved for the very wealthy (cf. Luke 16:19). Clothing styles also varied somewhat in the colder northern provinces (**7.176**).

Conclusion

Now that we've seen something of how Greco-Roman society of the first century A.D. was structured, how people ate, dressed, and organized their days, it's time to turn to the more vital question of their morality and standards of personal behavior. In those areas Christianity presented the greatest challenge to the world around it.

Notes

1. While it is difficult to establish equivalents between ancient and modern money, if we arbitrarily equate sesterces with dollars, we won't be far from an accurate picture. Assets of $400,000 would certainly make one upper-middle class today, and it is almost impossible to get into the U. S. Senate without being a millionaire.

2. See *The Beginnings of Christianity*, ed. F. J. Foakes-Jackson and K. Lake (London: Macmillan, 1920), vol. 5:148–149. Lake says the second-century pattern of "organized charity . . . prevailed . . . probably in the first." The "daily distribution of food" and the need to "wait on tables" in Acts 6:1–2 suggests a known practice in that Jewish-Christian milieu, and note Matthew 6:2–4, but we don't have direct evidence for non-Christian Jewish practice of organized charity.

3. The Romans experimented with secret ballots in elections toward the end of the Republic. Pliny reports that the senate introduced secret ballots at the end of the first century A.D. (*Ep.* 3.20). At first the novel practice worked well, but before long some of the distinguished members took to writing "jokes and obscenities" on their ballots (*Ep.* 4.25).

4. There does exist, though, one relief which shows a sword fight between two women clad in breastplates, helmets, and shields.

5. Tyrannus probably owned this large room and rented it out to traveling teachers, of the sort discussed in chapter 6. Or Tyrannus might have run his own school during the morning hours. We can probably assume that Paul worked at his trade during the morning, then spent the midday and early afternoon teaching. Tyrannus must have been pleased to derive income from the hall at a time when it would normally have been vacant. Did Paul get a lower, off-hours rate?

6. This pattern of gorging and purging obviously resembles the modern eating disorder known as bulimia. I've been unable to find any published studies on the subject, but a scholar named J. R. Pinault read a paper on "The Evidence for Bulimia in Antiquity" at a conference of the American Philological Association in 1988. She informs me that she is working on a book on eating disorders among the Greeks and Romans.

7. This garnish was made by allowing fish innards to sit until they liquified. The *liquamen* was then strained and refined. It must have been an acquired taste.

8. Now we can see why these professions were considered "unclean" by the Jews and why Simon the tanner's house was "by the seaside" (Acts 10:6), where it would get good ventilation from the sea breezes. The emperor Vespasian, notorious for his stinginess, taxed the tanners and fullers because, as he saw it, they were getting raw materials free. When his son Titus objected to such a tax as undignified, Vespasian handed him a coin and asked him to smell it. "Does it smell bad?" When Titus said no, Vespasian replied, "That's odd. It came right out of the latrine" (Suetonius, *Vesp.* 23).

9. For discussion of the origins of the number three and the names assigned to these men, see chapter 3.

BIBLIOGRAPHY

Social Classes

7.1.   Banks, R. "The Acts of the Apostles as a Historical Document." *AncSoc* 16(1986): 13–17.

7.2.   Bush, A. C. *Studies in Roman Social Structure.* Washington, DC: University Press of America, 1982.

7.3.   Cassidy, R. J. *Society and Politics in the Acts of the Apostles.* Maryknoll: Orbis Books, 1987.

7.4.   Gonzalez, J. L. *Faith and Wealth: A History of Early Christian Ideas on the Origin, Significance, and Use of Money.* San Francisco: Harper & Row, 1990.

7.5.   Jeffers, J. S. *Conflict at Rome: Social Order and Hierarchy in Early Christianity.* Minneapolis: Fortress Press, 1991.

7.6.   Joshel, S. R. *Work, Identity and Legal Status at Rome: A Study of the Occupational Inscriptions.* Norman, OK: University of Oklahoma Press, 1992.

7.7.   Judge, E. A. *Rank and Status in the World of the Caesars and St. Paul.* Christchurch, N.Z.: University of Canterbury Press, 1982.

7.8.   Kyrtatas, D. J. *The Social Structures of the Early Christian Communities.* London: Verso, 1987.

7.9.   Lyall, F. *Slaves, Citizens, Sons: Legal Metaphors in the Epistles.* Grand Rapids: Zondervan, 1984.

7.10.   May, D. M. "Leaving and Receiving: A Social-Scientific Exegesis of Mark 10:29–31." *Perspectives in Religious Studies* 17(1990): 141–151, 154.

7.11.   Mitchell, A. C. "Rich and Poor in the Courts of Corinth: Litigiousness and Status in 1 Corinthians 6.1–11." *NTS* 39(1993): 562–586.

7.12.   Neyrey, J. H., ed. *The Social World of Luke-Acts: Models for Interpretation.* Peabody, MA: Hendrickson, 1991.

The Free Classes

7.13.   Barnes, T. D. "Who Were the Nobility of the Roman Empire?" *Phoenix* 28(1974): 444–449.

7.14.   Bastomsky, S. J. "Rich and Poor: The Great Divide in Ancient Rome and Victorian England." *G&R* 37(1990): 37–43.

7.15.   Berry, C. J. "Luxury and the Politics of Need and Desire: The Roman Case." *HistPolTho* 10(1989): 597–613.

7.16.   Boatwright, M. T. "Theaters in the Roman Empire." *BiblArch* 53(1990): 184–192.

7.17.   Brunt, P. A. "Free Labour and Public Works at Rome." *JRS* 70(1980): 81–100.

7.18.   Burford, A. *Craftsmen in Greek and Roman Society.* Ithaca, NY: Cornell University Press, 1972.

7.19.   Cracco Ruggini, L. "Intolerance: Equal and Less Equal in the Roman World." *CPh* 82(1987): 187–205.

7.20.   D'Arms, J. H. *Commerce and Social Standing in Ancient Rome.* Cambridge, MA: Harvard University Press, 1981.

7.21.   Dewey, A. J. "A Matter of Honor: A Social-Historical Analysis of 2 Corinthians 10." *HThR* 78(1985): 209–217.

7.22.   Drachman, A. G. *The Mechanical Technology of Greek and Roman Antiquity: A Study of the Literary Sources.* Copenhagen: Munskgaard, 1963.

7.23.   Evans, J. K. "Wheat Production and Its Social Consequences in the Roman World." *CQ* 31(1981): 428–442.

7.24.   Fantham, E. "Censorship, Roman Style." *EMC* 21(1977): 41–53.

7.25.   Finley, M. I. "Technical Innovation and Economic Progress in the Ancient World." *Economic History Review* 18(1965): 29–45.

7.26.   ———. "Wealth and Work in the Ancient World." *PCA* 66(1969): 36–37.

7.27.   Finn, T. M. "Social Mobility, Imperial Civil Service, and the Spread of Early Christianity." *StudPatr* 18(1982): 31–37.

7.28. Foxhall, L. "The Dependent Tenant: Land Leasing and Labour in Italy and Greece." *JRS* 80(1990): 97–114.

7.29. Garnsey, P. "Slaves in Business." *Opus* 1(1982): 105–108.

7.30. Gelzer, M. *The Roman Nobility.* Oxford: Blackwell, 1969.

7.31. Hands, A. R. *Charities and Social Aid in Greece and Rome.* London: Thames & Hudson, 1968.

7.32. Henderson, M. I. "The Establishment of the *Equester ordo.*" *JRS* 53(1963): 61–72.

7.33. Hill, H. "The Equites as a Middle Class." *Athenaeum* 33(1955): 327–332.

7.34. ———. "*Nobilitas* in the Imperial Period." *Historia* 18(1969): 230–250.

7.35. Hock, R. F. "Paul's Tentmaking and the Problem of His Social Class." *JBL* 97(1978): 555–564.

7.36. Hopkins, K. "Elite Mobility in the Roman Empire." *P&P* 32(1965): 12–26.

7.37. Kidd, R. M. *Wealth and Beneficence in the Pastoral Epistles: A "Bourgeois" Form of Early Christianity?* Atlanta: Scholars Press, 1990

7.38. Louis, P. *Ancient Rome at Work: An Economic History of Rome from the Origins to the Empire.* New York: Barnes & Noble, 1965.

7.39. MacMullen, R. *Roman Social Relations 50 B.C. to A.D. 284.* New Haven, CT: Yale University Press, 1974.

7.40. Mossé, C. *The Ancient World at Work.* London: Chatto & Windus, 1969.

7.41. Reece, D. W. "The Technological Weakness of the Ancient World." *G&R* 16(1969): 32–47.

7.42. Reekmans, T. "Juvenal's View on Social Classes." *AncSoc* 2(1971): 117–161.

7.43. Reinhold, M. "On Status Symbols in the Ancient World." *CJ* 64(1969): 300–304.

7.44. Robinson, O. "The Water Supply of Rome." *SDHI* 46(1980): 44–86.

7.45. Rowland, R. J. "The 'Very Poor' and the Grain Dole at Rome and Oxyrhynchus." *ZPE* 21(1976): 69–72.

7.46. Schmidt, T. E. *Hostility to Wealth in the Synoptic Gospels.* Sheffield, UK: Academic Press, 1987.

7.47. Seccombe, D. "Was There Organized Charity in Jerusalem Before the Christians?" *JThS* 29(1978): 140–143.

7.48. Sippel, D. V. "Dietary Deficiency Among the Lower Classes of Late Republican and Early Imperial Rome." *AncW* 16(1987): 47–54.

7.49. Skemp, J. B. "Service to the Needy in the Graeco-Roman World." In *Parresia: Karl Barth zum 80. Geburtstag am 10. Mai 1966.* Ed. by E. Busch et al. Zurich: EVZ-Verlag, 1966: 17–26.

7.50. Suolahti, J. *The Roman Censors: A Study on Social Structure.* Helsinki: Finnish Academy of Science, 1963.

7.51. Syme, R. "Human Rights and Social Status in Ancient Rome." *CO* 64(1986–87): 37–41.

7.52. Treggiari, S. "Jobs for Women." *AJAH* 1(1976): 76–104.

7.53. ———. "Jobs in the Household of Livia." *PBSR* 43(1975): 48–77.

7.54. Winter, B. W. "The Public Honouring of Christian Benefactors: Romans 13:3–4 and I Peter 2:14–15." *JStudNT* 34(1988): 87–103.

7.55. Ziderman, I. I. "Seashells and Ancient Purple Dyeing." *BiblArch* 53(1990): 98–101.

Patrons and Clients

7.56. Argetsinger, K. "Birthday Rituals: Friends and Patrons in Roman Poetry and Culture." *ClassAnt* 11, no. 2, (1992): 175–193.

7.57. Bodel, J. "Patrons and Priests in Roman Society." *EMC* 36(1992): 387–407.

7.58. DeSilva, D. A. "Exchanging Favor for Wrath: Apostasy in Hebrews and Patron-Client Relationships." *JBL* 115(1996): 91–116.

7.59. Elliott, J. H. "Patronage and Clientism in Early Christian Society: A Short Reading Guide." *Forum* 3, no.4 (1987): 39–48.

7.60. Malina, B. J. "Patron and Client: The Analogy Behind Synoptic Theology." *Forum* 4, no.1, (1988): 2–32.

7.61. Nicols, J. "Pliny and the Patronage of Communities." *Hermes* 108(1980): 365–385.

7.62. ———. "Prefects, Patronage and the Administration of Justice." *ZPE* 72(1988): 201–217.

7.63. Pleket, H. W. "Labor and Unemployment in the Roman Empire: Some Preliminary Remarks." In *Soziale Randgruppen und Aussenseiter in Altertum.* Ed. by I. Weiler. Graz: Leykam, 1988: 267–276.

7.64. Saller, R. P. *Personal Patronage Under the Early Empire.* New York: Cambridge University Press, 1982.

7.65. Skydsgaard, J. E. "The Disintegration of the Roman Labour Market and the Clientela Theory." In *Studia Romana in honorem P. Krarup septuagenarii.* Ed. by K. Ascani et al. Odense: Odense University Press, 1976: 44–48.

7.66. Vyhmeister, N. J. "The Rich Man in James 2: Does Ancient Patronage Illumine the Text?" *AndUnivSemStud* 33(1995): 265–283.

7.67. Winter, B. W. "'If a Man Does Not Wish to Work . . .' A Cultural and Historical Setting for 2 Thessalonians 3:6–16." *TynBull* 40(1989): 303–315.

Slaves

7.68. Barclay, J. M. G. "Paul, Philemon, and the Dilemma of Christian Slave-Ownership." *NTS* 37(1991): 161–186.

7.69. Beavis, M. A. "Ancient Slavery as an Interpretive Context for the New Testament: Servant Parables with Special Reference to the Unjust Steward (Luke 16:1–8)." *JBL* 3(1992): 37–54.

7.70. Bradley, K. R. "The Problem of Slavery in Classical Culture." *CPh* 92(1997): 273–282.

7.71. ———. "The Regular, Daily Traffic in Slaves: Roman History and Contemporary History." *CJ* 87(1992): 125–138.

7.72. ———. *Slaves and Masters in the Roman Empire: A Study in Social Control.* Brussels: Soc. d'études Lat., 1984.

7.73. Christensen, K. A. "The *Theseion:* A Slave Refuge at Athens." *AJAH* 9(1984): 23–32.

7.74. Finley, M. I. "Between Slavery and Freedom. " *CSSH* 6(1963–64): 233–249.

7.75. Harper, J. "Slaves and Freedmen in Imperial Rome." *AJPh* 93(1972): 341–342.
7.76. Harrill, J. A. *The Manumission of Slaves in Early Christianity.* Tübingen: Mohr, 1995.

7.77. Martin, D. B. "Ancient Slavery, Class, and Early Christianity." *Fides & Historia* 23(1991): 105–113.

7.78. Smith, N. D. "Aristotle's Theory of Natural Slavery." *Phoenix* 37(1983): 109–122.

7.79. Szakats, A. "Slavery as a Social and Economic Institution in Antiquity with Special Reference to Roman Law." *Prudentia* 7(1975): 33–45.

7.80. Taylor, N. H. "Onesimus: A Case Study of Slave Conversion in Early Christianity." *Rel&Th* 3(1996): 259–281.

7.81. Vogt, J. *Ancient Slavery and the Ideal of Man.* Oxford: Blackwell, 1974.

7.82. Westermann, W. L. *The Slave System of Greek and Roman Antiquity.* Philadelphia: American Philosophy Society, 1955.

Freedmen

7.83. Saller, R. P. "Promotion and Patronage in Equestrian Careers." *JRS* 70(1980): 44–63.

Women

7.84. Aspegren, K. *The Male Woman: A Feminine Ideal in the Early Church.* Ed. by R. Kieffer. Uppsala: Uppsala University Press, 1990.

7.85. Baldwin, B. "The Women of Greece and Rome." *Helikon* 15–16(1975–76): 130–145.

7.86. Barron, B. "Putting Women in Their Place: 1 Timothy 2 and Evangelical Views of Women in Church Leadership." *JEvangThSoc* 33(1990): 451–459.

7.87. Best, E. E. "Cicero, Livy, and Educated Roman Women." *CJ* 65(1970): 199–204.

7.88. Boatwright, M. T. "The Imperial Women of the Early Second Century A.D." *AJPh* 112(1991): 513–540.

7.89. Bristow, J. T. *What Paul Really Said About Women.* San Francisco: Harper & Row, 1988.

7.90. Cameron, Averil, and A. Kuhrt, eds. *Images of Women in Antiquity.* Detroit: Wayne State University Press, 1983.

7.91. Carcopino, J. *Daily Life in Ancient Rome.* New Haven, CT: Yale University Press, 1965 reprint.

7.92. Clark, G. "Roman Women." *G&R* 28(1981): 193–212.

7.93. Cohen, D. "Seclusion, Separation, and the Status of Women in Classical Athens." *G&R* 36(1989): 3–15.

7.94. Coleman, K. M. "Some Roman Women c. A.D. 100." *Akroterion* 34(1989): 191–200.

7.95. Cracco Ruggini, L. "Juridical Status and Historical Role of Women in Roman Patriarchal Society." *Klio* 71(1989): 604–619.

7.96. D'Avino, M. *The Women of Pompeii.* Naples: Loffredo, 1967.

7.97. Dobson, E. S. "Pliny the Younger's Description of Women." *CB* 58(1982): 81–85.

7.98. Donalson, M. "More on Roman Women (Including 'Late' Ones)." *CJ* 86(1991): 171–175.

7.99. Duke, T. T. "Women and Pygmies in the Roman Arena." *CJ* 50(1955): 223–224.

7.100. Finley, M. I. "The Silent Women of Rome." *Horizon* 7, no. 1, (1965): 57–64.

7.101. Foley, H. P., ed. *Reflections of Women in Antiquity.* New York: Gordon & Breach, 1981.

7.102. Freckleton, I. "Women in Roman Law." *Classicum* 9(1983): 16–20.

7.103. Gardner, J. F. *Women in Roman Law and Society.* Bloomington: Indiana University Press, 1986.

7.104. Geddes, A. "The Philosophical Notion of Women in Antiquity." *Antichthon* 9(1975): 35–40.

7.105. Grant, M. *Roman History from Coins.* New York: Cambridge University Press, 1958.

7.106. Kampen, N. *Images and Status: Roman Working Women in Ostia.* Berlin: Mann, 1981.

7.107. Kroeger, C. C. "Women in the Church: A Classicist's View of 1 Timothy 2.11–15." *JBiblEqual* 1(1989): 3–31.

7.108. Lindboe, I. M. *Women in the New Testament: A Select Bibliography.* Oslo: University of Oslo, 1990.

7.109. MacMullen, R. "Women in Public in the Roman Empire." *Historia* 29(1980): 208–218.

7.110. Marshall, A. J. "Ladies at Law: The Role of Women in the Roman Civil Courts." In *Studies in Latin Literature and Roman History V.* Ed. by C. Derricks. Brussels: Soc. Latomus, 1989: 35–54.

7.111. Montgomery, H. "Women and Status in the Greco-Roman World." *StudTh* 43(1989): 115–124.

7.112. Moxnes, H. "Social Integration and the Problem of Gender in St. Paul's Letters." *StudTh* 43(1989): 99–113.

7.113. Pomeroy, S. B. *Goddesses, Whores, Wives and Slaves: Women in Classical Antiquity.* New York: Schocken Books, 1975.

7.114. Reis, P. "The Villa of Mysteries: Initiation into Woman's Midlife Passage." *Continuum* 1(1991): 64–91.

7.115. Rowe, A. "Silence and the Christian Women of Corinth: An Examination of 1 Corinthians 14:33b-36." *Communio Viatorum* 33(1990): 41–84. 7.116. Simon, S. J. "Women Who Pleaded Causes Before the Roman Magistrates." *CB* 66, nos. 3–4, (1990): 79–81.

7.117. Sullivan, J. P. "Lady Chatterley in Rome." *Pacific Coast Philology* 15(1980): 53–62.

7.118. Treggiari, S. "Family Life Among the Staff of the Volusii." *TAPhA* 105(1975): 393–401.

7.119. ———. "Libertine Ladies." *CW* 64(1971): 196–198.

7.120. ———. "Lower Class Women in the Roman Economy." *Florilegium* 1(1979): 65–86.

7.121. Viden, G. *Women in Roman Literature: Attitudes of Authors Under the Early Empire.* Göteborg: Acta Universitatis Gothoburgensis, 1993.

7.122. Wessels, G. F. "Ephesians 5:21–33. 'Wives, Be Subject to Your Husbands . . . . Husbands, Love Your Wives . . . .'" *JTheolSAfr* 67(1989): 67–76.

Daily Schedule

7.123. Davis, W. S. *A Day in Old Rome: A Picture of Roman Life.* New York: Biblo & Tannen, 1962.

7.124. Dilke, O. A. W. *The Ancient Romans: How They Lived and Worked.* Newton Abbott, UK: David & Charles, 1975.

7.125. Liversidge, J. *Everyday Life in the Roman Empire.* London: Bratsford, 1976.

7.126. Steiner, G. "The Fortunate Farmer: Life on the Small Farm in Ancient Italy." *CJ* 51(1955): 57–67.

7.127. White, K. D. *Country Life in Classical Times.* London: Elek, 1977.

7.128. ———. *Roman Farming.* Ithaca, NY: Cornell University Press, 1970.

Meals

7.129. Campbell, R. A. "Does Paul Acquiesce in Divisions at the Lord's Supper?" *NovT* 33(1991): 61–70.

7.130. Curtis, R. I. "In Defense of Garum." *CJ* 78(1983): 232–240.

7.131. D'Arms, J. H. "Control, Companionship, and Clientela: Some Social Functions of the Roman Communal Meal." *EMC* 28(1984): 327–348.

7.132. Evans, E. "Dining with the Ancients." *Archaeology* 43, no. 6, (1990): 55–61.

7.133. Flower, B., and E. Rosenbaum. *The Roman Cookery Book: A Translation of The Art of Cooking by Apicius, for Use in the Study and the Kitchen.* New York: British Book Centre, 1958.

7.134. Foxhall, L., and H. A. Forbes. "Sitometreia: The Role of Grain as a Staple Food in Classical Antiquity." *Chiron* 12(1982): 41–90.

7.135. Garnsey, P. "Grain for Rome." In *Trade in the Ancient Economy.* Ed. by P. Garnsey et al. London: Chatto & Windus, 1983: 118–130.

7.136. Hepper, F. N. *Baker Encyclopedia of Bible Plants: Flowers and Trees, Fruits and Vegetables, Ecology.* Grand Rapids: Baker, 1993.

7.137. Kim, C. H. "The Papyrus Invitation." *JBL* 94(1975): 391–402.

7.138. Lampe, P. "The Corinthian Eucharistic Dinner Party: Exegesis of a Cultural Context (1 Cor. 11:17–34)." *Affirmation* 4(1991): 1–15.

7.139. Rickman, G. *The Corn Supply of Ancient Rome.* London: Oxford University Press, 1980.

7.140. Safrai, S. "Religion in Everyday Life." In *The Jewish People in the First Century.* Ed. by S. Safrai et al. Amsterdam: Van Gorcum, 1976.

7.141. Slater, W. J., ed. *Dining in a Classical Context.* Ann Arbor: University of Michigan Press, 1992.

7.142. Smith, E. M. "Some Roman Dinner Tables." *CJ* 50(1955): 255–260.

Housing and Urban Life

7.143. Batey, R. A. "Sepphoris: An Urban Portrait of Jesus." *BAR* 18, no. 3, (1992): 50–62.

7.144. Beebe, H. K. "Domestic Architecture and the New Testament." *BiblArch* 38(1975): 89–104.

7.145. Birkey, D. "The House Church: A Missiological Model." *Missiology* 19(1991): 69–80.

7.146. Bourne, F. C. "Reflections on Rome's Urban Problems." *CW* 62(1969): 205–209.

7.147. Branick, V. P. *The House Church in the Writings of Paul.* Wilmington, DE: Glazier, 1989.

7.148. Brunn, C. *The Water Supply of Ancient Rome: A Study of Roman Imperial Administration.* Helsinki: Soc. Scient. Fennica, 1991.

7.149. Cilliers, L. "Public Health in Roman Legislation." *AClass* 36(1993): 1–10.

7.150. Collins, R. F. "House Churches in Early Christianity." *Tripod* 55(1990): 38–44.
7.151. Daugherty, G. N. "The *Cohortes Vigilium* and the Great Fire of 64 A.D." *CJ* 87(1992): 229–240.
7.152. Echols, E. "The Roman City Police." *CJ* 53(1958): 377–384.
7.153. Edelstein, G. "What's a Roman Villa Doing Outside Jerusalem?" *BAR* 16, no. 6, (1990): 32–42.
7.154. Frier, B. W. *Landlords and Tenants in Imperial Rome*. Princeton, NJ: Princeton University Press, 1980.
7.155. ———. "The Rental Market in Early Imperial Rome." *JRS* 67(1977): 27–37.
7.156. Hammond, M., and L. J. Bartson. *The City in the Ancient World*. Cambridge: Harvard University Press, 1972.
7.157. Harrison, R. K., ed. *Major Cities of the Biblical World*. Nashville: Thomas Nelson Publishers, 1985.
7.158. Hermansen, G. "*Domus* and *Insula* in the City of Rome." In *Classica et Mediaevalia F. Blatt Septuagenario Dedicata*. Ed. by O. S. Due, et al. Copenhagen: Glyendal, 1973: 333–341.
7.159. ———. "The Medianum and the Roman Apartment." *Phoenix* 24(1970): 342–347.
7.160. Ludwig, C. *Cities in New Testament Times*. Denver: Accent Books, 1976.
7.161. Marchese, R. T., ed. *Aspects of Graeco-Roman Urbanization: Essays on the Classical City*. Oxford: British Archeology Reports, 1983.
7.162. May, D. M. "Mark 2.15: The Home of Jesus or Levi?" *NTS* 39(1993): 147–149.
7.163. McKay, A. G. *Houses, Villas and Palaces in the Roman World*. Ithaca, NY: Cornell University Press, 1975.
7.164. Owens, E. J. *The City in the Greek and Roman World*. London: Routledge, 1991.
7.165. Rainbird, J. S. "The Fire Stations of Imperial Rome." *PBSR* 54(1986): 147–169.
7.166. Robinson, O. "Fire Prevention at Rome." *Revue internationale des droits de l'antiquité* 24(1977): 377–388.
7.167. Strange, J. F., and H. Shanks. "Has the House Where Jesus Stayed in Capernaum Been Found?" *BAR* 8, no. 6, (1982): 26–37.

Clothing

7.168. Hope, T. *Costumes of the Greeks and Romans*. New York: Dover, 1962.
7.169. Jackson, H. M. "Why the Youth Shed His Cloak and Fled Naked: The Meaning and Purpose of Mark 14:51–52." *JBL* 116(1997): 273–289.
7.170. Klepper, E. *Costume in Antiquity*. London: Thames & Hudson, 1964.
7.171. Muscarella, O. W. "Ancient Safety Pins: Their Function and Significance." *Expedition* 6, no. 2, (1964): 34–40.
7.172. Ross, J. M. "The Young Man Who Fled Naked." *IrBibStud* 13(1991): 170–174.
7.173. Rubens, A. A. *History of Jewish Costume*. New York: Crown Publishing, 1973.
7.174. Saunderson, B. "Gethsemane: The Missing Witness." *Biblica* 70(1989): 224–233.
7.175. Tracy, V. A. "Roman Dandies and Transvestites." *EMC* 20(1976): 60–63.
7.176. Wild, J. P. "Clothing in the Northwest Provinces of the Roman Empire." *Bonner Jahrbücher des Rheinischen Landesmuseums* 168(1968): 166–240.

CHAPTER 8

GRECO-ROMAN MORALITY AND PERSONAL RELATIONS

W HEN WE COME to the topic of morality in the ancient world, we reach the point at which we differ most fundamentally from pagan antiquity. The things we've studied thus far, from political organization to dress, are recognizable variations of things we do today. They may seem quaint, but we could probably imagine ourselves living under those conditions. Greco-Roman morality, however, rests on entirely different premises from ours. Few of us, conditioned by Christian teaching and living under laws which rest ultimately on the Judeo-Christian tradition, could imagine ourselves approaching morality on the bases which the Greeks and Romans used.

This is one area in which there is more than a modicum of truth to the popular perception, spread through paperback novels and gladiator movies, of Rome as a cruel, lascivious society. The fact is that, for the Romans of New Testament times, watching people die under the most barbaric conditions in the arena was a standard means of amusing the idle populace (though some intellectuals like Seneca and Pliny did object to it, as we saw in chapter 4); seduction and adultery were the pastimes of the self-indulgent rich; unwanted children were simply thrown away, sometimes even dumped in sewers (**8.3**).

The Greco-Roman view of morality was so different from the Christian that the Christians saw themselves as surrounded by evil (**8.2**). Paul says that the only way they could avoid associating with immoral people would be "to go out of the world" (1 Cor. 5:9–10). Even the more sensitive among the Romans admitted that they were a corrupt people, willing to stop at nothing to advance their own interests.

As Pliny says (*Ep.* 3.20), "Many people regard public opinion highly, but hardly anyone follows conscience." Lest we think him overly pessimistic, Sallust had a similar reaction when he began his political career in the first century B.C. He found that "recklessness, bribery, and greed flourished instead of decency, restraint, and virtue" (*Catiline* 3.4).

By the end of this chapter, the reader will see that such statements have minimal distortion and are rather fair assessments of the moral bankruptcy of ancient Rome (**6.130**). Unlike the earlier chapters, parallels with the New Testament will not be as obvious as contrasts.

The Basis of Greco-Roman Morality

The crux of the problem is that morality (from the Latin *mores*, meaning customs or habits) must rest on one of two sanctions: divine authority or communal wisdom (**8.9**). Anthropologists have shown that the laws which govern the behavior of any society are believed by the members of that society to have come from one source or the other. In some cases, as with the Confucian system which dominated the Orient for so long, one man's wisdom was taken as valid for the society as a whole.

In other cases the law-giver asserts the authority of his code on the basis of its divine origins. The Babylonian Code of Hammurabi (eighteenth century B.C.) acknowledges that the gods had given the laws to the king to be passed on to the people at large, a pattern familiar to us from Moses' experience on Mt. Sinai. The Judeo-Christian tradition which dominates modern Western society thus sees morality as having divine sanction. One does not commit adultery for example, because God says not to do that.

The Greeks and Romans, however, based their morality on laws given by an individual and validated by the community, not the gods. Each Greek city-state had its great lawgiver: prime examples are Solon for Athens and Lycurgus in Sparta. Much of Plato's thought was devoted to working out an ideal political system based on laws formulated by human reason. The Romans looked to the Twelve Tables of the law, first written down in the mid-fifth century B.C. and based on legislation allegedly handed down by Romulus, the founder of Rome, and Numa, another of its early kings. None of these law codes even pretends to have a divine origin (**8.7**).

The Greeks and Romans did teach that one should not commit adultery, but not because the act violates a divine prohibition. It was viewed as a violation of property rights. Greek and Roman men didn't want another man sleeping with their wives—who were their property—any more than they wanted someone stealing their farm animals. Under such a system, any reluctance which an individual feels to commit adultery comes not from fear of divine retribution but from the more prosaic fear of being caught by the woman's husband. If one believes that he can avoid detection, there is no reason not to commit the act.

The Greek view of morality is summed up by A. R. Burn, in a way also apt for the Romans (**8.4**:252). For these people, he says,

> Laws and customs exist not by nature or by the unalterable will of the gods, but simply by custom or convention. It was then also a perilously short step, for anyone who found traditional morality troublesome, to appealing from it to the law of nature or of the jungle, either in power politics or in personal relations.

Though the subject of morality covers business, politics, and interpersonal relations, it is fairly easy to describe Roman behavior in those first two areas but more difficult when it comes to the last. Self-interest and reciprocity were the dominant principles by which the Romans lived (**8.17**). The individual was expected to do what was to his advantage, regardless of its effect on others, so long as he did not violate another person's property. He was expected to repay favors and could count on having his favors returned.

These principles explain some of the surprising turns in Roman politics. When Julius Caesar was assassinated, for example, he left his wealth and power to his grandnephew, Octavian. This surprised and angered Caesar's chief lieutenant, Marc Antony, who had expected to inherit Caesar's position. Antony contested the legality of the will, and a deep animosity developed between him and Octavian. Yet they put their resentments aside long enough to defeat Caesar's assassins (Antony even married Octavian's sister), then turned on one another. At no point did either man seem to consider what might be advantageous for Rome or how they might reach some permanent compromise. The guiding impulse for both men, as for any Roman of the time, was to seek for their own personal advancement. (Perhaps it's worth pointing out that the Latin word for campaigning for office was *ambitio*.)

The Romans talked a lot about moral or upright behavior—using terms such as duty, loyalty, prudence, and utility (**8.12**)—and by the first century B.C., they were lamenting the decline in morality which they saw everywhere. But they never defined any basis for teaching morality other than admiration for the virtues of earlier generations. They were "decidedly against interfering by means of legislation in the development of moral behavior" (**8.14**:361).

Since, by the first century A.D., the population of Rome was a polyglot of former slaves and people drawn by commercial opportunity, the city had no traditions that meant anything to the mass of its people. The immigrants brought in by this flood "had literally been demoralized by uprootage from their native surroundings, cultures, and moral codes; years of slavery had destroyed in them that self-respect which is the backbone of upright conduct; and daily friction with groups of different customs had worn away still more of their custom-made morality" (**8.7**:366).

If a people lack a morality based on customs or traditions, they might turn to religion for a grounding of their social behaviors. But the Romans did not see that morality had any relation to their religious beliefs. The object of religion was to secure the goodwill of the gods and avert misfortune. In short, "Roman religion was concerned with success not with sin" (**8.15**:17). The gods weren't interested in the daily conduct of their worshipers. Blood guilt incurred by murder did render a person "unclean" and unsuitable for participating in rituals, but a man could seduce his neighbor's wife on the way to a pagan god's temple or cheat his neighbor in a business deal and still be acceptable to the deity. There were certain restrictions because of class or societal obligation, but no action in itself was immoral, except for incest, cannibalism, and murder of a blood relative, things that are taboo in almost every society anthropologists have studied. A "pious" person was one who observed the proper rituals, regardless of how he felt about them (**8.18**).

The gods themselves were bad examples of behavior. Merchants and thieves had their own god (Hermes/Mercury), and Zeus, Apollo, Poseidon, and other gods had seduced or raped countless young women, as well as the occasional young man. Several goddesses had also had affairs with mortal men. How could the behavior of the people be expected to excel that of their deities? That was precisely the problem Plato had seen when he forbade the telling of the old myths in the ideal state outlined in his *Republic*.

Whereas most Christians today would define their sexual morality as based on religious teaching, the Greeks and Romans made no such connection. In the words of R. Flaceliere, "The domains of religion and sexual morality were then regarded as completely separate" (**8.10**:70). The Romans' attitude toward sexual mores remained remarkably consistent over several centuries. As Durant describes it (**8.7**:68), "From beginning to end of Roman history the sexual morality of the common man remained essentially the same: coarse and free. . . . What increases with civilization is not so much immorality of intent as opportunity of expression."

Given the proper circumstances, any Roman man would attempt to sleep with any woman, provided only that any potential retribution from her male kin might not be too severe. An incident that illustrates this point is related in Apuleius' *Golden Ass* (2.6; ca. A.D. 180). The main character, a young man named Lucius, was staying with a friend of his family while visiting a foreign city. The host's wife was extremely attractive, and Lucius thought she might receive his attentions kindly. But he reflected that she was the wife of his host, and it would be a violation of his obligations as a guest if he tried to seduce her. It would also get him thrown out of the house if his host found out about it. Therefore he resolved not to seduce the wife but to try for the maid instead. Being of a lower class, she was fair game. The issue here is not whether it's right or wrong to have sexual relations with a woman he isn't married to, but which woman it would be more advantageous for Lucius to seduce.

Such a passage shows us that, from the Greco-Roman viewpoint, Jesus' blanket prohibition against adultery and against even desiring a woman would have been virtually incomprehensible, as would most of his ethical principles (**8.11**; Matt. 5:27–30). Paul must have sounded like he was preaching a strange doctrine, too, when he exhorted the Corinthians, "Do not seek your own advantage, but that of the other" (1 Cor. 10:24). This is not to claim that no Greek or Roman ever thought about doing something for someone else (**8.5**), but such altruism was a rare sentiment.

In his *Republic* (332d) Plato tried to refute the definition of justice as doing "good to friends and evil to enemies" (cf. Matt. 5:43: "You have heard that it was said, 'You shall love your neighbor and hate your enemy.'") Other Greek and Roman philosophers expressed altruistic sentiments similar to the Christian notion of loving the neighbor as oneself, as John Whittaker has shown (**8.19**), but the idea never seems to have gained wide popular acceptance (**8.16**). Seneca's advice is about the closest the Romans could come to a basis for morality that expressed some concern for others: treat your inferiors kindly because they, given the whims of Fate, could someday be your superiors (*Ep.* 47). Self-interest and reciprocity are still at the heart of that statement.

The Evidence for Roman Morality

If only one or two first-century writers displayed immoral or amoral attitudes, we might argue that they were expressing their personal views and did not represent their society at large. But the same themes reappear in one writer after another, and in the lives of one political figure after another, from the first century B.C. to the early second century A.D. Catullus was the first of the lyric poets to write about his affair with a (married) woman, whom he gave the pen name Lesbia. Propertius with his Cynthia and Ovid with his Corinna made this a popular model for the "jet set" of that day (**8.22**). Later in his life, after he had been exiled, Ovid tried to claim that Corinna was purely fictitious and that his life, if not his poetry, had been pure (*Tristia* 2.353–356). At the end of the century Martial would make the same claim.

Other writers, such as Petronius and Juvenal, show us that the situation got steadily worse until the early second century A.D. We can only conclude that, even allowing for literary exaggeration ("poets are allowed to lie," as Pliny says), the picture these writers present is true fundamentally, if not in every detail. And it is corroborated by pictorial evidence from Pompeii and Herculaneum, where today the guides

Ruins of Roman baths at Troas
(Photo by Howard Vos)

will—for a fee, of course—remove the covers concealing certain obscene paintings and mosaics (**8.25**). The Romans, who regularly encountered nudity in their baths, arenas, and theaters, seem to have been less impressed by it than the Greeks, who saw it as having overtones of heroism (**8.21**), as in the *gymnasion* (Greek, from *gymnazein*, "to exercise naked," 1 Macc. 1:14–15; 2 Macc. 4:9–17).

The study of morality in the first century A.D. does present a problem in choosing the best method. It is one kind of sociological survey, but as J. Crook (**8.23**:9) notes,

> sociology depends on measurement, upon statistical techniques for discovering what most people mostly do, and so upon measurable evidence. Notoriously, the ancient world very seldom provides such evidence, only particular statements of individual alleged facts.

That limitation should be born in mind, but it shouldn't prevent us from making some observations that will be generally applicable. We can use evidence from both Greek and Roman sources, since the distinctions between Greece and Rome had long since blurred, as noted earlier (**8.26**). We will break down our survey of Greco-Roman morality under several headings, beginning with the condition of the family.

Remains of the Circus Maximus (in the foreground) in Rome
(Photo by Howard Vos)

Family Life

It would be going too far to say, as one scholar once did, that the freedom enjoyed by Roman women led to the decline of morals in general and of family life in particular (**7.91**:90–95). Literary works and other sources provide graphic evidence that this decline was caused by a number of factors. It is a sad but instructive lesson to see how far the Roman sense of the family was degraded over the centuries. What was happening in the capital had repercussions all over the Empire (**8.35**).

The Roman Concept of Family

The early Romans (even more than the Greeks) had an austere, upright view of the family (**8.37**). Rome itself was seen as an extended family, with its sacred hearth and flame maintained by virgin priestesses devoted to Vesta, goddess of the purity of the home (**8.30**). Each family was a religious unit, with its own household gods and rituals, as well as being a group of people related by blood (**8.36**). All the families of the city joined together in worshiping certain tribal gods, such as Jupiter and Juno. Within each family the father, as priest and patriarch, had *patria potestas*, absolute control of the lives and affairs of his wife and children (**8.29**; **8.32**). The law allowed him to inflict capital punishment on them or sell them into slavery, though such things rarely

A Roman couple
(Photo from Alinari/Art Resource, NY)

happened. He arranged his children's marriages and planned his sons' careers.

This power continued in force as long as the father lived, regardless of the age of the children. Even after the sons were married and had families of their own, everything of theirs belonged to their father. A daughter did not completely escape his control, either, unless that was made a condition of her marriage contract. In some circumstances, a married woman's father could interfere in her affairs and even break up her marriage if he thought it advisable (**8.34**). The woman was expected to practice domestic crafts, manage the slaves, and behave herself with the utmost propriety (**8.31**). Early Roman law allowed a man to kill his wife if he caught her in adultery or divorce her if he detected the taste of wine on her lips. Though harsh, this view of the family produced a stable society in which adultery, divorce, and juvenile delinquency (**8.97**) were virtually nonexistent.

The Decline of the Roman Family

Several factors combined to undermine this foundation of Roman society (**8.42**). Only in retrospect did many Romans perceive the demoralizing effect of the inordinate wealth which they acquired through their conquests of the second century B.C. In the words of the historian Sallust (*Cat.* 10.2–4),

> To the men who had so easily endured toil and peril, anxiety and adversity, the leisure and riches which are generally regarded as so desirable proved a burden and a curse. Growing love of money, and the lust for power which followed it, engendered every kind of evil. Avarice destroyed honor, integrity, and every other virtue, and instead taught men to be proud and cruel, to neglect religion, and to hold nothing too sacred to sell.

Others believed the source of decay to be the Greek lifestyle which many Romans came to admire and imitate at that time, a lifestyle which found no harm in prostitution and homosexuality, for example.

As we saw in chapter 6, Cato the Elder, in the early second century B.C., saw Rome's fascination for Greek culture, especially philosophy, as detrimental to the old Roman virtues. In Cato's view Socrates was not a brilliant thinker but "a turbulent windbag, who did his best to tyrannize over his country by undermining its established customs and seducing his fellow-citizens into holding opinions which were contrary to the laws" (Plutarch, *Cato* 23). But his insistence that Rome be purged of Greek influences and return to the "tradition of the elders" made him a dinosaur in his own lifetime. His own sons grew up reading and speaking Greek.

One indisputable factor in the decline of the Roman family was the civil wars of the first century B.C., which left Rome bleeding and exhausted (Tacitus, *Ann.* 1.11). The effect of these wars on the family structure of Rome was catastrophic. Many women, especially among the aristocracy, were widowed, and there were few eligible men left to replace their husbands. Sons and daughters left without fathers were technically "free" from anyone's control, much like emancipated slaves.

By Augustus' day the family structure of Rome had all but evaporated, and many women, particularly of the upper classes, were living their lives unhindered by male control (**8.44**). A direct result of this shattered family structure was a decline in the birth rate. Once it became common for some people not to be married, others saw the advantages of that status. Many people made a conscious choice not to marry or have children (**8.41**). An astonishing number of family names vanish from census rolls during the first century A.D. as the last male member dies without heirs. Pliny the Elder left no children, nor did his nephew and adopted son, the younger Pliny. Since the younger Pliny was an only child, his death meant the end of two family lines, his biological father's as well as his adoptive father's.

Coupled with high infant mortality rates, the Romans' disinclination (or inability) to have children thinned the ranks of the upper classes drastically during the first century A.D. Pliny grieves for a man who has lost two daughters in childbirth: "Now only one of his three children survives, left as the sole prop and stay of a family which not so long ago had many members to support it." (*Ep.* 4.21).

Augustus attempted to reverse this trend by allowing only men who were married and the fathers of three children to hold political office and inherit property. His legislation produced little more than marriages in name only and a willingness on the part of Roman aristocrats not to inquire too closely into the paternity of children born to their wives. He soon had to begin granting exceptions to these rules or there would have been no one eligible to fill important government offices (**8.38–40; 8.43**).

Advice to Newlyweds

A good wife ought to be most visible when with her husband; when he is not there, she should stay home and keep to herself.

When two musical instruments play together, it is the deeper tone which carries the melody. In a well-ordered household every activity will be carried out by the husband and wife together, but it will be clear that the husband is leading and making decisions.

A mixture of wine and water is called wine, even if the greater portion of it is water. In the same way, a couple's property should be called the husband's, even if the wife has contributed the larger share.

Don't make a marriage on the basis of physical beauty or how much money your wife will bring you. Instead, consider what she will be like to live with.

The man who aspires to what is good and honorable will inspire his wife to become a woman of good sense and high principles.

Sensible women will keep quiet when their husbands are angry and shouting; when their husbands are silent, they will comfort them with soothing words.

Husbands and wives should try to avoid quarrelling under any circumstances, but especially when they are in bed. It is not easy to escape harsh words and disagreements which may arise there.

Plutarch, *On Marriage*, excerpts

Marriage

The foundation of the family, in Rome as anywhere, was the bond between a man and a woman. But, to understand the Roman concept of marriage, we must "make a clean break with all the Christian notions of marriage. To the Romans marriage . . . was not sacramental, not 'holy' matrimony; it was not thought to be maintained or sanctioned by anything beyond the will of those who were parties to it—or their heads of families" (**8.23**:99). No one asked whether the bride and groom loved each other. In most cases they had not met before the marriage or had only been introduced in the presence of their families. Mary's marriage to Joseph would have been arranged in this manner. It was certainly not unknown for a husband and wife to develop genuine affection for each other, but that was a bonus, not the foundation of the relationship. The basis of the relationship was the husband's domination, which ideally would be benign (see box).

There were several types of marriage in Rome, depending on the degree of power over the bride which was granted to the husband. None of them required a ceremony to make them official, though ceremonies were always held because the Romans liked an excuse for a party as much as anyone. The least formal type of Roman marriage amounted to little more than concubinage.

Marriage as a Contract

Across the Empire marriages were arranged by the fathers of the couple (**8.57**; **8.64**). This practice continued even as late as the second century A.D. (Pliny, *Ep.* 1.14). The bride's consent was not essential, but by the first century A.D., few marriages were arranged without it (**8.62**). Because she came from a place where different household gods were worshiped, the bride was regarded as an alien who had to be introduced to her husband's household gods so they would not attack her as an intruder (cf. Gen. 31:19). This notion is as old as Ruth's promise to Naomi that "your god shall be my god" (Ruth 1:16).

The bride brought to the marriage two things: her dowry and her virginity (**8.54**). Husbands were permitted to invest their wives' dowries or, in the case of property, to use it as they saw fit. In case of divorce, however, the dowry was returned to the wife. Even if the wife had been found guilty of adultery, the husband could keep only a portion of her dowry.

The chastity of unmarried women in the Greco-Roman world was a major concern. The father tried to insure his daughter's virginity so that when it came time to arrange a marriage for her, she would not be "damaged goods" (Pliny, *Ep.* 1.14). A woman who had engaged in sexual relations before marriage, whether willingly or not, was deemed to bear a permanent defilement that disqualified her from being a mother. Among the lower classes, this stigma mattered little, but it was a primary concern among the aristocracy (**8.55**). This attitude helps explain why upper-class men could have extramarital relationships with lower-class women without societal disapproval.

In order to insure their virginity at the time of the wedding, some girls were betrothed even before they reached puberty and began to live in their future husband's home at age ten or eleven. There is evidence to suggest that some Roman men consummated the relationship regardless of the girl's age. One of the most extreme cases is found in an inscription which reads in part: "My husband, whom, alas, I now have left . . . was truly like a father to me. When I was seven years old he embraced me. Now I am forty and in the power of death." In all ancient societies except the city of Sparta, girls typically married at the onset of puberty, as soon as their bodies were ready to bear children. In Epictetus' words, "Starting at fourteen years of age girls are addressed by men as ladies" (*Enchiridion* 40). This meant that a first-time bride older than fifteen was a rarity (**8.52**; **8.56**), and we should envision Jesus' mother Mary as being that age. Pliny poignantly describes preparations for the wedding of a girl of thirteen which were halted by her sudden death (see box, p. 232).[1]

The Roman groom was typically under twenty-five at the time of his first marriage. It was not unusual for Greek and Jewish men to be closer to thirty (**8.59**; **8.61**). Since brides were often so much younger than their husbands, the number of young widows in the Roman Empire was higher than the actuarial tables would predict. Because no mention of

Joseph is made after Jesus was twelve, most scholars conclude that he died before Jesus began his ministry. We know from inscriptions that many young widows married again. If they had demonstrated their fertility by having a child, they would be highly prized by potential husbands.

Greco-Roman marriages were contracts between families, not romantic attachments. The tender feelings Pliny expressed in several letters to his teenaged wife are so exceptional in antiquity that A. N. Sherwin-White describes him as "the first man known to have written a love-letter to his own wife" (**8.60**:79; *Epp.* 4.19; 6.4; 6.7; 7.5). Paul's admonition to husbands to love their wives (Eph. 5:25) may not have been meant, therefore, in quite the emotional sense which we usually give it on the basis of our experience. In Rome that sort of sentiment was reserved for one's mistress (**8.55**). But the Christian view of marriage was based on a radically different understanding of the relationship between husband and wife (**8.51**; **8.63**).

Death of a Child-Bride

I write this to you in the greatest grief. The younger daughter of our friend Fundanus has died. I've never known a girl brighter, more lovable. She deserved not just a long life but immortality. She hadn't reached her fourteenth birthday, and yet she possessed the prudence and seriousness of a mature woman along with the sweetness and modesty of a young girl.

How she would cling to her father's neck! How she would embrace us, his friends, with love and modesty. How she loved her nurses and her tutors because of the service each gave her! How eagerly and intelligently she read her lessons! With what modesty and restraint she enjoyed herself! With what patience and courage she bore her last illness!

(Continued on next page)

Divorce and Remarriage

Since a marriage was little more than an agreement to cohabit, divorce was easy. In the less formal types of Roman marriage, it could be initiated by either partner, simply by expressing publicly the intention to cancel the arrangement (**8.65**).

Reasons for divorce varied from the trivial to the compelling. Under early Roman law women were forbidden to drink wine because it was thought to have abortive properties. A man who found his wife drinking could divorce her on the grounds that she was endangering her ability to perform her primary function, child-bearing. (This provision was generally ignored by New Testament times, as wine was commonly drunk at meals; cf. **8.68**.) If one of the partners simply found someone else more interesting or another marriage more advantageous, that could be reason for divorce.

The most frequently mentioned cause for divorce was adultery. Even if there was no love in our sense between husband and wife, fidelity was expected on the part of the woman, if only to fulfill a condition of the contract. The wife who engaged in adultery was not only violating the contract, she was also disqualifying herself from becoming a fit mother. Once that happened, divorce was the natural consequence, since a man was supposed to have a wife in order to bear children.

Early Roman law required a man who caught his wife in an act of adultery to divorce her. The most stringent version of the law required him to kill her. If the roles were reversed, she was not allowed to lay a hand on him (**8.66**). By imperial times infidelity of either party was regarded more lightly. If the man tried to make an issue of it, he was often ridiculed as being unable to manage his own household (**8.67**; **8.74**).

If the Roman historians can be believed, divorce was unknown in Rome until the third century B.C. This does not mean that the Romans were any more virtuous in the early period of their history, just that social pressures in a closely knit community held marriages together. Exposure to the Greeks and increasing wealth seem to have given them the impetus to break the old bonds. This gradual erosion of marriage is a pattern repeated in many cultures. As Jesus said, Moses allowed divorce as a way of dealing with human weakness, "but from the beginning it was not so" (Matt. 19:8; cf. **8.71**).

> She obeyed her doctors, encouraged her sister and father, and sustained herself by her own strength of mind even after her bodily strength had given out. This willpower lasted right up to the end, unbroken by either the length of the illness or fear of death. Thus she has left us more and weightier reasons for longing and grief.
>
> O, what a profoundly sad and bitter death! And the timing of her death was worse than the death itself. She was already engaged to an outstanding young man; the wedding day had been chosen and everyone invited. So much joy, now turned into such sorrow! I can't find words to tell you what a wound I felt in my heart, when I heard Fundanus himself ordering that the money intended for a wedding gown and jewels be spent on incense, funeral ointments, and spices.
>
> Pliny, *Epistle* 5.16, 1–7

Once made acceptable, divorce and remarriage became rampant. Even the slightest suspicion of impropriety on the wife's part was cause to end the marriage. When Julius Caesar learned that his wife had attended a religious rite which had degenerated into an orgy, he divorced her, saying that "Caesar's wife must be above reproach" (Plutarch, *Caes.* 10.6). He himself, on the other hand, had the reputation of being "every woman's husband and every man's wife" (Suetonius, *Caes.* 52), a not very subtle hint at his bisexuality and a revealing insight into the double standard of sexual morality which prevailed at the time.

Virtually every notable Roman of the two centuries on either side of Christ's birth was divorced and remarried at least once, often to women also previously married. Cicero divorced his first wife after a difficult thirty-year marriage; he married a much younger woman, then

Wedding scenes from a Roman altar
(Photo from German Archaeological Institute)

almost immediately divorced her. Antony, already divorced from his first wife, married Augustus' sister to cement the political alliance between the two men, but divorced her to enjoy Cleopatra's company. By the late first century A.D., Martial (7.58) can point to men and women married six or seven times. Juvenal chides one woman for having "eight husbands in five autumns" (*Sat.* 6.230–231). Such cases may be extreme, but even Pliny, who moved in more conservative circles, was married three times, the last time at age forty-two to a girl of sixteen. Long, happy marriages were rare enough that Pliny can only occasionally point to one as an example (*Epp.* 7.19; 8.5).[2] Stepmothers, a common phenomenon because of the prevalence of remarriage, gained a distinctly bad press in Rome (**8.69**). Some of it could have been merited. If a second wife had children, it was in her and their interest to get as much of the father's inheritance as possible, even if this meant eliminating children from an earlier marriage.

To retain some historical objectivity, we should stop to remind ourselves that the writers who are our main sources for this study moved among the highest circles of Roman society, and the lifestyle they describe cannot be taken as normative for everyone. Among the lower classes, to judge from inscriptions on tombstones, a more stable family life was not so rare (**8.70**; **8.72**).[3] An epitaph from Rome can serve as an example: "To Cerellia Fortunata, dearest wife, with whom he lived forty years without the slightest cause for complaint, Marcus Antonius Encolpius built this."

However, even among the lower classes, the frequency of marriage was declining in the first century A.D., and divorce was becoming more common. And if Petronius' picture of lower-class morals is anywhere near accurate, extramarital affairs may have been almost as common among the masses as among the aristocracy (*Satyr.* 61). We do have a number of lead tablets and papyri with magical incantations placing curses on the owners' enemies, and unfaithful husbands and wives figure large in the sample (**5.88**).

Infidelity in Marriage

While divorce was not difficult, it was often not expedient. Most marriages had been contracted because the husband stood to gain something from his alliance with the wife's family. It sometimes happened that the husband invested the wife's dowry for her, then lost some of it. He could not divorce her because he could not return her dowry. For these and other reasons, many husbands and wives found themselves locked together in loveless, formal marriages. They often looked elsewhere for emotional gratification. Nothing in their ethical system forbade extramarital affairs; the only prohibition that applied was that against violating another person's property—or at least against getting caught at it.

The Greek orator Demosthenes summed up the classical male's view of extramarital arrangements in his prescription that men should have "mistresses for our enjoyment, concubines to serve our person, and wives for the bearing of legitimate offspring" (*Oration* 59.118–122). The Romans' casual attitude toward such matters is exemplified by Livy's description (39.9) of a young aristocrat whose affair with a freedwoman was "not at all harmful either to the young man's financial resources or to his reputation."

By the first century B.C., adultery was so common in Rome that Catullus could publish poems about his affair with "Lesbia," whose real name was Clodia, the wife of Metellus Celer (at least until she poisoned him). Ovid's relationship to Corinna and the difficulties which her marriage created for them were mentioned in chapter 7. His advice to men wanting to seduce women was intended to apply without regard to the marital status of the man or woman. In fact, if the woman was married, it made the "game" of seduction more exciting. In one poem he urges a husband to guard his wife more closely: "Easy things nobody wants, but what is forbidden is tempting" (*Amores* 2.19). The same game was still being played in Martial's day (1.73). In all fairness, one should point out that some Romans urged a different standard (see box), though they seem to have been a distinct minority.

A Stoic on Adultery

If we ignore the fidelity which is innate in us and seduce our neighbor's wife, what are we actually doing but destroying and ruining? Whom or what are we destroying? Human faithfulness, honor, and decency of behavior.

Are not women by nature common property? you may say. Yes, just as food placed on the table is common to all the invited guests. But, once it has been portioned out, should you snitch the share of the person next to you, or stretch out your hand and dip your fingers in someone else's meat sauce and lick them? A fine dinner companion you'd be! Likewise, the theater is shared by all citizens. But, once the seats are all taken, would you dare to come along and turn any man out of his place?

In a certain sense, then, women are common property by nature, but when they have been distributed by law, you, like everyone else, must be content with your share and must not steal or taste what belongs to someone else.

Epictetus, *Discourses* 2.4

Some husbands even helped their wives engage in affairs, apparently hoping to gain leverage with their wives' lovers (**8.75**). The most notorious example of such a thing is the Praetorian commander Macro, whose wife had an affair with the emperor-to-be, Caligula (Suetonius, *Calig.* 12). Caligula, however, eventually ordered Macro to commit suicide, so this was not a foolproof route to success.

Prostitution and Sexual Abuse of Slaves

In societies which place so little value on marital fidelity, we shouldn't be surprised to find prostitution flourishing. Indeed, it had from an early era in both Greece and Rome. The Greeks openly encouraged it. Many prostitutes became famous, especially in fifth-century Athens. Pericles, who governed the city from 462–429 B.C., left his wife and lived with a courtesan named Aspasia, a well-educated, witty woman who attracted even men like Socrates and the playwright Euripides to the dinners and erudite conversations which filled the evenings in her house.

Long before New Testament times, the city of Corinth had become famous for having some of the most uninhibited prostitutes in Greece and even contributed its name to a Greek verb, *korinthiazomai* (to practice fornication). Paul's strictures regarding women in 1 Corinthians 11 should be read against that background and probably not as universal prohibitions. The behavior of women in public was a particular problem in that city—especially among the class of people where Christianity was strongest—and Paul was attempting to cope with it on a local basis (**8.77**; **8.79**).

The Romans never officially permitted prostitutes to practice as openly as the Greeks did and never accorded them the status that the Greeks gave them. Yet Livy (1.4) acknowledges that the founders of Rome, Romulus and Remus, had been raised by such a woman. The Romans, he explains, used the word "wolf" much as modern Americans use "bitch" (a female dog) to describe a woman of low moral character. The story had been tidied up over the years, but its origin was undeniable. There are enough provisions in Roman law—including taxes imposed on brothels (**8.78**)—and enough references to prostitutes in the literature to assure us that such women were readily available (e. g., Juvenal, *Sat.* 11.172–173; Horace, *Ep.* 1.14; *Sat.* 1.2). The graffiti in Pompeii are replete with the names of such women, their specialties (sometimes illustrated), and their fees.

When Catullus' affair with Clodia went sour, he accused her of offering herself to men by the hundreds on street corners (Catull. 11). The fact that he could draw such an ugly picture of his former mistress suggests the presence of prostitutes in large enough numbers in Rome that his readers would recognize what he was talking about. Martial (11.45) says that both male and female prostitutes worked in portable booths on the sidewalks. The phenomenon of prostitution was empire-wide, as we can gauge from Jesus' references in Matthew 21:31 and Luke 15:30 and Paul's condemnation of the practice in 1 Corinthians 6 (**8.83**).

The most famous prostitute in the New Testament is Mary Magdalene, except that she almost certainly wasn't a prostitute. The creative tendency of early Christians to explain (and expand) the backgrounds of minor characters in the New Testament led them to link Mary with the woman caught in adultery (John 8:2–11) or the "sinner" who anointed Jesus' feet with her tears and dried them with her hair (Luke 7:36–50). Feminist scholars are now insisting on a re-evaluation of her reputation. She is, after all, listed first among the women who came to Jesus' tomb on Easter morning in Matthew, Mark, and Luke, and in John's Gospel Jesus appears first to her alone (**8.81**).

The existence of prostitution in Greco-Roman society should not surprise us; it is present in every civilized society. What is noteworthy is the degree to which the Greeks and Romans tolerated and even encouraged it. Today we cannot open a newspaper or magazine without seeing another frightening article on AIDS, herpes, or some other sexually transmitted disease. It may occur to us to ask how these promiscuous Greeks and Romans avoided or dealt with such things. The answer is that they didn't have to worry about it. There were no sexually transmitted diseases such as syphilis or gonorrhea in the ancient world. The first documented case of syphilis appeared in Europe in 1494. Columbus and his crew took smallpox to the New World and in exchange brought back this plague (**8.80**:208). Thus in antiquity a man could have affairs or visit prostitutes without concern about contracting such a disease.

Some Roman men, however, did not need to consort with prostitutes or go to all the trouble of seducing a woman. Instead, they forced themselves on their female slaves. These women were in a particularly unfortunate situation. Refusal could result in punishment from the master as a prelude to a sexual attack. Then, if the lady of the house discovered what was going on, she was also likely to punish the slave woman, since she couldn't take out her anger on her husband (Ovid, *Amores* 2.7; 2.8).

Childhood scenes from a Roman sarcophagus
(Photo from Giraudon)

The frequent references in the laws to children born of slave women and free men suggest that such liaisons were common (**8.82**). Most Roman aristocrats probably had an illegitimate child or two tucked away on their estates. Those who made no secret of the situation were the butt of jokes (Martial 1.84). As sometimes happens with Martial though, he may have been laughing at something of which he himself was guilty (**8.76**).[4] What we can seldom determine is the willingness of the slave women involved. But there was no double standard in this matter. By the first century A.D., many women were engaging in affairs with their male slaves (Martial 3.85).

Children and Education

The instability of marriage in Rome may have contributed to an ambivalence about having children. Many upper-class Romans of the first century A.D. were reluctant to take that step, in spite of the idea that it was their duty to the state (**8.90**; **8.113**). Children were no easier to raise in antiquity than they are today (**8.95**; **8.97**). Pliny reveals much about current attitudes on the topic in his description of a friend of his: "He has several children, for here too he has done his duty as a good citizen, and has chosen to enjoy the blessing of a fruitful marriage at a time when the advantages of remaining childless make most people feel a single child is a burden" (*Ep.* 4.15). He speaks of encouraging "our leading citizens . . . to undertake the responsibility of children" (*Ep.* 2.7). Martial (11.53) sings the praises of a woman who had actually borne three children to one husband.

One of the biggest differences between our life experience today and that of people in antiquity is the lack of a period of adolescence in the ancient world (**8.101**). People were expected to assume adult roles at a much earlier age than today. Girls, as already noted, typically married in their early teens. Boys became adults legally at sixteen. Pliny assumed the responsibilities of running his family's estates at seventeen and made his first speech in a law court at eighteen. As the most extreme example, Octavian inherited Julius Caesar's position at age eighteen, but Caesar's soldiers were willing to accept him as their leader. Childhood was not a stage of life to be cherished, in the ancient view. Children should be pushed through it to maturity as soon as possible.

Female children mixed freely with male children until they reached age seven. At that point boys went to school, and girls began learning what was necessary to run a home. It was not unusual for mothers or a household slave to teach girls to read and write, at least at an elementary level. Ovid assumes that any woman can write notes to her lover and read his in return. Some women enjoyed an education as sophisticated as any man's. Julia, daughter of the emperor Augustus, could hold her own in a philosophical discussion around the dinner table, Macrobius tells us (*Saturnalia* 2.5). By the early second century, Juvenal complains of women who take over the discussions (*Sat.* 6.434–437).

The male child's day centered around school. The schoolday began at dawn and, with a break in the early afternoon, ran until nearly dark. The educational theory of the day stressed rote memorization of huge chunks of Homer's *Iliad* and *Odyssey*. Other classical texts which were commonly used were sometimes anthologized (**8.98**). As the boy grew older, he would learn to deliver effective speeches, an important skill in a society where people spent much of their time in public assemblies and courts. Many writers complain of the harshness of the teachers, who often were former slaves with no other particular skills. The teachers, in their turn, complain of disinterested pupils, low fees which they had difficulty collecting, and lack of respect in society. Juvenal bitterly calculates that musicians and popular athletes earn more in a day than the teacher does in a year (*Sat.* 7.175–177, 240–243). (Some things change little over time!) Boys usually finished the equivalent of a secondary education at about age sixteen (**8.86**).

The purpose of this educational system was to produce young men who shared a body of knowledge, even if they did not think critically about it (**8.85**), and who were capable of making effective speeches in court or in debates in the Forum. Rhetoric had an importance in Roman society equal to that of television or computers in our age. Just as today's educational system is undergirded by the scientific worldview that has developed since the seventeenth century, the Roman system was founded on rhetorical categories. History, e. g., was not studied to learn the significance of important past events but to stockpile examples to insert in one's speeches (**8.90**). All types of literature were affected by rhetorical techniques (**8.87**; **8.96**), and the writers of the New Testament did not escape the impact of this rhetorical education (**8.84**; **8.103**). It shaped the way they thought and the way they composed written material, whether speeches (**8.92**; **8.114**), letters (**8.89**; **8.108**), or historical/biographical works (**8.88**; **8.104**). One can get a sense of the importance New Testament scholars now attribute to understanding this rhetorical background by merely scanning this section of the bibliography at the end of the chapter.

Woman giving birth, assisted by a midwife and companion/servant
(Photo from Cyprus Dept. of Antiquities)

Low Birth Rates and Infanticide

When it came to replenishing their numbers, the aristocracy had no model in the imperial household. Claudius was the only one of the first five emperors to father two children or to have a child outlive him. But his stepson Nero became his successor and murdered both of Claudius' children. Vespasian (A.D. 69–79) did produce two sons, who succeeded him in turn, but neither son had any children. No emperor of the second century had a child grow to adulthood until Marcus Aurelius (A.D. 161–180).

Children were never the center of the Greco-Roman family as they have become in our society. Some scholars even question whether the Greeks and Romans were emotionally attached to their children as we profess to be today (**8.124**). Under Greek and Roman law, a father could refuse to acknowledge a child as his if it was deformed or if he had any doubts about the paternity. The rejected child was "exposed," taken to some place at the edge of town and left to die (**8.115–116**; **8.126**). In actuality these children were often picked up by others who could not have children or by slave dealers.

Exposure of infants, especially of girls (**8.119**), continued to be practiced until the end of antiquity, among the fertile poor, and by others too. One of the best-known papyrus documents still extant is a letter, written about 1 A.D., from a traveling businessman to his wife which includes the offhand comment, "If the baby is a girl, get rid of it." Apuleius tells what was probably all too common a story about a woman who refused to obey the same command from her husband and entrusted her newborn daughter to a neighbor to be raised (*Golden Ass* 10.23).

As governor of Bithynia, Pliny had to deal with the legal problem of the status of foundlings when they reached adulthood (*Epp.* 10.65; 10.66).

Tertullian emphasized the cruelty of subjecting babies to death by "cold, starvation, and the dogs" (*Apol.* 9.7). Clement of Alexandria criticized the wealthy of the early third century for throwing away their children while keeping exotic pets. Many scholars today would argue that relying too heavily on such literary accounts gives us an exaggerated idea of the number of children who were exposed (**8.120**; **8.125**), but it is undeniable that the practice existed and was not alien to the ethics of Greco-Roman society.

For the upper classes, the more common problem was the scarcity of children. It has been suggested that the wealthier people, who had water piped into their homes through lead pipes, had gradually inflicted sterility on themselves (**8.127–128**; **8.131**). Another explanation holds that the extremely hot baths which Roman men, especially the wealthy, enjoyed each day decreased their sperm count (**8.118**; **8.130**).

Other scholars feel that wealthy Romans simply did not choose to have children. Pliny's praise for a friend who had three children was noted above, but an aristocratic family of that size was the exception. Childless aristocrats were courted by others who hoped to be included in their wills. They had gifts showered on them and were invited out to dine almost every evening (Juvenal *Sat.* 6.38–40). Some may have been reluctant to give up such amenities (**8.117**). Others, like Pliny, wanted children but were unable to have them; his young wife suffered a miscarriage (*Epp.* 8.10; 8.11). Whatever the cause, the childless aristocrat was a common figure by the late first century A.D. (Martial 11.44; 11.55; 11.83).

As noted earlier, in an attempt to reverse the declining birth rate among the aristocracy, the emperor Augustus decreed that no man could hold political office or inherit property from friends and distant relatives unless he was the father of three children. To meet this requirement, some men accepted whatever children their wives presented them with, even when they looked suspiciously like some gladiator or the neighborhood butcher (Juvenal *Sat.* 6.76–81; Martial 6.39). The women sometimes feigned pregnancy and then obtained children which had been exposed. The legislation had little real effect, and the emperors constantly made exceptions by granting "the right of three children"—the right to hold office and inherit property like a father of three children—to their friends or people whom their friends recommended (Pliny, *Ep.* 2.13). Pliny himself received the privilege (*Ep.* 10.2), as did Martial (2.92).

Many aristocratic women of this era did not want to have children because of the danger to themselves, due to inadequate medical care during delivery. Doctors gave little attention to gynecological problems, and a woman was likely to be assisted in childbirth by a midwife, possibly a slave in the household (**8.122**; **8.129**). As a result the mortality rate for both infants and mothers was high, as already noted in the case of Pliny's friend who had lost two daughters in childbirth (*Ep.* 4.21).

Contraception and Abortion

Some women found rearing children an inconvenience. There were simply more interesting things to do. As is so often the case, the upper-class people who could afford the children could also afford the means of preventing their birth, while the poor could not. Juvenal has no more love for lower-class women than for the noble ones, but he grudgingly admits, "These women at least endure the perils of childbirth, suffer the nuisance of nursing—but when did you ever discover labor pains in a golden bed?" (*Sat.* 6.593–594).

Women who did not desire to have children had recourse to various methods of contraception (**8.138; 8.142**) and, when those failed, to abortion (**8.134**). In Juvenal's words again, "There are potent prescriptions, fine professional skill, to be hired for inducing abortions, killing mankind in the womb" (*Sat.* 6.595–597). Ovid has two poems (*Amores* 2.13–14) reacting to his mistress' self-administered abortion, from which she nearly died. She's worse than a wild animal, he charges. At least lionesses don't tear their young out of their own bodies. She deserves to die, he concludes, but hopes the gods will forgive her this time. He sternly admonishes her not to do such a thing again.

Neither the Old Testament nor the New Testament contains a specific commandment against abortion, but the practice was widely condemned among first-century Jews (**8.135**).[5] A letter attributed to Paul's companion Barnabas and written around A.D. 100 expresses the Christian view when it says "You shall not procure abortion; you shall not commit infanticide" (19.5). The letter was reckoned as scriptural by some early churches but dropped from the canon by the fourth century. Christians continued, however, to abhor abortion (**8.136**). Early in the second century, the Didache prohibits it (2.2), and the Apocalypse of Peter envisions terrible punishments for women who practice it (Ethiopic, 8; Akhmim fragment, 26). Tertullian equates it with murder (*Apol.* 9.8). The Roman government took action early in the third century to outlaw the practice, but only on the basis that it deprived the father of his child, which was his property (**8.141**). Given their willingness to expose newborn infants, it is not to be expected that the Romans would have argued strongly for the right of the fetus to live.

Sexual "Deviance"

In modern discussions of moral standards, a popular argument is that, when it comes to sex, nothing is "abnormal" or "deviant." Whatever consenting adults wish to do with or to one another is acceptable. Such an attitude is certainly not biblical. The Old Testament sets out specific rules, governing even some of the more exotic varieties of sexual behavior (as in Lev. 20:10–16; Deut. 22:5), and Jesus raised the standards even higher when he said that whoever thinks of doing such things is as guilty as if having done them (Matt. 5:27–28).

Lacking this religious base for moral decisions, the Romans could justify virtually anything they wanted to do, for the novelty of it if for no other reason. On the basis of what we've seen thus far of their behavior, Paul's description of Roman morals doesn't seem too far off the mark:

> Their women exchanged natural intercourse for unnatural, and in the same way also the men, giving up natural intercourse with women, were consumed with passion for one another. . . . They were filled with every kind of wickedness, evil, covetousness, malice. Full of envy, murder, strife, deceit, craftiness, they are gossips, slanderers, God-haters, insolent, haughty, boastful, inventors of evil, rebellious toward parents, foolish, faithless, heartless, ruthless (Rom. 1:26–31).

The "unnatural" relations which Paul denounces were obviously homosexual, a form of personal interaction with which the church historically has never been comfortable (**8.144–145**; **8.147**; cf. chapter 1). The Greeks had exalted male homosexuality as the most meaningful form of personal relationship because women were too uneducated to form an intellectual bond with a man (**8.148**). On the other hand, some women, left to themselves at home and denied any active participation in Greek society, resorted to lesbianism as an outlet for their emotions. The writings of the poetess Sappho (ca. 600 B.C.), praising the beauty of the female students in her school, became popular among some groups of women (**8.152**).

By the time the Romans began imitating Greek culture in the second century B.C., homosexuality had been an accepted part of Hellenic life for centuries. The elite brigade of the Spartan army was the "Lovers," men who were required to join in pairs on the theory that no man would turn in battle and disgrace himself in front of his lover. Thebes had a similar corps. The Athenian tyrant Hipparchus had been murdered by two men with whom he was involved in a romantic triangle. His murderers became national heroes. Sophocles, Socrates, and other leading intellectuals of Greece had male lovers even when they were quite elderly (**8.143**; **8.153**).

The Romans began to engage in homosexuality as something of a fad, but they were never as comfortable with the practice as the Greeks were (**8.154–155**). Even though it remained slightly scandalous behavior, it was widely, if less openly, practiced among both sexes by the Romans. Juvenal's bitter second satire is devoted entirely to a denunciation of male homosexuals. Martial (1.90) and other sources make it clear that women also took lovers from their own gender (**8.151**).

Imperial leadership was sometimes an incentive to homosexual behavior. Nero engaged in numerous liaisons with persons of both genders. The emperor Hadrian, though married, preferred the company of his male lover Antinous, whose untimely death he commemorated in a poem. Those who sought to advance their own careers by flattering the emperor were more likely to adapt their morals to his (Martial 3.95).

It is clear from the artwork in Pompeii and from literary references that the Romans regularly engaged in sexual activities generally considered immoral in our day (**8.157**). Writers like Petronius (*Satyr.* 21; 25) and Martial are quite explicit in describing the sexual proclivities of their times (2.50; 11.61; 11.78; 11.104), and we cannot entirely dismiss their accounts as mere literary conventions (**8.149–150**). Sexual aggression plays a large part in Roman humor (**8.158**). What is lacking is a sense of shame. These are merely diversions for a jaded and amoral society, one which differed fundamentally from ours in its attitude toward sexuality (**8.159**).

This is the society to which the early church had to proclaim the teachings of Jesus (**8.156**). How strange his words must have sounded: "You have heard that it was said, 'You shall not commit adultery.' But I say to you that everyone who looks at a woman with lust has already committed adultery with her in his heart" (Matt. 5:27–28). Paul's description (Rom. 1:26, 29) of the "degrading passions" and "every kind of wickedness" among the Romans hits right at the mark once we see from their own records what they were like in this era.

Personal Grooming

Their devotion to the pleasures of the flesh prompted the Greeks and Romans to give more attention to personal grooming and hygiene than any society until modern times. The Greeks bathed frequently, the Romans obsessively. Cosmetics, dyes, ointments, and other beauty aids played an important part in Greco-Roman life (and in the economy). They were also significant for the Jews. The Talmud has a great deal to say about the use of such things. Archaeologists have discovered that even the Zealots who fled from Jerusalem in A.D. 70 and took refuge in the fortress of Masada carried combs, perfumes, mirrors, and equipment for applying make-up with them.

Baths

Public baths were a fixture of every town in the Empire, including Jerusalem. They were "the most important buildings of the Romans"

(*Oxford Classical Dictionary*, 2nd ed., 133). Even small towns like Pompeii and Herculaneum had several to handle the demand. The town of Baiae on the Bay of Naples was simply an outgrowth of the warm baths there, as was the town of Bath in England (**8.166**). Beginning as necessities, the baths became the center of social life in imperial times (**8.167**). People congregated there by the early afternoon, exercising (Petronius, *Satyr.* 27), initiating sexual liaisons (Martial 1.23; 3.51), wangling invitations for dinner (Martial 4.68), listening to gossip, and observing who was with whom. At the baths, which were more like our shopping malls than our health clubs, one could hear a poet reading his works, get a shave, buy clothes, or just while away a few pleasant hours (**7.91**:254–263).

The government recognized the value of such places for defusing the discontent of the masses and underwrote the costs of these magnificent establishments (**8.168**). Some baths in Rome were so large that surviving portions are used as churches and opera theaters. All over the Empire, homes of the wealthy had their own baths (Petronius, *Satyr.* 73). But it was expensive and time-consuming to heat the water for just a few people to bathe, so even the rich frequented the public baths (Pliny *Ep.* 2.17).

Bathers entered a dressing room, with a shelf running around it for their clothes. Theft was a frequent problem; those who could do so usually brought a slave to watch their garments (**8.165**). In the cold room (*frigidarium*) bathers sponged off. In the warm room (*tepidarium*) they accustomed themselves to warmer water before entering the hot room (*caldarium*), which was so hot that people sometimes fainted. A few deaths are even recorded (**8.164**). Warm air from the furnaces which heated the water circulated through ducts in the floors and walls so that the room was like a sauna. In the hot room bathers soaked in a pool of water, coated themselves with olive oil and scraped it off with curved metal scrapers called strigils. If they had the money and the time, they could enjoy a massage and even have unwanted body hair removed. Seneca once lived over a bathing establishment and complained about the screams of people having the hair pulled from their underarms (*Ep.* 56.2).

The literature shows that Christians needed to discern what was good or bad conduct at the baths. Late in the second century, Clement of Alexandria criticizes bathers who display wealth by using gold and silver vessels to sup and get drunk while bathing. He warns against baths "opened promiscuously to men and women" with accompanying lust and "licentious indulgence" (*The Instructor* 3.5). Men's bathing is to be for health only, women's for cleanliness and health. It is not necessary to bathe for the heat, and one should not bathe for pleasure, he says (3.9). Somewhat later the *Apostolic Constitutions* tell Christian women to avoid "that disorderly practice of bathing . . . with men" (1.3.9).

Hair

The Romans' attention to grooming began early in the morning. Women devoted great care to arranging their hair in the latest style. Aristocratic women had slaves who specialized as hairdressers. They often had their mistresses' ears because they spent so much time in such close contact. As we might suspect from Paul's reference to hairstyles (1 Cor. 11:14–15), women normally wore their hair long (**8.171**; **8.173**). Ovid describes his mistress' hair as coming almost to her knees (*Amores* 1.14). Apuleius rhapsodizes about women's hair as "the most important part of the body" (*Golden Ass* 1.8; cf. 1 Cor. 11:15) and concludes that "a woman cannot be considered decently dressed unless she has her hair fixed in a becoming style." References in the Talmud indicate that this fashion was followed in Judea. Jewish women wore such elaborate hairstyles, involving braids and hairpieces, that "it was forbidden to undo a woman's hairdo on the Sabbath because it involved transgressing the prohibitions of 'building' and 'demolishing'" (*Encyclopedia Judaica* 5:981).

Paintings and coins from the first century A.D. show that women's hairstyles changed every few years. Sometimes the hair was done up in a bun on the neck; at other times it was piled up on top of the head. Portrait busts of women "are sometimes found to possess detachable marble wigs which could be replaced as fashions altered" (**7.105**:42). Some women supplemented their natural locks with wigs and hairpieces, usually taken from slaves or war captives. At several points during the first century, braids were fashionable, especially with jewelry fastened into them. Both 1 Timothy 2:9 and 1 Peter 3:3 warn against women devoting too much attention to braiding and ornamenting their hair. One reason for considerable combing and brushing, however, may have been the removal of head lice (**8.172**).

Men's hair was worn short, seldom over the ears or any longer in the back than is considered normal today. Paul's admonition that men wear short hair (1 Cor. 11:14) suggests that this practice was commonplace among the Greeks and Romans of that time. Only fops and deviants did otherwise. Artistic evidence such as depictions of the Jews on the Arch of Titus shows that Eastern peoples wore their hair somewhat longer than the Romans and favored beards. A line in one of Martial's epigrams (2.36) urges a friend not to "let your beard be that of Orientals," meaning Persians.

By the first century A.D., however, rabbinic authorities permitted Jews who had frequent contacts with Romans to clip their beards and some Jewish men appear to have gone clean-shaven. The Talmud refers frequently to barbers and hairdressers, who also sold cosmetics, gave manicures and pedicures, and performed minor medical services.

Most Roman men began their day with a visit to a barber, which could be a painful experience (**8.170**; cf. Martial 11.84). In addition to shaving their faces, some Roman men had the hair plucked from their underarms. Men of questionable character depilated their arms and legs as well (Martial 2.62). Women also shaved or plucked their underarms and legs (Ovid, *Art of Love* 3.193–94), or used depilatory creams (Martial 6.93). Removal of body hair seems to have been the fashion for women all over the civilized world. A common jibe at barbarian women is their hairiness.

Brown or black was the dominant color of people's hair in New Testament times, but blonds were fairly common and greatly admired. The emperors Augustus and Nero had blond hair (Suetonius, *Aug.* 79; *Nero* 51). Some women bought wigs made from the blond hair of German captives. Ovid's mistress tried to dye her hair blond, with unfortunate results (see box).

> ### A Bad Hair Day
>
> I warned you to stop dyeing your hair.
> Now you don't have any hair that you can tint. . . .
> You know you did this to yourself;
> You kept on applying that poisonous mess to your head.
> Now Germany will send you a captive's hair and you'll
> be covered with a triumphal gift. . . .
>
> Oh, dear, she can't hold back the tears and with her hand she brushes tears from her reddened cheeks.
> In her lap she holds what used to be her hair and gazes at it, a treasure that doesn't belong there.
>
> Ovid, *Amores* 2.14

Cosmetics

In addition to all the attention they gave to their hair, the people of New Testament times used cosmetics heavily (**8.177**). A pale complexion was considered desirable for women, and those who had darker skin achieved the effect by using white powder, often in such thick layers that they were afraid to go out if rain threatened. Even a tear could plow a furrow down one of these heavily coated cheeks. Both Juvenal and Martial make such frequent comments about painted and powdered women that we might wonder if they looked more like Japanese geisha girls. The paintings from Pompeii help correct that impression (**8.176**). Aside from eye shadow, the women portrayed there do not appear to be overly made up, though their skin is generally paler than the men's (a common convention of ancient art). Heavy use of white powder may have been merely an affectation of the rich in the capital.

Ovid considered cosmetics such an important topic that he wrote a book on *The Art of Beauty*, which does not survive in its entirety. In it he gave formulas for making powders and ointments (**8.175**). In Book 3 of *The Art of Love* he gives a shorter version of some of the same advice but urges his readers to apply the techniques in the privacy of their rooms. A man wants to admire the effect, not learn how it was achieved: "Put on the finishing touch privately, out of my sight. Why do I have to know the cause of your lovely complexion?"

Jewish women also used cosmetics heavily, but in part for genuine health reasons. Makeup applied around the eyes and mouth prevented those sensitive areas from drying out in the arid Judean climate and may have helped cut down on infections.

Conclusion

Some of the things discussed in this chapter may have shocked some readers. That was not my primary purpose. I've tried to show how drastically the Greco-Roman view of morality and personal behavior differed from Christian conceptions. I hope that the reader now has a better understanding of what the early Christians were up against as they presented their message and how that opposition may have shaped their own views. Their view of how life should be lived was indeed so different from that of the people around them that they could be called "these people who have been turning the world upside down" (Acts 17:6).

Notes

1. The urn in which the ashes of this girl, Minicia Marcella, were buried has been found in her family's tomb outside Rome (cf. **8.53**). Her father became proconsul of the province of Asia in 124/125 and received from the emperor Hadrian a rescript limiting prosecutions against Christians to charges based on their actions which could be proved in open court (cf. Eusebius *Eccl. Hist.* 4.9).

2. Not long ago, when I attended the wedding of the daughter of some long-time friends, the minister made particular mention of how rare it was that the bride and groom both came from families which had not experienced a divorce. "Nothing new under the sun," as the saying goes.

3. Tombstone epitaphs must be read with some skepticism, of course (cf. **5.23**). No one advertises an unhappy marriage on a tombstone.

4. This situation is the foundation for my Christian historical novel, *Daughter of Lazarus* (St. Meinrad, IN: Abbey Press, 1988), which shows how a young woman, sold into slavery by her stepfather, tries to attain her freedom.

5. Exodus 21:22–25 deals with a case of miscarriage or induced abortion, which rabbis later deemed an act to be punished by a fine, not by death (Mekilta Nez. 8). The condemned "sorcerers" of Revelation 21:8 and 22:15 are called *pharmakoi*, perhaps referring to those who supplied drugs to induce abortions: S. D. Ricks, "Abortion in Antiquity," in *The Anchor Bible Dictionary*, 1:31–35.

BIBLIOGRAPHY

8.1. Friedländer, L. *Roman Life and Manners under the Early Empire*. London: Routledge, 1908–13.

8.2. Meeks, W. A. *The Moral World of the First Christians*. Philadelphia: Westminster Press, 1986.

8.3. Stager, L. E. "Eroticism and Infanticide at Ashkelon." *BAR* 17, no. 4, (1991): 34–53, 72.

The Basis of Greco-Roman Morality

8.4. Burn, A. R. *The Pelican History of Greece*. London: Penguin, 1966.

8.5. Dover, K. *Greek Popular Morality in the Time of Plato and Aristotle*. Berkeley: University of California Press, 1974.

8.6. Dupont, F. *Daily Life in Ancient Rome*. Oxford: Blackwell, 1992.

8.7. Durant, W. *Caesar and Christ: A History of Roman Civilization and of Christianity from Their Beginning to A.D. 325*. New York: Simon & Schuster, 1944.

8.8. Earl, D. *The Moral and Political Tradition of Rome*. London: Thames & Hudson, 1967.

8.9. Ferguson, J. *Moral Values in the Ancient World*. London: Methuen, 1958.

8.10. Flaceliere, R. *Love in Ancient Greece*. New York: Crown, 1962.

8.11. Kloppenborg, J. S. "Alms, Debt and Divorce: Jesus' Ethics in Their Mediterranean Context." *TorJTheol* 6(1990): 182–200.

8.12. Lind, L. R. "The Idea of the Republic and the Foundations of Roman Morality." In *Studies in Latin Literature and Roman History V*. Ed. by C. Derricks. Brussels: Soc. Latomus, 1989:5–34.

8.13. Meeks, W. A. *The Origins of Christian Morality: The First Two Centuries*. New Haven, CT: Yale University Press, 1993.

8.14. Noerr, D. "The Matrimonial Legislation of Augustus: An Early Instance of Social Engineering." *IrJur* 26(1981): 350–364.

8.15. Ogilvie, R. M. *The Romans and Their Gods in the Age of Augustus*. New York: Norton, 1969.

8.16. Quispel, G. "Love Thy Brother." *AncSoc* 1(1970): 83–93.

8.17. Sloan, I. "The Greatest and the Youngest: Greco-Roman Reciprocity in the Farewell Address, Luke 22:24–30." *SR* 22(1993): 63–73.

8.18. Tatum, J. "Ritual and Personal Morality in Roman Religion." *SyllClass* 4(1993): 13–20.

8.19. Whittaker, J. "Christianity and Morality in the Roman Empire." *VigChr* 33(1979): 209–225.

8.20. Zerbe, G. M. *Non-Retaliation in Early Jewish and New Testament Texts: Ethical Themes in Social Contexts*. Sheffield, UK: Academic Press, 1993.

The Evidence for Roman Morality

8.21. Bonfante, L. "The Naked Greek." *Archaeology* 43, no. 5 (1990): 28–35.

8.22. Cavander, K. "The World of Ovid." *Horizon* 15, no. 2, (1973): 38–43.

8.23. Crook, J. A. *Law and Life of Ancient Rome*. Ithaca, NY: Cornell University Press, 1967.

8.24. Garthwaite, J. "Martial, Book 6, on Domitian's Moral Censorship." *Prudentia* 22, no. 1, (1990): 13–22.

8.25. Grant. M., and A. Mulas. *Eros in Pompeii: The Secret Rooms of the National Museum of Naples*. New York: Bonanza Books, 1975.

8.26. Lindsay, J. *The Ancient World: Manners and Morals*. New York: Putnam, 1968.

Family Life

The Roman Concept of Family

8.27. Bradley, K. R. *Discovering the Roman Family: Studies in Roman Social History*. New York: Oxford University Press, 1991.

8.28.   ———. "Writing the History of the Roman Family." *CPh* 88(1993): 237–250.
8.29.   Crook, J. A. *"Patria Potestas." CQ* 17(1967): 113–122.
8.30.   DeWitt, N. W. "Vesta Unveiled." In *Studies in Honor of Ullman, Presented to Him on the Occasion of His Seventy-Fifth Birthday.* Ed. by L. B. Lawler, et al. St. Louis: The Classical Bulletin, 1960: 48–54.
8.31.   Dixon, S. *The Roman Mother.* Norman: University of Oklahoma Press, 1988.
8.32.   Hallett, J. P. *Fathers and Daughters in Roman Society: Women and the Elite Family.* Princeton, NJ: Princeton University Press, 1984.
8.33.   Osiek, C. "The Family in Early Christianity: 'Family Values' Revisited." *CBQ* 58(1996): 1–25.
8.34.   Pomeroy, S. B. "The Relationship of the Married Woman to Her Blood Relatives in Rome." *AncSoc* 7(1976): 215–227.
8.35.   Rawson, B. *The Family in Ancient Rome: New Perspectives.* Ithaca, NY: Cornell University Press, 1986.
8.36.   Saller, R. P. "Familia, Domus, and the Roman Conception of the Family." *Phoenix* 38(1984): 336–355.
8.37.   ———. *"Pietas,* Obligation and Authority in the Roman Family." In *Alte Geschichte und Wissenschaftsgeschichte: Festschrift für Karl Christ zum 65 Geburtstag.* Ed. by P. Kneissel and V. Losemann. Darmstadt: Wiss. Buchges, 1988: 393–410.

The Decline of the Roman Family

8.38.   Csillag, P. *The Augustan Laws on Family Relations.* Budapest: Akademiai Kiado, 1976.
8.39.   Frank, R. I. "Augustus' Legislation on Marriage and Children." *CSCA* 8(1975): 41–52.
8.40.   Galinsky, K. "Augustus' Legislation on Morals and Marriage." *Philologus* 125(1981): 126–144.
8.41.   Lambert, G. R. "Childless by Choice: Graeco-Roman Arguments and Their Uses." *Prudentia* 14(1982): 132–138.
8.42.   Levick, B. "Morals, Politics, and the Fall of the Roman Empire." *G&R* 29(1982): 53–62.
8.43.   Noerr, D. "The Matrimonial Legislation of Augustus: An Early Instance of Social Engineering." *IrJur* 26(1981): 350–364.
8.44.   Pearce, T. E. V. "The Role of the Wife as *Custos* in Ancient Rome." *Eranos* 72(1974): 17–33.

Marriage

8.45.   Corbett, P. E. *The Roman Law of Marriage.* Oxford: Clarendon Press, 1930; 1969 rpt.
8.46.   Deming, W. *Paul on Marriage and Celibacy: The Hellenistic Background of 1 Corinthians 7.* New York: Cambridge University Press, 1995.
8.47.   Looper-Friedman, S. E. "The Decline of *Manus*-Marriage in Rome." *RHD* 55(1987): 281–296.
8.48.   MacDonald, M. Y. "Early Christian Women Married to Unbelievers." *SR* 19(1990): 221–234.
8.49.   Rawson, B. "Roman Concubinage and Other de facto Marriages." *TAPhA* 104(1974): 279–305.
8.50.   Treggiari, S. "Concubinae." *PBSR* 49(1982): 59–81.
8.51.   Ward, R. B. "Musonius and Paul on Marriage." *NTS* 36(1990): 281–289.

Marriage as a Contract

8.52.   Amundsen, D., and C. J. Diers. "The Age of Menarche in Classical Greece and Rome." *Human Biology* 4(1969): 125–132.
8.53.   Bodel, J. "Minicia Marcella: Taken Before Her Time." *AJPh* 116(1995): 453–460.
8.54.   Cohen, B. "Dowry in Jewish and Roman Law." *Annuaire de l'institut de Philologie et d'Histoire Orientales de l'Université libre de Bruxelles* 13(1953): 57–85.
8.55.   Grimal, P. *Love in Ancient Rome.* Norman: University of Oklahoma Press, 1986.

8.56. Hopkins, M. K. "The Age of Roman Girls at Marriage." *Population Studies* 18(1965): 309–327.

8.57. MacCormack, G. "*Coemptio* and Marriage by Purchase." *Bulletino dell'Istituto di Diritto Romano* 81(1978): 179–199.

8.58. McGinn, T. A. J. "Concubinage and the *Lex Julia* on Adultery." *TAPhA* 121(1991): 335– 375.

8.59. Saller, R. P. "Men's Age at Marriage and Its Consequences in the Roman Family." *CPh* 82(1987): 21–34.

8.60. Sherwin-White, A. N. "Pliny: The Man and His Letters." *G&R* 16(1969): 76–90.

8.61. Thornton, T. C. G. "Jewish Bachelors in New Testament Times." *JThS* (1972): 444–445.

8.62. Treggiari, S. "Consent to Roman Marriage: Some Aspects of Law and Reality." *EMC* 26(1982): 34–44.

8.63. Ward, R. B. "Paul: How He Radically Redefined Marriage." *BibRev* 4, no. 4, (1988): 26–31.

8.64. Williams, G. "Some Aspects of Roman Marriage Ceremonies and Ideals." *JRS* 48(1958): 16–29.

Divorce and Remarriage

8.65. Arjava, A. "Divorce in Later Roman Law." *Arctos* 22(1988): 6–21.

8.66. Daube, D. "The Lex Julia Concerning Adultery." *IrJur* 7(1972): 373–380.

8.67. Dorey, T. A. "Adultery and Propaganda in the Early Roman Empire." *University of Birmingham Historical Journal* 18(1961): 1–6.

8.68. Dunbabin, K. M. D. "Wine and Water at the Roman *convivium.*" *Journal of Roman Archaeology* 6(1993): 116–141.

8.69. Gray-Fow, M. J. G. "The Wicked Stepmother in Roman Literature and History: An Evaluation." *Latomus* 47(1988): 741–757.

8.70. Kajanto, I. "On Divorce Among the Common People of Rome." In *Mélanges Marcel Drury.* Paris: Les Belles Lettres, 1970: 99–113.

8.71. Keener, C. S. *And Marries Another: Divorce and Remarriage in the Teaching of the New Testament.* Peabody, MA: Hendrickson, 1991.

8.72. Rawson, B. "Family Life Among the Lower Classes at Rome in the First Two Centuries of the Empire." *CPh* 61(1966): 71–83.

8.73. ——. *Marriage, Divorce, and Children in Ancient Rome.* Oxford: Clarendon Press, 1991.

8.74. Richlin, A. "Approaches to the Sources on Adultery at Rome." In *Reflections of Women in Antiquity.* Ed. by H. F. Foley. New York: Gordon & Breach, 1981: 379–404.

Infidelity in Marriage

8.75. Tracy, V. A. "The Leno-Maritus." *CJ* 72(1976): 62–64.

Prostitution and Sexual Abuse of Slaves

8.76. Bell, A. A., Jr. "Martial's Daughter?" *CW* 78(1984): 21–24.

8.77. MacDonald, M. Y. "Women Holy in Body and Spirit: The Social Setting of 1 Corinthians 7." *NTS* 36(1990): 161–181.

8.78. McGinn, T. A. J. "The Taxation of Roman Prostitutes." *Helios* 16(1989): 79–110.

8.79. McGraw, L. "The City of Corinth." *SWJourTheol* 32(1989): 5–10.

8.80. McNeil, W. H. *Plagues and Peoples.* New York: Doubleday, 1976.

8.81. Schaberg, J. "How Mary Magdalene Became a Whore." *BibRev* 8, no. 5, (1992): 30–37.

8.82. Syme, R. "Bastards in the Roman Aristocracy." *PAPhS* 104(1960): 323–327.

8.83. Wright, D. F. "Homosexuals or Prostitutes? The Meaning of *Arsenokoitai* (1 Corinthians 6:9, 1 Timothy 1:10)." *VigChr* 38(1984): 125–153.

Children and Education

8.84. Black, C. C. "Keeping Up With Recent Studies. XVI: Rhetorical Criticism and Biblical Interpretation." *ExposT* 100(1989): 252–258.

8.85. Bloomer, W. M. "Schooling in Persona: Imagination and Subordination in Roman Education." *ClassAnt* 16, no. 1, (1997): 57–78.

8.86. Booth, A. D. "Elementary and Secondary Education in the Roman Empire." *Florilegium* 1 (1979): 1–14.

8.87. Bullmore, M. A. *St. Paul's Theology of Rhetorical Style: An Examination of 1 Corinthians 2:1–5 in the Light of First-Century Graeco-Roman Rhetorical Culture.* San Francisco: International Scholars Publications, 1995.

8.88. Burridge, R. A. *What Are the Gospels? A Comparison with Graeco-Roman Biography.* Cambridge: Cambridge University Press, 1992.

8.89. Classen, C. J. "St. Paul's Epistles and Ancient Greek and Roman Rhetoric." *Rhetorica* 10 (1992): 319–344.

8.90. Cosby, M. R. *The Rhetorical Composition and Function of Hebrews 11 in Light of Example Lists in Antiquity.* Macon, GA: Mercer University Press, 1988.

8.91. Daube, D. "The Duty of Procreation." *PCA* 74 (1977): 10–25.

8.92. Dolamo, R T. H. "Rhetorical Speech in Galatians." *Theologia Viatorum* 17 (1989): 30– 37.

8.93. Ellens, J. H. "The Ancient Library of Alexandria: The West's Most Important Repository of Learning." *BibRev* 13, no. 1, (1997): 19–29, 46.

8.94. Evans, C. F. *The Theology of Rhetoric: The Epistle to the Hebrews.* London: Dr. Williams's Trust, 1988.

8.95. Eyben, E. *Restless Youth in Ancient Rome,* trans. by P. Daly. London: Routledge, 1993.

8.96. Forbes, C. "Comparison, Self-praise and Irony: Paul's Boasting and the Convention of Hellenistic Rhetoric." *NTS* 32 (1986): 1–30.

8.97. Garland, R. "Juvenile Delinquency in the Graeco-Roman World." *HT* 41 10 (1991): 12–19.

8.98. Grant, R. M. "Early Christianity and Greek Comic Poetry." *CPh* 60 (1965): 157–163.

8.99. Kennedy, G. A. *New Testament Interpretation Through Rhetorical Criticism.* Chapel Hill: University of NC Press, 1984.

8.100. Kinneavy, J. L. *Greek Rhetorical Origins of Christian Faith: An Inquiry.* New York: Oxford University Press, 1987.

8.101. Kleijwegt, M. *Ancient Youth: the Ambiguity of Youth and the Absence of Adolescence in Greco-Roman Society.* Amsterdam: Gieben, 1991.

8.102. Krentz, E. M. "Epideiktik and Hymnody: the New Testament and Its World." *BibRes* 40 (1995): 50–97.

8.103. Mack, B. L. *Rhetoric and the New Testament.* Minneapolis: Fortress Press, 1990.

8.104. Mealand, D. L. "Hellenistic Historians and the Style of Acts." *ZNTW* 82 (1991): 42–66.

8.105. Smit, J. "The Genre of 1 Corinthians 13 in the Light of Classical Rhetoric." *NovT* 23 (1991): 193–216.

8.106. ———. "The Letter of Paul to the Galatians: A Deliberative Speech." *NTS* 35 (1989): 1–26.

8.107. Sumney, J. L. "The Bearing of a Pauline Rhetorical Pattern on the Integrity of 2 Thessalonians." *ZNTW* 81 (1990): 192–204.

8.108. Watson, D. F. "James 2 in Light of Greco-Roman Schemes of Argumentation." *NTS* 39 (1993): 94–121.

8.109. ———. "The New Testament and Greco-Roman Rhetoric: A Bibliographical Update." *JEvangThSoc* 33 (1990): 513–524.

8.110. ———. "The New Testament and Greco-Roman Rhetoric: A Bibliography." *JEvangThSoc* 31 (1988): 465–472.

8.111. ———. "The Rhetoric of James 3.1–12 and a Classical Pattern of Argumentation." *NovT* 35 (1993): 48–64.

8.112. ———. "A Rhetorical Analysis of 2 John According to Greco-Roman Convention." *NTS* 35 (1989): 104–130.

8.113. Weidemann, T. *Adults and Children in the Roman Empire.* New Haven, CT: Yale University Press, 1989.

8.114. Zweck, D. "The Exordium of the Areopagus Speech, Acts 17:22–23." *NTS* 35(1989): 94–103.

Low Birth Rates and Infanticide

8.115. Boswell, J. "*Expositio* and *Oblatio*: The Abandonment of Children and the Ancient and Medieval Family." *AmHistR* 89(1984): 10–33.

8.116. Cameron, A. "The Exposure of Children and Greek Ethics." *Classical Review* 46(1932): 105–114.

8.117. Crook, J. A. "Intestacy in Roman Society." *PCPhS* 19(1973): 38–44.

8.118. Devine, A. M. "The Low Birth-Rate in Ancient Rome: A Possible Contributing Factor." *Rheinisches Museum* 128(1985): 313–317.

8.119. Engels. D. "The Problem of Female Infanticide in the Greco-Roman World." *CPh* 75(1980): 112–120.

8.120. ———. "The Use of Demography in Ancient History." *CQ* 34(1984): 386–393.

8.121. Eyben, E. "Family Planning in Graeco-Roman Antiquity." *AncSoc* 11–12(1980–81): 5–82.

8.122. French, V. "Midwives and Maternity Care in the Roman World." *Helios* 13(1986): 69–84.

8.123. Frier, B. W. "Natural Fertility and Family Limitation in Roman Marriage." *CPh* 89(1994): 318–333.

8.124. Golden, M. "Did the Ancients Care When Their Children Died?" *G&R* 35(1988): 152–163.

8.125. Harris, W. V. "The Theoretical Possibility of Extensive Infanticide in the Graeco-Roman World." *CQ* 32(1982): 114–116.

8.126. Hillman, J. "Abandoning the Child." *Eranos-Jahrbuch* 40(1971): 357–407.

8.127. Hodge, A. T. "A Plain Man's Guide to Roman Plumbing." *EMC* 27(1983): 311–328.

8.128. ———. "Vitruvius, Lead Pipes and Lead Poisoning." *AJA* 85(1981): 486–491.

8.129. Horstmannshoff, H. F. J. "The Ancient Physician: Craftsman or Scientist?" *Journal of the History of Medicine and Allied Sciences* 45(1990): 176–197.

8.130. Krenkel, W. A. "Hyperthermia in Ancient Rome." *Arethusa* 8(1975): 381–386.

8.131. Nriagu, J. O. *Lead and Lead Poisoning in Antiquity.* New York: Wiley and Sons, 1983.

8.132. Rawson, B. "*Spurii* and the Roman View of Illegitimacy." *Antichthon* 23(1989): 10–41.

8.133. Reinhartz, A. "Philo on Infanticide." *StPhilon* 4(1992): 42–58.

Contraception and Abortion

8.134. Dickison, S. "Abortion in Antiquity." *Arethusa* 6(1973): 159–166.

8.135. Freund, R. "The Ethics of Abortion in Hellenistic Judaism." *Helios* 10(1983): 125–137.

8.136. Gorman, M. J. *Abortion and the Early Church: Christian, Jewish, and Pagan Attitudes in the Greco-Roman World.* Ramsey, NJ: Paulist Press, 1982.

8.137. ———. "Why Is the New Testament Silent About Abortion?" *ChrT* 37, no. 1, (1993): 27–29; also in *Good News*, 1993, May/June: 20–23.

8.138. Hopkins, K. "Contraception in the Roman Empire." *CSSH* 8(1965–66): 124–151.

8.139. Laale, H. W. "Abortion in Roman Antiquity: Monarchy to Early Empire, I." *CML* 13(1992–93): 297–308.

8.140. ———. "Abortion in Roman Antiquity: Monarchy to Early Empire, II." *CML* 14(1993–94): 25–42.

8.141. Riddle, J. M. *Contraception and Abortion from the Ancient World to the Renaissance.* Cambridge, MA: Harvard University Press, 1992.

8.142. ———. "Oral Contraceptives and Early-term Abortifacients During Classical Antiquity and the Middle Ages." *P&P* 132(1992): 3–32.

Sexual "Deviance"

8.143. Africa, T. W. "Homosexuals in Greek History." *Journal of Psychohistory* 9(1982): 401–420.

8.144. Bailey, D. S. *Homosexuality and the Western Christian Tradition.* Hamden, CT: Archon Books, 1975.

8.145. Boswell, J. *Christianity, Social Tolerance and Homosexuality: Gay People in Western Europe from the Beginning of the Christian Era to the Fourteenth Century.* Chicago: University of Chicago Press, 1980.

8.146. Cantarella, E. *Bisexuality in the Ancient World.* New Haven, CT: Yale University Press, 1992.

8.147. de Young, J. B. "The Meaning of 'Nature' in Romans 1 and Its Implications for Biblical Proscriptions of Homosexual Behavior." *JEvangThSoc* 31 (1988): 429–441.

8.148. Dover, K. J. *Greek Homosexuality.* Cambridge, MA: Harvard University Press, 1978.

8.149. Green, P. M. "Sex and Classical Literature." In *The Sexual Dimension in Literature,* ed. by A. Bold. New York: Barnes & Noble, 1983: 19–48.

8.150. Griffin, J. "Augustan Poetry and the Life of Luxury." *JRS* 66 (1976): 87–105.

8.151. Hallett, J. P. "Female Homoeroticism and the Denial of Roman Reality in Latin Literature." *Yale Journal of Criticism* 3 (1989–90): 209–227.

8.152. Ide, A. F. *Loving Women: A Study of Lesbianism to 500 A.D.* Arlington, TX: Liberal Arts Press, 1985.

8.153. Konstan, D. "Friends and Lovers in Ancient Greece." *SyllClass* 4 (1993): 1–12.

8.154. Lilja, S. *Homosexuality in Republican and Augustan Rome.* Helsinki: Finnish Academy of Sciences, 1983.

8.155. MacMullen, R. "Roman Attitudes to Greek Love." *Historia* 31 (1982): 484–502.

8.156. Osborn, E. F. *Ethical Patterns in Early Christian Thought.* New York: Cambridge University Press, 1976.

8.157. Pike, E. R. *Love in Ancient Rome.* London: Muller, 1965.

8.158. Richlin, A. *The Gardens of Priapus: Sexuality and Aggression in Roman Humor.* New Haven, CT: Yale University Press, 1983.

8.159. Rousselle, A. *Porneia: On Desire and the Body in Antiquity.* Trans. by F. Pheasant. Oxford: Blackwell, 1988.

8.160. Smith, M. D. "Ancient Bisexuality and the Interpretation of Romans 1:26–27." *Journal of the American Academy of Religion* 64 (1996): 232–256.

8.161. Stegeman, W. "Paul and the Sexual Mentality of His World." *BTB* 23 (1993): 161–166.

8.162. Williams, C. A. "Greek Love at Rome." *CQ* 45 (1995): 517–539.

8.163. Wright, D. E. "Early Christian Attitudes to Homosexuality." *StudPatr* 18, no. 2, (1989): 329–334.

Personal Grooming

Baths

8.164. Bastomsky, S. J. "A Note on Some Hot Baths and Accelerated Deaths in Nero's Principate." *Latomus* 52 (1993): 612–616.

8.165. Brunn, C. "*Lotores*: Roman Bath-Attendants." *ZPE* 98 (1993): 222–228.

8.166. Dunbabin, K. M. D. "*Baiarum grata voluptas*: Pleasures and Dangers of the Baths." *PBSR* 64 (1989): 7–46.

8.167. Rook, T. "The Development and Operation of Roman Hypocausted Baths." *Journal of Archeological Science* 5 (1978): 269–282.

8.168. Wright, L. "Where the Romans Enjoyed 'Omnia Commoda.'" *Horizon* 2, no. 5, (1960): 39–41.

8.169. Yegül, F. K. *Baths and Bathing in Classical Antiquity.* Cambridge, MA: MIT Press, 1992.

Hair

8.170. Boon, G. C. "*Tonsor humanus*: Razor and Toilet-knife in Antiquity." *Britannia* 22 (1991): 21–32.

8.171. Gill, D. W. J. "The Importance of Roman Portraiture for Head-Coverings in 1 Corinthians 11:2–16." *TynBull* 41 (1990): 245–260.

8.172. Mumcuoglu, K. Y., and J. Zias. "How the Ancients De-Loused Themselves." *BAR* 15, no. 6, (1989): 66–69.

8.173. Thompson, C. L. "Hairstyles, Head-coverings, and St. Paul: Portraits from Roman Corinth." *BiblArch* 51 (1988): 99–115.

Cosmetics

8.174. Dayagi-Mendeles, M. *Perfumes and Cosmetics in the Ancient World.* Jerusalem: Israel Museum, 1989.

8.175. Matthews, K. D. "Saffron and Swan's Grease." *Expedition* 5, no. 4, (1967): 11–17.

8.176. Will, E. L. "Women in Pompeii." *Archaeology* 32, no. 5, (1979): 34–43.

8.177. Wiltshire, D. C. S. "Roman Aids to Beauty." *HT* 29 (1979): 332–335.

CHAPTER 9

TIME, DISTANCE, AND TRAVEL IN THE ROMAN WORLD

IN THE MODERN world we measure time and distance precisely on either end of a continuum, from nanoseconds and millimeters to millennia and light years. In his play *The Clouds*, the Athenian comic poet Aristophanes made fun of intellectuals who tried to measure how far fleas can jump. With our precise instruments, we can calculate what fraction of an inch they jump and what part of a second it takes them to do it—though we cannot answer any better than Aristophanes could the question of why anyone would want to know such things. Or we can plot a course to the moon and back. It is, therefore, difficult for us to imagine being content to know that it is "about midday" or "a three-day journey" to the next town.

In New Testament times people lived with just that sort of imprecision in their measurement of everything, from the hours of the day to the number of years they had lived. In general they had only vague notions of distances beyond their own town or the next town up the road. Soldiers and merchants had a better idea of distances, but even they figured largely in terms of a day's march or a day's journey. The farther they got from the Mediterranean coast, the sketchier their knowledge became.

Major highways had names, such as the Via Appia (Appian Way), but in towns the roads and streets rarely had names unless there was something distinctive about them, such as the "street called Straight" in Damascus (Acts 9:11), or some group of tradesmen concentrated in one area (such as the street of the bakers or tent makers).[1] One of the comic playwrights depicts a character trying to give directions to a stranger in Athens. The hilarity of the scene depends on the lack of street names and the stranger's lack of familiarity with local landmarks, which provided the only means of giving directions (**9.1**).

The Appian Way, outside of Rome
(Photo by Howard Vos)

Time

The modern Western obsession with time began in medieval monasteries, where the monks needed some reliable device to awaken them in the middle of the night for prayers (**9.2**). Their search has led us through pocket watches to wrist devices whose makers prefer to call them chronometers. We are seldom out of sight of a timepiece and are virtually enslaved to schedules—in school, at work, even in our entertainment (movie theaters, TV).

The ancients were not as dominated by time as we are. They never developed precise instruments to calculate it, though not for want of trying. They did invent elaborate waterclocks—which seldom agreed with one another, Seneca says (*Apocolocyntosis* 2)—and even had small sundials which could be worn on the wrist or around the neck (**9.11**). But most ancient peoples recognized that their timekeeping could only be approximate: "about the so-and-so hour" is the way times are usually given. Such a casual system says something about how fundamentally different these ancient people's world view was from ours (**9.3**).

The reckoning of the day varied from one culture to another (**9.8**). Pliny the Elder summed up the situation (*Nat. Hist.* 2.89):

> The actual period of a day has been differently kept by different people: the Babylonians count the period between two sunrises, the Athenians that between two sunsets, the Umbrians from midday to midday, the common people everywhere from dawn to dark, the Roman priests and the authorities who fixed the official day, and also the Egyptians, the period from midnight to midnight.

So, officially, the Greeks and Jews reckoned days from sunset to sunset while the Romans began at midnight, but for all ancient peoples, the day in ordinary terms began at sunrise (**9.5–7**).

Most peoples numbered days in a simple manner, such as "the fifth day of the month X." The Romans, however, contrived a cumbersome system based on three reference points, the kalends, the nones, and the ides. The kalends was always the first day of a month, but the nones and the ides varied, depending on the month. The nones usually fell around the fifth to the seventh day of the month, and the ides around the thirteenth to the fifteenth. Days were counted backward from the next one of these reference points. Thus any day after the ides of a month would be counted as so many days before the kalends of the next month (**9.9**).

Hours

Subdivisions of the day varied from culture to culture. The Greeks and Jews used no formal "hours," but described the parts of the day by the activities usually carried on at various times, such as "cock-crow," "market-time," "lamp-lighting" (**9.12**). The early Jews' lack of a formal system of timekeeping can be seen in the fact that there is no word for "hour" in the Old Testament except in the book of Daniel, which many scholars feel is quite late, from the Maccabean period (about 164 B.C.), when the Jews were under strong Hellenistic influences, as noted in chapter 2.

The Greeks developed the concept of the hour, a period of one-twelfth of the total daylight, but they didn't use it widely to reckon time until after the era of Alexander the Great (died 323 B.C.). Under this system the day was divided into twelve hours of equal length. Thus the hour did not have a fixed value, but would vary in length with the seasons, ranging from forty-five of our minutes in December to seventy-five minutes in June. An elaborate timekeeping mechanism, the Tower of the Winds, was built in Athens to serve as a public timepiece (**9.10**). The Romans borrowed this system from the Greeks, even though it was inaccurate in Rome because it was reckoned on latitudinal and longitudinal measurements taken in Greece.

Jesus takes the Greco-Roman time system as normative when he asks, "Are there not twelve hours of daylight?" (John 11:9). In the parable in Matthew 20:3–16, Jesus portrays the owner of a vineyard hiring laborers first at the beginning of the day, then at the third, sixth, ninth, and eleventh hours—roughly at 9:00 a.m., noon, 3:00 p.m., and 5:00 p.m. Except at the crucifixion, the hours of the day do not figure prominently in the first three Gospels. Jesus was apparently put on the cross

Tower of the Winds in Athens
(Photo by Howard Vos)

at the third hour; then there was darkness from the sixth to the ninth hours, at which point he died (Mark 15:25, 33 RSV).

In John's Gospel, however, probably written in the Greek city of Ephesus and less closely tied to a Judean background than are the other three, there are several references to hours. In 1:39 Andrew's first meeting with Jesus is set at "about the tenth hour" (RSV), i. e., 4:00 p.m. In 4:6 Jesus encounters the woman at the well at "about the sixth hour" (RSV), noon. A singular reference to the seventh hour occurs in 4:52 (1:00 p.m.). John places the crucifixion at "about the sixth hour" (19:14, RSV), noon, and does not mention the darkness.

References to the sixth and ninth hours are so common in ancient literature that they seem to have been a way of saying that the author did not know exactly when something happened, only that it was sometime around noon or just after the midday siesta. The exact time is not especially important to the meaning of the story. John's mention of the seventh and tenth hours thus becomes all the more peculiar and perhaps was a more historically accurate and original part of those stories, or it may have some symbolic significance which we no longer grasp.

The book of Acts also contains a number of references to the hours of the day and night. Peter defends the disciples against charges of inebriation on Pentecost by pointing out that it was only the third hour, nine in the morning, much too early to be drunk (2:15). In Acts 3:1 he and John are on their way to the temple "at the hour of prayer, the ninth hour" (RSV). That hour also figures in the story of Cornelius, the centurion, in chapter 10. He prayed at the ninth hour and saw an angel in a vision. The next day Peter also received a vision at about the sixth hour.

The night was also divided into hours, but it's rare to find these specified. Most commonly the Romans spoke of the watches of the night, four shifts of three hours each (Mark 6:48; Luke 12:38 RSV). Most things that happened late at night were described simply as occurring at "midnight." Paul and Silas were praying in prison "about midnight" when they were freed from their bonds (Acts 16:25). Paul once preached until midnight, with the unhappy result that a young man dozed off and fell out of the window where he was sitting (20:7–12). One of the few references to a specific time of night occurs in Acts 23:23. The tribune Claudius Lysias, who had arrested Paul in Jerusalem, sent him to the governor Felix "at the third hour of the night" (RSV) to avoid a plot on Paul's life.

There are enough references to the measuring of time in the New Testament to establish that the Jews of that day followed the Roman habit of counting the twelve hours of the day from dawn, but that, also like the Romans, they were never very precise in their reckoning, preferring vague terms like "toward evening" or "at early dawn."

Weeks

One of the demarcations of time most familiar to us, the week—a concept which determines the very rhythm of our lives—was lacking in ancient thought beyond Judaism. Notice Galatians 4:10: "You are observing special days, and months, and seasons, and years." No mention of weeks. The "special days" and "seasons" may be references to the fascination which some early Christians had with astrology (**9.30**), a phenomenon discussed in chapter 5. Astrologers did count a cycle of seven days, each one named after one of the heavenly bodies thought to govern it (sun, moon, and five planets). But no one other than the Jews lived by a fixed pattern of weeks.

This doesn't mean that ancient people never had a break from their drudgery. The normal workday ended at noon, as we saw in chapter 7. Market days were held several times a month, about every eighth or ninth day or in connection with a provincial magistrate's visit or with a religious festival (**9.15**). The Roman calendar contained 150 holidays. Each town or province had its own civic or religious celebrations as well. It seems unlikely that any free Greek or Roman ever worked himself to death. Slaves were generally included in these holidays (**9.13**).

Months

Months were reckoned by the phases of the moon, but a lunar year (355/6 days) doesn't coincide with a solar year. All ancient peoples inserted extra months periodically to make up the difference between the lunar and solar years (**9.21**; **9.34**). Some Jewish sects used a 360–day calendar (**9.20**) or one of 364 days (**9.17–18**). A primary function of the priests in all cultures was to keep track of the discrepancy between lunar and solar time and announce when an intercalary month needed to be added (**9.22**; **9.31**). The problem was that this process could be politically manipulated; the need for an extra month could be "discovered" just when a politician needed extra time in power. Greeks, Romans, and Jews each had their own names for the months (**9.33**). Contracts and other official documents often give the name of the month in two or more of these systems.

Julius Caesar greatly simplified this procedure when he introduced a system of months of artificial lengths (30 and 31 days) and a leap year with an extra day every fourth year. Though not universally popular when it was introduced (**9.25**), his Julian calendar is the one we still use, with slight modifications made in 1582 by Pope Gregory XIII. The update became necessary because Caesar's astronomers figured the solar year at 365 1/4 days when actually it is eleven minutes and fourteen seconds shorter. For greater precision, years divisible by 100 should be leap years, but not those years divisible by 400, to which people had been adding an extra day. That may not seem like much, but over sixteen centuries it added up, like compound interest, so that in correction, ten days were dropped from the calendar in 1582.

The earliest Roman year may have had only four months in it, with "weeks" of eight days (**9.23**). Some of the months got their names from certain activities associated with them (**9.24**). By the time of the early Republic (sixth century B.C.), the Roman year began in March. Thus the months of September through December were given names meaning seven through ten, because at that time they were the seventh to tenth months.

In the middle of the second century B.C., for reasons unknown to us, the Romans decided to begin the year in January (just after the winter solstice). Yet they retained the old names of the months (**9.25–29**) unless they decided to rename one in someone's honor. Quintilis was renamed July to flatter Julius Caesar. (Thankfully. "I'm a Yankee doodle dandy, born on the fourth of Quintilis" just doesn't have the same ring to it.) But then, of course, Augustus had to have Sextilis named after him (**9.19**). Nero tried to rename April in his honor, and Domitian changed September to Germanicus, to celebrate his triumph over some tribes north of the Danube; neither change outlived these unpopular emperors. The poet Ovid began work on a poem, the *Fasti*, about the origins of names of the months and the significant anniversaries but left it unfinished at his death (**9.24**).

Years

Years were counted in a chaotic fashion. Not only couldn't the Romans decide when to begin the year, they didn't have any starting point for counting them. (The foundation of Rome was a semilegendary event that took place in the forgotten past.) So they simply didn't count the years. They named each year after its two consuls and made no effort to number them. The problem was that all other cities had their own systems of reckoning years, and none of them coincided. The Athenians named their years after one of their archons (chief magistrates), but their year started in July (**9.35–36**).

Throughout antiquity kings counted years from the beginnings of their reigns, but that meant that the count started over whenever a new king came to power, and the count was different in each king's realm (cf. 2 Kings 18:9–10). This created utter confusion in trying to coordinate chronologies from one domain to another. Thus the year 225 B.C. would have been the twenty-first year of Ptolemy III, the second year of Seleucus III, and the sixteenth year of Attalus I. Imagine yourself a business person trying to date a contract under those conditions (**9.37**).

The Roman emperors provided a certain degree of standardization when they took to counting how many times certain of their powers had been renewed by the senate, a formality that took place once a year. So, when Luke refers to the fifteenth year of Tiberius, he at least knows how long that emperor has been on the throne, but he says nothing about how long anyone had ruled before or after that.

To illustrate how cumbersome this system was, let's figure, in Roman terms, how many years elapsed from the beginning of Jesus' ministry to the death of Paul (assuming Paul was executed in A.D. 64, the tenth year of Nero's reign). Jesus began his ministry in the fifteenth year of Tiberius' reign. We would have to know how much longer Tiberius ruled (8 years), the length of Caligula's reign (4) and of Claudius' (13)—and those figures don't even take parts of years into account. Add them up, plus ten to bring us up to the correct year of Nero's rule, and we have our answer.

To put it in modern terms, if someone claimed to be born in the eighth year of Franklin Roosevelt's presidency, how would we calculate that person's age? We would have to know how many years Roosevelt was in office, and the names and terms of all the presidents from that time to the present.

Perhaps now we can see why people in the first century would have been satisfied to say that it had been "about thirty or thirty-five years" from Jesus' death to Paul's and let it go at that. The precision that matters so much to us was of little concern to them, and they could not have achieved it if they had wanted to.

Birthdays

People who don't like to reveal their age would have been comfortable living in the ancient world. Whether or not people kept track of their age was left up to themselves. Some people did keep a record of their own birthdays. We have tombstones, from the second century A.D. and later, which give the age of the deceased, sometimes down to the month and day:

> To the eternal memory of Blandinia Martiola,
> most blameless girl
> who lived 18 years, 9 months, 5 days.

> Marcus Vodusius Crescens, freedman of Marcus, built this . . . for
> his son, Petronius Vocusianus,
> aged 18 years, 3 months, 18 days.

But the dating is sometimes vague, regardless of whether the person is young or old:

> To Aurelia Vercella, my wife most sweet, who lived seventeen years,
> more or less.

> Lucius Statius Onesimus . . . who lived sixty-eight years,
> more or less.

Just try to collect Social Security by telling them you're sixty-five, more or less.

People sometimes figured their ages by linking them with memorable events (**7.56**). Pliny the Younger knew he was seventeen when Vesuvius erupted (*Ep.* 6.16). But sometimes the events that stood out in people's memories were ones of local significance, such as a flood or a sensational crime. If an individual kept track of his own age, he could be assured of precision. If he didn't, though, no one was going to do it for him. Determining the exact age of a person who had lived in a remote part of the Empire and who was long since dead was virtually impossible. Luke (3:23) tells us all he can when he says that Jesus was "about thirty" when he began his ministry. We should not try to make that mean more than it does.

The Date of Jesus' Birth

We saw in chapter 5 that no one in the early church had reliable information about the month and day of Jesus' birth. Both Matthew and Luke tell us all they can about the year. Luke (2:2) ties it to a registration ordered by Augustus, which took place "while Quirinius was governor of Syria." This was likely a census, not a tax, although new taxes followed the census and triggered a revolt led by Judas the Galilean in A.D. 6–7 (Luke 5:37).

We've already discussed some of the problems connected with the dating of that census (see chapter 3). Augustus took several censuses, he tells us in the official history of his reign, the *Res Gestae* (sect. 8). But the one closest in time to the presumed date of Jesus' birth was begun in 8 B.C., the next in A.D. 14. This census of 8 B.C. covered only Judea (not Galilee) and was ordered because the Romans were converting Judea to a province. The Romans usually allowed five years to complete a census, so Jesus' birth could have occurred while this one was in progress. But there is still the problem of Quirinius' governorship.

Matthew 2:1 and Luke 1:5 both date the birth of Jesus to "the days of king Herod of Judea." That was sufficient information for the reader of that time, but since Herod ruled from 37–4 B.C., it only tantalizes us. When during those three decades was Jesus born? How could he have been born B.C., before Christ? Some have tried to maintain that Herod died later than 4 B.C., but there is little substance to that argument (**9.40**). It looks like there is a major chronological problem here. But there need not be if we remember that Luke said Jesus was "*about* thirty years old" when he began his ministry. Thirty-four or thirty-five is "about thirty" for people who treat numbers as carelessly as the Greeks and Romans did.

From other bits of information in Matthew's introduction, we can narrow the date down. He says (1:17 RSV) that fourteen generations lived "from the deportation to Babylon to the Christ." In the Jewish setting, a generation was normally reckoned as about forty years, though Herodotus (2.142) says that "three generations of men are one hundred years." So Matthew seems to be figuring on approximately 560 years from the fall of Jerusalem to the birth of Jesus. Jerusalem fell in 586 B.C., so that would date Christ's birth to 26 B.C. But Matthew would have emphasized the *about* forty years in each generation and the *approximately* 560 years. The date could easily be brought down a few more years. For the modern, fact-conscious reader, so imprecise a date is not enough, but for Matthew's readers it was. This should be a reminder that we can't expect ancient, non-scientific texts to be written with our standards of accuracy in mind.

Clement of Alexandria (*Stromata* 1.21) discussed this problem of chronology and provided what information he had about the reigns of emperors and the time that had elapsed since the birth of Christ. By his reckoning, Jesus was born in "the twenty-eighth year of Augustus." Modern scholars begin figuring Augustus' reign in 27 B.C., when he received the grants of powers which made him "emperor." But Clement appears to have been counting from the battle of Actium in 31 B.C., which would place Jesus' birth in 3 B.C. He admits that different sources give various figures for the reigns of some of the emperors.

Another clue to a more precise date is provided by the story of Herod's Slaughter of the Innocents, his command to slay all male children in Bethlehem under two years of age in an effort to destroy what he understood to be a rival king of the Jews (**9.42**). It seems from the story (Matt. 1:16–20) that this happened just before Herod's death, though that is not explicitly stated. Since Herod died early in 4 B.C., if he was looking for a child under two, it seems likely that Jesus was born around 6 B.C. Some scholars argue for 8–7 B.C. (**9.45**), others for 3–2 B.C. (**9.43**). On the basis of what appears to be a star map painted on the ceiling of a catacomb in Rome, one scholar maintains that Christ's birth took place on March 24–25 in 5 B.C. (**9.39**). In 1606 Johannes Kepler calculated that Jesus was born in 7–6 B.C., during a rare conjunction of Jupiter (the star of kings) and Saturn (the star of the Sabbath and sometimes of the Jews). Others have tried to identify the star (Matt. 2:2) with a nova or comet.

The major difficulty in using the story of the Slaughter of the Innocents as evidence is that it is not known from any other source, not even another New Testament source. There are some possible reasons for this silence. Bethlehem was small, and the infant mortality rate of the times was high. Since only males were sought out, the slaughter might have involved only a handful of babies. Thus it may not have seemed worthy of note to Josephus and other historians, especially in comparison to Herod's slaughter of members of his own family. They might have thought it unwise to mention the matter when it would only raise questions: What happened to this alleged king of the Jews? an inquiring Roman reader might want to know. We know that Josephus, as a client of Herod Agrippa II, tried to avoid delicate issues in his history of the Jews (**9.41**).

Although we can't know why Matthew alone records this incident, we don't have to disregard it simply because it is found in only one source. Other incidents from antiquity are accepted as historical even though recorded by only one author or in only one inscription. Our sources are limited in number, and they have a selective and unscientific approach to recording information. Hence, we should not be too quick to accept everything they tell us or too eager to reject any particular piece of data (**9.44**), even clues from the Dead Sea Scrolls (**9.38**) or from astronomy.

B.C./A.D.

Given all this confusion and lack of precision, it's little wonder that people interested in antiquity often have trouble understanding how we keep track of things. We've even complicated the problem by using the birth of Christ as our reference point. A student in one of my history courses once asked, in all seriousness, "Before Jesus was born, how did they know to count backwards so the dates would come out right?" My first reaction was disbelief. Could a college student actually have no notion at all of how our dating system works? Sad to say, I've encountered others since then. So, in brief, let me explain B.C. and A.D., and how we can correlate Roman and Greek and Christian dates.

Our modern system was worked out by Dionysius Exiguus, a monk living in Rome in the mid-sixth century. Using information like Luke's reference to Jesus beginning his ministry when he was about thirty in the fifteenth year of the emperor Tiberius, Dionysius decided to designate that year as the thirtieth "year of the Lord" (*anno Domini* in Latin, A.D.). He went on to construct a chronology of events up to his own time. His problem was complicated by the difficulty of performing calculations with Roman numerals and by the lack of a zero (**9.46–47; 9.49–50**; see chapter 1). Thus Jesus was born in A.D. 1, the "first year of the Lord," by Dionysius' calculations. Minor inaccuracies in record keeping meant that the system he devised was actually off by four to six years (**9.51; 9.53**).

We have seen the problems of correlating dates from one kingdom or city to another. When two cities fought one another, each would record the event in its own histories. Such cross-references allowed later historians to correlate events in one dating system with those in another (**9.52**). By the fourth century several elaborate chronologies had been worked out by Christian writers such as Eusebius and Jerome to show the connection between events from the Old Testament and Greco-Roman history.

Some modern scholarly publications add another twist to the time-keeping problem by trying to avoid the Christian implications of dating things B.C./A.D. The designations B.C.E. and C.E. are coming into wider use. They mean "before the Common Era" and "Common Era." The Common Era is the time period since the birth of Christ; the use of these phrases is intended to avoid offending non-Christians (**9.48**). The use of this system doesn't change any dates. The year 480 B.C. is also 480 B.C.E.; 79 C.E. is A.D. 79.

Distances

Not only did each ancient culture—practically each ancient city— have its own method of calculating time, they also had their own systems of measurements, whether for weights, volume, money, or distance. Weights and volume are of no particular importance for the study of the New Testament, and Roman coinage had become the standard medium of exchange all over the Mediterranean world (except at the temple in Jerusalem, where it had to be exchanged, at extortionate rates, for coins which did not bear an emperor's image). But an understanding of how distances were calculated can provide an introduction to the important topic of travel in the New Testament world.

The shortest distances were measured by comparison with body parts. Anything smaller than a foot was measured by the dactyl, the distance between two knuckles on a man's finger. The foot was the basic unit of measurement, but it varied from 296 millimeters (11 inches) at Rome to 320 mm in Olympia and 330 mm in Gaul. The Athenians used two different feet in measuring, one 295 mm, the other 326 mm. We have graphic evidence of the measurement of the Roman foot at a point where the Appian Way runs between the hills and the coastline of Italy. Engineers cut 126 feet off the cliff to construct the roadbed and marked off each foot.

The most common unit in the Near East was the cubit, the distance from the elbow to the tip of the middle finger. It continued in use in Roman times (Matt. 6:27, NRSV note) and resisted all efforts to standardize it (**9.58**).

Longer distances were measured rather arbitrarily. In their games, the Greeks used the *stadion*, the length of the running track. This was defined as six hundred feet; but since the foot varied from place to place, so did the *stadion*. The Romans were hardly more precise, using the *milia passus* (thousand steps) as their standard. The step was usually reckoned as five feet, making the Roman mile about three hundred feet shorter than our mile. The Greeks and Romans both used professional distance measurers and surveyors when calculating distances between cities, so they could achieve rough accuracy (**9.54**).

Distances were marked on Roman roads by milestones, large columns displaying the name of the road, the name and titles of the official who built or added to it, and the distance from the two towns which the road connected. These milestones were normally five to six feet tall. Construction and erection of them served to keep unemployed people occupied and provided propaganda for the current regime (**9.56–57**).

A milestone erected during Trajan's reign
(Photo by Gustav Jeeninga)

The most common measurement of a long distance was "a day's journey." Under optimum circumstances in antiquity, a person could cover about twenty of our miles in a day's travel on foot. But circumstances were rarely ideal and people rarely struck out alone on foot. Imperial couriers could cover as much as fifty miles a day (**9.55**); an ox-drawn wagon could manage only seven or eight (**9.59**). Since we don't know how Mary and Joseph were traveling, we cannot be certain how far they had gone when we read in Luke 2:44 that they left Jerusalem and "went a day's journey" before they realized that Jesus was not with

A modern-day caravan
(Photo from Denis Baly)

them. They had assumed him to be among the family and friends with whom they were traveling. That suggests a caravan of some sort, almost certainly with wagons, and reminds us of one of the most important conditions of ancient travel: safety in numbers.

The concept of the day's journey was almost as old as civilization in the Near East. In Genesis 30:36 and Exodus 3:18 we find references to "a three days' journey." Because of Sabbath restrictions, the Jews introduced a variation of this measurement, the Sabbath day's journey, barely more than half a mile (Acts 1:12).

Travel

The Greeks and Romans traveled for many of the same reasons we do today (**9.63**). They had business interests all over the Mediterranean basin, with contacts eventually extending to India and China (**9.64–67**). Government work kept a large number of people on the move. The wealthy moved several times a year to one or another of their villas, taking their entourages with them. People of all classes visited spas and shrines—especially those of Asclepius, god of healing—or attended famous festivals like the Olympic games. Roman doctors held sea voyages to be salubrious. The Romans added pure sightseeing to these reasons for being on the road. Tiberius' nephew Germanicus rubbernecked his way around Egypt like any modern tourist (Tacitus, *Ann.* 2.61). Seneca complains about people afflicted with "an unhealthy restlessness" who "undertake aimless journeys" (*On Peace of Mind* 2.13).

If we think about travel in the New Testament, Paul's journeys immediately come to mind (**9.60–62**). He combined land and sea travel and experienced many of the difficulties associated with both. But Mary and Joseph also traveled, first to Bethlehem (according to Luke), then to Egypt and back (according to Matthew). The Magi made a long journey to see Jesus. Jesus himself traveled all over Judea and Galilee and expected his disciples to travel, either in pairs around Judea or "to the ends of the earth" (Acts 1:8). What was travel like for these people?

Land Travel

The most natural form of travel in antiquity, but by no means the most comfortable, was by land. It required considerable time, and the dangers

A Roman road in Syria, paved with limestone blocks
(Photo by Ben Chapman)

inherent in it were not to be lightly disregarded. When Jesus told a story about a man who fell among thieves on a journey (Luke 10:30–35), his audience knew the reality about which he spoke. Paul also reeled off some of the perils which he had encountered on his frequent journeys: "danger from rivers, danger from bandits, . . . danger in the wilderness, danger at sea, . . . hungry and thirsty, often without food, cold and naked" (2 Cor. 11:26–27). Even in Italy itself, a wealthy Roman could simply disappear while traveling (Pliny, *Ep.* 6.25).

In spite of all these drawbacks, land travel was far safer and more convenient in the first century A.D. than it had ever been in human history. And it didn't get any better until the introduction of railroads in the middle of the nineteenth century. A trip from London to Rome in

Nero's time took twenty-eight days, assuming there were no major problems. At the beginning of Queen Victoria's reign, in 1832, the same trip took the same amount of time and was complicated by crossing several national borders.

Roman Roads

The Romans made relatively convenient travel possible by policing their territory to cut down on highway bandits, though they could never entirely eliminate them, and by providing superb roads that crisscrossed the Empire from Scotland to Arabia, from Morocco to the Black Sea (**9.69**). The Roman system of roads was unequaled until the development of the modern interstate highways after World War II.

The Romans began building roads in part for the same reason that the interstate system was begun by Franklin Roosevelt: the need to move troops quickly from one part of the Empire to another. For this reason Roman roads were as straight as possible, often bridging rivers or drilling through mountains. The highways they created were "graceful and beautiful as well as useful" (Plutarch, *Life of G. Gracchus* 7). Civilians could use the roads, but soldiers and persons on government business always had right of way. A large military contingent in passage could force all other traffic off a road for several hours—days in some cases.

Roman roads and bridges were engineered so well that stretches of them survive all over Europe today and in some cases are still used for local traffic. The roads were typically laid down on a base of gravel poured in a trench, covered by large stones in areas where traffic was especially heavy. Gravel or dirt might be the surface for roads used more lightly. The roads, always slightly higher in the middle than on the sides to ensure proper drainage, were lined with ditches and curbs. In 122 B.C. Gaius Gracchus began the practice of placing stones at frequent intervals to enable riders to mount their horses without assistance, a necessity because stirrups were unknown in western Europe before about A.D. 800 (**9.68**). Plutarch mentions people training their horses to kneel when they are "too feeble or lazy to mount them properly" (*On Marriage* 8).

Near cities, pedestrian paths were maintained alongside the major roads, but in the countryside people walked on the same surface used by vehicular traffic, with the result that they were sometimes run over. Some Romans apparently became maniacs once they got behind the reins. Nero's biological father, L. Domitius Ahenobarbus, once deliberately ran down a child in the road (Suetonius, *Nero* 5).

In addition to their system of major thoroughfares, the Romans built secondary roads with gravel or dirt surfaces. These were usually maintained by local governments and so were not as fine as the highways, but they made reasonably fast travel possible even between small towns. The usefulness of such roads is apparent when Pliny talks about a trip to one of his villas outside Rome (*Ep.* 2.17):

> It is seventeen miles from Rome, so that it is possible to spend the night there after necessary business is done, without having cut short or hurried the day's work, and it can be approached by more than one route; the roads to Laurentum and Ostia both lead in that direction, but you must leave the one at the fourteenth milestone and the other at the eleventh. Whichever way you go, the side road you take is sandy for some distance and rather heavy and slow-going if you drive, but soft and easily covered on horseback. The view on either side is full of variety, for sometimes the road narrows as it passes through the woods, and then it broadens and opens out through wide meadows.

We should recall that the day's work ended before noon, so Pliny had several hours to make the trip and still arrive in time for an early dinner. His comment about the width of the road is of interest. Eight feet was the minimum width for a Roman road, except where the need to build on the side of a mountain occasionally forced them down to one lane of five or six feet. In such cases they provided paved pullover areas wherever possible so that traffic going in opposite directions could pass. On flat ground a width of ten or twelve feet was common, broadening to thirty or forty feet as the road approached a major city.

Maps

We cannot envision Joseph and Mary calling AAA to get a map for their trip to Egypt. Yet well-educated ancients did in fact have a reasonably good sense of what their world looked like, at least until they got to the edges (**9.70**; **9.74**). The sphericity of the earth had been fairly common knowledge since the time of Pythagoras (540 B.C.). By 200 B.C. Eratosthenes of Alexandria had calculated the earth's circumference to within a few hundred miles and had devised a system of mapping the earth using lines of longitude and latitude.

Cicero gives one of the most explicit statements of the Roman view of the earth (*On the Nature of the Gods* 2.116). Ovid (*Metamorphoses* 1.32–37) also describes God as shaping the earth into a ball. The Romans portrayed the earth as a ball on their coins. The geographer Claudius Ptolemy provides directions for making maps on both flat and spherical surfaces (see box). The problem of distortion on a flat surface which he mentions is one that still plagues cartographers today. On a Mercator projection, Greenland appears sixteen times its actual size.

Before setting out on a journey, an ancient traveler could purchase a map, not to learn the distances between towns—the milestones told him that—but to learn what sorts of accommodations were available. Known as itineraries, these were commonplace in antiquity, but none survive except in the eleventh-century Peutinger Table, a copy of a third-century map of all the roads in the Roman Empire. It uses different symbols to indicate the various sorts of inns a traveler could expect to find (**9.72–73**).

Accommodations

Since the average traveler covered only twenty or so miles a day, it was necessary on long trips to plan to stop each night. Inns were available, but their quality varied dramatically. Some were large and comfortable and could provide meals, stabling for animals, and mechanics to repair vehicles (**9.77**). If the inn where Mary and Joseph stayed had a stable, it was not the shabby place it is often portrayed as being (**9.80**). Only the more substantial inns had such facilities. Others offered little more than a roof and a fire by which to sleep. It appears, however, that what was lacking was "a room" in our sense of the word (**9.78**); all the rooms were filled. This would suggest that the inn was particularly nice. Not all inns offered private rooms.

Mapping the Earth

Drawing a map on a sphere gives the likeness of the shape of the earth, but it's hard to make it large enough to allow room for all the details that must be indicated, and it's impossible to take the whole thing in one's sight at one time. Making a map on a flat surface overcomes these inconveniences, but requires some adjustments to correspond to the spherical shape in order to make the distances on the flat surface commensurate with the actual distances.

The decision as to the size of the sphere will depend on how detailed the mapmaker wishes his work to be. This is a function of his skill, for as the size of the sphere is increased, the amount of detail and the accuracy of the map will also be greater.

Ptolemy, *Geography* 1.20–22.

Judging from archaeological remains, inns were spaced closer together or farther apart, depending on the difficulty of the terrain. Inns were often dirty and infested with disreputable and dangerous characters (**9.76**). The poet Horace (40 B.C.) left a vivid portrayal of these places in his humorous description of a trip which he made from Rome to Brundisium, on the heel of Italy (*Sat.* 1.5). Both Petronius (A.D. 60) and Apuleius (A.D. 180) show that conditions in the inns did not improve noticeably with the passage of time. Characters in both their works are attacked while staying in inns.

If travelers found a decent inn, there was no guarantee it would have room for them. Even if other travelers hadn't filled it, someone on government business might commandeer rooms and services, and his needs would take precedence over any other, even a young woman about to become a mother.

An innkeeper was required by law to furnish anything requested by someone traveling with a pass from the emperor or a provincial governor, just as civilians were required to assist such persons by carrying burdens for a mile (Matt. 5:41). Only persons on official business, particularly the delivery of dispatches to and from Rome, were supposed to have these passes. The aim of the system was to speed communication between the provinces and the capital (**9.55**). The emperors strictly limited the number of passes in circulation at any given time so as not to overburden the system (Pliny *Epp.* 10.45; 10.64). But abuses of the privilege were common. Pliny himself, as governor of Bithynia, let his wife use a pass when she wanted to return home to her ailing mother; the emperor Trajan excused him with a mild scolding (*Ep.* 10.120).

Where possible, travelers stayed with friends or with friends of friends. Paul didn't even wait for an invitation from Philemon but just told him to "prepare a guest room for me" (verse 22). The obligation to entertain family friends was passed on from one generation to the next (**9.75**). Letters of introduction were a valuable commodity, for they insured that the bearer would find lodging in an unfamiliar city (**9.79**). Paul opened doors for some of his friends in passages like Romans 16:1–2: "I commend to you our sister Phoebe, a deaconess of the church at Cenchreae, so that you may welcome her in the Lord as is fitting for the saints, and help her in whatever she may require from you." Similar introductions are supplied in 1 Corinthians 16:10 and Colossians 4:7–10.

Travel Amenities

We typically think of people in the New Testament as walking, and many poorer people did travel in that fashion. But vehicular travel was much more common than we suppose. When Paul asks Timothy to bring his cloak along with some books and parchments (2 Tim. 4:13), we must conclude that Timothy would not be making the trip on foot. Considering Paul's health problems, one wonders whether he could have walked all over Asia Minor and Greece. Mary, being well along in her pregnancy, is not likely to have walked from Nazareth to Bethlehem. The mother of the poet Virgil set out on a short trip during her pregnancy and ended up giving birth in a ditch (Suetonius, *Life of Virgil* 3). Traditionally we picture Mary riding a donkey, but Luke never mentions her mode of transportation. Since Joseph was a man of some means, they might well have ridden in some sort of carriage.

Various styles of carriages or wagons could be rented in one town and left in another to be returned (**9.82**). A driver could also be hired if one wished to bargain with the drivers' guild, the ancient equivalent of the Teamsters' Union. But riding a donkey was cheaper and might have been more comfortable. Roman carriages had no springs, so the passengers felt every jolt of the road. Nor did the Romans ever develop an effective axle grease (**9.81**). Complaints about the screeching of wagon wheels are frequent in literature of the first century A.D. During chariot races slaves stood along the edge of the track and tossed water on the wheels to cool them down. The most comfortable way to travel without walking was to be carried in a litter. In town this chair or bed with

A model of a Roman grain ship. Note the captain's "cabin".
(Photo from Haifa Maritime Museum)

poles on the side was carried by slaves. On the open road, donkeys were sometimes used to carry the chair.

Travelers often needed some kind of vehicle because they had to bring their own supplies of food and water, as well as utensils, clothes, and whatever other necessities they may have required. Jesus counseled his disciples to go out preaching without a bag or bread or money. That would have sounded like madness to his contemporaries (Luke 9:3–5; 10:3–7). Cicero's brother Quintus turned back when the two of them were making their last effort to escape death at the hands of Antony's soldiers because, in their haste, neither of them had brought any money. Quintus knew they couldn't go anywhere or survive long, so he went back to see what resources he could scrape together, even though soldiers were pursuing them (Plutarch, *Cicero* 47).

Despite all their efforts to make travel comfortable, the Romans still had to contend with the weather. They tried as much as possible to limit their traveling to warmer months, May to October. Snow was not a problem in Greece and Asia Minor, except in the higher elevations. In Italy the Apennine Mountains, which divide the peninsula lengthwise like a spine, do retain their snow cover at the highest elevations until late June.

But all over the Mediterranean basin, rain and cold weather simply made a miserable combination for travel.

Paul clearly had land travel in mind when he told the Corinthians, "I intend to pass through Macedonia—and perhaps I will stay with you or even spend the winter" (1 Cor. 16:5–6). In two other passages, it's unclear whether he was concerned about land travel or sailing. In 2 Timothy 4:21 he urges Timothy, "Do your best to come before winter." In Titus 3:12 he announces his plan to spend the winter in Nicopolis, on the Adriatic Sea. In either case it's clear that travel of all sorts came to a virtual halt during the winter.

Sea Travel

Unlike the Greeks, the Romans and Jews did not take gladly to travel by sea. Cicero, trying to escape soldiers coming to put him to death, set out in a small boat. But the waves began to make him sick, so he ordered the boat turned around, and he went back ashore (Plutarch, *Cicero* 47). Seneca relates an almost comic incident when he tried to sail across the Bay of Naples instead of following the coastline, as any sensible sailor of the day did. With no compass or other navigational aid, one could quickly become lost if out of sight of land. A storm caught Seneca in the middle of the bay. He begged to be taken back to land. The helmsman told him it was more dangerous to try to get close to the shore in a storm than it was to ride it out on the open water. Seneca ordered the man to turn for shore, no matter what the risk. As soon as he could see that they were getting close, he leaped into the water and swam the rest of the way (*Ep.* 53).

But, once their empire had encircled the Mediterranean Sea, the landlubberly Romans had to come to terms with the water. They learned much from the Greeks about building and handling ships and improved on those techniques to construct vessels larger than anything that floated until the nineteenth century (**9.83**; **9.86**). These ships were powered by sail and wind. Ships with oars, sometimes several banks of oars, were normally used for military purposes. The oars would have been used for short periods when the wind was slack or in situations such as ramming another ship, where speed was essential. We still are not quite certain how the oars were arranged or manipulated.

The more common vessels, however, were merchant ships, designed to transport large quantities of grain and other commodities to feed the constantly gaping maw of the city of Rome (**9.94**). Shipping huge quantities of grain by water, whatever the distance, was always cheaper in antiquity than hauling cartloads of grain overland (**9.93**). There were no regular sailing schedules. Potential passengers had to find a ship going in the right direction, book passage, and wait until conditions (winds and omens) were right for sailing. Being extremely superstitious, the Romans placed great trust in dreams and omens. If a passenger or sailor had a premonition about misfortune, the voyage would be delayed. The centurion and the captain on Paul's ship probably would have paid attention to the apostle's warning if they had not been desperate for a safe harbor in which to spend the winter (Acts 27:10–11).

Once on board the ship, passengers found no facilities for them. Only the captain had a separate sleeping area. The passengers, like the crew, had to claim space on the open deck, perhaps with a small tent to keep the wind and salt spray off. They had to bring their own food and servants to prepare it for them, if they were wealthy enough. The number of people who might buy passage on a freighter was limited only by the boat's size and the willingness of the people to crowd together. One vessel sailed with six hundred passengers. When Paul sailed to Rome, there were 276 passengers and crew aboard (**9.88–89**; Acts 27:37).[2]

Since they had no reliable navigational aids, ships usually stopped at dark, pulling into a river mouth or beaching on the shore. Passengers could replenish their supply of fresh water and forage for whatever food the area might offer. This image was familiar enough that Epictetus' readers could recognize the scene: "Just as, on a sea voyage, when the ship rests at anchor, if you go ashore to draw water . . . your thoughts must be focused on the ship, so that you will hear the captain when he calls" (*Enchiridion* 7).

Sea travel in antiquity was totally dependent on the weather. With only one large square sail mounted perpendicular to the keel, Roman sailors could not "tack" the way a modern sailboat can and so found it extremely difficult to sail against unfavorable winds (**9.85**). The prevailing winds blowing out of the north, for example, made it an easy voyage from Asia Minor to Alexandria, but a laborious two-month journey going the other way (**9.91**). Pliny tried to sail north along the coast of Asia Minor, but finally had to abandon the effort and settle for land transportation (*Ep.* 10.17). That same wind delayed Paul's ship (Acts 27:4–7). The time required for a voyage between any two points could vary enormously from trip to trip. We have records indicating that the trip from Puteoli (near Naples) to Alexandria could take from nine to twenty-seven days (**9.59**).

Winter was the ancient sailor's dread. Only in extreme need did a ship put out to sea between October and May. The ship on which Paul started the last leg of his journey to Rome was Alexandrian, and the captain was frustrated by his battles against the winds. Seeing the end of the sailing season upon him, he had already given up hope of reaching Rome and knew he had to get to a suitable harbor to spend the winter (Acts 27:12). He would need a place that could supply lodging and food for a sizable contingent of people as well as a safe berth for his ship.

The details of Paul's shipwreck can be found in Acts 27:39–44, and the account, often praised for its clarity, can hardly be improved by retelling here (**9.90**; **9.92**).[3] This was a frequent hazard of sea travel. Paul reports that he was shipwrecked on three occasions (2 Cor. 11:25). Loss of cargoes was common and could mean financial ruin. But because of the risk, profits were high and the import business was one of the quickest paths to enormous wealth (Petronius, *Satyr.* 76).

Travel in New Testament times was safer than it had ever been or would be again until the twentieth century. And yet it was filled with peril, whether one undertook a relatively short overland journey like the one from Jerusalem to Jericho or a sea voyage halfway across the Mediterranean. Paul's decision to travel and spread the gospel involved a great deal more inconvenience and personal danger than we can possibly imagine in our age of jet planes and interstate highways. When we see the conditions under which these people labored to accomplish something that we take for granted, this should help us appreciate their achievement even more. It might also challenge us to use our advantages to the full.

Notes

1. Perhaps this is how Paul found Aquila and Priscilla in Corinth, since they were of the same trade (Acts 18:1–3).

2. Some manuscripts read seventy-six. Perhaps a later medieval copyist, not familiar with the size of Roman ships at the height of the Empire, changed the figure to something more reasonable in his experience.

3. See William Ramsay, *St. Paul, the Traveller and the Roman Citizen* (New York: Putnams, 1896; Grand Rapids: Baker, 1949 reprint), 314–343, for an exciting and classic treatment of Paul's voyage to Rome and the sailing techniques used.

BIBLIOGRAPHY

9.1. Ling, R. "A Stranger in Town: Finding the Way in an Ancient City." *G&R* 37(1990): 204–214.

Time

9.2. Brearly, H. C. *Time Telling through the Ages.* New York: Doubleday, 1919.

9.3. Malina, B. J. "Christ and Time: Swiss or Mediterranean?" *CBQ* 51(1989): 1–31.

9.4. Martin, T. "Pagan and Judeo-Christian Time-Keeping Schemes in Galatians 4.10 and Colossians 2.16." *NTS* 42(1996): 105–119.

9.5. Meritt, B. D. "The Count of Days in Athens." *AJPh* 95(1974): 268–279.

9.6. Pritchett, W. K. "The Athenian Count of Days." *CSCA* 9(1976): 181–195.

9.7. ———. "Calendars of Athens Again." *Bulletin de correspondance hellenique* 81(1957): 269–301.

9.8. Stroes, H. R. "Does the Day Begin in the Evening or Morning? Some Biblical Observations." *VetTest* 16(1966): 460–475.

9.9. Taisbak, C. M. "Ante diem: Did the Romans Count Their Days Backwards?" In *Studia Romana in Honorem P. Krarup Septuagenarii.* Ed. by K. Ascani et al. Odense University Press, 1976: 58–59.

Hours

9.10. de Solla Price, D. J. "The Tower of the Winds." *National Geographic* 157 (Apr. 1967): 587–596.

9.11. Gibbs, S. L. *Greek and Roman Sundials.* New Haven, CT: Yale University Press, 1976.

9.12. Kosmala, H. "The Time of Cock-Crow." *Annual of the Swedish Theological Institute* 2(1963): 118–120; 6(1967): 132–134.

Weeks

9.13. Bradley, K. R. "Holidays for Slaves." *Symbolae Osloenses* 54(1979): 111–118.

9.14. DeLigt, L. *Fairs and Markets in the Roman Empire: Economic and Social Aspects of Periodic Trade in a Pre-Industrial Society.* Amsterdam: Gieben, 1993.

9.15. MacMullen, R. "Market-Days in the Roman Empire." *Phoenix* 24(1970): 333–341.

9.16. Worp, K. A. "Remarks on Weekdays in Late Antiquity Occurring in Documentary Sources." *Tyche* 6(1991): 221–230.

Months

9.17. Baumgarten, J. M. "The Calendars of the Book of Jubilees and the Temple Scroll." *VetTest* 37(1987): 71–78.

9.18. Beckwith, R. T. "The Qumran Calendar and the Sacrifices of the Essenes." *RevQum* 7(1971): 587–591.

9.19. Bosworth, A. B. "Augustus and August: Some Pitfalls of Historical Fiction." *HSCP* 86(1982): 151–170.

9.20. Cryer, F. H. "The 360–Day Calendar Year and Early Judaic Sectarianism." *Scandinavian Journal of the Old Testament* 1(1987): 116–122.

9.21. Edmunds, L. "Alexander and the Calendar (Plut., *Alex.* 12.2)." *Historia* 28(1979): 112–117.

9.22. Gjerstad, E. "Notes on the Early Roman Calendar." *Acta Archaeologica* 32(1961): 193–214.

9.23. Hauben, H. "Some Observations on the Early Roman Calendar." *AncSoc* 11–12 (1980–81): 241–255.

9.24. Henderson, W. J. "What Ovid Tells Us About the Roman Calendar." *Akroterion* 17, no.4 (1972): 9–20.

9.25. Holleman, A. W. J. "Cicero's Reaction to the Julian Calendar (Plut. *Caes.* 59); January 4th (45)." *Historia* 27(1978): 496–498.

9.26. ———. "End and Beginning in the Ancient Roman Year: A Sabine Element." *Revue Belge de philologie et d'histoire* 54(1976): 52–65.

9.27.   ———. "The Pre-Julian Calendar." *Liverpool Classical Monthly* 9(1984): 6–7.
9.28.   Johnson, V. L. "The Primitive Basis of Our Calendar." *Archaeology* 21(1968): 14–21.
9.29.   ———. *The Roman Origins of Our Calendar.* Oxford, OH: American Classical League, 1958.
9.30.   Malina, B. J. "Jesus as Astral Prophet." *BTB* 27(1997): 83–98.
9.31.   Michels, A. K. *The Calendar of the Roman Republic.* Princeton, NJ: Princeton University Press, 1967.
9.32.   ———. "The Intercalary Month in the Pre-Julian Calendar." In *Hommages à A. Grenier.* Ed. by M. Renard. Brussels: Coll. Latomus, 1962: 1174–1178.
9.33.   Sarkady, J. "A Problem in the History of the Greek Calendar: The Date of the Origin of the Months' Names." *Acta Classica Universitatis Scientiarum Debreceniensis* 21(1985): 3–17.
9.34.   Thornton, T. C. G. "Jewish New Moon Festivals, Galatians 4:3–11 and Colossians 2:16." *JThS* 40(1989): 97–100.

Years
9.35.   Meritt, B. D. *The Athenian Year.* Berkeley: University of CA Press, 1961.
9.36.   Samuel, A. E. *Greek and Roman Chronology: Calendars and Years in Classical Antiquity.* Munich: Beck, 1972.
9.37.   Vardaman, J., and E. M. Yamauchi, eds. *Chronos, Kairos, Christos: Nativity and Chronological Studies Presented to Jack Finnegan.* Winona Lake, IN: Eisenbrauns, 1989.

The Date of Jesus' Birth
9.38.   Beckwith, R. T. "St. Luke, the Date of Christmas and the Priestly Courses at Qumran." *RevQum* 9(1977): 73–94.
9.39.   Beehler, C. M. "Follow the Star." *AD* Dec. 1980: 24–25.
9.40.   Bernegger, P. M. "Affirmation of Herod's Death in 4 B.C." *JThS* 34(1983): 526–531.
9.41.   Broshi, M. "The Credibility of Josephus." *JJewSt* 33(1982): 379–384.
9.42.   Maier, P. L. "Infant Massacre: History or Myth?" *ChrT* 20(Dec.19, 1975): 7–10.
9.43.   Martin, E. L. *The Birth of Christ Recalculated.* 2d ed. Alhambra, CA: Academy for Scriptural Knowledge, 1980.
9.44.   Mosley, A. W. "Historical Reporting in the Ancient World." *NTS* 12(1965–66): 10–26.
9.45.   Wojciechowski, M. "Mt 2.20: Herod and Antipater? A Supplementary Clue to Dating the Birth of Jesus." *Biblische Notizen* 44(1988): 61–62.

B.C./A.D.
9.46.   Anderson, W. "Arithmetical Computations in Roman Numerals." *CPh* 51(1956): 145–150.
9.47.   Jones, W. K. "Arithmetic, Latin Style." *CB* 33(1956): 7.
9.48.   Larn, R., and R. Davis. "Calendars and Dates in Research." *International Journal of Nautical Archaeology and Underwater Exploration* 6(1977): 242–244.
9.49.   Richardson, W. F. "The Greek Number System." *Prudentia* 9(1977): 15–26.
9.50.   Taisbak, C. M. "Roman Numerals and the Abacus." *C&M* 26(1965): 147–160.
9.51.   Teres, G. "Time Computations and Dionysius Exiguus." *Journal for the History of Astronomy* 15(1984): 177–188.
9.52.   van der Waerden, B. L. "Tables for the Egyptian and Alexandrian Calendar." *Isis* 17(1956): 387–390.
9.53.   Watkins, H. *Time Counts: The Story of the Calendar.* New York: Philosophical Library, 1954.

Distances
9.54.   Dilke, O. A. W. *The Roman Land Surveyors: An Introduction to the Agrimensores.* New York: Barnes & Noble, 1971.
9.55.   Eliot, C. W. J. "New Evidence for the Speed of the Roman Imperial Post." *Phoenix* 9(1955): 76–80.

9.56. French, D. *Roman Roads and Milestones of Asia Minor. Vol. 1.* Oxford: British Archeological Reports, 1981.

9.57. Isaac, B. "Milestones in Judaea, from Vespasian to Constantine." *PalExQ* 110(1978): 47–60.

9.58. Kaufman, A. S. "Determining the Length of the Medium Cubit." *PalExQ* 16(1984): 120–132.

9.59. Yeo, C. A. "Land and Sea Transportation in Imperial Italy." *TAPhA* 77(1946): 221–224.

Travel

Land Travel

9.60. Bradford, E. *Paul the Traveler.* London: Penguin, 1974.

9.61. Browrigg, R. *Pauline Places: In the Footsteps of Paul Through Turkey and Greece.* London: Hodder & Stoughton, 1989.

9.62. Bruce, F. F. *Jesus and Paul: Places They Knew.* Nashville: Thomas Nelson Publishers, 1983.

9.63. Casson, L. *Travel in the Ancient World.* Toronto: Hakkert, 1974.

9.64. Margabandhu, G. "Trade Contacts Between Western India and the Greco-Roman World in the Early Centuries of the Christian Era." *Journal of the Economic and Social History of the Orient* 8(1965): 316–322.

9.65. Parker, A. J. "Trade Within the Empire and Beyond the Frontiers." In *The Roman World.* Ed. by J. Wacher. London: Routledge & Kegan Paul, 1987: 635–657.

9.66. Raschke, M. "Roman Overland Trade with India and China." *EMC* 18(1974): 37–47.

9.67. Thorley, J. "The Development of Trade Between the Roman Empire and the East Under Augustus." *G&R* 16(1969): 209–223.

Roman Roads

9.68. de Camp, L. S. "Before Stirrups." *Isis* 51(1960): 159–160.

9.69. von Hagen, V. W. *The Roads That Led to Rome.* Cleveland: World Publishing Co. 1967.

Maps

9.70. Beitzel, B. J. "How to Draw Ancient Highways on Biblical Maps." *BibRev* 4, no. 5, (1988): 36–43.

9.71. Edson, E. "The Oldest World Maps: Classical Sources of Three VIIIth Century *Mappae Mundi.*" *AncW* 24(1993): 169–184.

9.72. Levi, A. C., and B. Trell. "An Ancient Tourist Map." *Archeology* 17(1964): 227–236.

9.73. Muhly, J. D. "Ancient Cartography." *Expedition* 20, no. 2, (1976): 26–31.

9.74. Romm, J. S. *The Edges of the Earth in Ancient Thought: Geography, Exploration, and Fiction.* Princeton, NJ: Princeton University Press, 1992.

Accommodations

9.75. Bolchazy, L. J. "From Xenophobia to Altruism: Homeric and Roman Hospitality." *AncW* 1(1978): 45–64.

9.76. Crane, T. "*Caveat Viator.* Roman Country Inns." *CB* 46(1969): 6–7.

9.77. Hermansen, G. "The Roman Inns and the Law: The Inns of Ostia." In *Polis and Imperium: Studies in Honour of Edward Togo Salmon.* Ed. by J. A. S. Evans. Toronto: Hakkert, 1974: 167–181.

9.78. Kerr, A. J. "'No Room in the *Kataluma.*'" *ExposT* 103(1991): 15–16.

9.79. Keyes, C.W. "The Greek Letter of Introduction." *AJPh* 56(1935): 28–44.

9.80 Trudinger, L.P. "'No Room in the Inn': A Note on Luke 2:7." *ExposT* 102(1991): 172–173.

Travel Amenities

9.81. Harris, H. A. "Lubrication in Antiquity." *G&R* 21(1971): 32–37.

9.82. Matthews, K. D. "The Embattled Driver in Ancient Rome." *Expedition* 2, no. 3, (1959–60): 22–27.

Sea Travel

9.83. Casson, L. "The Isis and Her Voyage." *TAPhA* 81(1950): 43–51.

9.84. ———. "The Mystery of the Trireme." *Horizon* 14, no. 1, (1972): 110–113.

9.85. ———. "New Light on Ancient Rigging and Boatbuilding." *The American Neptune* 24(1964): 81–94.

9.86. ———. *Ships and Seamanship in the Ancient World.* Princeton, NJ: Princeton University Press, 1971.

9.87. ———. "Speed Under Sail of Ancient Ships." *TAPhA* 82(1951): 136–148.

9.88. Fitzgerald, M. "The Ship of Saint Paul, Part I: Historical Background." *BiblArch* 53(1990): 25–30.

9.89. ———. "The Ship of Saint Paul, Part II: Comparative Archaeology." *BiblArch* 53(1990): 31–39.

9.90. Gilchrist, J. M. "The Historicity of Paul's Shipwreck." *JStudNT* 61(1996): 29–51.

9.91. Lake, K., and H. J. Cadbury. "The Winds." In *The Beginnings of Christianity.* Ed. by F. J. Foakes-Jackson and K. Lake. London: Macmillan, 1920, 5:338–344.

9.92. Praeder, S. M. "Acts 27:1–28:16. Sea Voyages in Ancient Literature and the Theology of Luke-Acts." *CBQ* 46(1984): 683–706.

9.93. Sippel, D. V. "Some Observations on the Means and Cost of the Transport of Bulk Commodities in the Late Republic and Early Empire." *AncW* 16(1987): 35–45.

9.94. Topham-Meekings, D. *The Hollow Ships: Trade and Seafaring in the Ancient World.* Basingstoke, UK: Macmillan, 1976.

CHAPTER *10*

KNOWING
AND
BELIEVING

IT'S DIFFICULT TO write a conclusion to this book. I don't feel that I'm finished with its subject matter in quite the same way I have finished with other writing projects. It took me three years to write my first novel, and when I typed the last page, I was relieved to be done with it and ready to go on to something else. When an editor accepted the book, he wanted me to make a few minor changes, which were not difficult with a word processor. But he also urged me to write a new chapter at one point to help develop the relationship between two of the characters. That was difficult, because by then I had been done with them and their story for a couple of years. But when you're an aspiring writer and an editor says, "I want to buy your book and I want you to write another chapter," you write another chapter. (The novel, a Christian historical set in first-century Rome, is called *Daughter of Lazarus*, published by Abbey Press, but no longer in print.)

But I don't feel that I'm finished with this subject, and I hope you, the reader, aren't either. This book I regard as a starting point. There will always be new chapters to write. In the course of researching and writing what you've read thus far, I've raised some questions for myself which will require further investigation. In addition to whatever information you've gleaned from it, I hope you've learned that the study of the New Testament is a continuous process.

Does that mean that one cannot achieve finality or certainty in this area? Can we undertake this kind of study and come out of it believing anything? People in my Sunday school and Bible study classes sometimes ask questions like that, and they are legitimate. I don't hesitate to answer yes to the second one, because I have been engaged in this sort of study for twenty-five years, and my faith is stronger now than it was when I began.

The first question requires a longer answer. Faith cannot be founded on the results of scholarship, for two reasons. First, as Sandmel pointed out in his article on "The Comfortable Theory" (**2.95**), modern scholars are sometimes no more nor less objective than the ancient writers they analyze. Feminists, such as Rawson and Pomeroy, tend to overcompensate for the lack of attention given to women in antiquity. An orthodox Jewish scholar like L. H. Feldman—under whom I have studied and whose friendship I prize—will not admit the possibility of Hellenizing influences on first-century Judaism. These biases—and all modern scholars have them, to some degree—must be kept in mind when one reads their studies of ancient authors' biases.

Second, the results of scholarly investigation cannot be the foundation of faith because the results of scholarship in this field, as in any other, may endure only until the next book on the subject appears. Today's "final" word on a problem can become a footnote in the next book or article presenting the new "final" word. (See the interest in rhetoric and its influence on the New Testament, in chapter 8).

All we have to do to illustrate this point is to look at trends in the study of the life of Jesus over the past century. In the early 1900s, Albert Schweitzer's *Quest of the Historical Jesus* held the field. It was not possible, Schweitzer said, to know anything historically reliable about Jesus because the Gospels weren't written as biographies.

By the late 1940s, Rudolf Bultmann was claiming that the early church had virtually invented the earthly Jesus. The kerygmatic Christ—Christ as the disciples experienced and proclaimed him after the resurrection—was the subject of the early church's preaching. (This is demonstrably true of Paul, who all but ignores the human Jesus and deliberately distances himself from those who knew Jesus during his earthly ministry; cf. Gal. 1:18–24.) According to Bultmann, whatever the early church said about Jesus was said in light of that resurrection experience and could not be taken literally. The illogical extension of this "demythologizing" trend was James Allegro's book *The Sacred Mushroom and the Cross* (1970), in which he claimed that Jesus was actually a cover-up for a cult centering around hallucinogenic mushrooms.

By 1961 Gunther Bornkamm, in *Jesus of Nazareth*, opened what came to be known as "the New Quest for the Historical Jesus." It was possible, he thought, to use the Gospels as historical sources with caution, recognizing that their authors were not unbiased observers and that everything they said was colored to some degree, however small, by their own experience. Some things in the Gospels could be believed as written. In other cases, critical principles had to be used to determine the original form of a saying or story.

This approach at least allows for the possibility of gaining limited knowledge about the historical Jesus, while admitting the difficulty of the process. The basic premise of this book has been a more confident version of Bornkamm's philosophy. I believe that we can know a great deal about Jesus and his teachings, though I am willing to concede that what we read in the New Testament, especially the Gospels, is shaped by the opinions, experiences, and purposes of the writers. That's why it's so important to know the background against which the New Testament was written.

To see how this approach applies to a specific text, let's go back to the centurion at the cross, mentioned in chapter 3. The story raises some problems, but they can be resolved if we look at it in its context.

In Matthew 27:54 and Mark 15:39, the centurion's reaction to the crucifixion was "truly this was the Son of God" (KJV) or "God's Son" (NRSV).[1] At least, that's the way it's usually taken. But the Greek text doesn't contain the article "the." The NRSV and RSV, in notes, concede that an equally valid translation would be "*a* son of God." The early Christian writer Justin Martyr recognized the subtle difference which the articles in this sentence can make: "Now the Son of God called Jesus, even if he was only a man born in the ordinary way, because of his wisdom deserves to be called a Son of God" (*First Apology* 22). In that age when the divine and human were believed to mingle much more easily than we can conceive (see chapter 5), such a statement probably meant no more than that this was an extraordinary person, a godly man, terms one might apply to Francis of Assisi, Luther, Gandhi, or a number of others. No doubt many believers later took his exclamation as an unknowing testimony (cf. Acts 5:39).

Another problem arises from the fact that Luke 23:47 records the centurion as saying, "Certainly this man was innocent." The skeptic can point to that inconsistency and claim that we cannot trust the Gospel account.

After this study, however, we can recognize that Luke's purpose differs from Matthew's and Mark's. Both of those Gospels seem to have been written primarily for internal consumption, for readers who were already Christian. But Luke was writing in an effort to legitimize the church in the eyes of the Romans. If a no-nonsense person like a centurion, the backbone of the army and thus of the Empire, could see that Jesus was innocent of any offense against Rome, then surely it must be evident to everyone. To Luke, this was a more important point than some vague declaration that Jesus was a godly person. To emphasize it, he had no compunctions about wording the centurion's "confession" in a way that served his own purpose. Likewise, Luke has the Roman governor (prefect) Pilate clearly state three times that Jesus is innocent (23:4, 14, 22), rather than merely raising the question, "Why, what evil has he done?" (Matt. 27:23 and Mark 15:14).

But for many Christians, admitting that the New Testament authors had such latitude opens the question of inspiration. It seems easiest to say that we have to believe everything in the New Testament because God inspired the writers to put those particular words on papyrus. But then we have to face the hard question: Why did God inspire Matthew and Mark to attribute certain words to the centurion and yet put other words in Luke's mind? At the risk of sounding irreverent, couldn't God make up his mind what the centurion had said? That's the sort of hostile question that critics of the New Testament will ask when they look at a passage like this, and we cannot ignore it if we expect to obey the biblical injunction to give a good account of our faith.

If we have some understanding of the background of the New Testament, however, we can see that the writers were inspired to write for their particular audiences. This does not mean that they invented or falsified material. They used their God-given creativity to proclaim the gospel in terms intelligible to their readers. For Paul, as we've seen, that meant adapting terms in general use in his day, terms that appear in the mystery cults and the Stoic school of philosophy. He redefined those terms, though we cannot be sure that his readers always kept the distinctions clear. That makes it all the more important for us to know where the terms came from and what new meaning Paul was reading into them.

For the evangelists, this kind of inspiration resulted in minor differences in the wording of their accounts, but not in the message. Look at Jesus' teaching on divorce as an example. In Mark 10:11–12 he says, "Whoever divorces his wife and marries another commits adultery against her; and if she divorces her husband and marries another, she commits adultery." That saying (*logion* in academic jargon) does not specifically forbid divorce. It does forbid remarriage after divorce. That's the way Paul understood it in 1 Corinthians 7:10–11. Luke 16:18 records it in a similar sense, but only mentions the man as responsible for divorcing and remarrying and committing adultery. Matthew, however, adds an exception: "Anyone who divorces his wife, except on the ground of unchastity, causes her to commit adultery; and whoever marries a divorced woman commits adultery" (5:32; cf. 19:9).

Matthew's wording is the peculiar one here. Mark and Luke reflect a Greco-Roman background. (Mark may have been written in Rome in the late A.D. 60s.) Paul is writing to an audience with that same world view. As we've seen, divorce was easy in Greco-Roman society and could be initiated by either party. This is reflected in Mark 10:11–12. Remarriage was as common as it is in our day. Mark, Luke, and Paul speak to readers from that background. But Matthew was written for a predominantly Jewish-Christian readership. In that tradition divorce was allowed in cases of the wife's unchastity, but a woman was not supposed to initiate the process. Notice that Matthew's version says nothing about a woman divorcing her husband. That possibility did not exist for his readers.

Regardless of the exact terminology in which it's couched, the essential message of this *logion* is that Jesus disapproved of divorce, in contrast to Jewish law and Greco-Roman customs. Yet he recognized that it would happen at times, human nature being what it is. But divorce alone does not break the marriage bond, so remarriage ordinarily constitutes adultery. Jesus does not require divorce after the spouse has been unfaithful, as Jewish law did then. Here the excepting clause (Matt. 5:32; 19:9) limits the guilt of the divorcing husband if the wife has already fractured the marriage by committing adultery, and after such a divorce, remarriage is assumed, though some are called to celibacy (Matt. 19:11–12; 1 Cor. 7:7, 11).

That much is consistent in all the versions. This was a difficult point to get across in a society where marriage had no more sanctity than a business contract. It's no surprise that the New Testament writers had to find various ways to get Jesus' meaning across in words that their readers could grasp.[2]

In approaching any passage in the New Testament, then, we need to be constantly asking ourselves, what is the substance of the passage and what form has it been cast in by the writer so that his readers could comprehend it? But we mustn't confuse those two elements.

Christian thinkers through the ages have tried to express timeless truths (substance) in contemporary terms (form). Paul was able to talk to the people of his time about a dying and rising Savior, and they understood perhaps partly because of similar language in the mystery cults. In the Middle Ages the Madonna and child became a helpful interpretation of who Christ was because people were frightened by the image of God as a stern, unforgiving judge. Who could be afraid of a baby in his mother's arms? In the thirteenth century, Thomas Aquinas blended Aristotelian philosophy with Christian theology and God became the Unmoved Mover, the First Cause. In the Christian literature of the late nineteenth century, God begins to sound like a successful American businessman or British imperialist, as in "Onward, Christian Soldiers." In the 1970s Jesus became "Jesus Christ Superstar," the hippie savior. All of those are culturally conditioned images designed to express a truth. None of these images *is* the truth.

The Christian who wants to see behind those images must not stop with this book. Don't limit yourself by accepting things just because that is what you've always heard. Ask yourself why somebody said it in the first place.

The story is told of a young man watching his new bride prepare a ham. She cut off each end of the ham before placing it in the pan to bake. "Why do you cut the ends off the ham?" her husband asked.

"My mother always did it that way," was her reply.

"Why?"

"I guess it lets the juices out, so you get. . . . I don't know," she finally admitted.

Some months later they were at a family get-together. The subject of the ham came up, and the bride's mother said that her mother had always cut the ends off. So they all went to ask grandmother why she prepared hams that way.

"When I got married," grandmother explained, "I had only one pan to bake in. An ordinary-sized ham wouldn't fit in it, so I cut the ends off. It just got to be a habit."

Some things are too important to be left to habit. We owe it to ourselves to understand our faith and grow in it at every opportunity. It is an ongoing task, and it is, for me, an essential part of what it means to lead a Christian life. Notice that when Jesus was asked, "Which commandment is the first of all?" he quoted Deuteronomy 6:5, but with an interesting addition, according to Mark 12:30: "You shall love the Lord your God with all your heart, and with all your soul, and with all your mind, and with all your strength." The phrase "with all your mind" is not in Deuteronomy. I don't think Jesus' inclusion of it here is accidental (cf. Rom. 12:2).

Where do you start?

Getting our souls or spirits involved is relatively easy. That's what we've been led to do for years in church. Giving of our strength—working to serve or witness to others—also seems natural to most of us. It's getting our minds involved that takes some effort. Some Christians, to judge from what people have told me, hesitate to begin to study the Bible seriously because they're afraid they'll learn something that will make them doubt what they've always believed. Such people should take comfort from the fact that when the Dead Sea Scrolls were discovered, some scholars, Jewish as well as Christian, were reluctant to investigate them for fear that they would undermine the Judeo-Christian tradition (**2.185**:5). Instead, they have enhanced our understanding of the background of the New Testament.

Do we really want to depend on a faith that cannot stand up to close examination? Isn't it better to find the weak spots in a house's foundation before we buy it? If they can be fixed, we fix them. If not, the house isn't worth buying. Socrates said that the unexamined life isn't worth living. Is the unexamined faith worth believing?

If you're going to examine the foundation of a house, you need to know something, even a little bit, about building. Or you need guidance from someone who can show you what to look for. If you're going to examine the foundation of your faith, the New Testament, you need a guide. I hope this book has been an incentive for you in that direction.

The items listed in the bibliography can direct you to the next step in your search for deeper understanding. Helpful articles on most of the subjects covered in this book can be found in the three-volume set *Civilization of the Ancient Mediterranean: Greece and Rome,* edited by M. Grant and R. Kitzinger (New York: Scribners, 1988). Make a commitment to yourself, set a goal. Read two books a year about the Bible or about the world in which the Bible was written. Read one of the Gospels in its entirety. Try reading Mark in one sitting. The average reader can get through it in less than an hour, less time than it takes to watch a TV show. Isn't it worth that much time to grow in your understanding of the gospel? Keep a notebook handy and ask yourself questions or write down your reactions to what you read.

It's not an easy task, but the rewards are worth the effort. Keep in mind the advice of Proverbs 16:16:

How much better to get wisdom than gold!
To get understanding is to be chosen rather than silver.

Notes

1. See D. C. Sim. "The 'Confession' of the Soldiers in Matthew 27:54." *HeyJ* 34(1993): 401–424.

2. On this issue see G. R. Ewald, *Jesus and Divorce: A Biblical Guide for Ministry to Divorced Persons* (Scottdale, PA: Herald Press, 1991).

APPENDIX 1

Sources

The ancient authors used most frequently in this study are discussed below in alphabetical order. All of their works are available in relatively inexpensive paperback translations. For further background information and bibliographic resources, see the entry for any particular author in the *Oxford Classical Dictionary (OCD)* or the *Oxford Dictionary of the Christian Church (ODCC)*. Most of the works mentioned below can be found in the Loeb Classical Library (LCL), a collection of ancient texts with translations published in America by Harvard University Press. The works of the Christian writers can be found in the *Ante-Nicene Fathers (ANF)*, an English translation of all the Christian writers active before the Council of Nicea in A.D. 325.

Clement of Alexandria

Apparently born in Athens ca. A.D. 150, but after his conversion he traveled extensively, listening to famous Christian teachers. He finally settled in Alexandria, where he became head of a school for Christian converts. He was forced to flee during a persecution of the church in 202 and did not return before his death in 215. He is the first Christian thinker to attempt a thorough synthesis of Greek and Christian points of view, trying to show that all earlier philosophical systems led up to Christianity. With his emphasis on knowledge and reason, he approaches Gnosticism at some points. His major surviving works are the *Protrepticus (Exhortation to the Greeks)* and the *Stromata (Miscellaneous Writings)*. The *Protrepticus* is included in the LCL. The other works are included in the *ANF*. The *Paedagogus (Instructor)* reveals many of the customs of Clement's day and guides Christians in living wisely, with good morals.

Epictetus

Ca. A.D. 55–135. Born in Hierapolis, in modern Turkey, he grew up as a slave in Rome. A kindly master allowed him to attend lectures by Musonius Rufus, whose Stoic teaching has points of contact with the New Testament (see chapter 6). Once Epictetus had been freed, he became a teacher in his own right. In 89, when Domitian banished philosophers from Rome, Epictetus settled in northern Greece, where he taught and attracted a large following until his death. His lectures were collected by one of his students into eight books, the *Discourses*, four of which still survive. The same student compiled a summary of Epictetus' teaching called the *Enchiridion*, or handbook.

Epictetus emphasized the brotherhood of all persons and our inability to control things that happen to us. Our happiness must not depend on external factors, and we must be indifferent to swings of fortune. The only thing we can control is ourselves and our will. Unlike earlier Stoics, he tried to reach a large popular audience. N. P. White's *The Handbook of Epictetus* (Indianapolis: Hackett, 1983) contains an introductory essay and a translation for the non-specialist.

Eusebius

Ca. A.D. 260–340. Author of the *Historia Ecclesiastica*, an account of the church from apostolic times to his own day. Unlike earlier classical historians, he did not attempt to rewrite material from his sources so that it would blend in with his own style of writing. He composed his history in more of a "scrapbook" style, inserting lengthy quotations from documents and earlier authors just as he found them. Thus he preserves much valuable material which would otherwise be lost. His interpretation of what he preserves is not always accurate, but this is "to be explained by his want of critical judgment and not by conscious perversion of the facts" (*ODCC*:481). Eusebius was imprisoned during a persecution of the church in 303, was later accused of heresy, but survived it all to become bishop of Caesarea. The *Ecclesiastical History* is available in the LCL and in a Penguin paperback.

Josephus

Ca. A.D. 37–100. Possibly a Pharisee who took part in the Jewish rebellion against Rome in 66 but surrendered early in the war. His first work was the *Jewish War*, written to explain why the Jews had revolted and how Rome had been destined to win. His *Antiquities of the Jews* is a compendium of rabbinic lore and more or less historical data parallelling the Old Testament and coming down to the outbreak of the war in 66. There is some overlap between portions of the *War* and the *Antiquities*, and Josephus sometimes contradicts himself; cf. S. Mason, "Will the Real Josephus Please Stand Up?" *BAR* 23, no. 5, (1997), 58–68. He also wrote an autobiography (the *Vita*) and a defense of Judaism called *Against Apion*, in which he contradicts some of what he says in his other works about his own activities in the war. All of his works are in the LCL. The *Jewish War* is also available in a Penguin paperback.

Justin Martyr

Born in Samaria ca. A.D. 100. After studying various Greek philosophers, he converted to Christianity about 130. He taught in Ephesus, where he wrote his *Dialogue with Trypho*, a Jewish opponent of his, and then in Rome, where he wrote two *Apologies* or defenses of Christianity. He attempted to reconcile faith and reason, believing that all knowledge is from God. Non-Christian systems of thought contain bits and pieces of the truth which was ultimately revealed in Christianity. Thus other schools of thought are not entirely invalid and are not to be discarded. He was martyred ca. 165.

Juvenal

Early in the second century A.D., the satirist Juvenal turned his barbed wit loose on his contemporaries. Rome is so decadent, he says, that it's difficult *not* to write satire (*Sat.* 1.30). All sixteen of his satires are devastating pictures of his society, but the second (against homosexuals) and the sixth (against "liberated" women) are the most scathing.

In *Satire* 3, Juvenal shows that Rome's moral corruption extended to all areas, not just to sexual behavior. A friend of his is leaving Rome because he cannot compete with people who cheat on contracts, lie and flatter their way into rich people's confidence, take bribes, and secure government jobs which require little and pay a lot (3.30–40). Juvenal does not pretend to have answers to Rome's problems. His satire is "a protest rather than a remedy" (*OCD*:572).

Virtually unread in his own lifetime, he was rediscovered in the late fourth century and has enjoyed a steady popularity since then. Samuel Johnson imitated several of his satires, turning them against London instead of Rome. There are several paperback translations of his satires, some of which omit the second and sixth; the most readily available (and complete) is probably the Penguin.

Martial

We might think Juvenal overly pessimistic about Roman morality if we did not also have the work of his older contemporary, Martial, who was Rome's favorite writer from A.D. 80–95. Prostitutes, homosexuals, lecherous old men (and women), and drunkards populate his pages. Pliny found the poems "remarkable for their combination of sincerity with pungency and wit" (*Ep.* 3.21). Though Martial is acclaimed for having perfected the epigram as a literary form, fully a third of his poems were deemed unsuitable for translation into English until modern standards changed in the late 1960s.

Martial claims at one point that his own life is pure (1.4), but in other poems he describes how he consorts with prostitutes (2.31; 6.23; 9.67) and how his wife caught him in bed with a young boy (11.43; 11.104). It's difficult to know where the poetic *persona* ends and where Martial is writing autobiographically. Was he married once or three times? Or was his wife a literary fiction? The only English translation of his complete epigrams is in the LCL (1970). Several paperback editions can supply excerpts.

Ovid

Nowhere is the Roman attitude toward morality shown more graphically than in the work of the poet Ovid, who died in A.D. 17. His *Art of Love* is history's first handbook on "how to pick up girls." He tells the ardent young men of Rome the best places to meet the opposite sex; one surprising place he mentions is the Jewish synagogue (1.75). Above all, he advises, "be a confident soul, and spread your nets with assurance. Women can always be caught; that's the first rule of the game" (1.270).

Ovid makes no secret of his numerous affairs. He boasts of his "rascally ways" (*Amores* 2.1). "There's not a sweetheart in town I'd be reluctant to love" (*Amores* 2.4). Later in life he tried to claim, like Martial, that his life was purer than his page. Admittedly, some of this may just be a pose he strikes for his audience, but we saw enough about Roman morals in chapter 8 to believe that what he relates are experiences typical of his circle. His readers would not have found his poetry entertaining if it did not reflect reality to some degree. Even in his mythological *Metamorphoses* most of the stories center around love and sex.

Born in Sulmona, a lovely mountain town east of Rome, and educated to be a lawyer, Ovid found amorous poetry more to his taste. Though popular in aristocratic circles, he was banished to what is now Romania for "a poem and a mistake" at the same time the emperor Augustus exiled his own daughter and granddaughter, both named Julia. The two women had apparently been extremely promiscuous, making a mockery of Augustus himself and his efforts to restore family life in Rome. Ovid, many scholars think, was either one of their lovers or knew what was going on. In his works from exile, the *Tristia* and the *Letters from Pontus*, he claims that his *error* was something he knew, not something he did. In any case, his gaily immoral poetry seemed to Augustus to encourage activities of which he disapproved. Ovid (and the two Julias) died in exile. Ovid's amorous poetry is most readily accessible in *The Art of Love*, published by Indiana University Press. The *Metamorphoses* is available in a Penguin paperback.

Petronius

There is at least a redeeming wit in Ovid's poetry which lifts it above the level of soft-core pornography. Petronius' *Satyricon*, written about A.D. 65, can boast of no such quality. (Until recently it was kept in the locked shelves or back rooms of many libraries.) The story, which survives only in fragmentary form, centers around two homosexuals who travel around southern Italy with their slave/lover, falling into and barely escaping from one comic situation after another.

The most difficult question associated with Petronius is whether he is to be identified with Nero's adviser of the same name. If he is, the work was probably written to criticize the manners of Nero's court. The grossly self-indulgent Trimalchio, who has the wealth of an emperor but behaves like a former slave (which he is), is almost certainly a parody of Nero himself. Suetonius and Tacitus provide ample evidence of Nero's excesses. Some of his interests are suspiciously close to Trimalchio's. The rhetorician Agamemnon, spouting platitudes and shallow philosophy, is probably a caricature of Nero's tutor and adviser, the philosopher Seneca, whose father was a teacher of rhetoric.

The *Satyricon* was not well received. It is hardly referred to at all by other ancient writers and survives only in fragments of late manuscripts. If Nero's adviser was the author, we have a description, in

Tacitus (*Ann.* 16.17–20), of his suicide on Nero's orders, which made a mockery of most of the rituals associated with that form of death. The Penguin edition of this work is the best now available for the general reader.

Philo of Alexandria

Ca. 20 B.C.–A.D. 50. Little is known about the life of Philo beyond the fact that he was part of a delegation of Alexandrian Jews in A.D. 39 who tried to get Caligula to recognize the political rights which had always been extended to them. His work focuses on the interpretation of Scripture from the standpoint of Hellenistic philosophy. He borrowed points of doctrine from various philosophical schools and from Jewish writers "without welding them into an harmonious whole" (*ODCC*:1083). Like the Greeks, he also tried to maintain the Jewish idea of God's concern for the world as a whole and for each individual; cf. D. Winston, "Judaism and Hellenism: Hidden Tensions in Philo's Thought," *StPhilon* 2(1990): 1–19.

Ignored in his lifetime, he came to have enormous influence on later Christian writers, particularly Clement of Alexandria, and through him, on Ambrose and other later thinkers. His use of allegory as a tool to interpret the Scriptures became a standard technique in the Middle Ages. His complete works occupy ten volumes in the LCL.

Pliny the Younger

Ca. A.D. 61–112. Nephew and adopted son of the elder Pliny, a government official and natural scientist. He declined his uncle's invitation to accompany him on an inspection of the eruption of Vesuvius in August of 79, during which the elder Pliny was overcome by fumes and died. The younger Pliny later became a politician and orator of note and was appointed governor of Bithynia in 112. We do not know if he ever returned to Rome. None of his letters can be dated later than that year.

His letters portray Roman high society of the late first century with a keen but self-satisfied eye. Most of his friends are provincials who have come to Rome but always look back happily to their roots. Some of the letters describe his country estates or his dealings with his home town, Comum. We often hear of his unhappiness with life in the capital. He urges others to retire to the country and devote themselves to literature, but he himself felt an obligation to public service, perhaps instilled in him by his uncle. A number of his letters discuss court cases or senate proceedings. His only other surviving work, a speech called the *Panegyricus*, demonstrates the lengths to which the aristocracy of the time had to go in order to flatter the emperor. The letters and the *Panegyricus*, in B. Radice's translation, are in the LCL. Her translation of the letters is also published by Penguin.

Plutarch

Ca. A.D. 50–120. He lived his entire life in the small town of Chaeronea, in Greece, although he did travel extensively, teaching Platonist philosophy and writing on a variety of subjects. He is best known for his biographies of famous Greeks and Romans, whom he paired (e. g., Alexander the Great and Julius Caesar) and compared. His purpose was to draw moralistic lessons from the way these great men had lived their lives. He also composed numerous treatises on philosophical and moral topics, which often provide insight into the life of the times through the analogies he uses and the off-hand comments he makes. His complete works are available in the LCL; various of the lives and moral essays have been published in Penguin translations, e. g., *Moral Essays*, trans. by R. Warner (Hammondsworth, UK: Penguin, 1971).

Seneca

Ca. 4 B.C.–A.D. 65. From Spain, son of a famous rhetorician and teacher. Little is known for certain of his life before ca. A.D. 41. He was a highly respected writer and orator by 37 but offended the emperor Caligula in some way—the charge was committing adultery with one of Caligula's sisters—and was forced into exile, where he remained until 49. He was recalled due to the influence of another of Caligula's sister, Agrippina the Younger, wife of the emperor Claudius and mother of Nero. Seneca served as Nero's tutor and adviser during the first five years of his reign. After Nero murdered Agrippina in 59 Seneca's influence over the emperor lessened. He "retired" in 62 and spent several years writing philosophical treatises. He was forced to commit suicide in 65 on a charge of conspiring to assassinate Nero.

Seneca's reputation as a Stoic philosopher rests on his numerous *Moral Epistles* and *Moral Essays*, on a wide range of topics. In addition he wrote nine plays, tragedies modeled on those of the great Greek playwrights. They were probably not staged but may have been performed as dramatic readings. They exercised considerable influence on Shakespeare. A tenth play, the *Octavia*, is sometimes attributed to him. Also probably by him is the *Apocolocyntosis*, a wicked satire on the deification of the emperor Claudius. His complete works are available in the LCL. A representative sample of his writings can be found in paperback in M. Hadas, *The Stoic Philosophy of Seneca: Essays and Letters*, New York: Norton, 1958.

Suetonius

Ca. A.D. 69–135. A friend of Pliny the Younger and secretary to the emperor Hadrian. Author of several biographical works, including the *Lives of the Caesars*, covering the emperors down to the end of the first century. He had access to the imperial archives and quotes letters and other documents from them. His simple, direct style made him popular and a model for later biographers. His work contains a number of salacious stories, leaving the impression that the emperors were too busy with their bedroom shenanigans to govern the Empire. Scholars question whether Suetonius gives an entirely accurate picture of life in the palace. The Penguin edition of the *Lives* is the most readily accessible. It was translated by Robert Graves, whose novels *I, Claudius* and *Claudius the God* are based on Suetonius.

Tacitus

Early second century A.D. Friend of Pliny and Suetonius and author of two historical works, the *Annals* and the *Histories*, which together covered the period from the death of the emperor Augustus through the reign of Domitian (A.D. 14–96). Unfortunately, only portions of his books survive. The account breaks off just as he is beginning to tell about the fall of Jerusalem in 70. He also wrote several minor works on topics such as the decline of oratory, the life of his father-in-law, and the Germans.

Because he was bitterly opposed to the imperial system, Tacitus' style is ironic, sometimes almost satiric. The incidents which he records may have been selected to put the emperors in the worst possible light, but modern critics have been unable to find any point at which he deliberately misrepresents anything. Both the *Annals* and the *Histories* are available in Penguin paperbacks.

Tertullian

Ca. A.D. 160–222. A lawyer from Carthage, in north Africa, who was converted to Christianity in his early middle age. His *Apology* made the case for the toleration of Christianity, contrasting it to the immorality and superstition of pagan cults and arguing that Christians were no danger to the state. In later life he turned to theological themes. A puritanical strain in his personality led him into the ascetic and eschatological Montanist sect, which was eventually deemed heretical. Because of the influence of his early works, however, the Catholic Church reckons him the Father of Latin Theology. His *Apology* is included in the LCL. His other works can be found in the *ANF.*

APPENDIX 2

GENEALOGIES

THE JULIO-CLAUDIAN EMPERORS

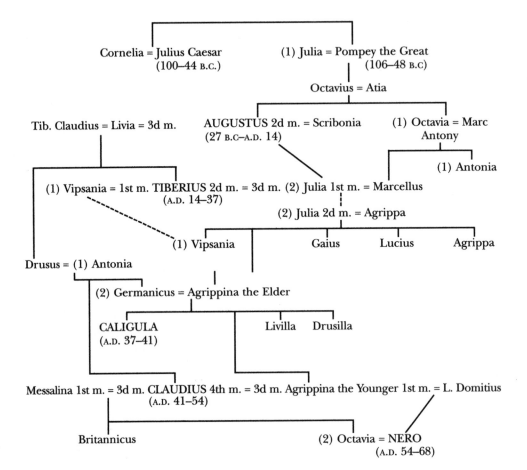

Julius Caesar was great-uncle and adoptive father to Augustus Caesar, the first Roman emperor, who in turn was the adoptive father of Tiberius. Vipsania was the daughter of M. Vipsanius Agrippa, Augustus' general and (2) Julia's second husband. Agrippina the Younger's third marriage was to her uncle CLAUDIUS, his fourth. Claudius adopted Nero as his heir.

The Family of Herod

Herod the Great (Matt. 2), King of Judea 37–4 B.C., married =

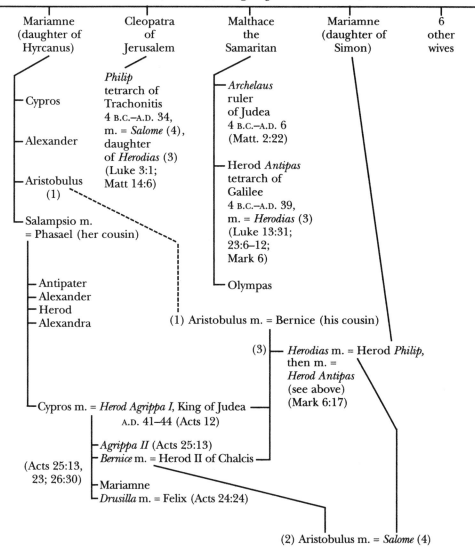

Mariamne (daughter of Hyrcanus)	Cleopatra of Jerusalem	Malthace the Samaritan	Mariamne (daughter of Simon)	6 other wives

— Cypros

— Alexander

— Aristobulus (1)

— Salampsio m. = Phasael (her cousin)

— Antipater
— Alexander
— Herod
— Alexandra

Philip tetrarch of Trachonitis 4 B.C.–A.D. 34, m. = *Salome* (4), daughter of *Herodias* (3) (Luke 3:1; Matt 14:6)

— *Archelaus* ruler of Judea 4 B.C.–A.D. 6 (Matt. 2:22)

— Herod *Antipas* tetrarch of Galilee 4 B.C.–A.D. 39, m. = *Herodias* (3) (Luke 13:31; 23:6–12; Mark 6)

— Olympas

(1) Aristobulus m. = Bernice (his cousin)

(3) — *Herodias* m. = Herod *Philip*, then m. = *Herod Antipas* (see above) (Mark 6:17)

— Cypros m. = *Herod Agrippa I*, King of Judea A.D. 41–44 (Acts 12)

(Acts 25:13, 23; 26:30)

— *Agrippa II* (Acts 25:13)
— *Bernice* m. = Herod II of Chalcis
— Mariamne
— *Drusilla* m. = Felix (Acts 24:24)

(2) Aristobulus m. = *Salome* (4)

Note: Names in italics appear in the Bible. Not all of Herod's family is charted above. The duplication of names causes confusion among ancient sources. Multiple marriages and intermarriage between cousins and aunts/uncles with nephews/nieces also make it difficult to identify some indivduals. Josephus (*Ant.* 18.128) says that within a century of his death, "all but a few of Herod's issue, and there were many, had perished." Few died a natural death.

Author Index

Scripture Index

Subject Index